SERENADE

SERENADE

A MEMOIR

OF MUSIC AND LOVE

FROM VIENNA AND PRAGUE TO LOS ANGELES

1927 to World War II to 2012

CAROL JEAN DELMAR

WILLOW LANE PRESS

Published by Willow Lane Press
P.O. Box 3513
Beverly Hills, California 90212

www.SerenadetheMemoir.com

ISBN: 978-0-9860359-0-6
Library of Congress Control Number: 2012946836

First Edition, 2013
Printed in the United States of America

Book Design: J.L. Saloff & Willow Lane Press

In memory of my mother and father.
Without their love and encouragement,
this story would have never been told.

To be joyful and sorrowful,
To be deep in thought;
To long and be fearful
In pending pain;
Heaven-high rejoicing,
Distressed unto death:
Happy alone is the soul who loves!

– Johann Wolfgang von Goethe

CONTENTS

Introductory Note

There is a melodic serenade which a lover sings to his beloved, the type that my father sang to my mother. But there is also a more symbolic serenade, one which sparks the senses and touches the emotions. This book is indeed my serenade to my parents.

After my mother died, my father spent many hours talking into a microphone and taping the story of his life as it had unfurled with my mother. He wanted me to keep the tapes, he said, so that I would truly understand my heritage.

My parents were Holocaust survivors. Their hopes and dreams had been shattered. But until after my mother's death, I knew very little about their early struggles.

At first I listened and transcribed the tapes. Later, I retraced my parents' journey from Vienna and Prague to the United States. Deeply moved by my parents' passionate, everlasting love for each other, I began typing out their story on my computer. But as I was conceiving their memoir, glancing at their photographs on the tables and shelves all around me, I occasionally allowed my imagination to carry me into their world.

The majority of the names, dates, places, and events are accurate. This is a nonfiction memoir. However on some occasions, I embellished to create probable creative dialogue and narrative based on what my father had described to me. If he couldn't remember a name or place, I created one. And if I couldn't find the date of an event, I approximated.

But make no mistake! This is indeed my parents' story – my serenade to them. I have turned back the clock to see and hear them vividly; so as you turn the following pages, I hope that you will envision them as well.

Carol Jean Delmar

Prologue

A Memorial Park
A Suburb of Los Angeles
October 24, 1998

My father and I often went to visit my mother at the site of her burial in the memorial park. He would sit on a little bench and talk to her. Although I walked away to give him some privacy, sometimes I could hear what he was saying to her.

$\mathcal{M}$y dear Franziska, my little Franzi: I am eighty-nine years old today. It seems like an eternity since you left me, yet at times, it seems like yesterday. I miss you so, but I know the day will come when this heavy piece of marble that I touch so longingly will no longer separate us. I yearn to be next to you, and I know that day will come soon.

It has become very difficult for me to visit you as much as I promised. My body is feeble with age, and the roundness of my back makes each step I take seem worthy of an Olympic medal. My heart beats in my throat and my breathing seems labored. But as I walk down the cement pathway that leads me here to your final resting place, I believe you feel my presence. I know you feel my love.

I've brought some flowers for you today. I picked them myself from our garden, but I don't think I'm going to do that again soon because when I was cutting some of the roses, I stuck my finger on one of the prickly stems, and there was blood everywhere. Anyway, I raced into the house to get a band-aid, and then I got blood on the carpet. But I know how much you love flowers, so I've arranged them in two vases, which attach to the small knobs under your plaque right in front of you.

This memorial park is such a beautiful place, in the wilderness, far from the city. There's such a feeling of serenity here. Today I saw a little rabbit, or maybe it was a hare. The little fellow was hopping along the grass oblivious to the contents therein. Then I saw a squirrel climbing a tree that was hovering over a vacant burial plot. The greenery is all-encompassing, and even in this courtyard, surrounded by the tall beige marble wall crypts that you and your neighbors now inhabit, there is, in the center, a place of solitude that is not merely vacant and secluded, but instead resembles a green pasture in wait of the proverbial shepherd who watches over his flock. Much like the shepherd, I always wanted to be your protector, but when illness engulfed your fragile body so that I could no longer care for you, I became helpless. When your body quivered and begged for the food of life that would sustain and nourish it back to health, I could only offer words of comfort.

For sixty-eight years, I felt as if we were one. We experienced the ravages of war together and accepted our fate by constructing building blocks to maintain our survival. When one of us was weak, the other became strong. There was never a thought of desertion, never a thought of separation. Yet, suddenly, the ties which had bonded us together for so many years were inexplicably being pulled apart. As you grasped on to my hand with all your strength to fend off the inevitable destiny, I could only grieve in silence.

But when I finally was forced to say good-bye and gazed upon you for the last time, I felt peace in knowing that you were free from pain and worry. Draped in a simple white tunic, your face framed with a delicate lace-trimmed veil and bonnet, you were once again my beautiful young bride, and I was your groom.

We were young then, but with a wisdom unfamiliar to those who are growing up in today's opportunistic America. Adolf Hitler removed the stars from our eyes. His regime stripped us of our arrogance and taught us the values of tolerance and humility. We learned to respect the dignity of all human beings and to cherish those we love unconditionally.

That is why, my Franziska, we were so special. Whenever our travels forced us to search for a new home, our love remained constant and unwavering. We embraced our desperate need for each other without fear, for we knew that as long as we were together, our lives would be fulfilled and complete.

Our story did not turn out as I had planned, but it was the incredible twists and turns that made it so unique. I will always be grateful to you for your willingness to make sacrifices when obstacles stood in the way of our stability. You unselfishly thought more of me and our daughter, Carie, than you did of yourself. And for that, I will always cherish you.

These last three years have been very empty for me. I keep quite busy though, reading magazines like *Time* and *Newsweek*, and watching informative television shows like *This Week* and *Face the Nation*. I try to keep my brain active, but worry that my failing eyesight could prove a hindrance to my independence.

I actually enjoy my frequent jaunts to the supermarket. Sometimes it takes me hours to select the canned, packaged, and frozen low-fat delicacies that my microwave oven will prepare consummately for me the following week. As I walk with leaden, tortoise-like steps from section to section, leaning on my shopping cart for support as I push it through the aisles, cordial, affable people routinely ask me if I need assistance. I usually decline their kind offers because I feel a need to remain self-sufficient; however, sometimes my weakness overcomes me, and I surrender vulnerably like a helpless sparrow with a broken wing. As I arrive home exhausted, my bittersweet feelings begin to overwhelm me. Although I greatly appreciate the generosity of others, I find it inconceivable to accept the visible physical changes that have been thrust upon me by my advancing age.

At times I am very lonely, but Carie telephones and visits often. Sometimes she cooks, and once in a while, we dine at a restaurant. It saddens me to think that she was never blessed with children, since they would have represented the missing branches on our family tree.

Without them, we will most likely be forgotten, but not as long as I can still see your angelic face in my dreams.

As I woke up this morning, I knew that I wanted to spend time with you today to reflect upon our past. Sometimes it gets extremely hot here in the afternoons, so I came well-prepared. I'm wearing a patriotic-looking red, white, and blue short-sleeved plaid shirt with lightweight summer pants. And I've covered what little hair I have left with a cotton baseball cap, to shield my face from the sun. I've placed a cushion on the wrought-iron bench where I'm sitting, and I've brought a bottle of water to drink, just in case I get thirsty. But the weather is really surprisingly pleasant. It is October now, so the temperature is no more than eighty degrees, and the swift breeze that rushes across my face reminds me of the sounds of ocean waves as they hurl themselves upon the sand.

I don't mean to sound overly sentimental here, but you know that I'm a sensitive person. Nevertheless, I'm sorry that I often conveniently forgot to buy you birthday and Valentine's Day presents. But I believe that one's love for another cannot be measured in material terms, but rather by deeds and actions. Besides, I think that you really enjoyed selecting those gifts for yourself.

I don't agree with the current sentiment that men are void of romance and only use it to capture their feminine prey. I have always had a great emotional range and tried to communicate my feelings toward you through music and literature. Since well before my birth, composers like Schubert and Brahms used the words of Goethe and Schiller to express their passions through songs they called German *Lieder*. They were not afraid to reveal their inner souls, and neither am I.

My faith in religion waned in the 1930s as I witnessed Hitler's brutally savage atrocities upon mankind. Only the artistry of music had the power to evoke my spirituality; and then I substituted you, my Franziska, for the art, and the art became merely your accompaniment. Oh, how many times I remember serenading you with this heartwarming Schubert *Lied*:

Oh dearest art, how often in dark hours of sadness,
When life's cruelties have encircled me,
Have you inspired a warm new love in my heart,
And brought me into a far better world!

Often a soft sigh rising from your harp,
A sweet and blessed chord sent from you
Has disclosed heavenly visions of better times for me.
O dearest art, for that I thank you now.

I am so sad, Franziska, because you can no longer be substituted for the art, and the art can never replace you. So when I yearn for a tender touch, I suddenly feel like the composer's lamenting "Wanderer" in another *Lied*, who roams aimlessly as he sings:

I go on silently with little joy,
And always my sigh begs: Where?
In a ghostly breath sounds the reply:
"There, where you are not, there is happiness!"

But I am not ready to make the transition: I want to hold our memories near. Each day, I look at pictures of us when first we met. I unseal the envelope that holds a lock of your hair; I caress our marriage certificate, now faded and yellow with age; I thumb through the pages of our tattered passports; and I read your treasured final bequest to me. Then I listen to old-fashioned phonograph records that bring me closer to the homeland we were forced to flee. I cry for friends and members of our families who were oppressed. And I cry for what I thought would have been, but for what could never be. Then, when I turn off the music and there is silence in the room, I realize how much more we had than most. We were the real characters in a truly beautiful love story. That is all that I wish for our Carie – our grown up Carol Jeanie. And then I will be ready to come to you, my dear Franziska. Only this time, I will never leave you alone again. I will embrace you lovingly, and we will always be together as one.

Statue of Johann Strauss II in the Stadtpark.

CHAPTER ONE

A Café and More

Vienna, Austria
3 September 1927

On the audiotapes that my father left me, he told me about the first time he met my mother. He couldn't quite remember the name of the café, but he told me where it was and described it to me. When I went to Vienna in 1998, I was sure that I had found it.

*F*ranz Jung (*pronounced "Yung"*) stumbled up the stairs nervously as he reached the entryway to the renowned Wiener Kursalon. He had never been inside before, but had walked by often on his way to his ballroom dancing classes, which took place in a building just across the street on the Ringstrasse – the long Viennese boulevard that encircled the inner part of the city. This was Franz's first five o'clock tea, and he'd put on a suit for the occasion. Today was his chance to show off the fancy footwork he'd perfected by waltzing with some old friends from the dance school, and hopefully with someone new, who might be entranced not only by his locomotor skills but by his charms as well. Little did he know that this innocent non-alcoholic cocktail-hour-type social for young people would serve to give structure to his actions for the rest of his life.

As he advanced into what was clearly a café, he couldn't help but think that no other café in Vienna resembled the one in the Kursalon. It wasn't simply lined up among many others on a particular street, but dwelled within the Kursalon building, which stood majestically independent on a corner adjoining the Stadtpark. Home to a few small concert halls as well, the Kursalon was much more than a coffeehouse. Its gold-colored Italian Renaissance style only served to enhance its reputation as the historical sight where the great composer Johann Strauss once conducted his immortal melodies.

Glancing into the café, Franz saw numerous small tables which seated three or four people each, but these people had not come to dance; they were eating pastries like *Apfelstrudel* and *Sachertorte*, and were sipping *Kaffee*.

"I think you're in the wrong place," he heard a soft voice say. "You're here for the Saturday social, aren't you?"

"Yes," Franz answered, noticing an attractive blond waitress dressed in a uniform-type long black skirt and white satin blouse.

"You took the wrong entrance. Just walk into that corridor;" she pointed to the right, "and you'll see where to go."

Franz thanked her and proceeded into a beautifully decorated passageway with regal-looking red-and-gold carpeting. One of the doorways in the back was open, and he could hear the sounds of laughter and music from within. He cautiously approached, not knowing what to expect. The room was filled with people. It was unquestionably different from the café. Here both small and large tables adorned with tablecloths and floral centerpieces were positioned unevenly in a U-shape around an unpretentious dance floor. And standing on top of a one-step platform-like stage were animated musicians who were dressed in the red-and-white imperial court ball uniforms of fifty years before. Their backdrop: tall arched windows cloaked almost to the ceiling with elaborate, lavish red velvet draperies cascading down into graceful folds. Franz was thoroughly impressed.

As he scrutinized the room, he spotted his friend Fritz Sachsel foxtrotting with a short, fat girl whose plunging décolleté and swinging ripe breasts had the young compatriot's full attention. Then there was Sigi

Levin. He was dancing with the amateur prostitute he told Franz he'd planned to escort.

She's not bad looking, Franz thought. *You could never tell.*

"Well, I guess it's time to make an entrance," he whispered under his breath. "Here we go. . . ."

First he handed the hostess his ticket. Then he walked all around the room with an approachable smile on his face, but he couldn't find a place to sit. None of the girls seemed to interest him either. Then, suddenly, his glances ceased. He couldn't move. *That's her*, he thought. *She's beautiful.*

His eyes were glued to the center of the dance floor. The music had just stopped and a nice-looking fellow was escorting her to a small round table on the left side of the stage. They said their adieus, and then Franz wondered: *How am I going to approach her? She's seated with another girl and they have a chaperone. Why should she be interested in me? I'm not tall. I'm nice-looking, but I don't think I'm exactly handsome. And at the age of seventeen, I don't even know what I want to do with my life. She could probably have anyone she wanted. She's gorgeous!*

Franz began to float toward his destination. With each new step, he became more enamoured with the girl who truly had a face fit to serve as the subject of many a fine painter. She had ravishing thick, long black hair which perfectly profiled her exquisite almost sculptured features. Her makeup was applied sparingly to a flawless olive complexion and served only to maximize the alluring quality of her unusual and stunning onyx-colored almond-shaped eyes. As dictated by the times, her eyebrows were penciled thin; her lips were painted red and full. Her nose, although not overly small, was slender and straight, and added a classicality to her face, which to Franz epitomized Cleopatra.

Her dress was also an illustration of style, he thought. He could appreciate that her skirt was short, just to the knee; yet the dress had buttons all the way up the front, from the hemline to the collar. The blue silk material was attractive, and the thin matching belt which tied just a fraction below the waistline revealed to Franz that this petite young lady not only had a bewitching face, but was endowed with a lovely figure as well.

He'd reached her table now. He was standing in front of her. She was even more beautiful up close than he had anticipated. He was speechless.

As her eyes met his questioningly, he felt as if time had stopped. He cleared his throat a little embarrassed and disconcerted, remembering what he had come to say.

"May I have the pleasure of this dance?" he tried to ask graciously.

Amused by the humor of the situation, the chaperone, a handsome-looking woman of about forty, couldn't help but laugh. She was wondering how her daughter would respond. The other girl just looked on vacantly.

"It would be my extreme pleasure to dance with you," Franz's damsel answered coquettishly, standing and offering him her hand. As they made their way onto the dance floor, Franz could feel his heart thumping inside his chest as if it were a gargantuan time bomb waiting to explode. Oh, no, his hands were starting to feel clammy; what if she noticed.

The musicians were beginning to play "An der schönen blauen Donau" ("On the Beautiful Blue Danube"). *I could waltz to this melody in my sleep*, Franz thought somewhat relieved. He then stood erect, faced his newly found partner, started to raise his arms into the dance position, and waited anxiously for her to reciprocate. As she gracefully placed her right hand in his left and her left around his right shoulder, he slipped his right arm around her back, looked deeply into her onyx-colored eyes, and drew her closer. They were ready to embark on their journey around the dance floor, and he felt as if he were going to faint.

They began dancing to his left. One, two, three; one, two, three . . .

The music seemed to carry them around the room. It felt to Franz as if they were flying. She was as graceful as a gazelle. But it was time to change directions. *Will she be able to follow my lead?* he wondered. *Will I step on her toes?*

As they stopped circling, he applied more pressure to her back, led her into a few repetitive steps in place, and guided her to begin dancing to his right. One, two, three; one, two, three. . . . The maneuver had been a success, and both were grinning. They continued to whirl from side to side until they heard the final beat of the music.

Then, instead of ushering his new treasure back to her table, Franz became more courageous and asked her for a second dance. This time, it was a slow fox trot. They could finally talk, he thought.

"My name is Franz . . . Franz Jung," he said as they began to dance again. He certainly didn't expect her response. She stopped dancing, started to laugh, and then led him to the side of the dance floor.

Within two seconds, he had lost his self-confidence and wondered once again if he had said something wrong or had stepped on her toes. Maybe she simply didn't like him and had never planned to have a conversation.

"Try to guess what my name is," she finally said flirtatiously, unlike someone who was angry or had been offended.

"Could it be Elisabeth or Maria?" he asked.

"Try again," she said smiling.

"Stefanie?"

"No, that's my mother," she replied.

"Okay. Maybe it's Brünnhilde," he joked.

"Try to think of something more familiar and familial," she hinted.

"I'm not very good at guessing games. I give up. Tell me, please. . . ."

"It's a perfect match with yours, Franz," she said. "It's Franziska . . . Franziska Perger."

He couldn't believe his ears. It was the way she told him. He was ecstatic. *She must like me*, he thought.

Then she grabbed his arm and walked quickly with him back onto the dance floor.

"Come on," she said. "We still have time to finish this fox trot."

While dancing, Franziska explained to Franz that she had just gotten over a bout with rheumatic fever but was feeling much better. Her mother was the chaperone, and the other girl at the table was a cousin visiting from Czechoslovakia.

"Is your mother very strict with you?" Franz inquired.

"Not really," Franziska responded. "She's just looking after me here because I'm only fifteen years old, but I'll be sixteen in a few months."

"I'm almost eighteen," Franz proclaimed, feeling very grown up. "I'm going to graduate soon from *Realgymnasium* (college-preparatory high school)."

"I attend a *Lyzeum* (upper class private high school and finishing school)," Franziska volunteered. "I love fashion. I'd like to study tailoring and learn how to design women's clothes."

"I have big ambitions too," Franz said to sound impressive. But as yet, he hadn't figured out what they were.

At the end of the dance, Franziska appeared visibly tired, so Franz considerately suggested that they stroll back to the table. A waiter was serving refreshments.

"I'd like to introduce you to my mother, Frau Perger," Franziska said as they reached their resting place. "Mother, this is Franz Jung."

"I enjoyed watching the two of you out on the dance floor," Frau Perger complimented. "Now let me make an introduction as well. This is my niece, Judith. She's staying with us for a few days."

Franz politely nodded and then pulled out a chair for Franziska. Judith didn't even vaguely resemble her younger relative, Franz observed. She appeared to be about eighteen years old, and although she was pretty and had an engaging smile, in the eyes of the beholder, she didn't radiate that certain sparkle that would distinguish her from other women. She wasn't particularly petite, her light-brown hair was clipped in a short bob, and she appeared to be wearing a slope-shouldered shapeless dress without a waistline. But as Franz took his place among the women at the table, he made a concerted effort to be approved by all.

During the ensuing minutes, the four discussed no more than idle pleasantries. They mentioned where they lived and then talked a little about their interests, families, the weather, and the movies they'd seen: nothing too controversial. A chance first meeting at a social event was not the place to reveal blemishes in the human psyche. Then at about seven o'clock, Franz was caught off guard when both Franziska and Judith were asked to dance. Initially he discovered that he already felt jealous; next he noticed that he had been awkwardly left sitting alone at the table with Frau Perger. Then she did what Franz thought was the unthinkable. "Why don't you ask *me* for a dance?" she requested, as if it were the most normal proposal a chaperone could present under the circumstances.

Franz knew what he had to do but he certainly didn't want to do it. *She must be forty*, he thought. *How can I dance with this old woman? She could be my mother.* Yet in spite of Franz's anxiety, he did ask Frau Perger for a dance. He didn't want to do anything that would jeopardize his future with Franziska.

Frau Perger was a pleasant-looking woman, he admitted to himself as they began waltzing to Johann Strauss's "Geschichten aus dem Wienerwald" ("Tales from the Vienna Woods"). She was wearing a light-weight suit with a silver-fox boa, and her short dark hair was ornamented with a cloche. She removed the boa before dancing, but still seemed adequately embellished with tastefully placed fine jewelry, including a ruby brooch on her lapel and matching earrings. She had remarkable energy and endurance as they sailed around the room, Franz thought, but then, she must have had a lot of practice. He actually enjoyed the experience when it was over and was grateful that he had not been called upon to do much talking.

Once back at the table, members of the quartet seated in their respective chairs, Franz realized that the music would soon cease, and a voice over the loudspeaker would bring the social event to a close. But he still wanted more time with Franziska to ensure that he would see her again.

"Frau Perger, would you allow me to take Franziska out into the garden so that we might speak to each other for a few moments?" he asked, hoping that his waltz with Franziska's mother had been for some advantage.

"Yes, of course," she answered. "It's getting late; we should leave soon. Let's meet in front of the Kursalon in ten minutes to say our good-byes."

"Thank you," Franz acknowledged. Then, as he listened to the musicians' rendition of the elder Johann Strauss's "Radetzky March," he grasped Franziska's hand and stepped with her in time to the music right out of the room into the corridor. They proceeded directly out the front door, and then started to run and laugh like the children which of course they were.

They raced up the steps outside on the Ringstrasse side of the building and found themselves standing on a veranda overlooking the Stadtpark, where they could see rows of tables which had been set up for future musical performances.

"It would be so romantic to hear a concert among the trees. Oh, let's go down there," Franziska said, grabbing Franz's hand and leading him down some steps into what she thought was sheer paradise.

Bushes were pruned into flawlessly shaped forms replicated to create a perfectly symmetrical design. Colorful lookalike floral patterns seemed to emerge magically from a meticulously nurtured grass meadow. And to complete the picture, a gazebo covered with lush green foliage was strategically positioned for the young and young at heart. It was a fairyland.

And once standing inside the gazebo, Franziska automatically envisioned her wedding day. She could imagine herself in a flowing bridal gown standing next to her prince charming. And although it was much too soon to suggest, she had a strange feeling that he was already there.

For some reason, Franz was reluctant to join her in the pavilion, so he continued to walk out into the Stadtpark, where the splendor of the back portion of the Kursalon was in full view. Finally he reached a walkway lined with benches, and he sat down. A few minutes later, she was sitting next to him.

"You're so pretty," he said, gazing into her unique eyes and gently stroking her cheek. It was as if he couldn't help himself. He didn't want to be too forward, but he needed to touch her.

She responded by bringing her own hand up to her face and placing it over his. It was her way of saying that what he did was okay. In fact, she liked it.

"I don't know how to phrase this," he said. "You must be very popular. Have you had a lot of boyfriends? Or rather, do you have a boyfriend now?

"You don't have to answer me," he continued indecisively. "I was just hoping that you might be available. I shouldn't say this, but I really like you, and I want to know what you like to do and where you like to go, and . . ."

She put her fingers to his lips. "I feel the same way about you," she said softly, "but boys *have* been known to ask for the pleasure of my company; my mother says that I'm too young to get serious though. But I'll know when the time is right."

Feeling somewhat encouraged and insecure at the very same time, Franz stood up and jumped over a hedge; he picked a pretty pink-and-white flower and then jumped back. "For you," he said to Franziska, handing the flower to her chivalrously on one knee.

"But I want something in return," he continued, standing. "I want you to promise that you'll go to a movie with me."

"I love movies," she said. "To which one?"

"I leave that up to you," Franz responded jubilantly. "You pick the time and place, and I'll be there."

"Hm . . . I really want to see *Flesh and the Devil*. Now before you make a face, I have to tell you that the title is deceiving; the film is a romantic drama, and Greta Garbo is supposed to be terrific. The movie's playing at the Gartenbau *Kino* (Cinema)."

"That sounds fine to me," Franz agreed. "Now when and where?"

"How about next Saturday afternoon? You could pick me up from my home at about four o'clock, and we could walk to the *Kino*. I live near the Prater at Blütengasse Neun (Nine)."

"That's easy to remember," Franz said smiling. "I'll be looking forward to it all week. . . . But now, I really think we should go back and meet your mother and your cousin; they're probably already waiting for us."

"I guess you're right," Franziska said, "but I would much rather stay here with you."

Upon hearing those words, Franz suddenly drew Franziska off the bench and kissed her firmly and quickly on the lips. Then they both stared at each other, stunned. His actions had occurred totally unexpected to both of them.

"I didn't know that I was going to do that," Franz told her. "I could say that I'm sorry, but I'm really not.

"Your mother said that we should meet in front of the Kursalon to say our good-byes; just think of that as my own personal and private farewell to you."

Franziska couldn't utter a word. She just stood mesmerized as Franz serenely took her hand and began leading her tranquilly back through the grass.

Frau Perger was indeed waiting for the twosome when they arrived. "I trust that you had a nice conversation," she said.

"Yes, we did," Franziska replied, trying to revive some of the vitality into her personality that was lacking.

"It's almost eight o'clock," Frau Perger continued. "We'd better start home. It was very nice meeting you, Franz."

"It was nice meeting you too," he echoed. "I really enjoyed our dance."

Now what had possessed him to say that, he wondered. He couldn't understand what was coming over him. He was doing all sorts of strange things.

"*Auf Wiedersehen*," he finally said to Franziska and her cousin.

"Then he gallantly took Frau Perger's hand in his, and kissed it. "*Gute Nacht*," he uttered.

Frau Perger didn't say a thing; she just smiled and began walking toward the Ringstrasse with the two girls following her. Franz remained there watching. Even from behind, Franziska looked beautiful to him; he could still see her long black hair in the distance. Then suddenly, she turned around and blew him a kiss.

CHAPTER TWO
Pötzleinsdorfer Strasse 130

Vienna, Austria
3 September 1927 and Before

When I went to Vienna, I had a Polish guide who took me to all of the places on my list. An elderly lady lived in the house where my father was raised. I contacted her nephew, an architect, and he arranged a tour of the house for me.

*F*ranz had always lived on Pötzleinsdorfer Strasse – at least that was the only address that he could remember. The admirable transportation system in Vienna had enabled many people to reside in districts far away from the central part of the city. On this particular Saturday evening, Franz was anxious to travel home to tell his sister all about his wonderful chance meeting with the girl of his dreams.

He raced up the tree-lined Ringstrasse to Schwarzenbergplatz, where he boarded a long red-and-white tram which consisted of three trolley cars on rails and looked to him like a caterpillar. Tram Number One took him around the Ring to Schottentor, and Number Forty-One took him northwest to the terminal near his home. Then, just a short walk through one of the most affluent and picturesque residential areas in Vienna, and he was there.

His parents had purchased the big three-story rustic-looking house just after he was born. It was positioned among so much natural beauty, his mother always said, that it would surely keep the dark clouds out of her family's life.

It was located just a few blocks from the legendary Vienna Woods where, as a child, Franz would often take leisurely strolls with his father. On some Sunday afternoons they'd continue into the little suburb of Neuwaldegg, where they'd stop at an outside tavern, and Franz would be allowed to sip off the foam from his father's beer.

The backyard extended farther than the human eye could see. Its velvety green grass bordered by evergreens and fruit trees contributed to making its vision one of fascination and awe. It was a miniature Vienna Woods, Franz's mother always thought, and she enjoyed serving friends the small purple-colored prune plums and fuzzy pink peaches which it produced.

The house looked much like a birthday cake to Franz. It seemed to have one layer piled on top of another, and the narrow width of the lot only served to make the effect even more noticeable.

Franz unlatched and opened the wrought-iron gate at the front. Then he ran down a path on the right side of the house, first passing the main entrance and then reaching another side entrance toward the back. He unlocked the door and entered the kitchen. "I'm home," he shouted.

It was a big comfortable kitchen with a combination of brown tile and dark wood paneling on the walls, and it had all of the latest appliances.

"Shhh," he heard his sister say. "Mother just went upstairs; she's tired."

Franz had grown very close to his older sister, Ilona. (*The "I" is pronounced like the "i" in "it."*) Their temperaments were quite different; maybe that's why they got along so well. Franz knew that she was a good person, and she could be lots of fun. And in the area of love, she was an expert.

"I met someone wonderful today at the five o'clock tea," he announced. "Do you believe in love at first sight?"

"Absolutely," Ilona answered. "Have you asked her to marry you yet?"

"Oh, you stop that," Franz said. "The wedding is next week."

Ilona was five years older than Franz, and definitely five years more mature. She was very confident around men, had a romantic nature, and was known to be somewhat of a flirt. Although only moderately pretty, she had an alluring, sensuous quality that was compelling and irresistible to the opposite sex.

Unlike the rest of the family, she was fair-skinned and her hair was blond. Although Franz never remembered her any other way, she was born with darker-colored hair. As the story went, one summer, Ilona and her mother took a vacation to the resort area of Wachau along the Danube River, and when they returned, Ilona's hair was blond. Her mother simply said that the sun had lightened it. Ilona was always a blonde from that time on.

"You probably haven't had anything to eat since this afternoon," she said, walking to the icebox. "Let me make you something."

"How about a *Kaisersemmel mit Schinken* (Kaiser roll with ham)?" Franz suggested.

"You must have read my mind," she responded, already holding the ingredients and placing them on the counter.

After a few minutes, the meal was ready. Ilona served Franz on the kitchen table, cleaned off the counter, and then sat next to him with a cup of tea.

He told her all about Franziska: how beautiful she was and how nervous he felt about their date the following week.

"How could she help but love you," Ilona said reassuringly, refraining from making the phrase sound too much like a question. "You're my brother."

This was the first time Franz had ever really talked seriously about a girl, so it was important for Ilona to make him feel that he could always count on her in the future for honest advice and support. Their father had died earlier that year of a heart attack, and the family was still in a state of upheaval. Ilona knew that Franz needed her now more than ever, just as she needed him, and just as both of them needed their mother.

Franz's father, Jakob Jung, was born in Siebenbürgen, which was part of the Austro-Hungarian Empire, but became part of Romania after World War I. Jakob's parents died when he was very young, and he was raised by his older brother, Ferenz. At the age of eighteen, he secured a job in Vienna, where he remained for the rest of his life. He was a mild-mannered man of slight build, and he always wore a square-shaped beard trimmed straight at the base. But it was his gentle, laughing eyes which distinguished him from others. Franz's mother, Olga, always said that when you looked into his eyes, you felt safe.

She was born, Olga Werner, in the Austro-Hungarian province of Moravia, which became part of Czechoslovakia after World War I. She had six sisters and a brother, and came from a very wealthy family. She was an attractive, strong-willed woman, with a resourcefulness that proved to be an asset in her later years. She met Jakob while on a holiday in Tyrol. And although he was thirteen years her senior, the two quickly became inseparable.

Olga moved to Vienna when she married Jakob in 1901. He was thirty-seven and already had an established business: "*Jung & Reichner Weisswarenerzeugung*" ("Jung & Reichner White Goods Manufacturing"). His partner had died shortly after the inception of the business, so Jakob Jung – who also called himself "Jacques" – became the sole proprietor. It was his vocation to subcontract with manufacturing plants to weave the linen and cotton yarns he purchased from them into cloth, to store the fabric in his warehouse, and then to sell it to companies that would turn it into table and bathroom linens, bedding, and sometimes clothing.

The business thrived and afforded the Jungs the income necessary to retain a maid, a cook, and a nanny in their home. The maid, Trude, and the cook, Vinzi, shared a bedroom on the second floor, and the nanny, Grete, lived in a room in the attic.

Trude loved to dust and polish the luxurious furniture in the living and dining rooms, located in front of the kitchen on the first floor. The two rooms, much like most of the rest of the house, were elegantly decorated in the Biedermeier tradition of the 1820s. The refined-looking couch and the round dining room table with matching chairs exhibited an artistic blend of delicately-carved light brown wood and fabric.

Then, just a few steps in front of these two rooms, Trude often found herself in an enclosed veranda dusting the baby grand Bösendorfer piano within. She sometimes sat on the bench and pretended to play as if she were a concert pianist; for in Vienna, no matter what one's station in life, the attainment of culture was a universal ideal. That's why Olga Jung surrounded her children with music, giving them both piano and violin lessons, hoping that at least one of them would be blessed with a talent and that an appreciation for music would be developed by both.

Although Trude enjoyed her job and her surroundings, her constant bickering with Vinzi often kept Olga and Jakob Jung awake at night, since the master bedroom and maids' room were on the same floor. Even though Jakob was forced to close his business for two years during World War I, he was indeed financially able to maintain Trude in his employ; but finally, one day toward the end of the war, Trude packed up her things, moved out, and Vinzi was left with all her chores. Vinzi never complained though; after all, she had the whole bedroom to herself; the children's rooms were upstairs on the next floor.

Franz's life was very carefree as a child; his parents never wanted to burden him. That gave him the license to be mischievous, and at times, he could be exasperating. It started when he was five and peed all the way down the stairs. His mother was so angry that she locked him in the basement. Within an hour, he'd hammered a hole in the door and had crawled out laughing.

At about the same age, Fräulein Grete sent him out to buy a loaf of bread. She watched him from a window as he walked back proudly with his purchase, dropped it by accident in the mud, picked it up, and then skillfully began cleaning it with spit.

The incident occurred a short time after World War I began. Little did Franz know how valuable a loaf of bread would become.

At the end of June in 1914, Archduke Franz Ferdinand, heir to the Austrian throne, and his wife, Sophie, were shot at Sarajevo, the capital of the Austrian province of Bosnia. The Austro-Hungarian government blamed Serbia for the assassination, and war was declared the following month.

At first, life continued as usual; later, the Jungs attempted to safeguard their children from feeling the war's effects. When food was rationed and stores began to run out of supplies, they planted vegetables: tomatoes, cucumbers, carrots, and spinach. Then they started a little farm: forty chickens, for eggs; three female goats, for milk; and a goose, for Franz. The animals were sheltered in a huge shed in the backyard. And sometimes Franz carried his goose around the house with him.

He never forgot how Vinzi had shoved corn into his pet's mouth to make it fat. Then one day when the bird appeared to be sufficiently plump, she stood Franz in front of it while she held its bill tightly closed and slit its throat. The animal struggled unhaltingly and then finally died. Franz cried and cried. And when the goose was served at the dinner table the next night, he cried some more.

But the most astounding surprise for the family occurred when Vinzi went to the shed one morning to fetch a few eggs for breakfast. "Come out," she screamed. "Come out here fast."

All of the Jungs, as well as Trude and Fräulein Grete, came racing out of the house, most only partially dressed. Then low and behold, they couldn't believe their eyes: They were looking at thirty-nine chicken heads . . . thirty-nine chicken heads without bodies.

"How gruesome!" Franz exclaimed.

"Someone most have stolen them," observed Ilona. "I feel sorry for those people; they must really be hungry."

A few hours later, Franz found the one surviving chicken. "This one must have somehow escaped," he said, petting the bird and showing it to Vinzi. "He must miss his brothers and sisters. Can we get him some new brothers and sisters?"

"I don't think so," Vinzi said. "I think our farming days are numbered."

The event, just one among many in the neighborhood, had prompted some of the homeowners to start a patrol as a precautionary measure, to prevent potential burglaries or riotous actions from the poor. Every evening, two men from the community marched up and down

Pötzleinsdorfer Strasse, armed with guns; and on some nights, one of these men was Jakob.

The Jungs were so nervous about crime that they chiseled a small alcove in the ceiling of their attic to hide food; they covered the vaultlike compartment with a piece of wood.

In the winter, many impoverished people had no heating and needed to burn wood or coal in their furnaces, so they went to and from the Vienna Woods via Pötzleinsdorfer Strasse. Franz often sat in his bedroom looking out the window as these poor people literally carried tree stumps and branches equaling pounds of wood on their backs.

It seemed that every younger able-bodied man was serving his country by being in the army; so once again, only the poor and weak were left to shovel the heaps of dirty, sludgy snow on the roadways so that buses and trams could move agilely by.

The war ended in 1918. Emperor Karl I abdicated; the Habsburg Austro-Hungarian empire crumbled; and the Republic of Austria was proclaimed. With the revision of boundaries, Austria's area had shrunk to about one-eighth of its former size as an empire. And with its depleted size and as yet unestablished government, the new republic faced a slow economic recovery.

Franz was beginning his fourth year of *Volksschule* (elementary school) then. The first two were very difficult on his parents. He simply didn't want to read or study. Oh, he was smart; he was just undisciplined and stubborn. Desperate, his parents paid to give him private lessons. Finally, only when his tutor presented him with pamphlets on football did he begin to read.

His aptitude for sports had already become evident. At the age of six, he was skiing on the slopes of the Vienna Woods. At thirteen, he was playing soccer as a member of the Hakoah, a sports organization for Jewish youths; and at fourteen, his coach recognized his speed and switched him to track running.

His disinterest in school continued, however. In fact, one winter when he was already in his first year of *Realgymnasium* (high school), his mother thought that he was leaving for school every morning, and when he returned in the afternoon, she thought that he had been there.

In reality, he and Fritz Sachsel were playing hooky. Oh, they were learning all right: They were going to museums on the Ringstrasse to keep
warm.

The boys continued with their little escapade for two weeks until
Franz's mother received a letter that asked her to make an appointment
with the principal. When she questioned Franz, he told her that he had
no idea regarding the purpose of the requested visit. However, he and
Fritz quickly began attending classes again.

When Olga arrived at the school on the day of her scheduled meeting, the principal expressed concern since Franz had been absent for
so long, but he was glad that Franz had returned. Olga was somewhat
surprised and dismayed, but she was well aware of her son's propensity
for shenanigans. She assured the principal that Franz would indeed be
attending school regularly and asked him to notify her if the pattern
ever reoccurred.

By then Fräulein Grete was serving as a nanny for some younger
children down the street, and only Vinzi remained to fill her shoes.
Vinzi was delegated to keep a close watch over Franz for the following
month. He was not allowed to leave the house after school, had to complete all of his homework, and was supposed to practice the violin for at
least an hour every day.

One late afternoon, Franz didn't want to practice and decided to
play a prank on Vinzi. He knew that there was an unloaded gun in his
father's bureau, so he went upstairs, took the gun out of one of the
drawers, and hid it in his knickers. Then he went up one more flight of
stairs to his bedroom and grabbed a *Knallerbse* (an explosive-sounding
noisemaking device wrapped in paper). He went downstairs and started
practicing the violin until Vinzi entered the room.

"I'm going to stop playing right now," he shouted, "and if you say
one word to Mother, I'm going to shoot you."

Vinzi wasn't about to let Franz have the upper hand. "You're going to
practice, and I *am* going to tell your mother," she said firmly.

Franz pulled out the gun, pointed it directly at Vinzi and cocked it.

Vinzi stood very still, afraid to move a muscle. And then he did it:
He dropped the *Knallerbse* on the floor and simultaneously pulled the

trigger of the unloaded gun. Vinzi heard a banging noise and thought she'd been shot. She didn't feel any pain, but she started to scream: "Oh, my God; oh, my God. . . ."

Franz began to laugh and laugh and laugh. When his mother came home and Vinzi told her the story, Franz's punishment was swiftly extended. Now he had to stay home every afternoon for two months.

Franz never became very proficient at playing either the violin or the piano. His teachers said that he was extremely musical and talented, but he simply refused to practice. He was also never an ideal student, but was for some unknown reason able to maintain high enough marks to remain in the *Realgymnasium*. Some of his peers thought that he might have attained some of the answers to exams from his friend, Franz Bauer, the class genius who sat directly behind him one year, but no one ever really knew for sure.

Then, when his father died in the winter of 1927, Franz's mother needed him to help her liquidate the business. It was a harrowing time. Jakob Jung's death had occurred completely unexpectedly. As usual, Jakob had eaten breakfast at half past seven that morning with the family and then went up to the master bedroom to finish dressing. Olga surmised that when he developed chest pain, he must have laid down; because at nine o'clock, when he had still not left the house for work, she grew suspicious and proceeded upstairs. She found him there, lying on the bed. He was already gone.

At first she went through a period of grief; then, a period of resourcefulness. She asked Franz to temporarily drop out of the *Realgymnasium*, and told the principal that as soon as the family's business matters were settled, he would return. Franz didn't really care if he ever went back or not. Most students who graduated from a *Realgymnasium* continued their educations at a university. The thought of more school and more studying was simply not appealing to Franz.

Olga hoped that as they liquidated the business together, Franz would possibly display an inclination toward commerce. Every day they went to Jakob's office and warehouse, located just a block away from Schottentor and the *Börse* (stock exchange), at Esslinggasse Zehn (Ten). They closed the accounts, settled outstanding debts with vendors and subcontractors, compensated former employees, and attempted to turn the merchandise into liquid assets. They sold some goods at a profit, some at fair market value, and the remainder at a loss. In August, just one month before Franz met Franziska, their accountant was able to finalize the books.

Olga had notified her landlord in July that she would be vacating the premises by the first of September, but she remained continuously worried that the family would suffer financial woes. Of course, Franz was almost eighteen and could secure a job, but Olga really wanted him to go back to school. And Ilona had an illustrious, wealthy boyfriend whom she would possibly marry.

Then toward the middle of August, Olga approached her landlord, J.Z. Schütz, with the idea of starting a cleaning business. Except for the space he had rented to Jakob – the whole first floor and the basement – Schütz had always utilized the entire building for his own purposes – he was the biggest furrier in Vienna. He had often complained that he needed more room, and although he was saddened by the demise of his longtime tenant, he was happy to be able to finally expand.

Olga begged him for some space in the front of the building on the first floor. At first he seemed reluctant; then he finally consented.

With the liquidation complete, Olga wanted Franz to assist her with the formulation of her new cleaning business, her *Putzerei*. She wanted the business to be somewhat established before he left her and went back to school.

Franz didn't really want to return to the *Realgymnasium* at all, so he tried to evade discussing the issue with his mother. But with Franziska, that was another matter.

"Ilona, what am I going to do?" Franz asked his sister agitatedly, continuing the conversation he had started earlier with her in the kitchen. "I told Franziska that I'm going to graduate from the *Realgymnasium* soon. When I go to pick her up next Saturday, the topic is sure to come up. She thinks I still attend school, and she thinks that I'm going to graduate."

"Well, maybe you are. You've always planned to go back," Ilona said soothingly, unaware of Franz's true feelings. "Mother wants you to go back too. Franziska will understand when you explain to her why you had to drop out."

"But I lied to her. She'll understand why I dropped out, but she's not going to understand the lie."

"You didn't really lie, Franz. You simply misled Franziska. Why did you do that?"

"I don't know, Ilona. Franziska didn't ask me about school; I just volunteered the information. I guess I wanted to seem mature and wanted to impress her."

"Well, I'm sure you did. But from now on, just try to be honest," Ilona advised.

"All right," Franz said pouting. Then he paused for a few seconds before blurting in an outburst: "I can't bear it anymore: more Latin, French, and English in a dreary, dismal classroom, sharing an uncomfortable wooden bench with a boring intellectual, and learning from a bunch of lifeless, lackluster teachers who probably don't even know my name. . . . I don't really want to go back to the *Realgymnasium*! How's that for honesty?"

"Hmm . . ."

"And by the time I'd go back, I'd most likely be a year older than everyone else; that would really make a difference to me. And even if I did graduate, I don't want to go to a university like the others, so what's the point in graduating?"

Ilona didn't know what to say.

"For appearances . . . Just to graduate," she responded. "Sometimes it's worthwhile just to finish things."

"But I don't care about appearances," Franz protested.

"If that's true, then why are you so worried about what Franziska thinks?"

"All right, Ilona, I guess I do care about appearances, but I still don't want to go back to that *Realgymnasium*."

"Then what are you going to do?" Ilona asked.

"I don't know. When I'm through helping Mother, maybe I'll get a job."

"You know, if you'd graduate, it would be easier for you to get that job."

"I'm *not* going back," Franz said stubbornly. "And that's that."

"Well, I think we have a problem that we need to discuss with Mother," Ilona proclaimed.

"Not now, Ilona. I plan to talk to Mother about it after her cleaning business is under way. I wouldn't be going back to school now anyhow, so what's the point in deliberating about it? This just isn't the right time."

"You're right," Ilona agreed. "So . . . where are you taking your fair maiden?"

"To the Gartenbau *Kino.* I'm going to pick her up and then we're going to walk."

"Wear something nice just in case you meet her parents."

"Oh, I've already met her mother," Franz recounted. "We danced at the five o'clock tea. I think she likes me.

"But her father . . . I don't think I want to meet him. Maybe he won't think that I'm good enough for Franziska."

"What is wrong with you, Franz? Maybe *she* isn't good enough for you."

"Now that is *not* the case," Franz said firmly, defending Franziska. "She's beautiful and lovely and refined and . . ."

"All right, you've made your point," Ilona conceded. "Since she's so special, I think the least that I can do is offer you a few extra Schillings. Would you like a few Schillings extra?"

"Sure. I'd never turn down an offer like that," Franz answered.

"I want you to be able to take Franziska out after the movie for some nice pastries. My purse is upstairs, so I'll give you the money tomorrow. Now that you're officially dating, I don't think your allowance is going to be sufficient anymore. Of course, Mother may give you a small salary while you're working for her. But if you're ever in a bind, Franz, come to me. I'm your big sister."

With that, Ilona started to clear the kitchen table and then placed the dishes in the sink for Vinzi. "I'm going to go upstairs now," she said. "Tomorrow is Sunday. I'm going to sleep and sleep and sleep. Good night, Franz."

"Good night, Sis."

CHAPTER THREE
Blütengasse 9

Vienna, Austria
10 September 1927 and Before

I also visited the apartment where my mother was raised. The inside had been remodeled.

It was surprising for me to learn that the people who lived there were Orthodox Jews. My parents were forced to leave Vienna because of Hitler's occupation. Yet in 1998, many years after the Holocaust, Jews were finding peace and sustenance with their families in Vienna, remembering the atrocities of the past, but still able to move forward.

𝓕ranziska was in a daze. She'd spent the whole week walking around her home at Blütengasse Neun as if the people and objects within it were invisible. Her mother worried that she'd bump into something and get hurt. Her father was preoccupied with work and didn't even notice.

But today was the day she had to snap out of it. It was ten o'clock on Saturday morning. Franz was coming to pick her up in just six hours. She wanted everything to be perfect. She had planned out her day accordingly. She would relax until eleven, then take a bath and be completely dressed by one. At one, she'd sit down with her family for their main midday meal, and then at about half past two, she'd freshen up and be completely ready about three, just in case Franz came early. She'd even forewarned the maid, Hilde, that this was the day that the living room had to be spotless.

It was a lavish living room in an expensive, roomy apartment. Her parents had moved there just after she was born. Her father, Heinrich, liked the location. He could take a tram to the junction of the Ringstrasse and Franz-Josefs-Kai along the Danube Canal, and then, within a few minutes, walk directly to his office. Or he could walk on Sundays with his children to Vienna's amusement park, the Prater, and they could ride and ride on the colossal *Riesenrad*, one of the largest and oldest Ferris wheels in the world.

Their apartment, just east of the city center on the corner of Blütengasse and Löwengasse, was in a brown-colored five-story Renaissance-style building. The ancient-looking façade, adorned with ornamental pilasters and decorative moldings around the windows, was not unlike many of the more celebrated structures along the Ringstrasse.

The inside was plush; however, some rooms, like the living and dining rooms, were almost ostentatious. When guests arrived at the entrance, they were ushered down an immense hallway which seemed to lead to another front door at its point of termination. This second front door opened up into the gold accented Baroque-furnished living and dining rooms. The door to these rooms was almost always closed. In fact, when the children were very young, it was usually locked.

However, just before reaching this second front door, guests would find a narrow hallway extending to the right and left of it. This hall was the path to all of the other rooms in the apartment. Walking to the right, a guest would find three bedrooms and a bathroom on the left side, and the kitchen and maids' rooms on the right. Walking a few steps to the left of the door, the guest would find a den on the left side, and the master bedroom at the end of the hall on the right.

But guests didn't usually frequent very far down the narrow hallway. Either they were escorted into the living room or den, or they were led from the entry hall directly outside to the patio. Franziska wanted Franz to see the opulent-looking living room. Although the den was furnished with expensive, modern, heavy leather furniture, it was meant to be a comfortable family room. Franziska's father would surely consent to meeting Franz in the living room, she thought; he had never rejected her anything.

She was the oldest of four children: Her sister, Lilly, was fourteen; Fritz was thirteen; and her brother Paul was a few years younger. But she was her father's favorite; he treated her like a little princess. All of the children were attractive, with olive complexions and dark-brown or black hair, but none was blessed with the fetching beauty of Franziska.

Her father had taken her on one of his recent business trips to Czechoslovakia. While eating dinner in the hotel restaurant in Prague, the waiter brought a bouquet of flowers to the table. "These are for you, madam," he said, setting them down.

"Who are they from?" Franziska asked inquisitively.

At that moment, an extremely attractive gentleman in a finely tailored hand-made suit appeared. He must have been about thirty-five, Franziska presumed.

"Pardon my indiscretion," he told her father. "I couldn't resist sending these roses to your lovely bride." Then he took Franziska's hand and kissed it.

Franziska's father almost choked on the goulash he was eating and then said to the stranger: "This is not my bride; I'm very proud to say that I'm her father." For years later, he told the story to friends and family members. They always read into the anecdote that he was flattered by the incident because it had appeared to this stranger that he was married to a stunning younger woman. In reality, that had never even crossed his mind; he was simply bursting with pride for his daughter. Franziska loved him dearly, and she thought that he loved her too.

He had always been comfortable in Prague: He was born near there in 1873, when it was the largest city in the Austro-Hungarian region known as Bohemia, which became part of Czechoslovakia after World War I. And although he lived in Vienna since the age of twenty, he never renounced his Czechoslovakian citizenship, thus making his wife and children Czech citizens as well.

Heinrich Perger had come to Vienna to make his fortune. Although not tall in height, he hoped to one day have height in stature. Even his face carried an air of determination, which could, if mistaken, prove to be intimidating. Somewhat stout and overweight with short-trimmed hair and a neatly combed mustache, he dressed immaculately, usually in a business suit, and seemed to his family to look like the typical chairman-of-the-board.

By the time he actually had a family, he had achieved much of the success he had always yearned for. He possessed a lucrative wholesale jewelry business, and his office was filled with rare and beautiful gems sought by many of the fashionable, exclusive jewelry stores in Vienna, Prague, and Budapest. He never reached his potential earning power, however, because of his reluctance to hire salesmen and his desire to travel only for short durations of time to nearby cities.

To his family, he was a king. Both Lilly and Franziska loved to go to his office and look through his drawers of costly and extravagant jewels. But he refused to allow them to visit him there often because he didn't want them to develop a false sense of ideals. However, when it was Franziska's fourteenth birthday and she wanted her first strand of pearls, he granted her wish. And when Lilly wanted a little animal pendant with sapphires, he granted hers as well. But nothing pleased him more than showering gifts of jewelry upon his wife, Stefanie.

Heinrich met Stefanie purely by accident. She was browsing at necklaces in a posh jewelry store on the Kärntner Strasse, one of Vienna's most stylish shopping boulevards within the Ring, and he entered the store to sell his wares to the owner. When he glanced at Stefanie, he sensed an attraction and began talking to her.

When they became better acquainted, he learned that she had two brothers and a sister, was born in Poland, and had moved to Vienna when she was eight. Her parents didn't approve of her relationship with Heinrich because of the fifteen year difference in their ages. However, when Stefanie Popper turned twenty-one in 1909, she married Heinrich and became Stefanie Perger forever.

She tried to be a good mother, but sometimes became overwhelmed, especially in the middle of World War I when Franziska, Lilly, and Fritz were very small. Just about that time, Emperor Franz Josef died, and his funeral became the main event. On that morning in November of 1916, Heinrich took the whole family to his office to watch the majestic procession which paraded by right in front of it. Generals, kings, and presidents from many countries all over the world marched afoot or rode on horses toward the funeral service in Stephansdom, Vienna's foremost Gothic cathedral. Their uniforms were magnificent. Then they proceeded to the imperial burial vault in the Capuchin Church, where Emperor Franz Josef was laid to rest among some one hundred-forty other members of the Habsburg dynasty.

After the regal spectacle, Stefanie decided she needed more help with the children, so she employed a governess to look after them and teach them French and English; the governess remained with the family until Franziska was fourteen. Then, in moments of crisis, Stefanie began to rely on Franziska, who was always responsible and level-headed. But something had happened to Franziska since she met Franz. Stefanie hoped it wasn't permanent.

It was noon. Franziska had bathed and was ready to apply makeup to her cleanly scrubbed face. Powder, lipstick, eyebrow pencil, mascara, and rouge were sprawled all over a table next to the bathroom sink. Franziska looked into the mirror above the basin and liked what she saw: Her skin was perfectly clear like a flawless diamond – her features symmetrically arranged on her face – and her unique onyx-colored eyes likened some of the exquisite, priceless, unattainable gems sought by her father. Yet, in spite of her natural God-given good looks, on this particular day, she thought that she appeared somewhat drab; a little color was in order, she thought.

She reached into the medicine cabinet and took out a small, unlabeled bottle. One day about six months earlier when her parents were out visiting some friends, she sneaked into the bathroom in their bedroom and poured a little of her mother's foundation into her bottle. She was saving the makeup for moments just like this, when she wanted to look exceptionally good for someone special.

She shook the bottle, screwed off the lid, and then slowly poured some of the makeup onto the second and third fingers of her right hand. She remembered that the printing on the outside of the original bottle had said that the foundation would give her skin a "velvety matte finish." She started to apply some of the makeup to her chin. "Oh, no!" she uttered, staring at herself in the mirror. It was the wrong color; it was too light. She quickly rubbed the makeup off her face with a washcloth and some soap and water.

"Well, I guess it's time to start over," she whispered as she dried her skin with a towel. Then she heard her brother Fritz's voice.

"Get out of the bathroom, Franzi," he shouted. "You've spent enough time in there. Paul and I won't be ready for the *Mittagessen* (the main midday meal)."

Many of Franziska's relatives and friends called her "Franzi" (*pronounced "Frahnzi"*). It was a shorter name and far less formal. Still, she liked "Franziska" because it made her feel sophisticated, but "Franzi" was okay, too.

"Just give me a few more minutes," she shouted back.

She quickly powdered her face, thinly penciled her eyebrows and the inside of her lower eyelids, brushed some mascara onto her lashes, and . . .

"Get out of there," Paul yelled. "I don't understand what you women do in there for so long."

"I'll be out soon," she called back out.

She outlined her lips with a lipstick brush and filled them in with red lipstick. Then she smeared a touch of rouge on her cheeks, and her makeup was complete. She quickly grabbed a comb, parted her hair in the center, and then began brushing ferociously. When she was finished, she shoved all of the makeup on the table into a plastic bag and ran out of the bathroom with it into her bedroom next door.

Now she really had to rush. It was already half past twelve. She started grabbing dresses out of her closet and throwing them on the bed. Finally she pulled out a purple dress that she thought might do the trick. No, it was wrong. It was very fashionable, but it didn't have much of a waistline and was really too dressy to wear to a *Kino*. Franz wouldn't like it. She threw it on the bed with the others.

Then she decided on something very simple and casual: a dark blue pleated short skirt with a matching sweater, and a light blue blouse with a round Peter Pan collar. She dressed quickly, slipped into some dark blue leather pumps, placed the clothes laying on the bed back into the closet, and began to walk toward the door. Oh, she forgot; she needed a necklace. She opened the jewelry box on top of her chest of drawers and selected a strand of burgundy-colored beads. She placed them around her neck, arranged her hair neatly over them and walked toward the door again. Oh, she'd forgotten to look at herself in the full-length mirror. She rushed back into the room again and appraised herself. "Not bad," she said, nodding her head up and down. "Not bad at all." Then she walked toward the dining room.

Her father was seated at the head of the table, her mother at the other end. The boys were sitting on one side and Lilly on the other. The room was very elegant. The walls were ivory with accents of gold, a magnificent Gobelin tapestry panorama of Vienna hanging on one of them. The rectangular dining room table with cabriole legs seated eight, with a capacity for four more. It was embellished with a finely made linen tablecloth bordered with damascene lace. The chairs were reminiscent of those that graced the royal dining room in the imperial palace of Austria's rulers. They were upholstered in rich crimson velvet and framed with antique white-finished wood.

It was a few minutes past one.

"I'm sorry I'm late," Franziska said as she entered the room and took her place next to Lilly.

"We've been waiting for you," Heinrich responded.

Then he pushed a button on the wall behind him, and Hilde appeared.

"We're ready for *Mittagessen* now," he said.

"Yes, sir." She nodded and left.

"Father," Franziska began to speak. "I have something special to ask of you."

"So grown up and formal," Heinrich responded. "Father and not Papa? This must be important."

"Well, you see, Papa," Franziska continued, "I've met someone nice, and he's going to take me to the *Kino* this afternoon. He's coming here to pick me up at four."

"This fellow, how old is he and where did you meet him?"

"He's almost eighteen, and I met him last Saturday when *Mutti* (Mother) took me to a five o'clock tea."

Heinrich looked across the table directly into Stefanie's eyes, a perturbed look emerging on his face. "You took Franziska to a five o'clock tea?" he questioned Stefanie. "You know that I don't want her to date until she's seventeen."

"Yes, well, Judith was here; she's older, and I didn't think there would be any harm . . ."

"Have you taken Franziska to other such social events in the past?" Heinrich cut Stefanie off.

"Well, no . . ."

"I think we need to discuss this matter later in private," Heinrich concluded.

Just then, Hilde entered, served the soup and withdrew.

No one uttered a word. They just ate. . . . Finally . . .

"Franziska, I see that you're wearing more makeup than usual. I think that you'd look more natural without all of that lipstick and rouge," Heinrich remarked.

"Well, I'm going to *eat* off the lipstick," Franziska answered somewhat dismayed.

Both Paul and Fritz began to laugh.

Heinrich raised his eyebrows. "Please take some of the makeup off after *Mittagessen*," he continued.

Then Hilde removed the soup bowls and brought in the main course: *Wiener Schnitzel mit Petersilienkartoffeln* (breaded veal cutlet with parsley potatoes).

"Thank you," Heinrich said when she was finished serving. She promptly nodded once again and returned to the kitchen.

"Papa," Franziska tried to be more brazen. "The boy that's coming to pick me up . . . Franz . . . when he rings the doorbell, could I have him meet you and Mama in the living room instead of the den? It's so much nicer in there."

Heinrich declined to give Franziska an answer. "Does . . . Franz . . . go to school? Does he work? What does he do?" Heinrich asked.

"He attends a *Realgymnasium*. He told me he's going to graduate soon," Franziska said a little despairingly.

"Does he plan to go to a university?"

"I don't know, Papa. I just met him."

"Do you know any of his friends?"

"No. . . ."

"Have you met anyone from his family?"

"No, Papa. . . . But I know he has a mother and a sister; his father died; and he lives in Pötzleinsdorf."

"What kind of a career did his father have? How is his mother supporting the family?"

"I don't know, Papa," Franziska said, feeling a little frenzied.

"Heinrich," Stefanie finally interceded. "I think that your questioning is somewhat excessive. I met Franz myself last week, and he seems to be a very admirable young gentleman. Now let's eat our meal in peace. We can discuss this matter later."

They finished their *Wiener Schnitzel* with very little conversation. Then Hilde brought in some *Palatschinken* (rolled pancakes filled with jam) for dessert.

"Oh, boy," Paul shouted. "I'm glad I saved some room for this. What kind of marmalade is inside?"

"Your favorite," Hilde answered. "Apricot."

"I'll take a double serving of that." Paul smiled with glee.

"I don't want any," Franziska said to Hilde. "I still want to be able to close my skirt before I go out today."

There was a strange sadness in Franziska's voice. She couldn't understand her father's behavior. She thought that when she told him about Franz, he'd be happy for her. Instead, it seemed the reverse held true.

After *Mittagessen*, Fritz and Paul went back to the bedroom they shared, and the others proceeded into the den. Heinrich sat on the big brown leather easy chair and began reading Vienna's leading newspaper, the *Neue Freie Presse*. Stefanie settled on the couch with some knitting, and Lilly sat next to her with a book.

"I'm going to go freshen up," Franziska said somewhat insecurely, standing in the middle of the room. "It's almost three. Franz will be here in a little more than an hour. Oh, and Papa, I don't care anymore where you meet him. If you're more comfortable here in the den than in the living room, that's fine with me too." Then Franziska started to turn toward the door.

"Franziska, wait a minute," Heinrich suddenly said, setting his newspaper down. "We never finished the conversation we started earlier."

Hearing his remarks, Stefanie put her knitting aside and looked up curiously.

"Franziska," Heinrich said almost unexpectedly even to himself. "I don't want you to go out this afternoon with Franz."

Franziska was stunned. She started to get dizzy and thought she was going to fall, but she remained standing. Then she began to feel shaky inside.

"But, Papa, I don't understand. . . . Why? Why can't I go out with Franz?" she asked, feeling a choking pain in her throat, holding back the tears.

"You're simply too young to go on a date," Heinrich said firmly, even though it was secretly breaking his heart to see her so unhappy. "Seventeen . . . when you're seventeen you can start dating. Your mother shouldn't have taken you to that five o'clock tea."

"But she *did* take me, and I met someone nice," Franziska pleaded. "Can't you make an exception just this one time?"

"No, no I can't, Franziska." Heinrich refused to bend. "One time leads to another. And it appears that you like this boy much too much; you're definitely too young to get serious with anyone."

"But Franz is going to be here in an hour. I don't have his telephone number, and even if I did, it would be too late to call and tell him not to come. What am I going to do?"

"Don't worry about it," Heinrich assured her. "When he arrives, I'll simply explain to him that you aren't feeling well and regret that you didn't have any way of reaching him."

"But that's not even the truth," Franziska began to cry.

"No, but it will be the easiest, least painful reason to communicate to him."

Suddenly, for the first time in her life, Franziska had a feeling of disrespect for her father. Although she would never tell him outright, she thought that he was acting cowardly. Then she tried another approach.

"Mutti, you met Franz. Tell Papa all about him."

Stefanie nodded her head affirmatively at Franziska. Then her eyes turned toward her husband. "Well, Heinrich, as I told you before, Franz seems to be a very commendable young gentleman," she confirmed. "In fact, I even had the pleasure of dancing with him. And before he took Franzi out into the garden, I asked him to bring her back in precisely ten minutes, and that's exactly what he did."

"You mean that you allowed the children to go out alone into a garden?" Heinrich asked her, somewhat disconcertedly. "What time was it? Was it dark?"

"It was about half past seven," Stefanie responded. "I don't know what is wrong with you, Heinrich. Franziska has always been trustworthy."

"Yes, but she's maturing, and she's starting to have different sensations that she might not be able to contain," Heinrich muttered. "And the boy's almost eighteen. . . . But I do not want to discuss that particular aspect of it right here and now with you."

Franziska could not understand her father. Instead of helping her cause, Stefanie seemed to have unintentionally harmed it.

"I will not change my mind," Heinrich reiterated. "Franziska is *not* to go out with Franz today."

Franziska looked into her mother's helpless eyes as her own filled with tears. She turned toward the door and rushed out of the den down the hallway into her bedroom. She slammed the door shut, threw herself onto the bed, and cried "Why, Papa? Why, Papa?" so many times that it seemed like every muscle in her body had gone limp. Why had her father hurt her like this? Why had he broken her heart?

The doorbell rang precisely at four o'clock. Just a few minutes before, Franz had entered the lobby of Blütengasse Neun and climbed the marble stairway on the right, thus avoiding the elevator, which had looked to him like a metal animal cage, on the left. He'd been waiting a whole week to see Franziska again. He could hardly contain himself.

When he rang the doorbell on the first floor, he expected to meet the maid. Instead, it was Franziska's father who greeted him.

"*Guten Tag* (Good afternoon)," Heinrich said, opening the door. "Why don't you come in?"

"*Guten Tag*, Herr Perger," Franz duplicated. "I have a date with your daughter. I'm Franz Jung."

"Yes, I've been expecting you. Let's go out onto the patio," Heinrich said, leading Franz through a door in the entry hall directly to the outside. "Please, have a seat."

For some reason, Franz already felt uncertain and insecure as he sat down on one of the garden chairs next to Heinrich.

"I've heard so many nice things about you from Franziska and my wife," Heinrich complimented, attempting to start a cordial conversation. Franz looked so young and impressionable that Heinrich didn't want to jolt the poor boy too suddenly with the bad news. "Franziska tells me that you hope to graduate from a *Realgymnasium* soon."

"Yes, sir, I do."

"That's very commendable of you."

"Thank you, sir."

"What do you plan to do after that?" Heinrich asked.

"I don't know, sir." Franz was beginning to get nervous. "My father died earlier this year, and I'm trying to help my mother get started in a new little *Putzerei*."

"Oh, very nice," Heinrich said, nodding his head approvingly, yet thinking that Franz obviously did not come from a well-to-do enough family to have an alliance with his daughter. It wasn't that Franz wasn't good enough for Franziska; Heinrich simply wanted to safeguard her from any financial woes in the future. He'd made the right decision, he concluded; he was doing what was best for his daughter.

"Herr Perger, is Franziska getting ready?" Franz then asked with anticipation. "How long do you think it will be before she joins us?"

"I'm afraid I have some disappointing news," Heinrich said, trying not to look directly into Franz's eyes. "Franziska isn't feeling well, and she won't be able to go out with you this afternoon. She's very sorry, but she didn't know how to reach you."

Heinrich's disclosure had been totally unexpected. Franz was caught completely off guard. He sat on his chair immobile and totally confused. Was this an excuse? Did it mean that he would never see Franziska again? Or was she really sick? She'd just recovered from rheumatic fever; maybe she'd had a relapse. In any event, Franz was too intimidated by Heinrich to ask many questions.

"Oh, I'm so sorry," he told Heinrich very sincerely. "I hope she feels better soon. I was so looking forward to this date. We were going to walk to the *Kino*; then I was going to take her for some pastries."

Franz was hoping that Heinrich would respond by saying something like: "Another time, perhaps." But he didn't.

Franz assumed the worst: He would never see Franziska again. But, why? He would probably never know for sure. It was as if an arrow had pierced his heart. He grew very pale and became unaware of his surroundings. He almost felt numb.

"It's been very nice chatting with you," he told Heinrich, attempting to raise himself up from his chair, "but I really think that I should go."

"I understand," Heinrich said, grasping Franz's forearm and leading him cautiously back into the entry hall.

Once in front of the door, Franz had the presence of mind to take a pen and some paper from his pocket, and to write down his name and telephone number. In addition, he simply wrote the words: *"I'm waiting."*

"Please give this note to Franziska," he said to Heinrich, folding the piece of paper and handing it to him. "I would really appreciate that."

Heinrich took the note, and the boy and the man just stood at the door and looked at each other without speaking. Franz felt his face becoming a little flushed, and the tears started to well up into his eyes. He was almost grown up – this wasn't supposed to happen.

"I have to go," he said, quickly reaching out and shaking Heinrich's hand. "*Auf Wiedersehen.*"

He pulled the door open and rushed out, leaving Heinrich alone in the entry hall with the note. Heinrich felt sorry for the boy, but he was not about to lose his little girl yet. He closed the door and started to walk back toward the den. Then, without even reading the note, he began to tear it up into a million little pieces.

CHAPTER FOUR

Around and About

Vienna, Austria
10 September to 20 October 1927

$\mathcal{F}$ranz was convinced that he was not suffering from puppy love; this was the real thing. Puppy love wouldn't hurt this much. When he arrived back in Pötzleinsdorf, he was completely spent and didn't have the energy to speak to anyone. He couldn't face Ilona; she was so excited for him that she said she would wait up for him so that he could tell her all the "marvelous details." He wanted to postpone the humiliation, so instead of walking directly home from the tramway terminal, he wandered around the neighborhood instead. Two losses in one year was too much for him: first, the biggest in his life – his father; and now, Franziska.

He hadn't even felt this empty inside when he'd been out on his first, and only, hunting expedition. He was about thirteen then. Fritz Sachsel's father had invited some boys from the *Realgymnasium* to partake in the excursion. The boys were led to a remote area in the Vienna Woods and were instructed to shake the bushes and trees with the sticks that they were given. The hunters positioned themselves about three kilometers (two miles) away. And as the boys rustled the shrubbery and the petrified animals sallied forth, the scheming game hunters fired at their outmaneuvered prey.

When Franz was safely home, he remembered that a little squirrel had been shot by accident, and no one had seemed to care. Well, he cared; he cared very deeply, so he declared to Vinzi that he was about to go back into the woods to search for the victimized creature. At about five o'clock, she offered to escort him; they rummaged through foliage and dirt, but they were unable to locate the squirrel. Franz was very discouraged and disheartened, but the two decided to abandon their endeavor and return home. However, when they arrived at ten o'clock, a surprise delegation was waiting there for them: Franz's parents had been so worried that they'd called the police and alerted the neighbors. And although Franz felt grateful for the reception, he couldn't help but think about the poor dejected squirrel. He was downhearted about the ill-fated animal for weeks.

And now, this pain that he felt inside was even much greater. How would he ever survive it? He was still walking in the Pötzleinsdorfer-Schlosspark across the street from his house when the sun was beginning to set behind the hills. A tall, thin man wearing a white smock was illuminating the gaslit streetlights with a long stick. In the morning, another man would smother the burning gas jets out. It was time for Franz to leave the solitude of the park and go home.

Both Ilona and his mother sensed there was something wrong when he didn't enter through the main entrance to greet them in the living room, but opted for the back entrance instead. Then they heard him go upstairs.

"You better find out what happened," his mother said to Ilona. "Why don't you go and look in on him?"

Ilona nodded, then advanced toward the stairway.

A few seconds later, she knocked on his bedroom door. "Franz," she said warmly. "It's me; can I come in?"

"Sure," Franz responded almost inaudibly. "Do you want your Schillings back?"

"Very funny," she said as she entered and found him sitting at his desk with his back hunched over and his head cradled on his arms. She made herself comfortable on his bed, and then he told her the whole story.

"I need to know what happened," he said, with a sound of desperation in his voice. "Is Franziska really sick or did Herr Perger make up an excuse? And if the excuse was fabricated, why? Did Franziska's mother or father dislike something about me? Or did Franziska change her mind?"

"Oh, how could she change her mind about you?" Ilona tried to console him.

"I handed her father a piece of paper with my telephone number on it. I hope he gave it to her. . . . Oh, I just had a terrible thought. What if she really is seriously ill? I'm so worried. I can't even let her know that I care."

"Now don't jump to conclusions," Ilona advised. "Why don't you wait a few days? Maybe Franziska will call you."

Franz waited, but Franziska didn't call. He tried to take his mind off her by helping his mother organize her *Putzerei*. Since most of the dry-cleaning and laundering would be done off the premises, Olga needed to contract with a laundry and dry-cleaning plant to pick up her customers' garments and linens, clean or wash them, and then return them to her *Putzerei* when finished. Franz was doing the preliminary ground-work for his mother. He was locating businesses and speaking to their owners to determine which would be suitable, efficient, and comparatively moderately priced.

At the same time, Olga was creating storage spaces and installing clothes racks for outgoing garments and for those which would be returned. She was setting up a customer-service counter, devising a garment labeling system, and was retaining part of Jakob's old office to set up files. She still had a lot of work in front of her before the *Putzerei* would be ready for opening; however, she was aware of what had to be done, and she knew she was capable of accomplishing it.

Even though Franz went there every day and drowned himself in work, he couldn't stop longing for Franziska. Every time he went to a soccer game at the stadium in the Prater, he was reminded of her, because she lived only minutes away. And every time he ran around the track, which was located in the same vicinity, he was reminded of her again. He had to do something about his dilemma.

He finally made a decision that he wouldn't tell anyone. He'd go to her apartment and wait for her to either leave or come home, he thought. But then what? If she was with her father, he certainly wouldn't be able to approach her. But then he could go back and try again. Franz suddenly felt better; he had a plan.

Now, when should he attempt it? He thought and thought. He couldn't go when she left for school in the morning because he had to work at the *Putzerei*; he didn't want anyone in his own family to get suspicious. He'd try one afternoon. He'd tell his mother that he planned to run around the track. It was Tuesday; he'd go on Thursday.

The fateful day arrived. Franz jumped on the tram at the terminal by the *Börse* and was standing in front of Franziska's apartment at half past four. Even though the building was on the corner of Blütengasse and Löwengasse, the main entrance to Blütengasse Neun was halfway up the block. Franz didn't want to be noticed, so he hurried down Blütengasse to the corner, crossed the street, and then slid into a small coffeehouse that looked like a miniature Café Central, the famous coffeehouse near the city center where many literary and political figures often gathered. Similarly, this café had small round tables without tablecloths scattered throughout, and a refrigerated glass-enclosed display of pastries at the back. Franz sat at a table near the window where he had an unobstructed bird's-eye view of Franziska's apartment building.

"*Guten Tag*," a waiter said, standing in front of him.

"*Eine Tasse Kaffee, bitte*," Franz said, ordering a cup of coffee.

Then he sat and watched. The waiter brought the *Kaffee*; Franz sipped it slowly and continued to sit and watch. At half past five, he ordered another *Kaffee*. He was beginning to feel fidgety and nervous. At six, he paid the check and left. He walked up Löwengasse to Hetzgasse and then paced back to the corner. There was no sign of Franziska.

Then Franz watched two automobiles almost collide at the intersection under scrutiny. One was a green Duesenberg with a black top; the other, a black Mercedes-Benz. Franz observed the Duesenberg move up Blütengasse in the direction of Franziska's apartment and then turn right onto Löwengasse. The Benz, which was moving through the intersection down Löwengasse, then almost clipped the back left side of the

Duesenberg. The driver of the Benz was obviously very impatient and hadn't been paying attention; the driver of the Duesenberg wasn't even aware that anything had happened. Franz watched with bated breath; then he sighed with relief.

He looked at his watch; it was almost six-thirty. Then suddenly he saw a kind of stodgy man in a business suit walking down the other side of the street. It was Franziska's father. *He must be coming home from work; he must have just gotten off the tram*, Franz thought. *Oh, my gosh! If I can see him, he can probably see me. What should I do? I know . . . I'll run. . . .*

With that notion in mind, Franz took off as fast as his legs would carry him. It was as if he'd become airborne. Now he knew what all of that long-distance track running was really about. He raced down Blüten-gasse, realizing that Franziska's father would be walking in the opposite direction, turned right at Blattgasse, turned right again at Hetzgasse, and then virtually leaped onto the tram when he came back around again to the station at Löwengasse. He was out of breath and drops of perspiration were trickling down his face. *That was enough detective work for one day*, he thought. *I'll have to try again some other time.*

Franz went back twice the following week, but Franziska never appeared. He refused to get discouraged though; he was convinced that with perseverance, he would prevail. Hopefully his fortuitous day would be on the fourteenth day of October, which was just one day shy of six weeks since he'd met Franziska. He literally ached to see her again. This was his lucky Friday; he felt it. At three o'clock, he was staked out at the coffeehouse across the street from her apartment building. He was tearing the napkin at his table into bits. He drank one cup of *Kaffee*, then another. Where was she? Then suddenly it started to rain; it started to pour. He was glad that he was wearing an overcoat and had remembered to take an umbrella. October could be a cold month in Vienna, and rain often came unexpectedly. Then finally, finally he saw her. She was getting out of a blue Ford across the street at the corner. She waved as the Ford pulled away and then started to run up Blüten-gasse toward her apartment. She was wearing a coat but didn't seem to have an umbrella. Then she slipped and fell. She was sitting on the wet sidewalk, her beautiful black hair getting sopping wet. She was crying.

Franz quickly threw some money on his table to cover the check and ran out the door. Luckily there weren't very many cars on the road because his eyes were fixed on Franziska as he crossed the intersection. He hadn't bothered to open his umbrella. He was getting drenched, but he didn't even notice. Both the street and the sidewalk were slippery and he almost fell himself a few times, but he resisted. The water was already so high that it bounced up onto the legs of his trousers. Finally he reached Franziska and bent down so that she could see his eyes. "It's going to be okay," he said, putting his arms around her.

She was more frightened than anything else. He let her cry. Then he pushed her back gently. "Are you all right?" he asked softly, wiping the rain and tears from her cheeks.

"I think so," she said. "I'm sure I just scraped my leg, that's all. . . . Oh, I'm so glad to see you. I thought I'd never see you again."

"Me too," he said elatedly, helping Franziska to her feet and opening his umbrella to shelter them. "What happened? Please tell me what happened? Didn't you get my note? I gave it to your father."

"No, I never got it," she said. "But that's understandable. What did it say?"

"It said that I'd be waiting for you," Franz responded shyly. "It had my telephone number on it."

"Oh, how sweet," Franziska said with a tenderness in her eyes. "And I *would* have called you."

"So you didn't change your mind about me?"

"Oh, no!" Franziska responded almost instantaneously. "On that Saturday, the day of our date, I was very excited. I'd spent hours getting dressed. Then at *Mittagessen*, my father announced that he wouldn't allow me to go out with you. He said that I can't start dating until I'm seventeen."

"I'll wait," Franz said playfully. "But until then, can we see each other a little bit on the sly?"

"I'm afraid that's what we'll have to do if I decide to disobey my father," Franziska answered. "I just don't understand him. He's never denied me anything. Even my mother tried to reason with him. . . . And then he came up with that cowardly excuse."

"Well, I'm grateful that you're not sick," Franz admitted. "I was really worried for a while."

"You were?"

"Yes, I was."

For some reason, hearing that was like music to Franziska's ears. Someone had "worried" about her. She couldn't have been more flattered.

"Franziska, can you think of any reason why your father might not like me?" Franz asked.

"Not that I know of. . . . He doesn't really even know you; well, for that matter, neither do I."

"I'd like you to get to know me, Franziska, and I'd like to get to know you, too. . . . It's raining, and this isn't a very good place to talk. Do you think we could meet sometime? Maybe some afternoon?"

"Yes, I'd like that very much, except I'd be doing something against my father's wishes. . . . Well, all right. I really *do* want to see you again."

"How about next Thursday?" Franz suggested. We could meet at the *Praterstern* (Prater Star) near the *Riesenrad* and then walk and talk to get to know each other."

"That's a good idea," Franziska responded. "The location is convenient. It's close to home. I'll just stop off at home after school and then meet you there."

Franz wanted to ask the whereabouts of Franziska's *Lyzeum*, but he didn't want to breach upon the subject of education lest it would lead to a discussion about the *Realgymnasium* he allegedly attended as well. "Is half past three a good time?" he asked.

"Perfect. I'll see you there."

Franz walked Franziska to the doorway of her building. Then just as he had done almost five weeks earlier, he took a pen and a piece of paper from his pocket, wrote a note, and folded it. "Please keep this piece of paper in case you want to reach me," he said, handing the note to Franziska.

She opened it. Once again, he had written his name and telephone number; however, this time, he had added the words: "*If you need me for any reason, I am yours.*"

Franziska smiled at Franz and held the note to her heart. Then she reached around him, stretched up onto her toes, and planted a quick, soft kiss on his cheek.

"See you at the Prater," she whispered in his ear. Then she swiftly opened the door to her apartment building and disappeared.

The Prater, originally an imperial hunting ground of woods and meadows between the Danube River and Danube Canal, was opened to the public in 1766. Its chestnut tree-lined *Hauptallee* (main avenue) became the haunt of members of the aristocracy and upper classes, who paraded up and down it by foot and in carriages. Prater cafés remained fashionable until after World War I; then many were closed as the Prater slowly became more of an amusement park and the home of sports facilities, with the *Riesenrad* at the western end and the remaining Lusthaus café and restaurant at the other.

Franziska's father had often taken Franziska and the rest of the family to the Lusthaus for Sunday *Mittagessen*. The former imperial hunting lodge had been redesigned into a two-story octagonal pavilion with a balcony, columns, and a pyramid-shaped roof. Franziska always felt like such a lady when she ate there. She was daydreaming about the restaurant while waiting at the *Praterstern* for Franz to appear for their first real date.

I love it here, she thought, inhaling deeply. *I love the way the trees smell.*

It was autumn and most of the leaves were yellowish-brown and falling from the trees in preparation for winter. The weather was already quite cold, yet Franziska enjoyed the fresh, crisp quality of the air; she found it invigorating. And although the dying leaves often made her feel sad, she knew that much as in all life, the cycle would continue and a generation of new leaves would be born in the spring. As she stood there deep in thought, she felt a tap on her shoulder. "Oh!" she jumped.

"I didn't mean to scare you; it's only me," Franz said.

She started to laugh. Then he started to laugh. They hugged each other intensely and unyieldingly. Then he took her hand, placing his fingers between hers, and began walking with her toward the *Hauptallee*.

"I should have been born years ago," Franziska said, as they started to walk down the lovely boulevard.

"Why is that?" Franz asked.

"Because I would have adored dressing up finely for you and having you escort me down this street in a *Fiaker* (horse-drawn carriage). We could have even waltzed at one of the stylish cafés."

"One day you could dress up and we could dine at the Lusthaus," Franz suggested.

"I would like that," she responded. "But right now, why don't we go on the *Riesenrad*?"

Within a short time, they were sitting in a red-and-white cabin on the two hundred twelve-foot-high giant Ferris wheel, which moved slowly at thirty inches per second and made one complete rotation every twenty minutes. Even though both had ridden on the park's major attraction many times, this particular instance somehow seemed different, as they sat hand in hand alone together sharing the spectacular view of their city from what seemed to be the top of the world. They didn't say much; they just wanted to enjoy the warmth of their bodies next to each other. Franziska felt an elated happiness inside that she never knew existed, and Franz felt a oneness with her that gave him peace.

When the wheel brought them safely down to earth, they left their cabin feeling as if they'd been jolted from euphoria back into reality. They shared some cotton candy: first he took a bite, then she. Then they walked back to the *Hauptallee* and continued to promenade down the boulevard. He told her virtually everything about his family and interests; and likewise, she did the same. Then they sat on a bench along the way, and she described her plans to attend a specialized tailoring and design school when she graduated from the *Lyzeum*. Franz realized that his moment of reckoning had finally arrived.

"Franziska," he said. "I have something to tell you, and I beg you to try to be understanding."

"Why, what is it, Franz?" she asked, searching for the answer in his sad hazel eyes.

"I've misled you, Franziska. I'm so sorry. You see . . . I *did* attend a *Realgymnasium*, and I *was* supposed to graduate the end of this school year; but when my father died, my mother asked me to drop out of school temporarily to help her liquidate my father's business and to assist her in establishing her own. She wants me to go back to the *Realgymnasium* to graduate, but I don't know if I want to or not. I'm so sorry if I misled you. . . . You're so beautiful. You could have your pick of so many young men who probably have much better futures than I do. . . . I just wanted you to like me."

At first Franziska didn't say anything. Then: "Franz, I like you because you're kind and sensitive. It's true that you misled me, but I also drew my own conclusions. You never really said that you were attending school right now. I just assumed you were because you told me that you'd be graduating soon. Of course, now you don't really know if you want to or not. . . . Franz, I want you to do what makes you happy, but from now on, please be truthful with me."

"I will," Franz said as if the load on his back had finally been lifted. "When I thought that I'd lost you, I couldn't bear it. I don't want anything to ever stand in the way of your trust."

"I appreciate your honesty with me. . . . Now come on, let's stop being so serious. I didn't come here to frown."

Franziska stood up, grabbed Franz's forearm and pulled him up from the bench. Then she started running down the *Hauptallee*, and he chased after her. The leaves of the chestnut trees seemed to semi-cloak the boulevard much as an umbrella with multiple tears would, allowing the light and warmth of the sun to filter through. Franziska ran and ran until Franz caught up to her; after all, he was a long-distance track runner. She held on to the trunk of one of the chestnut trees and started to circle it; then she vacillated from one side to the other. He held her hands in place on the trunk. "What are you doing?" he asked laughingly.

"I'm trying to get away from you," she flirted coquettishly.

"Well, we'll see about that." He kissed her boldly on the lips.

She broke away from his grasp and started to run into the park. Few people seemed to be frequenting the area on this late Thursday afternoon. She swerved in between the trees as he faithfully followed. "I've got you; I've got you," he shouted, gently dragging her down to the grass.

"Oh no, no, no!" she screamed, as he started to move his body over hers.

She wriggled backward until she was cornered up against a tree. "I like you, I like you, I like you; but I'm too young," she blurted out. "My mother knows I'm seeing you and she trusts me."

"You mean you told her?" Franz asked, surprised.

"Yes. She promised to keep our dating a secret from my father. She likes you and somehow feels responsible for our meeting."

"Well, I like her too, but I like her daughter better. . . . Oh, Franziska, I just want to hold you and kiss you, that's all."

"That's all?" Franziska uttered somewhat perplexed, sitting on the ground quite still.

"That's all for now," Franz amended, sitting next to her and putting his arms around her protectingly.

Then he placed her face between both of his hands. "You are so special," he said. "You have to promise me that you will always let me know what you want and what you think. I will never do anything to hurt you, and I will always respect your wishes."

"I promise to tell you what I think," she said mesmerized.

He kissed her forehead and her nose, and then she closed her eyes as he kissed her left eyelid and then her right. Then she could feel his mouth on hers, forcing her lips apart. She couldn't resist. She allowed him to kiss her deeply and completely as she began to feel new, unknown tingling sensations writhing throughout her body. He moved away; she drew him toward her. They kissed passionately, surrendering to each other's impulses.

He unbuttoned her wool tweed coat and placed his arms under it, holding her tight. He moved his hands up and down her back, dreaming of slipping them first underneath her sweater and then her blouse. *Oh, what ecstasy to be able to feel her soft skin*, he thought. As he fantasized, he became more-and-more excited, more-and-more impassioned. He didn't want to stop, yet he knew he must. He was already aware of how very much he cared for her.

"That's enough," he said, pulling his arms away. "This could lead to a place we shouldn't go."

"You're right," she answered. "But, oh, what fun."

He gave the tip of her nose an affectionate pat with his forefinger. "You are so cute," he said, buttoning up her coat. He took her hand, and they both struggled to their feet. Then he put his arm around her waist, and they began to walk out of the woody area and back up the *Hauptallee.*

When they reached the place where their date had begun, they both seemed content and fulfilled. They put their arms around each other one more time.

Then she would return to Blütengasse Neun to tell her mother how happy she was.

And he would return to Pötzleinsdorfer Strasse One Hundred Thirty to tell his sister that he'd finally had the opportunity to spend her Schillings, and that he was going to have a happy eighteenth birthday after all.

CHAPTER FIVE
Bits and Pieces

Vienna, Austria
November 1927 to October 1931

*N*ovember and December of 1927 were very good months for Franz and Franziska. They saw each other often. Franz usually picked Franziska up at her *Lyzeum*, and the two of them walked to the Kai, or as far as the weather would allow. Sometimes to vary the scenery, they took a tram to an outer district of the city and strolled there. They usually stopped for *Kaffee*, and then Franz escorted Franziska back into her neighborhood. They said their farewells a few blocks from her home and then went their separate ways. When they were together, they were blissfully happy and the outside world ceased to exist.

On Franziska's sixteenth birthday – Monday, the twenty-eighth of November – Franz arrived at her *Lyzeum* with a bouquet of roses. When she read the enclosed note, she began to cry.

Dear Franziska,

Last night I dreamt that my heart was creeping away from me, and when I asked it where it was going, it said that it was leaving me because it could not bear to be away from you. So you see, my little Franziska, without you, my heart is forsaking me.

So please do not be frightened if I say that I believe I love you. I am not sure, but I think that the feelings exploding like firecrackers inside of my body must mean that I do. I only hope that you will one day feel the same way. Although we met less than three months ago, you have changed my life completely. I do not know what lies in the future, but I would like to be with you always, shield you from harm, and give you my devotion.

Happy Birthday, my sweet Franziska!

Franz

Franziska was indeed touched. She knew that she loved him too; however, she would not reveal her true feelings just yet.

The Christmas season was a beautiful time of year in Vienna. The city was a spectacle of lights and decorations. Even though Franziska was Jewish, she couldn't help but enjoy wandering through the various Christmas markets which displayed the work of some of Vienna's most talented craftsmen. This year she enlisted Franz, who was also Jewish, to walk with her. The market in front of the Gothic-style *Rathaus* (City Hall) was particularly inviting. There were decorations, toys, and beautiful gifts for sale amid a fairy-tale atmosphere with music, homemade desserts, and hot punch.

On New Year's Eve, Franziska's mother told Heinrich that their daughter was going to a *Kino* with a girlfriend. In reality, she went to the Deutsches Volkstheater with Franz to see two comedians: Farkasch and Grünbaum.

In January, Franz's mother opened her *Putzerei*. All of the details had been accomplished, including her hiring of a delivery person and her purchase of a large rotary presser, or mangle, which Vinzi would use to flatten clean but wrinkled linens and garments returned from the laundry. One last touch: a sign with the word, "*Putzerei*," and Olga Jung was in business.

At the beginning, the *Putzerei* was a family affair. Naturally Olga was there all day. Franz arrived with her in the morning, but often left early to meet Franziska. Ilona came at about one, usually with Vinzi, who brought the family a homemade *Mittagessen* and then spent the rest of the afternoon pressing.

Olga was amazed how quickly people became aware of the *Putzerei* and began enlisting her services. There were no other *Putzereien* in the area, so those who lived and worked in the neighborhood were grateful to have hers nearby.

Franz and Franziska continued to see each other and develop their relationship. Once in a while, Franziska met Franz at the *Putzerei*. On these occasions, she always tried to have a polite conversation with Franz's mother and sister. They received her warmly, and she quickly began to feel like one of the family.

In June, Franziska graduated from the *Lyzeum* and immediately made plans to attend a school of tailoring and design in the fall. She selected one that was located near the juncture of the northeast portion of the Ringstrasse and the Kai.

Beginning that July, Franz and Franziska usually met at the Urania, a bizarre, unconventional-looking building situated at that juncture. Then one Tuesday, Franziska telephoned Franz at the *Putzerei* to say that she wouldn't be able to meet him for a few weeks. Her brother, Paul, had contracted whooping cough. And because the disease was so contagious, her mother had sent Lilly and Fritz to live with their grandparents. The conversation continued as follows:

"So if the disease is so contagious, what are you doing in the apartment?" Franz asked a little perturbed.

"Mother is going through one of her moments of crisis," Franziska answered. "That's when she depends on me."

"Aren't you afraid you're going to catch it?"

"Sure. It's only been a year since I had rheumatic fever; I don't want to be sick again."

"What are the symptoms?"

"Well, first Paul just started sneezing and seemed to have a cold; then he developed a dry cough," Franziska described. "The doctor made some cultures and determined that he had whooping cough."

"What's next?"

"Well, he's supposed to start coughing five to fifteen times in succession ending with a deep indrawn breath that creates the whooping sound of a high-pitched crow. When he coughs, I'm supposed to stay away from the spray; that's what's so contagious. He has to have all of his own dishes and linens, and the doctor wants him to be isolated."

"How long is this going to last?" Franz continued to delve.

"The doctor said about six weeks. After three weeks, Paul probably won't be contagious anymore, and after four-to-five weeks, the coughing is supposed to slowly subside. He's taking some fairly heavy medication."

"Anything else?"

"Well, he could hemorrhage or develop pneumonia, which could be fatal, but Mama and I are going to take good care of him so that he doesn't."

"How long are your brother and sister going to be away?"

"Mama hopes they can come home in about three or four weeks."

"You know, Franzi, maybe I shouldn't be saying this, but I'm somewhat angry that your mother didn't send you to live with your grandparents too. I think she was being selfish and inconsiderate."

"Don't be so hard on her, Franz; she gets so flustered sometimes."

"And your father, what did he say?"

"He stayed out of it. He just wants peace in the house when he comes home at night."

"Okay," Franz started to soften. "You know I'll miss you terribly. If you need help of any kind, please telephone me."

"I will," Franziska said. "I'm going to call you a lot during the day when Papa isn't home."

"Great," Franz responded. "Please take good care of yourself. I worry so."

"I know," Franziska replied. *"That's why I love you."*

She'd finally said it. Franz wasn't sure he'd heard correctly.

"You do?" he asked, hoping she'd repeat the words again.

"Yes, I love you; and the next time I see you in person, I plan to tell you face-to-face and lips-to-lips. I only told you now because I thought you needed to hear it."

"Oh, Franziska, I'm so happy. You've given me an early birthday present."

"I'm so glad. . . . Now I better go and help Mama."

"Please stay well, my darling little girl," Franz said lovingly. *"Auf Wiedersehen."*

"Auf Wiedersehen, my sweet."

After the conversation, the two smitten teen-agers felt quite hollow inside. Franz knew that he had to wait for Franziska to contact him since he'd made it a policy never to telephone her at home.

About a week later, she called the *Putzerei.* "Could you do me a huge favor?" she asked.

Her voice warmed him inside when he heard it. "Anything," he replied.

"Come over and stand outside the building in front my apartment. I'll tell you what I need from the window."

"I've waited for days to see your dark gorgeous eyes. . . . I'll be right over."

When he arrived, Franziska was waiting. Just seeing her from the window made his heart beat strongly inside his chest.

Franziska didn't really need anything; she just wanted to be near Franz. She felt as if she'd go mad if she had to stay cooped up in her apartment for one more day without seeing him.

"Well, here I am," he shouted up to her. "I guess I'm Romeo and you're my Juliet."

Then Franziska began reciting Shakespeare's lines from Juliet's balcony scene.

Franz was amazed. "I didn't know you had such talents. That was beautiful," he uttered, realizing that on this day, the words were meant for him.

"I love to go to the Burgtheater, and Shakespeare is one of my favorite playwrights," Franziska revealed.

"Well, I'll have to take you there sometime. . . . Now, what is it that you need?"

"Actually . . . I need you," she announced.

"Oh, Franzi, I need you too. Why don't you come downstairs for a few minutes?"

"I can't," she explained. "I could be carrying whooping cough bacteria in me, and I don't want you to catch it."

"I don't care. I'll take my chances," Franz responded.

"Well, I care. In fact, when Paul stops being contagious, I'm still not going to see you for at least a week to make absolutely sure that I haven't caught it."

The conversation continued until Franz began to worry that Franziska's father would soon be seen walking up the street. Franz left sadly without receiving the kisses Franziska had promised him when she first vowed her love; however, he had all good intentions of claiming them later.

Toward the end of August, Franziska finally telephoned Franz to inform him that her brother and sister had moved back home. Paul was no longer contagious; and even though he was still sick, the worst part of the disease was over. Franziska wanted to meet Franz at the Urania.

The Urania was an odd-shaped multi-story building, educational institution and observatory, which also housed a *Kino* that featured educational films. It had a style all its own and didn't seem to fit with the other buildings along the Ring, which were a potpourri of the past. Franz and Franziska never went inside the *Kino*; they liked the building for other reasons.

It was Monday, the third of September. Franziska was wearing a clinging jersey two-piece dress that completely revealed the contour of her body. She wanted Franz to notice her every curve. As she stood at the entrance to the Urania, her stomach was fluttering uncontrollably. "Stop this," she kept whispering to herself. "There is absolutely no reason to be nervous."

When she saw Franz's face as he crossed Uraniastrasse and walked toward her, all of her jittery uneasiness vanished. They ran toward each other and embraced. "Is it you? Is it really you?" Franz kept asking, as he moved his hands up and down her body, beginning to kiss her impetuously without reserve.

They held hands and ran past the front of the Urania to the side that was adjacent to the Danube Canal just below. They walked toward the back of the building and down some steps that went under it like a subterranean crosswalk. But they didn't come out at the other end, which was level with the canal. "Oh, I've missed you; I've missed you so much," Franz said, holding Franziska's face in his hands and kissing her gently. Then as the passion began to surge through his body, he held her close and began kissing her with fervent desire. The little alcove that sheltered them was dark as Franz pulled Franziska down to one of the steps. Their lips were parted now, their mouths hungry for fulfillment. She began to feel the heat sizzling through her every pore. She wanted him desperately and completely; her appetite seemed insatiable.

He was kissing her face now: her forehead, her nose, and her eyes. His hands were brushing up and down her back and along the outside of her thighs. Then they moved up the sides of her torso until they reached her breasts. But the jersey material had become encumbering. She sensed it, grasped one of his hands and guided it under the top of her dress. Her skin was soft to the touch, his rapture increasing. He unfastened her bra and began caressing her breasts. He lifted the top of her dress and kissed one and then the other, then glided his tongue in between them.

She untucked his shirt and snuck her hands underneath it. Up and down his back they journeyed. She explored her new territory with the tips of her fingers. She was touching his chest now, responding sensually to his masculine physique. He kissed her longingly as his hands began gravitating back down to her thighs. His right hand moved under her skirt and up the inside of her leg until it reached the core of her sexuality. Then he felt her hand on his. She was signaling him to go no further. She was right, he knew. They had time; they had their whole lives. But still at this moment of animalistic fervor, it was difficult for him to refrain. Yet he did.

He helped her to her feet and hugged her tightly. As he held her entwined in his arms, gently stroking her lustrous hair with his fingers, she felt such love emanating from him that her eyes began to fill with tears. "You're crying again? What's this all about?" he asked, taking a handkerchief from his pocket and wiping the moisture from under her eyes.

"I'm just so grateful that I found you," she uttered. "Promise me that we'll always be together."

"I promise," he said endearingly. And this time, he intended to keep his word.

She fastened her bra; he tucked in his shirt; and they soon appeared at the other end of the steps. They walked arm in arm on a paved walkway, looking at the Danube Canal and talking about their future.

"I've decided not to return to the *Realgymnasium*," Franz revealed.

"Oh. . . ." Franziska responded.

"I'd be older than everyone else, and I don't want to go to a university. I've told my mother; and although she's not happy, she's being tolerant of my wishes."

"Well, I suppose I'll do the same," Franziska said, a little disappointed. "So what are you going to do?"

"For the time being, I'm going to continue helping my mother at the *Putzerei*; she gives me a small salary. And then I'm going to look for a job."

"What kind of a job?" Franziska asked.

"I don't know. . . . Maybe I'll do something in the field of athletics."

They didn't talk about the matter anymore. They reminisced about their meeting exactly one year before. And then they returned to their secret hiding place for a few more kisses, climbed the steps, and said their good-byes in front of the *Kino*. On this occasion, Franz was not going to escort Franziska home. She often felt it was unnecessary, since they lived in opposite directions and since he was never welcome inside.

"Well, I guess I've claimed most of my kisses," Franz said jokingly. "Will you promise me a few more?"

"Always," Franziska responded. "Always."

෴

In October, Franz celebrated his nineteenth birthday. Franziska gave him a silver *tabatiere* (cigarette case) inlaid in gold with a matching lighter. She thought that if he smoked, he'd appear more worldly and mature. Smoking did make him feel more grown up, he discovered, but it never really appealed to him. However, to make her happy, he smoked when they were together.

In November, Franziska turned seventeen. She thought that she'd finally be able to openly date Franz. In December, she announced to her father that she'd met him by accident in a store near the Kai. She told her father that nothing had been said about that ill-fated day the year before when Franz had come to pick her up for their first date.

"He still wants to take me out, Papa, and now that I'm seventeen, I plan to go."

Franziska felt like it was a scene revisited: a déjà vu. They were in the den again; her father was sitting on his easy chair reading the newspaper, and her mother was settled on the couch, knitting.

"Has Franz graduated from the *Realgymnasium*?" Heinrich asked.

"No. He dropped out to help his mother open her *Putzerei* after his father died."

"Is he going back to school?"

"No. He's going to work with his mother for a while and then get a job."

"I'm sorry, Franziska. I still don't want you to see him."

"But why, Papa? You said that I could date when I'm seventeen."

"You *can* date. But you can only date young men who come from wealthy families or who have secure futures in front of them."

"Well . . . Franz *does* come from a family of means. He lives in a big house in Pötzleinsdorf."

"Yes, but now that his father has died, his family's source of income has obviously diminished, or his mother wouldn't have opened a *Putzerei*."

"And how do you know that he doesn't have a good future ahead of him?" Franziska upheld.

"Because you haven't given me any indication that he does. He can't enroll in a university now, and you haven't mentioned that he has any particular talents. . . . You can't go out with him, Franziska. I forbid you to see him."

Franziska wanted to cry, but she didn't. The hurt she felt inside had turned to rage.

"A year ago, you told me that I couldn't date Franz because I was too young. That was the only reason you gave."

"It was the only reason," Heinrich responded. "At that time, you told me that Franz was going to graduate from a *Realgymnasium*. His plans have changed."

"You told me that I could date when I turned seventeen," Franziska reiterated slowly, trying to contain herself. "I thought that meant that I could date the men of my own choosing, not yours."

"Well, I'd hoped that your judgment in selections would match mine," Heinrich quipped back.

"I hate to inform you, Papa, but one day when I decide to get married, I'm going to marry the man that *I* want to marry," Franziska screamed.

"Well, hopefully, when that day comes, the man will be someone that we both want you to marry," Heinrich acknowledged.

Franziska was getting angrier and angrier. She knew that she was knocking her head against a wall. She wanted to tell her father that she was going to see Franz whether he approved or not. But she didn't. She respected her father too much to be that antagonistic, so she simply glared into his eyes ready to explode, took a deep breath and left the room. She was just going to have to continue to see Franz in secrecy. She knew that she could depend on her mother to remain silent.

When she told Franz what had occurred, he became infuriated. That's when she discovered what a temper he had. However, as she grew to know and love him, she learned that he was all bark and no bite; he had a heart of gold.

The Christmas season was a busy time for everyone. Franziska went to the Christmas markets again; and this year, she dragged Franz ice-skating. With his athletic prowess, he picked the sport up very quickly and was soon ice-dancing with Franziska all around the *Wiener Eis-laufverein* (Viennese Ice Skating Club) near the Stadtpark.

The year 1929 was fraught with changes. Ilona married her longtime boyfriend, Hans Beck, whom she'd met four years earlier when visiting her best girlfriend, Nellie Humburger. Hans lived in the same apartment building and had passed Ilona in the lobby one afternoon when she was on her way to Nellie's apartment. Ilona gave Hans a flirtatious smile, and that was the beginning of their romance.

Hans came from a very prosperous family. His father represented several prominent yarn companies, acting as their liaison to large manufacturers. Hans, who was just a few years older than Ilona, went into business with his father.

After their wedding, Ilona and Hans moved into a spacious, luxurious apartment located behind the *Rathaus*, near the northwest portion of the Ring. It was within walking distance of the *Putzerei*, thus enabling Ilona to continue to help her mother every afternoon. Ilona immediately employed a maid and purchased a dog. And at the age of twenty-four, she was finally the wealthy married lady she'd always dreamed of being.

But most others were not as fortunate as Ilona. The economy in Vienna had improved since the end of World War I but suddenly took a downturn in October of 1929, with the collapse of the city's leading bank and then the historic stock market crash in the United States, which signaled the Great Depression. Austrian production slumped and unemployment became widespread.

In addition, political strife existed between the Social Democratic and Christian Social parties, the latter being the more conservative. And the lesser Nazi German National Party was gaining in strength. Although anti-Semitism did exist in Austria, it did not plague most Jews. But the failing economy set the stage for the rise of Adolf Hitler and the Nazi Party. People were looking for radical change; they were looking for a cure for their economic woes. For many, following Hitler's anti-Semitic racial theory was a small price to pay for financial solvency.

In spite of the poor economy, Olga's *Putzerei* was turning into a lucrative business. Yet she was anxious for Franz to become self-sufficient. It was time for him to get a job. She discussed the situation with one of her husband's old friends, Hugo Flegman, a wholesale glove dealer who employed a number of salesmen and agreed to hire Franz. Olga broke the news to her son one morning in the office of her *Putzerei*.

"I would like you to get a job, Franz," she announced hesitantly.

"Oh?" Franz replied.

"The economy is very depressed and my income is declining," she explained, hoping that he would buy her story. "Although I really appreciate your help here in the shop, I realize that my proceeds would be the same whether you were here or not. If you went out and got a job, you could help increase the family's assets. You could take from your salary whatever you needed, and then save the rest so that it would be available in case of an emergency."

Of course Olga never planned to really utilize Franz's salary; she simply wanted to make a convincing argument.

"I don't want to leave the *Putzerei*," Franz exclaimed. "Are you sure it's absolutely necessary?"

"Yes, I'm afraid so." Olga put a downtrodden expression on her face. "We really need the extra money."

"All right, Mother," Franz sighed. "I'll start looking tomorrow."

"Don't worry about doing that yet; I may be able to help you," Olga reported. "You know Hugo Flegman."

"Yes."

"He may have a sales position available. I told him about my dilemma, and he said that he'd be willing to talk to you. Why don't you go to see him tomorrow?"

"Gloves? I've never really thought of selling gloves before. I don't know if I'd be any good at it," Franz deliberated. "Well, I guess I'd be willing to try. . . . All right, Mother, I'll go tomorrow."

The following day, Franz walked to Hugo Flegman's apartment on Schwedenplatz, near the central portion of the Kai. A few of the rooms in the apartment had been designated for business. Hugo Flegman asked Franz numerous questions about his education and interests. Then he ushered Franz into another room that contained drawers and drawers of gloves from various manufacturing companies in Czechoslovakia. "Do you think that you could sell these gloves to retailers?" he asked. And when Franz replied in the affirmative, he offered him a job.

Franz began working for Hugo Flegman the end of 1929. Because he worked full time now, it was much more difficult for him to meet Franziska in secrecy. He could rarely leave his job in the afternoons, so the two lovebirds had to see each other in the evenings and on weekends. Franziska was becoming an excellent storyteller.

However, she soon realized that she probably needn't have been such a convincing actress. For some reason, her father never seemed interested in anything anymore. He went to work every morning, came home in the evening, had something light to eat, relaxed for a while in the den, and went to sleep. Franziska could have told him that she was going to fly to America, and it probably wouldn't have phased him. In fact, in the middle of April 1930, she accepted a wonderful job as a seamstress and design apprentice at a ladies' dress shop: *Sonnenfeld*, the store was called – *Béla Sonnenfeld*. It was located on Mariahilferstrasse, a commercial boulevard which extended from the southwestern portion of the Ring. Franziska was thrilled; she was going to start working there as soon as she completed her studies that June at her school of design. When she approached her father with the good news, he barely congratulated her.

The dwindling economy had affected his business and he was forced to travel more in order to promote his wares. In times of abundance, retailers from neighboring countries had always come to him; now he was compelled to reach out. At the end of April 1930, he took a trip to Zagreb, a leading financial and trading center of Yugoslavia. He was scheduled to be gone for a week; however, the week stretched on, and he simply never returned.

The family was devastated. The children couldn't understand why he had abandoned them. Stefanie simply explained that as the economy had worsened, their father had obtained much of his jewelry on consignment. Instead of only keeping the profits, he had retained the full amount of each sale. If he had remained in Vienna, he would have faced numerous lawsuits. He would send money, she assured them; they needn't worry.

At the beginning, Heinrich did send the funds necessary to sustain them. However, the checks soon became smaller and more infrequent, and Stefanie began to worry. She had no employable skills, and she wanted her children to complete their education. At first, only Franziska contributed a portion of her salary. Then Lilly dropped out of business school and found a menial clerical job; and Fritz gave up his studies at a *Realgymnasium* and became an electrical apprentice. Only the youngest sibling, Paul, remained in school. And of course, they could no longer afford to keep Hilde.

Then, as if things couldn't have possibly gotten any worse, the Perger's apartment became infested with bedbugs. The little bloodsucking vermin were rampant all over Vienna; but for some unknown reason, they lingered in some buildings while rejecting others. In the course of a few weeks, Franziska's body was covered with bites. Although the other members of her family often saw the insects crawling on their beds at night, they were never bitten. "You must have *sweet* blood," they always told Franziska, teasingly. But she failed to see the humor in their comments; she was suffering too much.

Each bed consisted of three small mattresses. Every morning after all of her children had left home for either work or school, Stefanie stripped the beds of all their linens and lined the mattresses up on the window sills to air out. Later, she returned the mattresses to their rightful places and covered them with fresh linens. But nothing helped.

The bugs were reddish-brown in color and about one-fifth of an inch long. Their bodies were very flat during the day when hiding between the floor boards, in the cracks of plaster, and along the seams of mattresses; but their trunks grew quite plump and dark red in color after a full meal. And Franziska seemed to satisfy their appetites. They pierced her skin unceasingly with their sharp beaks, and they drew out her blood.

"Aaaaaa . . ." Franziska screamed from her bedroom one Saturday at two o'clock in the morning. "Aaaaaaaaaaa!"

The whole family came running. Stefanie was tying the sash around her robe when she entered the room. "What is it, darling? What is it? Did you have a bad dream?" she asked.

Franziska was sitting upright in her bed, pushing the covers away from her body, and kicking her feet up and down as if she'd been in a swimming competition. She was screaming at the top of her lungs. "Get them away from me! Get them away!"

At least ten bedbugs were crawling around Franziska's bed, and she was swishing another two or three off her legs. "Do something," she continued to scream. "I can't take it anymore. I cannot take it."

"Now calm down, Franzi," her mother said, trying to soothe her daughter's nerves. "Come on. You get out of bed, and come and sleep the rest of the night with me."

Stefanie held her daughter comfortingly and helped her down the hall to the master bedroom. Lilly, Fritz, and Paul yawned a few times and meandered back into their beds.

But Franziska only calmed down momentarily. For the next week, she took her linens to the den and slept on the leather-covered sofa, but the ravenous pests followed her there too. Finally in the spring of 1931, she decided to move out. Even though her job was an excellent first step toward realizing her dreams of one day becoming a dress designer, she earned a very meager salary. Yet she would have enough, she hoped, to rent a room.

"You cannot move out," her mother told her angrily. "We count on your salary to help pull us through. I don't know when or if your father is ever going to come home. How can you turn your back on your own family?"

"I'm not doing this to spite you, Mama. I'm trying to survive too. Do you think I want to live in some dingy room in an apartment with a family I don't even know? I simply cannot take the bedbugs anymore. I'm getting so tired and sick that pretty soon I won't be able to go to work at all."

"Please reconsider your decision, Franziska."

"And if you're so concerned about the family's well-being, Mutti, why don't you sell some of your jewelry? Papa has given you so many gorgeous pieces; surely you could part with a few."

Franziska had caught her mother off-guard. Stefanie didn't know what to say. "I keep the jewelry for sentimental reasons. It seems I've lost your father; at least I want to remember what we had together."

"If jewelry is all you had together, then I can understand why Papa left," Franziska shouted almost maliciously. "I think it's time you started thinking more practically."

Evading what she'd just heard, Stefanie hollered in return: "If you move out now, your sister and brothers will never forgive you."

"I'm not doing anything to hurt them, so I don't expect them to have to forgive me," Franziska responded. "I simply hope that they'll understand why I'm leaving."

But they didn't understand. Most children never left home in Vienna until they were married. Nevertheless, Franziska packed her clothes and belongings and moved out. She found a room in an apartment near the store where she worked. It was a modest apartment, and the room was small; but it was clean. She had a bed, a chest of drawers, and a small table with two chairs. A bathroom was located just outside her door, and she could use the kitchen whenever she chose. Her landlords – Ernst Grünwald, a retired professor, and his wife, Magda – seemed friendly and warm-hearted. Franziska had all that she needed. She'd just have to become accustomed to it, she concluded; that's all.

But Franziska missed her family terribly in the months ahead. Whenever she telephoned, she was received coldly, so she finally stopped calling altogether. She had Franz, and he was enough.

Franz felt the same way about Franziska. As long as he had her, he knew he could survive. But life was not that simple. He knew that he had to be able to provide for her, but his job was not working out as he had planned. At the beginning, he appeared to be the ideal salesman. All of the retailers he approached seemed to like both him and his product. In fact, he'd decided to one day start a wholesale glove business of his own after he'd made the appropriate contacts. Then the product began to go sour and so did his sales. Storekeepers and managers were calling Hugo Flegman to complain about the merchandise they'd purchased; the gloves were ripping and tearing. Either they were poorly made or the leather was inferior, the retailers complained, because their customers were returning the goods.

Hugo Flegman always apologized profusely and generously delivered his purchasers a new shipment. Yet when Franz returned to these same retailers, they were no longer interested in dealing with him. His future hopes of starting a similar business had disintegrated, and he could find no other option except to quit his job.

So in October of 1931, Franz was unemployed and Franziska was estranged from her family. Sometimes Franz would pick Franziska up in the evening after she finished work, and they'd walk along Mariahilferstrasse without saying a word. Even though they never questioned their feelings for each other, the bleakness of their situations affected them greatly. They looked to each other for answers. But the answers would not come.

Franz Jung as a 10-year-old child.

Franz's sister Ilona Jung.

The remodeled Jung house on Pötzleinsdorfer Strasse in Vienna with the original on top. (*Photo of the remodeled house taken in 1998 by the author.*)

Olga Jung pictured on a streetcar pass.

Jakob Jung portrait.

My grandfather Jakob Jung's grave in the Zentralfriedhof in Vienna, one of the largest cemeteries in the world -- the home of composers including Franz Schubert, Arnold Schoenberg, Johann Strauss, Ludwig van Beethoven, Johannes Brahms, and others. My grandfather was also known as "Jacques."

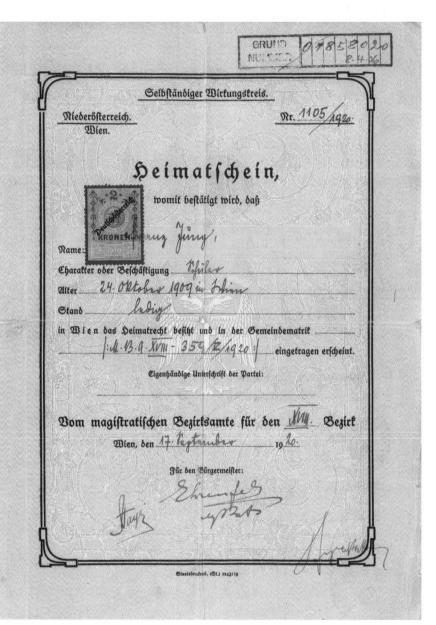

Selbständiger Wirkungskreis.

Niederösterreich.
Wien.

Nr. 1105/1920.

Heimatschein,

womit bestätigt wird, daß

Name: _Franz Jung,_

Charakter oder Beschäftigung _Schüler_

Alter _24. Oktober 1909 in Wien_

Stand _ledig_

in W i e n das Heimatrecht besitzt und in der Gemeindematrik

: M. 13. g. XVIII – 359/II/1920 : eingetragen erscheint.

Eigenhändige Unterschrift der Partei:

Vom magistratischen Bezirksamte für den _XVIII._ Bezirk

Wien, den _17. September_ 19 _20._

Für den Bürgermeister:

Ehrenfeld

Staatsdruckerei. (St.) 124311 9

My father's *Heimatschein* (citizenship certificate or certificate of family origin).

Vinzi Dočkal, the Jungs' cook and nanny.

Vinzi worked in Olga Jung's *Putzerei* on the first floor of the building at Esslinggasse Zehn. (*Photo taken by the author in 1998.*)

Franziska Perger at about 11 years of age in Vienna.

My mother, Franziska Perger (seated front left), with her family (left to right: Fritz, my grandfather Heinrich, my grandmother Stefanie, Paul, Lilly).

The Prater: Historical postcard of the *Praterstern, Riesenrad* (Ferris Wheel), and *Hauptallee* in the early 1900s. (© *Lebrecht Music & Arts/Corbis*)

The *Hauptallee* in autumn with the trees cloaking the pathway. (*Getty Images*)

The Prater *Riesenrad* in 1998.

Advertisement-Poster for Sonnenfeld in Vienna, my mother's first place of employment from 1930-1936. The actual ad was dated 1927. (*ADSandBRANDS.com*)

The Urania in the early 1900s.

The Musikverein.
(*© Stuart Black/Robert Harding World Imagery/Corbis*)

CHAPTER SIX

Discovery

Vienna, Austria
January 1932 to July 1933

$\mathcal{T}$he winter of 1932 was a cold season for Franz and Franziska. Franziska's job was not at all what she had expected. She was supposed to be a seamstress, yes, but she was also hired to be a design apprentice. However, whenever she tried to present a sketch to her employer, who produced a reputable line of clothing, or to one of the other managers – her work was praised, the sketch was thrown on top of an immense pile, and she never heard anything about it again. She was sent on numerous errands. And once in a while she was called upon to bring her chalk and pins to do a fitting. But as long as she worked at Sonnenfeld, she knew that she would never become a designer, or even a dressmaker, yet she couldn't afford to give up the job.

Franz's situation was even worse. He was unemployed and didn't know in which direction to proceed, so he spent most of his days brooding at the *Putzerei*. His mother and sister were beside themselves. Franz dismissed all of their suggestions with a stubborn attitude that enraged them, and he threw temper tantrums whenever they asked him to help.

He was even taking out his frustrations on Franziska. On one Saturday evening, they went to the Erika-*Kino* to see *The Sin of Madelon Claudet*, a new American film starring actress Helen Hayes. Franz seemed normal enough inside the darkened theater. While watching the movie, he often pulled Franziska toward him and kissed her amorously. He held her hand throughout, and at one point, guided it inside the pocket of the trench coat he was wearing so that she could feel just exactly how much he desired her. And while she watched the teary parts of the movie, he nibbled on her ear. Sometimes she responded lovingly in kind, sometimes she giggled, and sometimes she whispered: "Wait, wait, wait – I want to see this. . . ."

For some reason, the story of Madelon Claudet had completely captivated Franziska. Madelon was a young Parisian girl who had fallen in love with an American who went back to his home country and married another woman. Madelon gave birth to his illegitimate baby, and was then compelled to become a mistress and prostitute to support her unsuspecting son. The tears streamed down Franziska's face as she walked out of the *Kino* with Franz.

"Madelon gave up so much for her son," Franziska uttered.

"Uh-huh," Franz responded obliviously.

"It's amazing how much people sacrifice for the people they love."

"Uh-huh," Franz repeated.

"If we had a child, would you take any menial job, if you had to, just to ensure that we had food on the table?"

"What?" Franz asked.

"If we had a child, would you take any menial job . . ."

"We don't have a child," Franz interrupted, "so I can wait until the right job comes along."

"I wasn't referring to your present situation," Franziska tried to explain. "I was just talking hypothetically. For example, I know that if we had a child and you were sick, I would work as a scrubwoman if I had to in order to support us."

"Well, I don't live in the world of fairy tales," Franz responded somewhat irritated. "I live in the real world. So if we're ever in that position, I'll worry about it then."

"If we were married and didn't even have a child, if you were sick and couldn't work, I'd still find a job as a cleaning woman if necessary in order to support us," Franziska recounted sweetly, refusing to change the direction of the conversation.

"You don't have to get a job as a maid, Franziska, because you're working as a seamstress, so will you please drop the subject?"

Franziska was clinging on to Franz's arm as he began to increase his pace. The weather was nippy, and the tip of Franziska's nose was turning red from the cold, but she was wearing a virgin wool coat and a soft-brimmed hat to keep warm.

"Oh, you have no romance in you," Franziska replied.

Franz stopped walking suddenly and kissed Franziska abruptly. "How's that for romance?" he said strongly.

"What is wrong with you, Franz?"

"I'm going crazy," he screamed. "I want a job, but I want the *right* job. I want a job with a future. I want a job for me and for you."

"Just have a little patience," Franziska said, trying to comfort him. But he remained agitated for the rest of the evening.

Life was becoming more-and-more complicated for everyone in Vienna. Since the Nazi Party was now the second largest party in Germany, its success was spiraling into Vienna, and the tide of anti-Semitism was flowing. More swastikas were becoming visible, and the newspapers were reporting repeated incidents of Nazi violence in Jewish coffeehouses and businesses. Rowdies were kicking and mauling Jewish students in front of the main building of the University of Vienna, thus blocking them from entering; and the police were slow to respond. Even in Parliament, when a Jewish member of the Social Democratic Party was speaking, insults from members of the anti-Semitic Christian Social and German National parties were often heard surging toward the speaker's podium. The newspapers were full of lurid details. Some of the beauty of Vienna was turning ugly, Franz thought. Anti-Semitism was like a contagious disease that was spreading.

He tried to be realistic. What kind of a job could he get now? He wanted to work in a business that consisted of Jews and dealt only with Jews. He wanted to avoid any unsettling confrontations. But maybe he

was jumping to conclusions unnecessarily. After all, he hadn't personally been exposed to any radical behavior. Maybe the newspapers were
exaggerating.

Finally in the spring, Ilona came up with a solution to Franz's dilemma. "You're always shouting around the house, Franz. It's amazing
that the neighbors have never complained," she said out of the blue one
afternoon at the *Putzerei*.

"Yeh, so what?" Franz answered gruffly, thinking that Ilona was
about to criticize him for his unruly temper.

"Sometimes your singing is almost as loud, and I can't tell if you're
singing or shouting," she continued.

"I guess I'm not as musical as I ought to be," Franz said.

"No, that's not the point," Ilona explained. "Opera singers have big
voices, and you seem have a big voice too; maybe you should find out if
it's good enough to sing opera."

"Opera . . . I've never thought of singing. I like opera, and I love German *Lieder*, but me . . . a singer . . . I don't know."

"Why don't you go to a teacher and find out?"

"And if I do have talent, I'd probably have to study for years without
earning a Schilling. And how could I afford the cost of the training?"

"Don't worry about that now," Ilona said. "Just go and find out what
you've got."

"All right, Ilona. You've certainly come up with a unique suggestion.
The thought of becoming an opera singer is actually kind of compelling. All right; I'll go and find out. . . . All right."

Ilona remembered the name and telephone number of her old piano
teacher. She called the gentleman, and he recommended a voice teacher for Franz: Albert Lindemann.

The day of Franz's appointment arrived; Franz didn't know what to
expect. As he approached the teacher's apartment building, he could
hear the sounds of a piano and singing radiating from one of the open
windows on the second floor. He was getting a little nervous. He entered the lobby and began to climb the stairs. The building reminded

him of Blütengasse Neun: The style and coloring of the outside and lobby were much the same. However, this building was much closer to his home; it was located in the neighboring suburb of Sievering.

He knocked on the door and was greeted by an elderly, refined-looking man with white hair. "*Guten Tag*," the man said. He was comfortably dressed in lightweight wool trousers, a shirt with a bow tie, and a loose-fitting sweater.

"*Guten Tag*, Herr Lindemann," Franz replied. "I'm Franz Jung."

"Ah, won't you come in?" Albert Lindemann responded pleasantly.

Then he said good-bye to the student that was walking toward the doorway from behind. "You had a good lesson," he told the young woman. "Remember to yawn and keep your throat open when you practice, and I'll see you next week."

The student nodded and then smiled at Franz as she walked past him and out the door.

"Come this way," the voice teacher said, directing Franz into what seemed to be a combination living room and studio.

"Why don't you stand on this side of the piano facing me as I play?" he pointed as he sat down in front of the keyboard. "Now then, have you ever sung before?"

"No," Franz answered. "Just around the house."

"Ah, and you would like to find out if you have a great operatic voice?"

"Well, I'd just like to know if I have a voice?" Franz replied humbly.

"Then let's begin – shall we?"

Franz nodded.

"First, I will play a few notes – a scale – and you will then sing what I have played. Don't worry about words; just sing the vowel *ah*. "

Herr Lindemann played a simple scale consisting of five notes up and five notes back. Franz then sang the scale. "Good. Now sing the same notes with *aye* and *ee*, " Herr Lindemann directed. Franz then sang the scale with the two new vowels.

Herr Lindemann started Franz on the second B below middle C. He played the scale three times to indicate to Franz that he should sing it on all three vowels.

Franz then sang the scale: "*Ah—aye—ee—*." Then Herr Lindemann moved to the next note on the keyboard and played the scale on the C below middle C. And Franz sang: "*Ah—aye—ee—.*"

They continued up the keyboard until Franz began to feel tight in his throat. He tried to push the tones out nevertheless, but he finally stopped the progression with a cough.

"I think we've gone high enough," Herr Lindemann said. "Now let's sing the scale again on the C below middle C. Only this time, we'll work down the keyboard. So Franz sang the scale on C, then B, and so-on.

Herr Lindemann led Franz through a few other quick scales and then decided on one that was slower. "Each two consecutive notes should be sung smoothly and connected without any breaks – *legato* – and after each set of notes, you can sneak in a short breath," he said, playing a scale on the piano that consisted of eight notes up and eight notes back, with a brief pause between every two successive notes.

He demonstrated by playing the scale on the piano and by singing it himself: "*Ah—ah; ah—ah; ah—ah; ah—ah,*" he sang up the keyboard. "*Ah-–ah; ah—ah; ah—ah; ah—*ah," he sang down.

"Now you – " he said, striking the second A below middle C.

"*Ah—ah; ah—ah; ah—ah; ah—ah,*" Franz sang. "*Ah—ah; ah—ah; ah—ah; ah—ah.*" Franz loved the scale; his voice sounded so full and melodious.

Herr Lindemann led Franz up the keyboard again until he began to strain. "Well, young man," he said, concluding the scales. "I can tell that you have a wonderful voice. At this time, I believe that you are a baritone. That could change as you develop your technique. You must learn to sing with a relaxed, open throat; and you must learn about breathing and placement."

Franz was pleased, but he didn't really know what to ask next, so he remained silent.

"Can you read notes?" Herr Lindemann asked.

"Yes, sir. I've studied piano and violin."

"Do you have a piano at home?"

"Yes, sir. I have a Bösendorfer."

"Good. . . . I want you to learn Wolfram's song to the evening star – 'O du mein holder Abendstern' – from Richard Wagner's opera, *Tannhäuser.* In the opera, Wolfram secretly loves Elisabeth, but she is only interested in Tannhäuser. When she believes that she will never see Tannhäuser again, she prays sacrificially to the Virgin Mary. Wolfram, who overhears her, then asks the evening star to greet Elisabeth as she approaches heaven. . . . You can pick up the sheet music at the store down the street. Learn the music, and come back in three weeks."

"Yes, Herr Lindemann. Thank you, Herr Lindemann," Franz said, going over to the vocal teacher and shaking his hand.

Franz felt elated as he left the voice teacher's apartment. He suddenly had hope. That was enough for the time being. He purchased the sheet music and arrived home with a smile on his face. And when Vinzi and his mother entered later that evening, he was already standing in front of the piano trying to learn the song.

Olga was very happy when she heard what had occurred; but of course, she had some reservations. However, she didn't want to spoil this time of happiness for Franz, so she refrained from expressing any skepticism.

Franz practiced the aria every day. The music said *"dolce"* ("sweetly"); however Franz was practicing it as if it were a march. He loved to hear his tones bellow out. But soon, he started to get hoarse. His throat became so sore that he could barely sing, or even talk, for that matter. He must be doing something wrong, he thought, but he didn't know what it was. However he did know that he didn't want to go back to Albert Lindemann.

Once again, Ilona came to the rescue. She learned from her husband that he had a distant cousin, *Kammersänger* Arthur Fleischer, who was a renowned opera singer and had sung at the major opera houses and concert halls in Dresden, Berlin, and Vienna. *"Kammersänger"* was an esteemed honorary title awarded to distinguished singers by the German and Austrian governments. Ilona telephoned Arthur Fleischer and told him about Franz. He was very polite and invited her to send Franz to his home a few days later for an assessment.

The day of Franz's appointment arrived; and again, Franz didn't know what to expect. Arthur Fleischer's apartment was in the Neubau district, the district where numerous artists and musicians made their homes. It was in an attractive nineteenth century building on Kaiserstrasse, close to shops, restaurants, and cafés, and with a tram stop conveniently positioned right in front of it. Yet although the apartment was centrally located, it was hardly a display of majestic opulence. It was furnished simply, Franz noticed, as he was led through the living room and into the stark-looking studio. No drapes. No carpeting. Just a beautiful grand piano with a bench and music stand.

"So . . . you want to determine if you have a voice?" Herr Fleischer addressed Franz.

He was much more jovial than Herr Lindemann, Franz decided. Somewhat tall and portly, he was in his early fifties, Franz surmised. He was fair-skinned with sandy reddish-blond hair, small blue eyes and a fleshy nose, and he was wearing a medium gray-colored suit.

"Yes. I've been trying to learn this song from *Tannhäuser,* " Franz replied somewhat hoarsely, handing the *Kammersänger* his sheet music.

"Oh, Wolfram's song to the evening star . . . it's lovely. I'm afraid I can't accompany you. I'll give you the first note, and you can begin."

Franz nodded as Herr Fleischer played the G below middle C on the piano. He began singing: "O my fair evening star . . ."

Herr Fleischer didn't let him get very far before interrupting him. "I'm sorry, Franz; you might have a good voice, but I'm not sure. You're simply too hoarse for me to assess it. I want you to go to Doktor Wilfried Witte; he's a specialist for opera singers. I want him to check your vocal cords."

Herr Fleischer wrote Doktor Witte's telephone number down on a piece of paper and handed it to Franz along with his sheet music.

"Now don't sing anymore until you've seen him," Herr Fleischer recommended. "And then call me."

Franz went to Doktor Witte's office, which was located near his sister's apartment just behind the *Rathaus.* Doktor Witte told him that his vocal cords were inflamed and that he shouldn't talk for six weeks; and if he absolutely had to make a sound, he should whisper.

The six weeks were difficult for Franz, but he obeyed the doctor's orders. Vinzi and Olga were delighted to have such peace and quiet in the house, and they were also amazed at Franz's sudden sense of discipline. Franz made good use of his handicap with Franziska as well; they spent more time at *Kinos* and in Franziska's room – kissing and making out.

In June, Franz returned to Doktor Witte and was given a clean bill of health. Then he went back to Arthur Fleischer to be reassessed.

"Yes, you have a very promising voice," Herr Fleischer told Franz after leading him through a few elementary scales. "If you're willing to work hard, I'd like to teach you."

Franz went for a singing lesson every day. Herr Fleischer was so sure of Franz's potential that after a couple of months, he presented Franz with a contract binding him to pay for the lessons after he began his career. Until that time, Ilona agreed to pay two hundred Schillings per month.

"Technique is everything," Herr Fleischer drilled into Franz. "You should never feel anything in your throat; it should be completely relaxed. You breathe with your diaphragm; that is the foundation. The air then flies upward like the stream of a fountain. The diaphragm is the faucet where you turn the fountain on. The tone floats on the air like an eggshell resting on top of the stream of the fountain. The tone, or the eggshell, should move up into the head and should be curved forward, with some tones aimed toward the nose, yet not in the nose. The higher the tone, the higher you must place it in the head. This is where imagination comes into play. Of course, the tone really is formed by the vocal cords and comes out of the mouth, which holds truer for the low tones, but as they move up, you must imagine what I have just described, and you will feel the tone resonating in the mask: in the cheeks and sinuses and sometimes in the forehead. If there is tension in your throat, the air will not flow freely, and your vocal cords will not produce a mellow sound; but if your throat is relaxed and the air is allowed to flow freely, the tone will rest where it should. The only pressure that should be felt is the pressure exerted by the faucet, or diaphragm: The higher the stream goes, the more water pressure is required from the faucet; the higher the tone or eggshell sits, the more air pressure is required from the diaphragm. But once again, if your throat is relaxed and your

imagination is working correctly, all of the elements will come together almost simultaneously."

Franz was obsessed with his music training. He had never shown so much enthusiasm about anything in his life before. He sang scales and more scales. Herr Fleischer told him that he must perfect his technique before learning opera parts, German *Lieder* or oratorios. He was a bass-baritone, he learned, and because of his relatively short stature, would probably be limited in the roles he could portray. So Herr Fleischer decided that Franz would learn the roles for character baritones and for comic basso buffos.

In the fall, Franz enrolled at the Neues Wiener Konservatorium, the prestigious music conservatory housed in the Musikvereinsgebäude (Music Society Building), which also contained two magnificent concert halls and was the headquarters of the Vienna Philharmonic Orchestra. Arthur Fleischer was a member of the faculty and remained Franz's predominant vocal teacher; however, other faculty members helped him develop a well-rounded understanding of music.

By now, Franz realized that as a Jew, he would no longer be able to sing in Germany where many young singers flocked to begin their careers. Hitler's Nazi Party – the National Socialist German Workers' Party – was now the largest party in that country. And even in Vienna, the fate of the Jews was uncertain since Engelbert Dollfuss had recently become Chancellor of Austria. A member of the Christian Social Party, Chancellor Dollfuss did everything he could to stifle the Nazi Party; however his party was also anti-Semitic and fought unceasingly against the more liberal and often Jewish Social Democrats.

However Franz tried not to think about politics; he immersed himself in his music instead. He was singing oratorios and *Lieder* now and was becoming familiar with the scores of the operas he would soon learn. He studied at the Konservatorium approximately three times a week, usually entering from the side of the building that was directly behind the luxurious Hotel Imperial. As he walked down the main hallway, he always looked at the posted notices to learn which great artists would be performing in the concert halls next. There were small rooms scattered throughout the Musikverein building on different floors. It was in these rooms that Franz and the other students spent most of their days.

One day a class had been called from one to five. Seven students were crammed into a tiny room which contained an upright piano and a few flimsy chairs under some shaky tables. Five students were seated in front of the makeshift desks while Franz remained standing. The final student was under fire so-to-speak. She was standing next to the piano facing Arthur Fleischer and the accompanist; she was singing Musetta's playful waltz from *La Bohème*.

"A little more flair next time . . . but good," Herr Fleischer said when she was finished. "Now let's go on. . . . Karl . . . where is Karl Edelmann?"

"I think he wandered out into the corridor. He must be listening to the singer who will be giving a recital in the *Grossen Saal* (Grand Hall)," Fritz Bergar commented.

"Well, will you go out and get him? He's supposed to be working on *Falstaff.* "

Fritz left the room, but he never returned.

"How bizarre; now I've lost two students," Herr Fleischer remarked. "It seems I'm being paid to be a baby-sitter." He made a few clownish grimaces to get the students laughing. "Franz, will you please go and bring them both back?"

Franz nodded and was out the door.

As he quietly entered the Grossen Saal and sat in the front row of the balcony, he felt so fortunate to have access to such a magnificent concert hall, one of the most highly regarded in Europe. Its neo-Renaissance décor – with gilded columns, statues, and balustrades – flawlessly imitated classical antiquity. With the richness of music reverberating throughout the hall due to its almost unparalleled acoustical capabilities, Franz sometimes felt that the room had a spiritual quality not unlike a Roman temple.

He was sitting next to his two lost comrades, but no one said a word. What they were hearing was indescribable. It seemed like the singer was baring his soul.

Franz was motivated to strive for a prestigious career, and he knew that he had a wonderful girlfriend. What more could he ask for?

Franziska was always very supportive, and she was relieved that he finally had a vocation, even though it would be years before he would earn a living.

Sometimes after his lessons at the Konservatorium, Franz needed to practice but didn't want to take a tram all the way home to Pötzleinsdorf; so since his sister had a piano, he went to her apartment instead. Then in the evening, he would meet Franziska with music and pitchpipe in hand; and as soon as they entered her room, he would begin singing. Franziska was always amazed at the beauty of the sounds he was capable of delivering. In fact, sometimes her landlords invited Franz to do a little concertizing for them in the living room. That's when Franziska always thought about her family and how much she missed her brothers and her sister, her mother and her father. She wondered if they'd ever be together again.

On the thirtieth day of January in 1933, Adolf Hitler was appointed Chancellor of Germany by President Paul von Hindenburg. And on that Monday, the Viennese Nazis celebrated in front of the Karlskirche: the Church of St. Charles Borromeo. News of the victory rally spread quickly to the music students in the nearby Konservatorium. A number of them, including Franz, ran out to see what the commotion was all about. Because Franz was a Jew, he was afraid to go too close; however he could hear and see perfectly from where he was standing.

A lot of students were there, but there were also white-collar workers, professional people in business suits, and well-dressed women; and of course, there were also some rowdies. They cheered as the Nazi orators praised Hitler:

"He is the great son of this country. It is God's will that he will achieve greatness and take Wien, his native land, into the Reich," one chanted.

"This city is a gem; we must entrust it to the entire German Reich," echoed another.

"Hitler will pull us out of our economic depression. With him as our leader, we can overcome any obstacle, no matter how overwhelming.

We must become part of the Reich; the Reich is destined to become the greatest power in the world."

The people were cheering wildly now. Many were wearing swastika armlets.

"*Heil Hitler!*" they shouted. "One people, one Reich, one Führer!"

Then the orators started talking about racial purity:

"Adolf Hitler believes in the biological and cultural superiority of the Aryan race. The strengths and weaknesses in mankind rest solely in the blood. We, the Nazis, are Aryans: Our bloodline reigns supreme."

"The Aryan bloodline has suffered a loss in purity, thus causing a loss of culture. The German decline and Jewish problem must be acknowledged. German nationalism cannot be reborn until the Jewish menace is eliminated."

The crowd was exhilarated. People were shouting: "*Juda verrecke! Sau Jud!* (Judah, croak! Jew pig!)"

The orators were likening Hitler's conceived government to an ecclesiastical order; they were likening him to an infallible pope. Now Franz knew why they were in front of the Karlskirche. He was getting sick to his stomach, and he could feel the perspiration seeping through the pores of his skin. He'd always thought that the Karlskirche was such a beautiful Baroque church, with its domed rotunda and gigantic columns on either side, and its pagoda-like gatehouses and Roman portico. The Karlskirche would never look the same to him again.

The rally seemed to be coming to an end. A few people were starting to leave. Franz had almost been hidden in the park-like area in front of the Karlskirche; but now, some of the Nazi sympathizers appeared to be coming toward him. He decided to walk back toward the Konservatorium when suddenly he saw a familiar face. It was Bruno Eichler, an old schoolmate from the *Realgymnasium*. Pretty soon Bruno was standing right in front of him. Both young men froze; their eyes met, but neither spoke. Then Bruno suddenly spit into Franz's face and continued walking.

Franz was completely shaken up. He felt flushed and began to tremble. He hadn't seen Bruno in a few years; but at school, they had always been friends. Bruno wasn't Jewish; he had blond hair and looked very

Aryan; however Franz had never known him to be anti-Semitic. Franz was shocked by the change in Bruno's behavior. He was beginning to realize just how dangerous Hitler could be.

At the end of February 1933, the German Reichstag building was set ablaze. The Nazis blamed the Communist Party; however most people believed that the Nazis set the building on fire themselves to create a crisis atmosphere. The next day, a presidential decree was issued that granted emergency powers for Hitler to restrict civil liberties. The Enabling Act gave him dictatorial powers; he directed the Nazis to stage a boycott of Jewish businesses. And by the summer, the first labor camps had been established.

In Austria, Chancellor Engelbert Dollfuss was fighting dauntlessly to weaken the power of the Social Democrats and to curb the rise in power of the Nazis. He also implemented a law that enabled him to govern without Parliament, and thus to proceed on his own dictatorial path. But the Nazis were becoming more violent. They were painting swastikas on buildings, setting off firecrackers and tear gas in department stores, and even detonating bombs. Although Dollfuss banned all Nazi Party uniforms and activities throughout Austria, the terrorism continued.

Most Viennese still seemed unconcerned with the happenings occurring around them. After all, Hitler was in Germany, not in Austria. Chancellor Dollfuss would ensure that Austria remained independent.

But Franz was worried. He had seen first-hand how minds could be exploited and maneuvered. Franziska felt apprehensive as well. Every morning when she walked along Mariahilferstrasse to begin a day of work at Sonnenfeld, she was frightened that tear gas would be released that afternoon or that a bomb would explode before it was time for her to go home. But when Franz and Franziska were together, they forgot their anxieties. They felt safe.

CHAPTER SEVEN
The Lobau

Vienna, Austria
16 July 1933

*My father told me about his visits with my mother to the Lobau. He
wasn't sure that it still existed. He thought that the site was probably filled
with buildings. But I found it.*

*The Lobau has been a protected area since 1978, which assures its lon-
gevity, and it has been part of the Danube-Auen National Park since 1996.
It has also been the site of some nudity and skinny-dipping. Hmmmm. I
guess that my parents are part of its history. In all fairness to them, I must
add that in writing this chapter, I used my imagination. I might have been
too graphic in dreaming up the details. Yet my father was not displeased. He
read it and smiled.*

$\mathcal{F}$ranziska was in a terrible hurry. It was eleven o'clock on a beautiful summer Sunday in July, and Franz was going to pick her up in half
an hour. Although her landlords had given her access to the kitchen,
she'd always tried not to abuse the privilege and rarely cooked anything
elaborate. But she wanted this to be a special picnic, so she'd baked a
chicken the night before and placed it in the ice box. She was cutting
it in quarters now and wrapping it in wax paper. Food ingredients were

spread all over the counter. She'd made potato salad and had baked a small, round chocolate *Sachertorte* for dessert. She piled everything into a large straw picnic basket, and then added some fruit and soda water. She attempted to hastily clean up the kitchen when the doorbell rang.

"Oh, no, I'm not ready," she said frantically.

"I'll clean up; don't worry about it," she heard Frau Grünwald's voice calling from the living room. "I'll answer the door if you like."

"*Danke, danke* (Thank you)," Franziska shouted back.

Franziska took off her apron, grabbed her purse and picnic basket, ran her fingers through her hair hurriedly without even looking into a mirror, and rushed into the living room. "Now I'm ready; I'm ready," she said, a little out of breath.

Franz seemed amused. "We're not in a rush, so take it easy," he said. "We have plenty of time."

"Well, I want to make sure we catch the sun," she answered.

"Have a good time, you two," Frau Grünwald said as they walked out the door.

Three tram rides later, they'd reached their destination. They went to the Lobau often during the summers to sunbathe and to be alone. It was located quite a distance southeast of the city center along the Danube River. Sometimes Franziska thought of it as a neglected park area that nobody had as yet discovered. At other times, she referred to it as a field of high grass, overgrown foliage, and intermingling trees. But whatever the Lobau was or wasn't, it was Franz and Franziska's hideaway.

As usual, the area was uninhabited. "Why don't we go way over there?" Franziska said, reaching her arm out and pointing.

"We'll barely be able to see the Danube from there," Franz commented. "There's nothing but greenery."

"Exactly," Franziska responded.

They walked to their spot, and Franz laid out the blankets that he'd been carrying.

"You seem awfully cheery today," Franz commented. "Have you got something up your sleeve?"

"Not that I've noticed," Franziska said, setting her purse and picnic basket down on one of the blankets and then removing the blouse and denim wrap skirt that were covering her bathing suit.

"Ooo la, la . . . I like that," Franz said. "I like the way it fits."

"Good," Franziska answered. "It's the latest style; it's made out of elasticized yarn."

"I see," Franz commented, nodding his head up and down.

Franziska had purchased the tight-fitting one-piece swimsuit the previous week. It was emerald green.

"Your hair and complexion look fantastic in that color."

"I'm so glad that you approve."

"I do," Franz said, taking off the shirt and slacks which were covering his swim trunks, and then slipping off his shoes.

"Why don't you give those to me? I'll set them down next to my things."

Franz handed Franziska his clothes; she folded them neatly and placed them on the corner of the blanket next to hers. Then she kicked off her sandals.

"Now, how about some food? Are you hungry?" she asked.

"Well, actually . . . yes, I am."

"Good! If we eat right now, nothing will get spoiled."

Franz couldn't believe what he was seeing. Franziska had all sorts of surprises in her picnic basket. First she took out a colorful tablecloth and laid it on top of the blanket. Then she proceeded to set the tablecloth with napkins and silverware. She took out two plates and put a portion of chicken, potato salad, and fruit on each, and then she set the plates down next to the place settings.

"*Mittagessen* is served," she said. "Oh, wait a minute. . . . I've forgotten something." She pulled out a thin metallic vase, placed a long-stemmed red rose in it, and stood the vase in the center of the tablecloth.

Franz just stared and smiled. They'd come to the Lobau so many times before, but she'd never made him a picnic like this.

"Here's something to drink," she said, handing him a bottle of soda water.

They both sat down on the blanket in front of the tablecloth and began to eat.

"Mmmm. . . . I like the chicken," Franz said, picking up a drumstick. "And the salad is delicious too."

The wind was blowing and Franziska noticed that the vase had fallen over. "I guess I should have just laid the rose down in the center of the tablecloth without a vase," she said. "Oh, well, it was all for effect. . . . I'm glad I didn't put any water in it."

"Just relax, Franzi; everything is perfect. I love what you've done, and I love you for doing it."

Franziska smiled like a little girl, but she wasn't so little anymore; she was already twenty-one, and Franz was twenty-three. She was an expert at making out and petting by now; in fact, she and Franz had done everything sexually except the real thing. He was always respectful of her wishes. But today was going to be different, she'd decided. Her wishes had changed.

Sometimes at night she felt so lonely and frightened. She'd been alienated from her family; her job didn't meet her expectations; and she never knew where the Nazis were going to strike next. Franz was the only person she trusted; she wanted to feel so close to him that nothing could tear them apart.

While the two ate, they looked deeply into each other's eyes. Franz sensed that something was different about Franziska. She always seemed so independent and secure; yet today, her eyes were searching. He wanted to be amorous, but he wanted to approach her light-heartedly. Her onyx eyes revealed so much need; he wasn't sure he could fill her longings.

As he bit off a piece of his chicken, she bit off a piece of hers, and they seemed to chew in unison as they looked at each other. Then he licked the juice from his lips, and she licked the juice from hers. Their appetites were turning from food to each other.

"Are you finished?" she asked.

"Not really," he replied lasciviously.

"Oh, would you like some more? There's plenty to eat."

"I know," he said, maintaining the same intent in his demeanor.

"I mean there's dessert; you have to save room for dessert; I made something special."

"Yes, I'd like dessert," he said, trying to focus his attentions on the box she was taking out of the picnic basket and placing near him.

"What's that?"

"First let me take away your plate," she said, clearing the tablecloth. "Here . . . I've put some water on these napkins so that you can clean up."

As she handed Franz the napkins, he drew her toward him and kissed her tempestuously with his juice-covered lips. Then he took a napkin and wiped her mouth and each of her fingers; and when he was finished, she did the same for him. Then she started to move back toward the mysterious box. She lifted a small *Sachertorte* out, just big enough for two. She glided her forefinger around the side of the cake until it was covered with chocolate icing; she licked a little bit off, moved toward Franz and offered him a taste for himself. He held her wrist as his tongue indulged in the creamy glaze.

"What's this?" he said, pulling a little note from the center of the cake. He opened it and read it to himself:

Dear Franz,

You once wrote: "If you need me for any reason, I am yours." Well, I need you, Franz. I need you more than you will ever know.

So are you to my thoughts, as food to life,
Or as sweet seasoned showers are to the ground.

I love you, my darling. And today, I would like to be yours completely. I would like us to be together as one.

Franziska

Franz didn't speak. He reached out for her and drew her into his arms. He held her tightly. They remained that way, unmoving. Then he stroked her lustrous black hair with the palm of his hand and kissed her eyes: those undeniably singular onyx-colored almond-shaped eyes that looked back at him now vulnerably, yet with desire.

"That's beautiful," Franz said, breaking the silence.

"It's exactly how I feel."

"Me too. . . . Did Shakespeare write the verse?"

"Uh-huh."

"That's what I assumed. . . . So . . . you're sure that you want to . . ."

"Uh-huh."

"Why don't we have a piece of *Sachertorte* first?"

"Why don't we share one?"

"Uh-huh."

Franziska cut the cake in half and set it on a plate in front of Franz. She lifted a piece with her fork and placed it in his mouth. He then reciprocated. They were looking at each other lustfully now and began to kiss passionately.

"Let's grab the empty blanket and go into that secluded woodsy area over there." Franziska pointed, trying to stand, reach for the blanket, and still continue kissing.

The area was full of high grass and shrubbery. They threw the blanket down and almost fell to the ground holding on to each other. His hands were all over her now: her back, her breasts, her neck, her buttocks. She was pressing him against her, running her hands up and down his back so that he could feel her fingernails imprinting a pattern.

He needed to feel his skin next to hers now. He reached inside the top of her swimsuit and caressed her right breast, cupping his hand around it. Then he took both hands and dragged the top of her swimsuit down to her waist. Her breasts were so beautiful, so smooth and so round and erect. He put his lips to them and sucked them gently. Then his tongue roamed around her body, between her breasts and down to her belly. His hands were moving up and down the insides of her legs. He grasped for her bathing suit again. Now he was pulling it down below her waist, down past her knees, now over her ankles. Her body was gorgeous. He had seen it before, but never like this. She was waiting for him now; she wanted to be his.

He moved his head downward and glided his tongue up the inside of her leg from her ankle to her knee to her thigh. She felt so much pleasure that her body began to quiver. He was tasting her now; his tongue was caressing her. "I love you," she said. "I want to be yours."

He moved on top of her so that she could feel his arousal. His hands were behind her head, and he was kissing her devouringly. She tried to maneuver his swim trunks down, but wasn't able. Finally, she reached under his waistband, and he seemed to shudder.

"Have I hurt you?" she cried.

"No . . . no, that feels wonderful," he whispered, pulling his trunks down and kicking them aside. "Are you sure this is what you want? Are you sure?"

"Oh, yes, Franz. Oh, yes. I've waited my whole life for this. You'll be my first . . . and only."

"I love you so much, Franziska. I would never want to hurt you."

"I know, Franz. I want to be yours."

She wrapped her legs around his waist because he seemed to hesitate.

"Now . . . now," she cried. "I'm ready. Now!"

He entered her gently. She uttered a whimper of pain . . . then one of joy.

"Are you all right?" he asked feverishly.

"Oh, yes," she answered. "Now *I* feel wonderful. But I want more. I want to feel you deeper."

His thrusts became stronger now; he wanted her to feel his rapture. They were free of all inhibitions; their rhythm was quickening.

"You're setting off sparks, Franz."

"I love you, Franziska."

They were riding the waves now, their minds in euphoria. Heatedly they went from one swell to the other: their hips moving tirelessly, their energies unceasing. And then when it seemed as if they could bear it no longer, they reached their highest crest, their juices blending simultaneously. He had taken her where she wanted to go, and she was his.

They lay there motionless and exhausted, neither moving; it was as if their bodies were inseparable. They had never experienced such closeness before, such heated love, yet such tenderness and fulfillment. Finally Franz lifted himself slowly, settling on his side as Franziska nestled her body up close to him.

"Oh, how I love you. I'll love you forever," she said, rolling him onto his back and positioning herself atop him.

She looked into his eyes, painting the lines of his face with her fingers. Then she kissed him gently on his forehead and cheeks, his neck, his chest, and his belly. She enjoyed the feel of his masculinity so and wanted to hold on to the moment.

He placed his hands on her shoulders as she moved back up toward him. One last quick kiss on the lips, a fading look of love, and she fell fast asleep. At first he smiled lovingly, then tenderly stroked her hair. The cheek of her face on his chest felt so right to him. He wrapped his arms around her and held her close. He didn't want to sleep now; he wanted to smell her and feel her. But a few minutes later, he closed his eyes just for a moment, and they rested together that way until the sun set.

CHAPTER EIGHT

Wiener Staatsoper; Burgtheater

Vienna, Austria
Spring to 25 July 1934

*F*ranz and Franziska had always tried to spend almost every evening of the week together, except for Monday; Franz reserved that day for his mother. But there was one extenuating circumstance that necessitated a break in their routine: singing.

Franz was studying opera roles now, and it was extremely beneficial for him to attend performances at the Wiener Staatsoper, one of the foremost opera houses in the world. Tickets were very expensive, so Franz opted for standing room in the highest gallery. Sometimes Franziska did go along; but more often, she either stayed home or went to a play. She realized that Franz needed space to concentrate on the music, and to discuss what he was seeing and hearing with some of the other opera students present.

On one spring weekday, Franz started out as usual, taking a tram ride from Pötzleinsdorf to the Ring. He sat in the streetcar studying an aria from the score of the opera he planned to see that night. He could hear the orchestra in his head, so he began mouthing the words, his body swaying to the imaginary music and his hand marking time like a silent metronome.

"Pardon me," the conductor said. "Your ticket, please."

Franz looked up from his score a little embarrassed. "Oh, yes, of course . . . here it is," he stammered, clumsily pulling out a pass from the wallet in his pocket.

"*Danke*," the conductor said moving on.

But Franz wasn't the only peculiar passenger on the tram. He watched as a rather thin man, also carrying a music score, seemed to hallucinate similarly. The gentleman was wearing a felt porkpie hat and a shirt with a bow tie, and he sat on the wooden bench of the streetcar conducting. Later that day, Franz described him to some of his classmates at the Konservatorium. "He might be Kurt Herbert Adler," one of them finally announced. "He's going places as a conductor and impresario."

On Friday, the sixth of April, Franz left the Konservatorium in the early evening, crossed the Ringstrasse and had a bite to eat at a café. A couple minutes of walking, and he was in front of the Staatsoper. He just stood looking at it for a moment, at the magnificent neo-Renaissance stone façade with its grand arcades and ornamental dome. After purchasing a ticket, he entered the opera house and began climbing its superb marble staircase. As he traveled upstairs, he passed a grandiose foyer decorated with the busts of famous composers and frescoes representing scenes from famous operas. By the time he reached the top floor, he was in awe of the beautiful archways, chandeliers, and statues.

He always stood behind the last row in the gallery until everyone was seated. The ivory, red and gold décor was opulent. He could see everything perfectly: the fashionably-dressed men and women taking their seats on the main floor, and the boxes and balcony surrounding them.

It was seven o'clock now. The opera was about to begin and the houselights were dimming. The conductor approached the orchestra, and the audience started applauding. There were aisles of steps leading downward to the gallery seats. And as the overture began, Franz sat down on the uppermost step in the center and opened up his opera score.

The opera was Giuseppe Verdi's *Don Carlos*, the action taking place in Spain in the sixteenth century at the time of the Spanish Inquisition. Don Carlos, Prince of Spain, had planned to wed Elisabeth of Valois from France; but his father, King Philip II, married her instead. As the curtain rises, the grief-stricken Carlos has sought refuge in a monastery in Madrid. He is soon greeted by his friend, Rodrigo, Marquis of Posa, who consoles him, entreating him to go to the Netherlands to help restore religious and economic freedoms for the Flemish, who were then oppressed by Spanish rule.

As Franz skimmed his finger from bar to bar and page to page in his score, he tried to focus his attentions on Rodrigo, a role that he hoped to learn. He rarely looked down at the costumes or set because he was too preoccupied with the music. He loved the duet in the first act when Carlos and Rodrigo sing a series of ringing thirds to pledge their everlasting friendship.

At the end of the second act, Franz did look down at the stage, however. The inquisitors were about to burn some heretics in the crowded square outside of a cathedral in Madrid. Philip arrived with Elisabeth after his coronation to the sound of pleas from the crowd for his mercy. Franz just had to look at the pageantry of the procession and the regality of the costumes: tight-fitting gowns with long-waisted bodices and multiple petticoats for women; and doublets and ruffs at the collar, breeches and stockings, boots, armor, and cloaks for the men.

It was intermission and Franz went out into the a foyer where he met some opera students who looked familiar, and some who didn't. As usual, they all gravitated toward each other to critique the singing. However this conversation was destined to be far less artistic.

"Did you hear about it?" one of them asked.

"Hear about what?" Franz responded.

"Chancellor Dollfuss announced a new constitution, and since then, the political parties that were supposed to disappear have gone underground, and the Nazis are growing stronger and more defiant."

"How do you know?"

"It was on the radio."

The chimes began signaling the end of intermission. Franz found that he was getting nervous. Nothing had really happened, but he wanted to be with Franziska. She was attending a performance at the Burgtheater. He didn't know whether to go back into the auditorium, or to leave and go to the Burgtheater. Realizing that she probably wasn't even aware of the situation, he decided to return to his step in the gallery.

He opened his score to the beginning of the third act. Once again, the conductor Clemens Krauss entered, and the audience applauded. Franz was anxious to hear Philip's soliloquy. Although he never planned to learn the role, since Philip was always a bass, he had learned the aria for recitals.

As the curtain rose, Philip was sitting alone in the palace study, musing over his inability to win the Queen's love.

"*Sie hat mich nie geliebt,*" the bass on the stage was singing. "She never loved me."

Franz liked the singer's interpretation. He had heard a phonograph record of the great bass Alexander Kipnis singing the aria, but this bass, Josef von Manowarda, was comparable, which was not an easy feat.

By this time, Franz realized that he was having trouble concentrating, since he was still thinking about Franziska. He really wanted to stay to see Rodrigo's death scene; however, he also wanted to make sure that Franziska was all right. So after Philip's aria, while the audience was still applauding, he stood up and walked into the foyer, down the steps, and out the door to the nearest tram.

Franziska was indeed at the Burgtheater, which was located on the Ringstrasse across from the *Rathaus*. It was another grand building in the neo-Renaissance tradition, with a central convex façade and a lavish Baroque interior of red, gold, and ivory. Franziska was comfortably seated in the highest balcony, but she wasn't paying much attention to the last scene of Hanns Sassmann's *Maria Theresia und Friedrich II*. Instead, since she knew that Franz was at the Staatsoper hearing Verdi's *Don Carlos*, she started visualizing the last act of Friedrich von Schiller's *Don Carlos* – the play from which the opera was composed. Although not identical, the stories were similar. Franziska had seen the play at the Burgtheater less than two years before.

She envisioned that the Marquis of Posa had just been shot after falsely revealing that he'd been in love with the Queen, having lied to save his enduring friend, Carlos, who explained to his father that he and Posa had been like brothers and that Posa's loyalty had led to his death.

Then Franziska envisioned the final scene: Carlos bidding a sad farewell to the Queen and revealing his plans to aid the Flemish against his father. Franziska imagined that Philip had entered with the Grand Inquisitor, that the Queen had fallen unconscious with Carlos catching her, and she could hear Philip saying that he had done his part and that the Cardinal should do likewise. Philip's final lines always gave Franziska the chills.

She was suddenly jolted back into the real world as the real curtain fell. The audience was applauding enthusiastically. The actors reappeared on the apron of the stage for their curtain calls.

Franziska rose from her seat, walked into the foyer and down the stairs. She was intellectually and emotionally exhausted. As she started to leave, she noticed that some people were milling around and whispering, and there were armed Austrian soldiers standing strategically on all sides of the theater and along the street. Franziska concluded that maybe the government had anticipated some terrorist outbreaks or demonstrations. As she walked out apprehensively in front of the theater, she bumped into an elderly well-dressed gentleman, and her program and opera glasses fell to the ground. He bent down to retrieve them and attempted to start a conversation. Franziska merely wanted to leave her immediate surroundings, so she thanked him and continued walking. It was half past ten, and she was starting to shiver. It was a warm summer evening, and she was wearing a long, full-sleeved softly draped dress. There was no reason for her to be cold; she was just apprehensive, and she really didn't know why.

By now Franz had arrived in front of the theater. As the people were leaving, he weaved in and out among them, looking for Franziska; but it seemed as if he was roaming back and forth in semicircles. Finally he spotted her getting on a tram. He crossed a path in front of the theater reserved for *Fiakers* and shouted:

"Franziska . . . Franzi! . . . Wait!"

He reached her just in time and climbed onto the tram behind her.

"Franz," she said, turning around, surprised. "What are you doing here?"

"I just wanted to make sure that you are all right."

She looked at him questioningly as they sat down.

"There are so many soldiers all around. Has something happened?"

"Not really. The Nazis are picking up their momentum. I was just worried about you."

But then on July 25th, Chancellor Engelbert Dollfuss was killed by the Nazis.

About a hundred men had invaded the government headquarters in Ballhausplatz before a scheduled cabinet meeting. Chancellor Dollfus had tried to escape from his office through a secret passage, but was locked in. He was shot in the neck and shoulder. Most of the men were immediately apprehended.

Franz and Franziska were together that night. Franz was walking Franzi home. Once inside, they heard on the radio that Kurt von Schuschnigg, Austria's minister of justice, had been appointed the new chancellor.

"He's a Christian Socialist like Dollfuss; he'll put up a good fight against the Nazis," Franz said, sitting next to Franziska on her bed.

"But what if Hitler comes into Austria and takes over? What will we do then?"

"That won't happen, Franzi. He's in Germany, and he's going to stay there."

"But I saw *Don Carlos* at the Burgtheater, and you saw the opera at the Staatsoper. The Netherlands was taken over by Spanish rule, and the people lost all of their liberties. Protestants and Jews were cast out and labeled heretics by the Inquisition, and only Catholicism prevailed."

Franziska began to cry.

"It could happen again, Franz, or even worse. The Flemish people were fighting for religious freedom and for their independence from Spain. Can you imagine the reaction if that play had been performed today?

"You were at that rally almost two years ago; you saw how the Nazis want to make Austria part of the Reich. . . . "

"But it's not going to happen."

"Oh, what are we going to do? What are we going to do?" Franziska cried. And Franz held her until she fell asleep.

Wolfgang Amadeus Mozart.
(*Drawing by Dora Stock.*)

CHAPTER NINE
Musikvereinsgebäude

Vienna, Austria
1935

My father talked glowingly when I asked him about his début. Plus he felt so privileged to have heard the glorious Marian Anderson in recital. I spent many an afternoon as a child listening to an old phonograph record of Marian Anderson singing Schubert's "Die Forelle." I played it over and over again and was mortified one day when I sat on the record. I never found another version that I cherished as much.

$\mathcal{F}$ranz was rehearsing for a student production of Mozart's *The Marriage of Figaro*. The performance was less than three weeks away, yet this was the first time the entire cast was singing together. The production was scheduled in the last minute when a teacher at the Konservatorium discovered that the opera would soon be performed by students of the Akademie, the competing music school housed in the nearby Konzerthaus. It was the goal of the directors of the Konservatorium to present the opera first, and to make the performance superior.

After much debate among the opera department's directors, Franz was awarded the role of Figaro. He was very excited because the performance would mark his opera début. At this early rehearsal, the students were standing next to each other in a small room. Their music scores were open, and they were being accompanied by Fritz Bland, one of the directors. Herr Bland was a thin man of medium height. Franz thought that he had a mean face, probably because the two always seemed to lock horns on matters regarding musicianship. But Franz was determined to behave himself, at least until after the performance. However he was looking forward to the last week of rehearsals, which would be with the student orchestra; those rehearsals would be conducted by a much more amiable department director, Rudolf Nilius.

The cast had reached the end of the third act when a voice teacher entered the rehearsal room and whispered something into Fritz Bland's ear. Herr Bland clapped his hands together and told everyone to take a break and go into the theater to hear an American contralto who had been receiving rave reviews from critics all over Europe, but was still unknown in Vienna.

Grateful for a chance to rest, the group of eleven left the rehearsal room and sat in the back of the theater. The contralto was standing in front of a grand piano on the stage; there was no orchestra. She was singing Schubert's "Der Tod und das Mädchen" ("Death and the Maiden"). First her voice took on the characteristics of the terrified young girl who feared dying, and then it became the solemn voice of death, luring in its victim. Franz thought her voice was magnificent; it had a spiritual quality. Her higher tones were opulent; her lower notes, hauntingly rich; and her legato line enabled her to glide from one register to the other seamlessly.

Although the hall was almost empty, the critics were amply represented. And when the reviews called her "the sensation of the music season," her name spread throughout Vienna, and by her second concert a few days later, the hall was completely filled.

A black woman, her career wasn't progressing as quickly as she'd hoped in America, so she came to Europe, where the critics and audiences rated her solely on her phenomenal talent. Her name was Marian Anderson, and she was never to suffer from obscurity again.

But although she found Europe to be a land of equal opportunity, many others, including Alexander Kipnis, were living and working on a far different continent. When German President Paul von Hindenburg died in 1934, Hitler merged the offices of chancellor and president, and thus became Germany's supreme leader. By the time Marian Anderson was singing in Vienna, Jews in Germany were excluded from the arts, from civil service and government jobs, and their children were barred from public schools. At about the same time, when Alexander Kipnis left Berlin to become a member of the Wiener Staatsoper, he left to escape persecution.

Franz had no idea where he would sing when he graduated from the Konservatorium. Although he sometimes studied individual songs and arias in different languages for possible future concert dates, he had been learning complete operatic roles only in German. But he wasn't going to worry about it. In less than three weeks, he would make his opera début in the same theater he'd heard Marian Anderson.

The big day finally arrived. Franz felt ready, but he was extremely nervous. The production was being presented in the Brahms-Saal, which was much smaller, more intimate, and less ornate than the Grosser Saal. There was a small, slightly elevated stage; a space in front for an orchestra; and rows of burnt sienna-colored chairs. There were no boxes, but there was seating on the second tier, which – much more like the Grosse Saal – was decorated in the gold neo-Renaissance tradition. It was six o'clock. Franz was sitting in a dressing room with the other male students in the cast. He had just finished applying makeup and was about to put on his costume. The performance would begin in an hour. A number of agents had been invited. It would either be the beginning or the end of his life, he thought.

He took his costume from the rack in the center of the dressing room and laid it down on a chair. He put on the shirt, stockings, breeches, and buckled pumps; he slipped into the waistcoat, and then he covered everything with a long apron. He was dressed.

"Are you going to go onstage like that?" Paul Hofbauer asked. Paul was going to sing the part of the lawyer, Don Curzio.

"I think so," Franz responded, looking into the mirror. "Oh, you're right. I have forgotten something."

Franz reached over to the dressing table and lifted a tie wig off the stand. He carefully placed it on his head and secured it with some hairpins.

"Now I'm dressed," he whispered to himself. "But can I sing?" He took out a pitchpipe and sang a couple of scales, and then he sang a few phrases from some of his arias.

A few minutes before seven, he walked out of his dressing room and into the wings.

By this time, the orchestra members were seated in front of the stage, some of them still tuning their instruments.

Franziska and Franz's mother and sister were seated next to each other near the front of the hall. Franziska was wearing a lovely two-piece ensemble with a lacy white collar and cuffs; Ilona had on a flowing yellow chiffon dress; and Franz's mother was wearing a dressy suit.

"Oh, look, there's Franz's name," Franziska said, pointing to the program. "I'm so excited; I've never heard him sing with an orchestra before."

"Neither have we," Ilona responded.

"I never thought I'd see this day," Olga commented. "Jakob would have been so proud."

The three sat silently for a moment.

"*Marriage of Figaro* is one of my favorites," Franziska announced. "Can you believe the medieval custom that gave a ruler the right to sleep with the women who worked for him on the eve of their weddings?"

"That was quite a custom," Ilona laughed. "I'm not sure that I'd mind it."

"Oh, be quiet," Franz's mother remarked.

"But think of the poor ruler's wife; she must have felt terrible. I'm glad that Mozart wrote an opera to comment on such practices. They were simply immoral."

"But Franziska, even though the Count abolished the policy, he was really sorry," Ilona responded. "It just proves that men always have a roving eye and seem to stray. . . ."

"Not my Franz." Franziska cut her off quickly.

But Ilona continued: "And in the olden days, and even today, the behavior is often accepted."

Franziska felt her face growing flushed. Fortunately for Ilona, the performance was about to start. Rudolf Nilius, the conductor, was approaching the podium, and the audience was applauding. When the overture began, Franz and the girl who was playing his fiancée, Susanna, were already standing behind the curtain on the stage. Franz had heard the overture so many times that he'd almost memorized it. The curtain was opened at the overture's conclusion.

"*Fünf . . . zehn . . . zwanzig . . . dreissig . . .*" Figaro (Franz) sang. "Five . . . ten . . . twenty . . . thirty . . ."

He was measuring the bedroom that he and Susanna would soon share to determine if their new bed would fit. The bed and room were given to them by Count and Countess Almaviva of Spain, their employers. Figaro was the Count's valet and Susanna, the Countess's personal maid. Figaro liked the location of the room, between the Count's quarters and the Countess's boudoir. But Susanna didn't.

After Susanna explained to Figaro about the Count's seductive intentions, she left him alone on the stage to vent out his dismay to a pair of boots that represented the invisible Count.

Franz received a thunderous applause after he concluded the aria, and he left the stage. The extreme tension in his body had finally dissipated as he discarded his apron and slipped on a knee-length coat that was waiting for him on a chair in the wings.

When Franz returned to the stage as Figaro, the Count had been displeased with Cherubino, his lovesick page, for having made eyes at the Countess. Nevertheless, the Count pardoned Cherubino by making him an officer in his regiment. Then, after the Count made his exit, Figaro sang his second aria to the squeamish page, explaining to Cherubino that he would be living among soldiers – marching through the mud with bullets thundering past his ears on to victory. Figaro and Susanna saluted heroically and marched off the stage with Cherubino.

The curtain was closed; and the stage crew, mostly students, hustled to change the scenery. Since this was a school production on a small stage, the scenery was sparse. The stagehands lifted flats and moved furniture out and in and altered props, while the electrical crew changed the lighting levels.

The setting for the second act was in the Countess's boudoir. Susanna and the Countess were dressed in the eighteenth century clothes of the times: gowns with stiff, fitted bodices; scooped necklines filled with ruffles; and full, cumbersome skirts with whalebone hoops underneath.

First the women botched up a masquerade they'd planned to catch the Count making advances to Susanna. Then Marcellina, the Count's housekeeper, demanded that Figaro honor his signed agreement to marry her or pay her back the money she lent him years before. The announcement created havoc in the boudoir as the act concluded before the commencement of intermission.

The stagehands and electrical crew plunged back into their work, this time creating a large meagerly-furnished room in the chateau, spacious enough for a celebration. While the stagehands were working behind the curtain, Franz was drinking a glass of water and trying to relax for a few minutes in his dressing room. The three ladies in his life were visiting the powder room where they left ample coinage for the attendant who was providing clean towels to everyone while checking the cleanliness of each of the stalls.

Back in their seats, they waited anxiously for the next act to begin.

"I like the part in this act when Figaro shows Marcellina the birthmark on his arm, and she determines that he's really her son," Franziska commented.

"Yes . . . and that Dr. Bartolo is really his father," Ilona added, smiling. "That Marcellina was really a sly one; she must have had some fun when she worked for Dr. Bartolo."

"But remember, they finally decided to get married."

"Shhh," Olga said interrupting them. "Herr Nilius is coming in; the performance is going to start."

The scenes moved rapidly. Ilona and Franziska couldn't help but giggle when Susanna was introduced over and over again to Figaro's newly discovered parents. Susanna's rival for Figaro's attentions would now become her new mother-in-law.

"*Seine Mutter?*" Susanna sang with disbelief. "His mother?"

"*Seine Mutter,*" Dr. Bartolo responded.

"*Seine Mutter?*" she asked the Count.

"*Seine Mutter,*" the Count responded.

Then she asked Don Curzio and Marcellina, and their responses were the same.

Finally: "*Deine Mutter?*" she asked Figaro. "Your mother?"

And so Figaro introduced her to his father as well.

"*Sein Vater?*" Susanna sang. "His father?"

"*Sein Vater,*" Dr. Bartolo responded.

Susanna also asked the Count, and he confirmed it.

And so the scene progressed. . . .

In Act Four, Figaro had reason to believe that Susanna was actually going to have a rendezvous with the Count. The stagehands had changed the lighting and scenery again, this time to produce the garden of the chateau in the darkness of evening. While Figaro waited impatiently in the garden hoping to catch Susanna in the act, he sang his final aria: a warning to all men on the heartlessness and infidelity of women.

"Just open your eyes," he sang, then likened women to witches who do not love and have no pity.

When he finished singing, he was once again given a resounding applause. He ran to hide in the garden when he heard voices. It was Susanna and the Countess attempting to carry out another masquerade. They exchanged cloaks so that the Count would think he was about to make love to Susanna, when in reality, he would actually be with his own wife. This time the scheme proved successful, and the Count finally apologized for all of his roguery.

As the opera concluded, the applause seemed deafening, probably because most of the audience members were parents, relatives, and friends of the performers. The whole cast, including Rudolf Nilius, walked onto the stage, Herr Nilius signaling the orchestra to rise. The applause and *bravos* continued until the people's hands and throats became sore.

Franziska raced backstage and arrived in Franz's dressing room at the same time he did. She gave him a big hug and told him how wonderful he'd sung. A few minutes later, Ilona and Olga arrived, echoing her sentiments.

By now the dressing room was really quite crowded because all of the male cast members were there with their families and friends. Fritz Bland and Rudolf Nilius came back to congratulate the cast, as well as Hans Wohlmuth, the acting teacher, and Josef Reitler, the head director of the Konservatorium and music critic for the *Neue Freie Presse*.

Franz hoped that the room would clear out soon so that he could take off his costume and makeup. Then he saw Doktor Witte approaching him. Franz had made many trips to Doktor Witte's office since that first time he'd met him almost three years before, but this was the first time that the doctor had heard him sing.

"Wonderful," Doktor Witte said, grabbing both of Franz's shoulders in what appeared to be a strong masculine embrace.

"You will go far. You are the only one here with real talent," he whispered into Franz's ear and pulled away.

"Why, thank you, Herr Doktor," Franz replied a little astonished. Doktor Witte's patients had included many great singers from the Wiener Staatsoper. Franz held such a compliment from him in high esteem.

Next, Arthur Fleischer congratulated him, moving on to his other students in the production: Fritz Bergar, who played the Count; and Paul Hofbauer, Don Curzio.

Then an unknown face approached Franz.

"*Guten Abend* (Good evening)," the gentleman said. "My name is Wilhelm Stein; I'm an agent with Artur Hohenberg."

Franz opened his eyes wide and listened. Artur Hohenberg was the largest theatrical agency in Vienna.

"I'm in charge of the opera department," Herr Stein continued. "And I'm interested in representing you when you finish studying at the Konservatorium. I think you show great promise."

"Thank you," Franz said again.

"Our office is in the Konzerthaus building. When you're ready, please give me a call."

Herr Stein gave Franz his card and walked out the door without speaking to any of the other students.

"Did you hear what he said?" Franz asked Franziska and his family exuberantly.

"Yes," they all responded in unison.

"I'm on my way. It looks like I'll be able to pay Arthur Fleischer back for all of those lessons after all."

"I guess I made a good investment," Ilona commented, hugging her brother. "This is a happy day for all of us."

Alexander Kipnis as Hermann in Tannhäuser, 1935.
(© *Hulton-Deutsch Collection/CORBIS*)

CHAPTER TEN

Beginnings

Vienna, Austria
January to November 1936

$\mathcal{F}$ranziska was extremely depressed, but she tried to hide her melancholy from Franz since he was always so happy. She'd worked at Sonnenfeld for more than five years now and was still really no more than a seamstress. But how could she find a job somewhere else?

The eerie feeling of anti-Semitism spreading throughout Vienna had been exacerbated by Hitler's enactment of the Nürnberg Laws which, in Germany, redefined who Jews were, stripped them of their political rights, forbade marriage and sexual relations between Aryan Germans and Jews, and required medical examinations before marriage licenses could be attained. Germans who violated these laws faced imprisonment and fines.

Franziska always had the feeling that many Viennese would have embraced these laws, welcoming Hitler into Austria, but Franz never allowed her to dwell on the subject. She wanted to find another job, and she wanted it to be in a store owned by Jews. She had a break every day for *Mittagessen*, so she walked from store to store on Mariahilferstrasse while munching on bites of the food she'd brought from home. She did this for a number of weeks without any success. But she was determined.

She was also still unhappy about her relationship with her family. Every time she called her mother, her mother continued to reproach her for having moved out and for refraining to help sustain the family with a portion of her salary. She couldn't bear listening to her mother anymore, so she rarely called. However she was still able to talk cordially to Lilly and Fritz, but Paul refused to speak to her at all. Like the other siblings, he had finally dropped out of school to work in a plumbing supply store, and he blamed Franziska in part for his inability to complete his education.

Then one Sunday at about eight in the morning, the telephone rang and Frau Grünwald answered it. There was only one phone in the household, so Franziska always used it sparingly.

"*Ja . . . ja* . . . I'll see if she's available," Frau Grünwald told the person on the other end of the line.

Then she knocked on Franziska's door.

"Franziska . . . are you up? Can you come out? There's a telephone call for you. It's your mother."

"Coming," Franziska answered, opening her door, then walking toward the phone in the living room. She was still a little groggy since she'd gotten home late the night before. She was wearing a full-length knitted pink robe with a satin sash and trim.

"Hello, Mutti," she said, almost sounding a little annoyed.

Then the expression on her face changed, and she suddenly grew pale.

"Dead? . . . How?"

As she posed questions to her mother, her mother responded, and then she delved deeper.

"Of a heart attack? . . . Where? . . . Who found him? . . . Oh, how awful. . . . *SHE* called to tell you? . . . Oh, how awful. . . . Are you going? . . . How can you? . . . I know he left because of financial problems, and I shouldn't have probably believed that he was alone for all of those years; but he was my father, and I guess I always hoped he'd come back. . . . Oh, I'm fine. . . . Yes, he's doing very well; he's going to start singing professionally soon. . . . Marriage? No, we haven't really talked about it. One day. He has to start his career first. But Mutti, back to Papa: You're not going there alone, are you? . . . Good. Yes, take Paul. By the way, how is everyone taking it? . . . Yes, I feel strange too. I feel sad and a little numb; I don't think I can cry though. But Mama, how about you? How do you feel? . . . Oh, Mutti, don't cry. You have to be strong. When are you going? . . . Yes, I promise I'll stop by to see Lilly and Fritz while you're gone. Take care of yourself, Mama. . . . Me too. Bye."

Franziska hung up the receiver and slowly walked back into her room. Frau Grünwald had gone into the kitchen to make breakfast when she realized the personal nature of the conversation. Franziska didn't say anything to her; she wanted to digest the news alone.

When Franz came to pick her up that afternoon, she told him all of the details. And she did start to cry, but not just because her father had died; it was her whole situation. Franz tried to cheer her up, telling her about his hopeful future and how he'd one day be able to take care of her. And for a while, he had her convinced.

But on Monday, it was back to work, and all of her realities were once again inescapable. During her *Mittagessen* break, she continued her job search, bundled in a coat, boots, and scarf, walking from one store to another as the snowflakes floated down atop her head like graceful feathers.

In the evening, she visited Lilly and Fritz. She hadn't seen the apartment in more than a year, but everything looked the same, just maybe not as neat or clean. It was good to see her brother and sister; however the conversation was strained, and the three seemed somehow distant. Then when Franziska was about to leave, she heard a key turning in the door, and footsteps. It was her mother and Paul. They'd been turned back at the border because they couldn't produce passports. They never traveled, so they never applied for them; now they were sorry.

"Can you imagine? We got all the way to the Yugoslavian border and then had to come back," Franziska's mother explained as Fritz, Lilly, and Franziska ran into the hallway. "It's good to see you, Franzi. . . . You don't look like you're eating enough though."

Exhausted, Stefanie and Paul set down their suitcases and then started to unbutton their coats.

"I'm just going to have to call that *woman* up and tell her that she'll have to take care of the funeral arrangements herself," Stefanie reported. "If not, I'll just have to send the money and do it by phone."

Then she began to cry. "Oh, I never thought it would come to this. I loved your father. We just weren't able to talk to each other anymore. He just couldn't discuss his problems with me. He had too much pride, and he didn't want the family to know. Oh, if we'd only been able to talk, maybe he wouldn't have left."

Lilly and Fritz comforted their mother, leading her to the sofa in the den as Paul and Franziska followed. There was no doubt that they were a family and that this was a sad moment in their lives.

Then Paul started talking antagonistically: "So, Franzi, how's the big designer?"

Franziska didn't say a word.

"Paul, this isn't the time," Lilly uttered.

"Oh I think it's the perfect time," Paul continued.

"Please, Paul."

After a pause: "Well, I think I'd better be going."

"No, please stay," Lilly offered warmly.

"No, I'd better go. It's getting late. . . . I'll talk to you soon."

Franziska went to her mother and kissed her on the forehead. "Goodbye, Mama. Everything's going to be all right."

Franziska walked out of the den, through the hallway and out the door, and then she sighed. She knew she could never move home again; she'd somehow outgrown it. She could never go back; she had to move forward.

So the next day, she tried to look for a job with a more optimistic attitude. As she walked down Mariahilferstrasse and along Neubaugasse, she found herself in front of a dress shop that resembled all of the others. She looked up at the sign: "*Appenzeller*," it said. *I think I'll give it a try*, she thought.

She walked into the store and immediately liked what she saw. It was smaller than Sonnenfeld, and there were fewer dresses on display. The store was made to look more like a living room with a sofa and a few comfortable chairs. This meant to Franziska that it was more exclusive and that more clothes were probably made to order. In this type of store, women didn't search for dresses on numerous racks, but sat patiently instead, making selections as salespeople presented the dresses to them.

"I'm Gustav Appenzeller, one of the owners of this store. May I help you find something?"

Franziska always dressed well and looked attractive because she was able to sew. She could pick up a sale item that was two sizes too large, alter it and add some trim, and she looked fantastic. Of course, Herr Appenzeller couldn't see the lovely suit she was wearing because it was covered with a coat; however the coat was quite elegant, so she probably appeared to him to be a customer.

"Oh, Herr Appenzeller," Franziska said somewhat shyly. "I'm looking for a job as a designer."

"Well, we have our own label," Herr Appenzeller explained. "But we sell different lines as well, and we make clothes to order in different fabrics. . . . Tell me something about your experience."

Franziska told him about her education and about her position as a design apprentice at a neighboring store. She didn't want another job as a seamstress, so she enhanced her experiences.

"Do you have a portfolio?"

"It's at home," she said, making an excuse. "I didn't really intend to look for a job today; but I saw your store, and it looked inviting."

Herr Appenzeller sensed that she was not an established designer by her manner; however, he liked her. She seemed capable, professional, and warm.

"I am looking for someone," he said. "However I employ an excellent designer. Of course, I would give you an opportunity to show me your designs, and once in a while, I might use one. But the job basically entails making patterns, cutting fabric, and purchasing materials for me. And if you do well, I could use a buyer."

The job sounded impressive to Franziska. However, she remembered the promises that had been made to her at Sonnenfeld, promises that had never been kept. Maybe Herr Appenzeller would be more true to his word, she thought. He offered her more money than she was making, so she accepted the job.

After just a few weeks at Appenzeller, Franziska realized that she had made a wise decision. She was truly no longer a seamstress. In fact, most of her days were spent purchasing materials. At the beginning, she just bought what she was told. But Herr Appenzeller soon began showing her dresses and telling her that he wanted to make them up in different materials. Then she was allowed to select the fabrics and purchase them. She had good taste and seemed to know what the customers wanted. He was satisfied with her, and she was satisfied with the job.

On the twenty-fifth of March, Franz was finally able to hear Alexander Kipnis give a recital in the Grossen Saal of the Musikverein. His voice was beautifully rounded and resonant; his lower tones were deep and melodious; and he had the ability to sing sweetly or with great power and intensity.

In Schubert's "Der Doppelgänger" to words by Heinrich Heine, the singer must transform himself into a man who sees someone standing in front of his former sweetheart's house, and then realizes that the grief-stricken someone is really himself.

The *Lied* was sung so mournfully. Franz was listening to a singer who really knew how to put pain and suffering into his voice. However, the next *Lied* moved Franz even more. In "Der Erlkönig," Kipnis fused the music of Schubert with the poetry of Goethe to create what seemed to be a musical play in which all of the characters were portrayed by one person. First his voice was the narrator; next a strong, but comforting father; then a panic-stricken son; and finally the Erl King, an imaginary supernatural being connoting death.

With a limitless range of colors in his voice, Kipnis was singing the story of a father who rides home through the forest one night with his young son in his arms. The child tells his father that he hears the Erl King trying to lure him away. The father assures his son that what he hears is only the wind. Finally the Erl King injures the young boy, and by the time the father arrives home, his son is dead.

Franz couldn't believe what he was hearing. When Kipnis portrayed the Erl King beckoning the child to come away with him, his voice was delicate and lyrical. When he was the father attempting to calm his son and dissuade his fears, his voice was robust and authoritarian, yet consoling. And when he was the young boy crying out in terror, his voice was frantic and desperate.

The interpretation was chilling. Kipnis's ability to communicate emotions and feelings to an audience with his dark, splendrous voice was awe-inspiring to Franz. He knew that he wanted to sing technically correct, but he also wanted to be able to move an audience emotionally with the colors of his voice. Alexander Kipnis had become his role model.

In April, Franz graduated from the Konservatorium, but continued to study privately with Arthur Fleischer, whose son, Thomas, often accompanied him. Franz also sang before a board of examiners, who certified him as an official opera singer in the Austrian theater artists association. He was ready to work, so he contacted Wilhelm Stein.

Herr Stein was delighted to hear from him and asked him for a list of the current roles in his repertoire. Franz was prepared to sing Mozart's Figaro and Papageno, Rossini's Dr. Bartolo, Verdi's Elder Germont and Baron Douphol, Puccini's Marcello and Schaunard, Wagner's Alberich, Klingsor and Beckmesser, and a few other roles.

Herr Stein explained that it was too late to secure a contract with a particular opera house for the 1936-37 season, but that he could probably guarantee one for the following year; and in the interim, he would be able to keep Franz busy at the Wiener Volksoper and a few other nearby theaters.

The summer months seemed to fly by, and Franz began singing at the Volksoper in September. It was a small opera house found northwest of the Ring; in fact, Franz always passed it whenever he rode a tram from the Ring to Pötzleinsdorf, or vice versa. Many excellent young singers started their careers at the Volksoper. Franz was happy. He was spending his first professional season getting experience, and he was able to remain in the same city with Franziska.

CHAPTER ELEVEN

The *Opernball*

Vienna, Austria
February 1937

Since Franziska had been a child, she'd always dreamt of going to a ball in an exquisitely designed long evening gown, and now she was finally going. But in what? That was the question.

The *Opernball* (Opera Ball) was a regal social event held at the Wiener Staatsoper, where prominent artists, local and international government officials, business magnates, and the crème de la crème of Viennese society mixed together under one roof to spend a lavish evening of dancing and merriment. Franz's agency purchased tickets, and because Wilhelm Stein was so pleased with Franz's progress, he gave Franz two tickets a few days before. Franziska didn't know how she would find an evening gown on such short notice or how she'd be able to pay for it. She also worried that since the ball was on Thursday evening, she'd be so tired after work that she wouldn't be able to enjoy it. And then how would she be able to coax herself into work the next morning? The ball was in just two days on the Thursday before Ash Wednesday, the fourth of February, and she still didn't have a dress. Herr Appenzeller sensed that something was wrong because she seemed so preoccupied.

"You know, Franziska, I'm a little worried about you," he told her. "You don't seem like yourself lately, and your work is suffering."

In reality, Herr Appenzeller had no intentions of criticizing Franziska's work; he simply wanted to coax the problem out of her. He soon discovered that his strategy had been a success when a worried look crossed her face. She was not about to lose her job over a silly ball, she was thinking.

"Herr Appenzeller, please excuse me for my behavior. Franz and I were given tickets to attend the *Opernball*, and I still don't have a gown."

"When is the ball?" Herr Appenzeller asked.

"On Thursday."

"Oh, that doesn't give you much time, does it?"

"No," Franziska sulked. "I promise that I'll try to concentrate more. I have to go out now and buy some fabric. I'll be back in a few hours."

Franziska put her coat on and left. When she returned, Herr Appenzeller asked her to sit down on the sofa just as if she were a customer. Then he and his wife, Bertha, brought two dresses out and laid them down in front of her. She was speechless.

"These dresses can't be sold to the public because there are slight flaws in the material. One would require just a little altering, while the other is really much too big for you and would require more. Choose the one you like, and it will be ready for you on Thursday," Herr Appenzeller said.

Franziska couldn't believe how generous her employers were. They appeared to be a very average hard-working couple in their early sixties. He was tall and thin with graying hair; and she was short, round, and motherly-looking. Franziska had never told them a great deal about her life, but they knew she rented a room nearby and had a boyfriend who was an opera singer. In fact, they'd met Franz a few times when he'd picked her up.

"I really don't know how to thank you," Franziska said. "You're making me feel a little like Cinderella."

"Well, which one do you want?" Frau Appenzeller asked. "We have to begin working on it."

One gown was made of ivory-colored jersey and ornamented with gold sequined embroidery over the bust, down the long flowing sleeves, and around the waistline like a cummerbund. It was simple and stylish.

The other was made of pale pink chiffon trimmed with satin appliquéd flowers, and it came with a matching stole embellished with feathers.

"I'd like the gown without all the fluff," Franziska said. "It has more of a classic look."

"It's yours," Herr Appenzeller affirmed. "And I'm pleased to say that you've selected the one that requires the least amount of altering. Now go and try it on so that we can get busy."

So Franziska did as she was told. She was fitted by the head seamstress; then she dressed in her own clothes and went back to work making a pattern.

As promised, the gown was finished on Thursday. And to confirm that Franziska really wasn't Cinderella, the Appenzellers gave her Friday off.

"Have a wonderful time and stay out as long as you like," Frau Appenzeller said at about four o'clock. "Go home now and get dressed."

"Yes, Fairy Godmother," Franziska said with a glow on her face, running to Frau Appenzeller and giving her a quick kiss on the cheek.

She thanked them both, took her evening gown from the sold rack, and carefully carried it over her arm out the door.

Franziska was dressed and waiting for Franz in the living room of the Grünwalds' apartment at about seven o'clock. That's when Magda Grünwald asked her husband to retrieve the camera from the bedroom to take some photographs. Franziska really looked stunning. The flowing gown fit perfectly. It wasn't a showy dress – it had a high neckline and long sleeves – but it was smart-looking and chic, just like Franziska, and the sequins made it just dressy enough for a ball. As for accessories, her feet were graced with suede pumps – not glass slippers – and she was carrying a brown calfskin leather bag with a bracelet handle that slipped over her wrist.

She was wearing her hair shorter now; it was somewhat smooth on top, breaking into curls that extended just below her shoulders. And on this special evening, her makeup was applied heavier than usual; but as always, it flawlessly accentuated her onyx-colored almond-shaped eyes because of an almost artistic utilization of eye shadow, mascara, and penciling on her thinly curved eyebrows and on the inside of her lower eyelids. Her lips were painted red, and there was a hint of rouge over her creamy foundation.

Herr Grünwald was earnestly snapping pictures when the doorbell rang. Then he and his wife departed as Franziska opened the door. Franz was so loaded down that Franziska couldn't see what he was wearing.

"Wow! You look gorgeous," he said.

"Let me help you. What all do you have here?"

"An umbrella just in case," Franz said sticking out one of his hands. "And a corsage for you," he divulged, bearing the other. "I'm sorry that I can't pin it on your dress right now, but . . ."

"Oh, how pretty," Franziska said, taking the corsage from him and placing it on a table as he dropped the umbrella onto the floor. "And what's this?"

"It's a fur coat. I knew you didn't have a wrap for tonight, so I borrowed it from Ilona. It's fox."

"Oh, how lovely."

Franziska took the coat from Franz and placed it around her shoulders twirling around the room. Then she laid it down on the couch.

"And where did you get your coat?" she asked. "It's very impressive-looking."

"I rented it along with everything else."

It was an alpaca Chesterfield with a black velvet collar. Franz took the overcoat off so that Franziska could see his formal evening attire underneath.

"Don't you look handsome," Franziska said. "I hear that when you become a famous opera singer, you'll be required to dress like this all the time."

Franz smiled. He was wearing a stiff white dress shirt with a white bow tie and waistcoat, black trousers with silk braided side seams, and a tailcoat of black broadcloth with a wing collar and silk lapels.

He took the corsage from the table and pinned it on Franziska's dress. "I wanted us to go in style tonight, so I telephoned for a taxi before I left home and told the driver when to come. The taxi's probably outside by now, so shall we go?" Franz asked, helping Franziska into the fox jacket.

"It would be my supreme pleasure."

"Wait, wait," Ernst Grünwald shouted, entering the room and taking a few pictures of the couple together. "Now you can go. Have fun!"

With that final edict, Franz put on his overcoat, grabbed the umbrella, and escorted Franziska out the door.

Franz and Franziska arrived at the Staatsoper about ten minutes later. All lit up at night, the building looked as if it were made of fourteen karat gold. Franz and Franziska felt regal as they entered the foyer, handed their tickets to an usher, and began ascending the grand marble staircase. They didn't have to walk far this time because they would be sitting at a table on the main floor in the proximity of the stage, not on a balcony or gallery. They checked in their coats and then continued walking into the auditorium.

Franz had never seen the opera house bedecked like this before. All of the seats on the main floor had been covered with a wooden floor that was actually level with the stage, the stage becoming part of the ballroom. People were standing all around, leaving the dance floor in the center vacant. The room was decorated with thousands of red carnations, many bunched in bouquets gracefully garnishing the front of the boxes, balcony, and gallery. As Franz and Franziska approached their table, they continually looked up and all around at the splendor of the room. People were standing and sitting everywhere, all of them looking very noble and aristocratic.

"I think this is our table," Franz said.

"Let me see your ticket," a young gentleman remarked, standing. "Yes, you're at the right place. This is a certified Artur Hohenberg table. Welcome, I'm an up-and-coming violinist; who are you?"

"An up-and-coming opera singer, I suppose," Franz said laughing.

The two men introduced each other to their significant others. Then Franz pulled the chair out for Franzi, and everyone sat down. Another couple joined them a few minutes later. He was the general manager of one of the major theaters in Vienna, and she was an actress.

Franz and Franziska sat quietly waiting for the gala to begin. And when it did, their eyes were glued to the dance floor, where more than one hundred fifty young ladies in long white evening gowns were partnered with an equal number of young gentlemen in black tails to dance the opening polonaise. These young women were the debutantes of the ball, celebrating their introduction into high society. They held bouquets of red-and-white carnations as they promenaded across the dance floor with their partners, creating carefully choreographed patterns of black and white.

"Oh, how beautiful they all look," Franziska whispered to Franz. "Did you ever learn the polonaise?"

"Not that I can recall."

"It's more like a stately ceremonial procession than a dance, isn't it?"

"I guess so."

"I wonder if any of those girls are Jewish."

"I don't know," Franz responded, also whispering: "I doubt it."

Soon later, all of the young debutantes were waltzing, and it was time for the audience to join in the party. The other two couples at the table decided to wander around.

"Look," Franz said. "Look up there at the *Mitelloge* (a large box located one level above the first row of boxes in the back of the auditorium directly opposite the center of the stage).

"Who are they?"

"They look like government officials and maybe diplomats from other countries. In fact . . . that looks like Franz von Papen, the German ambassador to Austria. Many people say that he's responsible for Hitler's rise to power."

"Oh, no." Franziska panicked. "Maybe he's trying to help Hitler gain power in Austria too."

"Please, Franziska, don't start trying to determine the significance of his presence here. . . . I'm not even sure if it's him. . . . This is the *Opernball*. It's a worthwhile event for any international diplomat to attend."

"If Hitler appointed him, the two must think alike. He must be an anti-Semitic Nazi, and in that case, he's a dangerous man."

"Really, then how do you explain that just a few months ago, he engineered an agreement whereby Hitler consented to respect Austria's independence?"

"Did you read the agreement, Franz? I'll bet there were a lot of Austrian concessions that went along with it."

"Come on, Franzi, don't spoil the evening for both of us. . . ."

"But how can you trust a man like Hitler? He blatantly violated the Versailles Treaty by sending troops into the Rhineland, and the French yielded their territory without hardly any resistance. That little coup only served to bolster Hitler's confidence, and now Austria's going to be next."

"Franziska, we did not come here to talk politics. So please, stop!" Franz said firmly. "Let's look around and dance and have some fun."

Franziska scrutinized Franz's eyes. She didn't say a word because she knew that he was right. Her demeanor changed; she put a smile on her face, and the two began walking around the ballroom. They wandered into foyers and other rooms in the opera house where they heard Strauss waltzes and Viennese folk music, sampled tasty hors d'oeuvres and pastries, and watched a lot of other people indulge at the bars.

"Are you sure you don't want anything to drink?" Franz asked. "Not even some wine or champagne?"

"No, I don't like drinking alone. You know, you're no fun anymore since you started singing and swore off liquor and smoking."

"I think they affect my voice."

"I know. I was just kidding. Let's go back into the ballroom and waltz."

So back they went straight to the dance floor. The orchestra was playing "An der schönen blauen Donau." They put their arms into the dance position and began waltzing around the room – smiling, laughing, and remembering the first time they'd met at the Kursalon and had danced to the same melody so many years ago. They danced like that for hours until they were so tired that they became slaphappy and seemed to slip into a state of exaggerated euphoria.

"I know that people stay here until three o'clock in the morning, but I think it's time for us to go home," Franziska said, sounding a little punchy.

"My sentiments exactly," Franz responded, leading Franziska back to their table. "It's too late to take a tram; so since I'm so rich, I'll go and call a taxi."

"You better look out the door first; there might be some waiting on the Kärntner Strasse."

While Franz was gone, Franziska could see that many people had already left. When he returned, he was wearing his overcoat and holding her wrap and the umbrella.

"Here, let me help you on with this," he said as she stood and put her arms into the sleeves of the jacket. "You were right; there are plenty of taxicabs outside."

"What, not a *Fiaker*?"

"Oh, stop joking. You know it's too late: it's after one in the morning."

Then Franz put his arm around Franziska's waist as she placed hers around his. They strolled out of the ballroom slowly, trying to catch one last glimpse, walked down the grand marble staircase into the foyer, out the door, and to the taxi.

When Franz and Franziska arrived at the Grünwalds' apartment, Franz didn't know what to do. He wanted to go inside with Franziska, but then he wouldn't probably be able to get another taxi until the morning. Since Franziska rented a room from the Grünwalds, he didn't want to find himself in a precarious situation.

"Oh, I can't leave you like this, looking so beautiful," he said. "I'll take my chances and come in."

He paid the taxicab driver, and they quietly entered the apartment and went to Franziska's room. She took off the fur jacket and laid it on the table, and he removed his overcoat and placed it on a chair.

"You know, you were the most exquisite-looking woman there," he said, starting to unfasten the hooks down the front of her dress. He reached inside and began caressing her breasts as she struggled to undo her cummerbund.

"You know, this isn't going to work," she whispered. "I'm a little worried about my evening gown, and you're in rented clothes, so why don't we undress ourselves, and then . . ."

So the two stood facing each other, slowly disrobing inch by inch and piece by piece. As Franziska's dress fell to the floor, she stepped over it, revealing her slender silhouette covered delicately with a satin slip. She released the strap from one shoulder, then the other, freeing her arms and pulling the garment down provocatively. She removed her bra as Franz lunged his body close to her, kissing her breasts and then allowing his tongue to rove around what was his devouringly. He kissed her lips with hunger, and then in an almost animalistic fashion, reached between her legs, cupping his hand around her crotch possessively. She had to catch her breath from the surprise of the maneuver; then as she felt her heart pulsating, his hand remained in place as the two fell onto the bed entwined. He detached her garter belt from her stockings, leaving them untouched as he slid down her panties. "Oh, how I long for you," he said, pulling off his undershorts and then gliding his body atop her.

They made love deeply and completely throughout the night, meeting each other's needs both physically and emotionally, both dreaming of a time when they would be able to spend their nights together always. They slept on and off in each other's arms, neither wanting to see daybreak, both wishing the moments would last. But as light began to glimmer through the shades, Franz awoke and softly kissed Franziska's eyes. She opened them, still looking very far away as he whispered: "You bring me so much sunshine and pleasure. My heart couldn't bear to live without you. Please don't ever leave me."

Franziska smiled as he kissed her on the forehead and rose from the bed. She watched as he dressed himself, understanding that he hoped to sneak out before the Grünwalds would notice him. Then he bent down over her and held her face between both of his hands, kissing her lips tenderly. "Thank you for a wonderful evening," he said. "I love you."

He walked toward the door with the fur coat draped over his arm and the umbrella hanging from his wrist. He stopped to take one more look at her, turned the doorknob, and was gone.

CHAPTER TWELVE
Björling

Vienna, Austria
Winter 1937

After hearing the following incident on my father's audiotapes, I started listening to the great tenor, Jussi Björling. I also read the autobiography written by his wife and was so involved in it that I thought I should be made an honorary member of their family. I bought my father some Björling CDs, and we spent hours sitting together on the couch – listening and agreeing about the phenomenal beauty of Björling's voice. For my father, who was a young artist in 1937, the following incident lingered vividly in his mind until well after the last chapter of this memoir. He told me that if I were to speak to Anna-Lisa Björling, he was sure that she would remember that evening. Alas, I never had the opportunity.

$\mathcal{T}$he reviews were encouraging:

> *Franz Jung's loveable Papageno was delightful.*

> *As Rossini's Dr. Bartolo, Franz Jung's comedic timing was beyond reproach.*

> *A first-rate Figaro in the Mozartian tradition, Franz Jung sang with vocal ease and musicianship, impeccable phrasing and finesse.*

The exceptional reviews served to bolster Wilhelm Stein's confidence in his new client. He was attempting to secure a contract for Franz in either Graz, Zürich, or Prague. In the meantime, he wanted to show-case his young protégé's talents whenever possible. At the beginning of February, Stein decided to throw a party for the musical élite of Vienna and for the phenomenal Swedish tenor, Jussi Björling, who would be singing an array of roles at the Wiener Staatsoper. He invited Franz to the party, telling him to bring his music.

Franz was so nervous on the day of the party that he asked Franziska to meet him at Wilhelm Stein's apartment; under normal circumstances, he would have naturally picked her up. Franz rested all day, practiced a few scales, and sang the aria he had selected once through. He ate something light at about four o'clock and dressed in his best black suit.

At half past seven, he was standing in front of Wilhelm Stein's apartment building, which was centrally located just outside the northwest portion of the Ring. Franziska was already there. She looked beautiful as always, in a lush purple velvet dinner dress partially covered with a stylish, collarless, slightly flaring coat with voguish sleeves.

"You look lovely," Franz said, placing his arm in hers as they walked into the building. The apartment was easy to find; they simply let their ears guide them. The entry door was open, and the soirée was already well under way.

The apartment was spacious, and the furniture that still remained was elegant. Most of it had apparently been moved out to make room for the evening festivities, since there were small round tables and chairs placed everywhere. As Franz and Franziska entered, Wilhelm Stein rushed over to greet them.

"I'm so glad to see you," he said. "Good! You have your music."

Franz smiled. "This is Franziska. She was with me in the dressing room that first time you came backstage after hearing me sing in the Musikvereinssaal, but I didn't have a chance to introduce you to her then. She's been the supportive light in my life."

"Well, it sounds like Franz is very lucky to have you, my dear," Stein said, taking Franziska's hand and kissing it. "It appears you're lovely both inside . . . and out."

Now Franziska smiled.

"Why don't you mingle around for a while and have something to eat? I'll probably call upon you to sing, Franz, at about nine o'clock."

Herr Stein moved on to the other guests while Franz and Franziska seated themselves at one of the tables. Franziska took off her coat and Franz placed it around the chair behind her. She looked so luscious that he would have normally flirted with her, but he was already thinking and focusing on what he would be singing.

As the two lovebirds looked around, they could see that people were walking in and out of all of the rooms in the apartment. "There must be two hundred people here," Franz said. "And most of them probably really understand music. This audience will be much harder to please than any other."

"Don't be so apprehensive," Franziska said. "You have a beautiful voice. Just sing the way you always do, and you'll be fine."

Then another couple joined them at the table. Franz didn't really want to speak to anyone until after he'd sung, so he let Franziska do most of the talking. Like Stein, the gentleman was an agent with Artur Hohenberg, only he represented instrumental artists. Franz briefly told him about his operatic career and that he would be singing later. Then one of the waiters served them hors d'oeuvres, and another brought glasses of wine.

"Aren't you going to eat anything?" the agent asked Franz.

"Later. I can't sing after I've eaten," he responded.

Then he looked across the room and recognized Jussi Björling. Franz had heard him sing the year before at the Staatsoper. His voice was magnificent. It had a singular timbre, an almost lamenting quality that other tenors tried to put into their voices, yet Jussi Björling could call upon the tear whenever he needed it. His technique was superb, enabling him to sing clear, brilliant tones, never faltering on high B's or C's. He was about the same age as Franz, yet he was years older in experience. He was sitting with his beautiful wife. She had blond hair and looked very Swedish, Franz thought.

It must have been nine o'clock because Herr Stein went to the grand piano near the center of the living room and played a few chords. Everyone stopped talking and looked.

"We're going to have some entertainment now," he said. "Please find seats so that we can begin."

About five minutes later, all of the chairs in the room were taken, and a number of people were left standing. A few guests were still whispering, but most were waiting attentively and curiously.

"First, let me welcome you to my home," Stein said. "I hope that you're all enjoying yourselves."

Everyone applauded.

Wilhelm Stein was a dark-haired average-looking man of medium height and build, but he had intelligence and warmth, and he could be a terrific salesman.

"Next, I'd like you to join me in welcoming Jussi Björling to Vienna. Some of you were fortunate enough to have heard him when he was here briefly last year; but this time, it gives me great personal pleasure to say that he'll be gracing Vienna with his splendid vocal cords for more than a month. So I don't want any of you telling me that you missed the opportunity to hear him. He's a rising star, and if you don't believe me, just read the reviews."

Everyone applauded again. Jussi Björling stood halfway up from his chair to acknowledge the applause and then sat back down again. He looked friendly, Franz thought. He was somewhat stout and had blondish-brown-colored hair, and he seemed surprised by the grand introduction, maybe even a little embarrassed.

"And now for the entertainment," Stein said. "You all know that I enjoy launching new careers, and that I delight in reaping the benefits of such discoveries."

Everyone laughed.

"So without further ado, please listen to and remember Franz Jung."

Herr Stein motioned to Franz. He stood and walked toward the piano with his music. At the same time, a nice-looking gentleman, probably about forty-five, also approached and sat down in front of it.

"Carl Alwin," Stein announced, making a hand gesture toward the gentleman as everyone applauded again.

Carl Alwin, Franz thought. *HE'S going to accompany me. He's one of the conductors of the Wiener Staatsoper.*

Franz tried to contain himself as he handed Carl Alwin his music. The maestro set it down on the music rack, opened it, and adjusted the knobs on the artist's bench. When he was comfortably seated at the right height, he sat patiently and waited for Franz to signal him to begin.

Franz was standing in front of the piano facing the audience. The aria he had selected to sing needed no introduction; he was sure that everyone in the room would recognize it as soon as he sang the first few words. In the "Catalogue Song" from Mozart's *Don Giovanni*, Leporello, Don Giovanni's servant, cites his master's feminine conquests for Donna Elvira, one of the abandoned many. The aria is light, lively, and somewhat comical.

Franz was ready to begin. He nodded his head. And they were off and running. He had to come in on the second bar and Carl Alwin was playing the accompaniment faster than was customary, at least to Franz.

"Schöne Donna!" Franz sang as Leporello, explaining to an imaginary Donna Elvira that he was holding the list of all the beauties his master had loved.

He enumerated that there were six hundred forty in Italy; two hundred thirty-one in Germany; a hundred in France; and one thousand three in Spain.

Finally: "If she wears a petticoat, then you know what he does."

A warm applause followed the aria. Carl Alwin stood and handed Franz his music, smiling and nodding his head in approval. Franz walked back to his table and sat down. He felt a little strange because from these people, the music intelligentsia of Vienna, he could not expect an overwhelming declaration of his talent. He simply had to acknowledge to himself that he'd sung well. Of course, he could always depend on Franziska to elevate his self-confidence.

"You sang beautifully," she said. "I knew you had nothing to worry about."

The couple who had been sitting at the table were now socializing. So Franz and Franziska decided to do the same, except they were somewhat shy and didn't know anyone. Nevertheless, they walked around the room smiling and talking to each other, and feeling very out of place.

Then suddenly, without even being aware of how it happened, Jussi Björling and his wife were standing next to them. "I liked your singing," Björling said in a friendly, straightforward manner in excellent German.

Franz thanked him.

"But if you don't mind, I'd like to make a few suggestions."

"Please do."

"Your vocal placement was good, but you sang without support."

The two talked about vocal technique as if they'd known each other for years.

"I concentrate so much on placing my tones in the mask and relaxing my throat that I don't think enough about the diaphragm," Franz said.

"Put your hands here above my waistline below my ribs," Jussi said, showing Franz where he meant. They were already calling each other by their first names.

So Franz placed his hands on Jussi's torso. Then Jussi sang a relatively high note, probably an A or B-flat. Franz could feel how firm Jussi's abdominal muscles became after he took a breath and attacked the note. Jussi explained that a high note was like a skyscraper that needed a good foundation to build on. Singing with support takes tension away from the throat, he said.

"But how do you get it?" Franz asked.

"When I sing a tone, it's just there. I don't do anything about it. If you practice correctly, it happens."

Franz was still a little confused, but he didn't want to ask any more questions. He remembered what Arthur Fleischer had drilled into him, yet he realized that he'd neglected to put the complete theory into action.

"It's getting late. We should really go," Jussi's wife said.

"Let's stay just a little while longer. I'm enjoying myself."

"You look a bit tipsy. Let's go now. You have to sing tomorrow."

"All right, Anna-Lisa. . . . Good luck, Franz. I'm sure we'll see each other again."

"It was nice meeting you," Anna-Lisa said smiling pleasantly.

Franz and Franziska watched the couple walk toward Wilhelm Stein. They exchanged a few words and left. Franz assumed that there must have been a car waiting to escort them back to their hotel or to wherever they were staying.

He was very stimulated by the conversation and doubted that he'd be able to sleep that night. It was late and the room had thinned out.

"I suppose we'd better go too," he told Franziska.

Then Wilhelm Stein approached them. "You sang well," he complimented. "Everyone seemed to like you, and in this business, that's important."

"Thank you, Herr Stein," Franz said. "This has been a very special evening for me."

"And for me as well," Franziska echoed. "Good night."

"*Auf Wiedersehen*," Stein said.

The two walked out the door hand in hand, to a tram, and home.

The party on the thirteenth of February was one of the most special evenings of my father's life. Jussi Björling sang La Bohème *at the Staatsoper the following night, and my father told me that everyone told him that Björling sang beautifully.*

Paul Eger.
(Courtesy of Státní Opera Praha.)

CHAPTER THIRTEEN

Paul Eger

Vienna, Austria
Prague, Czechoslovakia
Spring to Summer 1937

$\mathcal{F}$irst Wilhelm Stein received a contract for Franz to sing in Graz, the second largest city in Austria, located one hundred forty miles south-west of Vienna. Stein told Franz that the general manager had been very anxious to hire him, yet Franz didn't want to sign the contract because he was hoping to sing in either Zürich or Prague, two larger cities with better established and more noteworthy opera companies. Then without giving any specific explanation, the general manager of the theater in Graz withdrew the contract. Franz assumed that the manager must have learned that he was Jewish, and because of political pressures, was obliged to rescind the offer.

Then another general manager, Karl Schmid-Bloss, notified Stein that he had heard Franz sing the role of Alberich at the Stadttheater Baden bei Wien. Unlike the Wiener Staatsoper – Austria's state opera house – the Stadttheater Baden was a small civic theater, yet it had a fine reputation. The role of Alberich, a deformed dwarf in three of the four operas of Richard Wagner's *Ring*, was difficult to cast since few opera singers had the appropriate voice, physical stature and acting ability to undertake the part. So when Karl Schmid-Bloss heard Franz as Alberich in Wagner's *Siegfried*, he immediately wanted to offer the young singer a contract for the following season in Zürich. But Herr Schmid-Bloss wasn't very expeditious in sending the contract.

Finally a third theater director, Paul Eger, called Stein to set up an audition for Franz at the New German Theater in Prague. He'd heard Franz sing Figaro in Vienna and was impressed. Stein immediately began making the arrangements. The audition was set for the eighteenth of May. Herr Eger would send the train tickets and make the hotel reservations. And he wanted to know which aria Franz planned to sing so that the orchestra would be prepared.

Franz decided on the "Catalogue Song" from *Don Giovanni*, the aria he'd sung for Jussi Björling. So Wilhelm Stein passed the information on to Paul Eger. And although Franz didn't mention anything about it to Stein, he also hoped to sing the "Prologue" from Leoncavallo's *Pagliacci*.

On the seventeenth day of May, Franz took the train to Czechoslovakia. The main train station in Prague was on the same street as the New German Theater, and the theater was just across the street from Franz's hotel. He was only staying one night, so he simply packed one small piece of luggage. It was seven o'clock in the evening when he arrived; he'd been traveling for more than seven hours, and he was tired. As he walked out of the train station not knowing in which direction to turn, he showed the address of his hotel to an old woman who was sitting on a bench in a little park. He motioned to the right with one hand and to the left with the other, and she pointed left. He walked a short distance and found himself in front of the New German Theater. It looked about the same size as the Volksoper, maybe a little larger, but the architecture reminded him more of a miniature Wiener Staatsoper, with its neo-Renaissance stone façade of columns, pilasters, and balustrades. The theater looked closed, so Franz assumed that there hadn't been a performance that night. He walked up a few steps into an imposing loggia, set his luggage down, and attempted to see the inside of the theater through one of the wood-framed glass doors. No luck: it was too dark inside. He picked up his bag, proceeded down the steps, and crossed a boulevard. He could see his hotel to the right: the Esplanade.

So he continued walking up a narrow street, Washingtonova ulice, until he was in front of the hotel's outdoor café. Glancing at more columns, arched windows and doors, he made his way into the lobby to a long reception desk on the right.

"*Sprechen Sie Deutsch?*" he asked, appearing a little befuddled.

"*Ja,*" the woman behind the front desk replied. She explained that almost everyone in Prague spoke German, so he needn't worry. She located his name in the reservation book and gave him a few registration papers to sign. Then she reached into one of the slots of the finely-carved mahogany cabinet behind her, pulled out a room key attached to a decorative gold-engraved tag, and laid it down on the counter in front of him.

"Everything is being taken care of by the management of the New German Theater," she said. "We're aware of the circumstances of your visit, so you may check out anytime tomorrow. Enjoy your stay. If you have questions, do not hesitate to ask the concierge."

A bellboy led Franz up an elevator to his room. Franz gave him a tip at the door, walked into the room, unpacked the suit he'd brought to wear for the audition, and sat on the edge of the bed feeling the mattress. The room wasn't nearly as plush as the rest of the hotel, but it was comfortable and clean. Franz really wanted to go to sleep but decided that he'd better go downstairs to the hotel restaurant and get something to eat first. He didn't want to eat anything heavy on the day of the audition, so this was his last chance to have a big meal.

But later as he sat in the restaurant, he began to feel lonely. He looked at a couple across the room and immediately thought of Franziska. If he was fortunate enough to secure an engagement in Prague, how would he be able to live without her? He tried not to think about the situation as he ate the chicken and dumplings that were on his plate. The décor in the restaurant was really quite lovely; the green and burgundy flowered upholstery on the chairs matched the carpeting, and the dark wooden tables served as a flattering accent. The hotel and restaurant were quiet and stately – a perfect complement for Franz's mood.

When he returned to his room, his bed had been turned down. He ate the piece of chocolate that was left on the pillow and undressed without even hanging his clothes up, opting to lay them down on top of the dresser instead. He cleaned his teeth, then fell limp into bed. Once buried under the covers feeling like he was in a strait jacket, he crawled down to the foot of the bed and untucked the blanket and sheets. He tried to sleep for almost an hour but kept hearing the "Prologue" from *Pagliacci* in his mind, and then the "Catalogue Aria." Maybe he'd had too much *Kaffee* to drink. Finally, after taking Franziska's picture out of his wallet and setting it on the nightstand, he was able to fall asleep.

The next morning, he arose at eleven o'clock, took a bath and shaved, sang a few scales, ate a light breakfast in his room, and dressed in a dark blue suit. A few more scales and he felt ready for the audition. At fifteen minutes past one, he looked at Franziska's picture again and slid it back into its rightful place in his wallet. He glanced at his music and carried it out of the room, down the elevator and out of the hotel, routing it directly to the New German Theater.

He was told that there was an artists' entrance on the side of the theater which would be open. He entered precautiously, finding himself in the wings. He told a stagehand that he had an audition and was looking for Paul Eger. The crew member directed him onto the stage.

"I'm Paul Eger," the director said, greeting him. "I hope you had a pleasant trip."

"Yes, I did. Thank you," Franz answered, shaking his hand.

Paul Eger seemed very astute and businesslike. "We just finished a rehearsal, and I've held the orchestra back for your audition. You're going to sing Leporello?"

"Yes."

"Just wait until I go down into the house."

Franz set his music on a table and stood in the center of the stage. He wanted to draw a picture of the theater in his mind, but he didn't really have time to look around. All he could see was a lot of ornate gold and red.

Paul Eger stood two-thirds of the way back in the auditorium. When he motioned to the orchestra members, they began playing. Then Franz sang: "*Schöne Donna. . . .*"

Franz, as Leporello, didn't have time to show the "dear lady" a list of very many of his master's conquests because just after he sang, "In Germany, two hundred thirty-one," Herr Eger cut him off.

"Thank you," Paul Eger said. "You can go home now."

Franz didn't know if Eger was talking to him or to the orchestra. But he couldn't understand what had happened. He'd only sung a few bars.

"I couldn't hear your voice over the orchestra," Herr Eger shouted up to the stage as the orchestra members began leaving.

Franz felt a rush of anger building inside of him: anger directed at himself, at Arthur Fleischer, and at Paul Eger. He'd still been pressing some of his tones and wasn't singing with enough support, so Fleischer had coached him to loosen up at the beginning by refraining to sing with full voice and to save his best tones for later. Franz was annoyed at himself for having listened to Fleischer, and he was displeased that his longtime vocal teacher had given him the wrong advice. But he was even more furious at Paul Eger.

"You didn't even let me finish," Franz said as Eger walked back onto the stage.

"Well, I couldn't hear you."

"At least let me sing something else," Franz said a little exasperated.

So Herr Eger agreed and called an accompanist to the stage. A member of the crew rolled a piano forward as Franz seized his music from the table and handed it to the accompanist.

"Tonio's 'Prologue,' " he said

In the "Prologue" to Leoncavallo's *Pagliacci*, Tonio, a member of a troupe of strolling actors, announces that a play – a tragedy of true life – will soon begin.

Franz's general feelings of indignation toward Paul Eger provoked him to sing unassailably with verve and élan. When he sang, "I am the Prologue," he displayed full, robust tones.

When Franz (as Tonio) sang of the playwright's desire to paint a picture of real life by drawing from his own memories of tears and sorrows, Franz sang with lyricism and a great outpouring of feeling.

And when he disclosed that the audience would soon witness the emotions of hate, grief, rage, and bitter laughter, he sang with urgency, his crescendo building until there could be no doubt that his voice would easily ring over any orchestra. A few more intense, heartrending high tones, and Franz had proved to himself, at least, that his voice had depth, splendor and volume, and that he could be a dramatic presence on any stage.

Paul Eger was flabbergasted. "Why didn't you sing like that before?" he asked.

"You didn't give me a chance."

Eger concluded that Franz must have been nervous at the beginning of the audition. Franz's talent was undeniable, but could he produce what would be required of him if contracted as a character baritone and basso buffo at the New German Theater? Paul Eger was uncertain. Maybe Franz needed more experience.

"You do have an excellent voice," he told Franz. "Thank you for coming to Prague, and have an agreeable trip home."

Herr Eger shook Franz's hand again, and that was the end of the audition. Franz collected his music and left the theater via the artists' entrance. He felt hollow inside as he walked back to his hotel, retrieved his luggage, and checked out.

The many hours on the train back to Vienna were arduous ones for Franz. He didn't want to read anything, he refused to think about music, and he couldn't care less about the scenery. The train was relatively empty, so he had his compartment all to himself. About once every hour, he evacuated it for a few minutes to pace up and down the walkway of his car. He grew more-and-more restless and more-and-more angry at the events of the day. By the time he arrived in Vienna, he was incensed. Maybe he should give up singing and become an agent, he thought.

That's what he told his mother when he arrived home, and that's what he told Franziska the next day. But he didn't tell it to Wilhelm Stein: He told Wilhelm Stein the truth.

"You have enough good reviews and performances behind you for me to sustain my confidence in you," Stein told Franz. "There will be other opportunities. Just have a little patience."

A few weeks later, Stein called Franz with some unexpected news.

"Paul Eger just telephoned me. He's sending a contract for you to sing at the New German Theater next season."

"What?" Franz said.

"There is a catch though. Apparently he feels that you need more experience, so you will also be singing at the Stadttheater in Aussig."

Aussig was a small Czechoslovakian city north of Prague that was part of the Sudetenland, a mountainous region inhabited by German descendants.

"I guess that's all right," Franz said. "When do I leave?"

"Why don't you plan to move the end of August. But first, let's wait until I receive the contract. You know what happened with Zürich."

The contract did arrive and was signed by all of the concerned parties. Then in July, the contract from Zürich arrived as well; but it had come too late. Franz was packed and ready to move to Prague on the twenty-second day of August.

It was a Sunday morning. Franz and his mother met Franziska at the train station at ten-fifteen. Franziska looked like she hadn't slept at all that night. She was happy that Franz had secured an engagement for the coming opera season, but she was worried that their separation would lead to the downfall of their relationship. In Franz's eyes, he couldn't afford to support Franziska, so he couldn't afford to marry her. As for Franziska, she knew that she needed to maintain her job. In fact, she'd shown Herr Appenzeller one of her designs just the previous week, and he'd asked her to make a pattern of it and purchase some material; he thought that it would make a perfect dress for one of his customers. Franziska was thrilled that she'd finally made some progress with her career. But without Franz, she knew that she'd feel lost.

The three of them were standing on the loading platform now. Franz was taking his luggage on the train with him. Because he hadn't acquired a massive wardrobe, he'd just packed two large suitcases, and the majority of one of them was filled with music.

"This is the beginning of your life," Franz's mother told him. "I'm so proud of you. Maybe one day you'll be able to come back here and sing at the Staatsoper when all of this Hitler-Nazi scare resolves itself."

Crying, Olga hugged Franz for a long time. She pulled away wiping her tears.

The tension was broken a little when one of Franz's as yet unknown colleagues greeted him. "I'm waiting for the train to Prague. What about you?"

"Yes, me too," Franz replied.

"I'm going to be singing at the New German Theater."

"What a coincidence, so am I," Franz responded.

"Well, it's really not such a coincidence, I expect. The management of the theater is paying for our tickets, and we both have to report for rehearsals at about the same time, so . . ."

"I don't mean to be unfriendly," Franz explained. "Maybe we could share a compartment and talk on the train; but right now, I'd really like to say good-bye to my family."

"I understand perfectly. I'll see you on the train." The young comrade then moved discretely to another part of the platform.

"Good-bye, Son," Olga said, kissing Franz's cheek and then wiping her lipstick off his face with a handkerchief. Then she walked away to give him some privacy with Franziska.

"Well, here we are," Franziska uttered in a low voice. "I'm going to miss you terribly."

"And me, you."

"Oh, you won't have time. You'll be too busy, and you'll be meeting so many new people."

All at once Franziska broke down sobbing. Franz held her in his arms, stroking her hair comfortingly. "Don't cry, Franziska. You're going to get a Czech passport, and you're going to come to visit me."

"I know, but I'm so used to being with you almost every day. Now I probably won't see you for months."

"But we can write, and there are telephones now."

"You might forget me."

"Forget you? Franzi – I love you. You've supported everything that

I've done all of these years. You're the reason that I've gotten this far. I want you to share all of my successes with me."

Franz wiped her tears with his handkerchief and kissed her eyes tenderly. She threw her arms around him and kissed him on his mouth searchingly. Then she rested the side of her face on his chest as he held her until the train arrived.

"Well, I suppose I'd better go now. You know these trains; if I wait too long, mine could leave without me."

Franziska didn't want to let go of Franz. She felt him releasing her gently, yet she was still holding on strong. Finally she relaxed her arms and moved away slowly. "Good-bye, my love," she said, the tears welling up in her eyes again.

Then Franz's mother walked back toward them. "Enough, enough," she said. "You've got to get going." She placed her arm around Franziska's waist, and the two stood there supporting each other as Franz grabbed his suitcases and climbed aboard. Then they stood there waving until the train rolled its way out of sight.

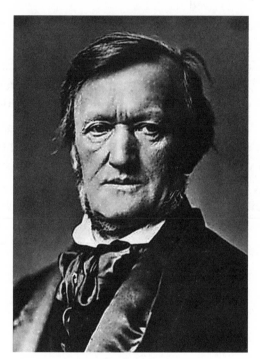

Richard Wagner.

CHAPTER FOURTEEN
Beckmesser

Prague, Czechoslovakia
Vienna, Austria
September 1937 to January 1938

5 September 1937

Dear Franziska,

Despite the distance between us, please know that I am always beside you, just as you are always in my heart and mind. Do not ever doubt the constancy of my love, for it is as unwavering as the liaison between the sun and earth. There could never be anyone for me but you.

The other night I dreamt that I had sung in Baden and that we had gone to our favorite holiday spot in nearby Bad Vöslau. I watched you swim in the thermal spa, the ends of your bountiful black hair dipping into the turquoise-blue aromatic elixir. Then you came running toward me as I was lying on the velvety-green grass. You were wearing the clinging emerald-green swimsuit you'd captivated me with the first time we gave ourselves completely to one another. You threw yourself down on the towel beside me, your body moist and warm from the brimming, percolating spring. I soothed your tepid, silky skin with a sweet, fragrant balm of jasmine blossoms, applying just enough to your torso to ensure the longevity of

155

your sheath's polished, even glow. Then you reciprocated by strok-ing my body with a creamy, soft emollient which exposed the fresh, natural scent of a pine tree. We bathed in the sunlight until my skin could no longer withstand its effects, yours thriving steadfastly under its golden beams. You chased me over a bridge into a cabana where we forgot our longings and desires by consuming each other's pas-sions. But then I awoke; and I was alone, missing you despairingly, realizing how much you have given me, and how much more of my-self I was born to give you. I dressed quickly, rushing to a rehearsal, finally comprehending that my passion for music had only grown out of your compassion for me. I discovered the necessity to be suc-cessful – not for myself, but for both of us, so that we could one day always be together.

So, my Franziska, I miss you. I missed you the days I spent at the Hotel Esplanade; I missed you while looking for a place to stay; and I miss you now that I am settled in a small furnished apartment that a singer I know vacated. Please come and visit! And please write often, addressing your letters to me at Petrská Twenty-Four, Prague Two.

I sing Schubert's "Ständchen" to you now, my darling. If you try very hard to listen, maybe you will be able to hear me sing his "Serenade":

Leise flehen meine Lieder
Durch die Nacht zu dir. . . .

Softly my songs cry
Through the night to you;
Beloved, come to me,
To the quiet grove. . . .

Trembling, I await you.
Come make me happy!

I love you!

Franz

15 September 1937

Dear Franz,

Your letter moves me deeply each time I read it, which is every night before I close my eyes to sleep. I usually doze off just after I picture you sitting at the foot of my bed singing "Ständchen" to me. Oh, how I long to be near you!

I am very busy at work. Herr Appenzeller is making up another one of my designs; he thinks it will sell well this fall. Of course, I continue to run all over town for materials, so I remain perpetually exhausted.

I don't know when I will be able to visit you; that will depend on the Appenzellers. I wanted so much to be in the audience for your opening performances. But since I cannot make that happen, I will just have to be there in mind and spirit. And I will be there, my love.

In the dark hours, I often find solace by reading Shakespeare's sonnets. Somehow they reach my soul like no other poetry.

> *So, either by thy picture or my love,*
> *Thyself away are present still with me;*
> *For thou not farther than my thoughts canst move,*
> *And I am still with them and they with thee;*
> *Or, if they sleep, thy picture in my sight*
> *Awakes my heart to heart's and eye's delight.*

Sing well, my dearest! I am always with you.

Franziska

15 October 1937

Dear Franzi,

I have had some success already. One of the news critics wrote that I am "the bright new face in opera" here, with an "excellent voice" and a promising career ahead of me. Another one wrote that my voice was "round and mellifluous at just the right moments," and that my portrayal was both "mature and sensitive." But of course, you know that I will never allow myself to be stirred by reviews – good or bad. I only wish that you could have been here to tell me the truth.

I've rented a room in a comfortable home in Aussig. My land-lords have three children and a dog, are quite pleasant, and seem to love opera. In fact, they even came to hear me sing the other night. However I have to admit that sometimes I don't get enough sleep because the family faithfully rises early.

The Stadttheater is really quite charming, in the Baroque tradi-tion with an off-white stone exterior. The building is laid out much like the Burgtheater – only it is much smaller and simpler – with a convex center and wing sections on either side that somehow make it appear circular. I actually enjoy going to the little town of Aussig that encircles it; the community somehow seems so separate and isolated from the city of Prague.

I've made a few friends during the time I have been here in Czechoslovakia. One is the singer who introduced himself to me at the train station in Vienna the day I left. Josef Olaf is a baritone from Budapest, and he told me that he's sung with the Royal Hun-garian Opera. His voice is average and his technique leaves much to be desired; but he always has a lot to say, and he helps me camou-flage my loneliness.

I am learning a great deal from the very talented opera director and conductor, Franz Allers. Oh, and my other new friend – really just an acquaintance – is a soprano from Berlin. She likes my voice.

In closing, my darling, I ask you again to please come and visit me soon. Writing back and forth just doesn't seem to be enough. I need your love, and I miss seeing the glimmer in your beautiful onyx eyes. Right now I walk from my apartment to the New German Theater and back. I'm waiting to explore the rest of Prague with you. So please don't disappoint me. Come soon!

Your loving opera-singer-boyfriend,

Franz

$\mathcal{W}$hen Franziska read Franz's letter, she wanted to instantaneously board a train to Prague. *Hmmm . . . I wonder what else that soprano likes besides his voice,* she thought. But she knew that she couldn't leave Vienna until after Christmas. The Appenzellers would never let her go. So she continued to correspond by letter to Franz, nervously awaiting the holidays to arrive. Then . . .

5 December 1937

Dear Franz,

I'm coming! I'm finally coming! I have a Czech passport and I'll see you the day after Christmas! And since you wrote me that you're not performing that Sunday, I expect you to pick me up at the main train station at four o'clock. I'm staying for a week, so you better rest up.

I've been calling your mother about twice a month to make sure she doesn't get too lonely. Talking to her somehow makes me feel a little closer to you. But now I'm going to get the real thing. I'm so excited. I want to see all of Prague; I want to watch you sing at the German Theater; and of course, I want to meet your new friends.

I love you, Franz! I love you much more than words could ever say.

I'll see you on the twenty-sixth of December!

Franziska

On Christmas, Franz spent the day cleaning his apartment. It was small. The living room was furnished with a worn-looking couch, coffee table, and armchair. The bedroom had what bedrooms have; the kitchen had a table and two chairs and came equipped with an ice box, a stove, dishes, and a few pots and pans; and of course, there was a bathroom. Despite the apartment's frayed-looking condition, Franz rented it because some of the singers from the New German Theater lived in the building; he knew the previous tenant; and an upright piano was sitting in the living room.

The apartment hadn't been cleaned since October, so Franz thought it was about time to give it a once-over. And on Sunday, a few hours before Franziska was due to arrive, he purchased some flowers and set them conspicuously in a vase on the coffee table.

At three-fifteen, he walked out of his apartment building onto Petrská ulice, walked a few blocks until he was on Wilsonova, and then followed the street directly down to the train station. It was cold out, though not snowing; and although Franz was clad in an warm woolen overcoat and gloves, the nippy air induced a reddish-blue tint to his cheeks and nose.

He entered the railway terminal, eyed the display monitor above, and then followed arrows and signs until he found the track listed for the four o'clock arrival from Vienna. The terminal wasn't very busy, probably because it was the Sunday after Christmas. Franz waited, but Franziska's train was late. When it finally arrived at half past four, Franz could see Franziska waving from one of the windows.

As the brakes screeched bringing the train to a halt, Franziska carried her luggage to the exit of her passenger car. She opened the door with all her strength, pushed her suitcase out so that it landed on the ground below, and squeezed her body through, jumping down as the door slammed shut behind her.

Franz saw her instantly and ran to meet her. They embraced, happily holding on to each other for a very long time. And then they just looked at each other as if they couldn't believe that what they were seeing was real. Franz picked up Franziska's bag, and they made their way out of the terminal. As they walked to Franz's apartment, they talked and talked: about his singing, about her designing, and about how much they'd missed each other. When they were in front of Petrská Twenty-Four, Franziska looked up at the prosaic tan-colored building which would be her new home for the next week, commenting that she hadn't expected it to look so contemporary. No arches, no domes, no columns: it was a five-story structure with a concrete frame, and it had bands of rectangular windows.

Franz led Franziska into the building and to his apartment. He set her bag down as she unbuttoned her coat and laid it on the couch. She was wearing a stylish blue wool suit, consisting of a skirt, blouse, and three-quarter-length padded-shouldered jacket. Franz went over to her and hugged her again, this time placing his arms under her jacket and around her. "Oh, you feel so good," he said. And the two smooched until:

"Mmm . . . I have something for you," Franziska said, rushing to her suitcase and pulling out a gift wrapped in tissue paper. "Happy holidays!"

"What could this be? I don't have anything for you except flowers," Franz said, pointing to the coffee table.

"Oh, they're beautiful." Franziska leaned down to smell them.

Franz tore off the tissue paper and found a long tan-colored cashmere scarf. The enclosed note said:

My dearest Franz,

When I am near you, it is my responsibility to keep you warm. This little present will help you to maintain that kind of heat if I'm not around. And when you wear it, I know you will think of me.

Franziska

Franz threw the scarf around his neck and his arms back around Franziska. He was still wearing his overcoat, so Franziska pushed him away gently, unbuttoned the top buttons of his coat and draped the scarf inside. "Now that's how it's supposed to be worn," she said. And they continued where they'd left off.

They stayed in the apartment that night, eating snacks and making love, making love and eating snacks. The next day, they walked around Prague. Franziska was actually more familiar with the sights than Franz, since her father had taken her to visit the city a number of times while she was growing up.

They walked along Wilsonova, passing the train station and the New German Theater, continuing until they reached the colossal neo-Renaissance National Museum seated at the head of Wenceslas Square near the statue of the saint for whom the area was named. The square was really more rectangular than anything else, as it was a long, broad boulevard with cobblestone walkways down the center and on either side, and it was lined with buildings of various sizes, heights and architectural styles, from neo-Renaissance and Baroque to Art Nouveau. Franz and Franziska walked from one end of the boulevard to the other, stopping for something to eat at the café in the very gold Grand Hotel Europa. They walked from Wenceslas Square, which was in the New Town section of Prague, to the Old Town Square, which really was a square. Bordered with Baroque and medieval buildings of all imaginable hues, the area was originally a marketplace in the eleventh century. The atmosphere was festive, so Franz and Franziska looked at the wares of the artisans and browsed in the charming shops which edged the square and extended into the nearby crooked streets and alleyways. Just before leaving, they stood in front of the tower of the Old Town Hall, looking above its astronomical clock as tiny wooden figures enacted a medieval morality tale, which concluded with a rooster's crow at the moment that the clock below marked the hour.

Next, they walked along Karlova ulice and began crossing the Charles Bridge, a fourteenth-century Gothic stone structure named after Charles IV. They stopped to look at the statues that adorned it and gazed at the beautiful Moldau River below. They continued uphill on Mostecká ulice to a square in the Little Quarter, where they had a spectacular view of the Prague Castle: a complex of palaces and churches joined by gardens and courtyards and enclosed by a grandiose façade.

Franz and Franziska had been walking for hours. They were cold and tired, so they started strolling back toward the apartment, picking up some food at a small market along the way. That evening Franziska cooked a sumptuous dinner for Franz. He had always been accustomed to having his main meal in the middle of the day, but his eating habits had become more flexible and now tended to revolve around his singing schedule: nothing heavy before a performance. On this evening he wasn't singing, and he and Franziska had worked up a powerful appetite from all of their hiking in the cold winter air. After they'd finished eating, Franz helped Franzi with the dishes, and then they listened to the radio and kept each other warm.

For the next few days, Franz had rehearsals at the New German Theater while Franziska searched for some out-of-the-way shops and restaurants. She learned that Old Town was indeed ancient, but that New Town was quite antiquated as well, having been conceived in the fourteenth century. Each day she met Franz back at the apartment in the late afternoon and then took him to one of her new discoveries.

On New Year's Eve, they went to a party at Josef Olaf's apartment. Franz didn't have to worry about singing that evening or the next. Josef Olaf was a very personable fellow. He had blond hair, blue eyes, and was somewhat stout. Although Hungarian, he looked more Swedish than anything else. Franz's other new friend, the soprano, was at the party as well, with a date. She was pretty with blond hair, but Franziska didn't think that she was Franz's type.

Could he become attached to her solely because of her vocal skills?

Franziska purged the thought from her mind.

The evening was quite amusing to Franziska, though. Of the fourteen people there, eight were singers, and all they talked about was opera. It was like they were competing against each other. One would talk about his or her superior training, and another would respond with a resumé of experiences. Then they started debating about technique. Should the voice be placed out in front or in the mask? And so the evening proceeded until the clock struck twelve. Then everyone kissed their wives, husbands, and dates, or whatever. A toast and a glass of champagne – in Franz's case, a sip – and the evening was complete.

On New Year's Day, Franziska wanted to be alone with Franz. And even though it was a lazy day because almost everything was closed, Franziska dragged Franz along Wenceslas Square so that he could take her picture in front of the statue of St. Wenceslas. The air was extremely crisp since it was snowing. Franziska hadn't brought the right kind of shoes, so she was slipping and sliding, and Franz was constantly holding her up by the elbow. They were both wearing warm coats, gloves and hats, but they were still cold. After wandering around for a while, they ended up in a vacant Charles Square. Franziska thought the area looked like a park, but that was difficult for her to verify since all of the leafless branches looked like brittle sticks against the misty sky. The two of them chased each other around the barren parkland throwing snowballs back and forth as if they were children. As they laughed and hugged one another playfully, they fell on the white powdery flakes that coated the grass and earth beneath them. They tried to shake off the snowy crystals when they stood, but patchwork designs of watery ice remained affixed to their clothing. Continuing to act somewhat giddy, they made their way home into the warmth of Franz's apartment where Franziska cooked two plentiful servings of *Leberknödelsuppe* (beef broth with liver dumplings). A piece of *Guglhupf* (a round, high coffee cake) for dessert, and they went to bed.

On Monday morning, the two stayed home resting since Franz would be singing later. Franziska tried to adhere to his schedule. She woke up, bathed, dressed in a skirt and sweater, and prepared a light meal for the two of them. Franz didn't budge out of bed until his nose detected the smell of *Schinken und Spiegeleiern* (ham and eggs) coming from the kitchen. Before doing anything else, he tried out his voice to make sure it was still there. When it was, he proceeded into the kitchen to eat with Franziska. A little later, he sang a few scales at the piano, thumbed through his score, dressed in a suit and overcoat, and announced to Franziska that he was going to the theater. Since it was a few hours before the dress rehearsal, Franziska told Franz that she'd see him at the theater later.

After he left, she freshened up her makeup and changed into the same purple velvet dinner dress she'd worn to Wilhelm Stein's party the

winter before. She didn't wear the same coat though; it was quite dressy
and wouldn't have fit with her other clothes. Since she'd only wanted
to bring one coat on the trip, she'd opted for something tailored. She
threw it over her dress, grabbed the spare apartment key that Franz had
left for her on a dish in the kitchen; and hurried out of the apartment.

Franziska was sitting in the auditorium of the New German Theater
now. It was very ostentatious, she thought, very Rococo. She was seated
in the center of the sixth row, looking all around at the boxes and balconies and then bending her head back to see the ceiling. It was gorgeous.
A Gobelin-type tapestry covered it all around, and in the center, there
was a gold-framed mirror which accentuated the dazzling crystal chandelier suspended below. The auditorium was very red and very gold, as
many theaters were, but the gold in this one seemed more ornate to
Franziska; the detail-work, more intricate. At first she thought that the
décor was a little overpowering for the theater, which was much smaller
than the Wiener Staatsoper, but as she sat waiting for the performance
to begin, she started to warm up to it. It made her feel regal.

Franz was covering for the singer who would be singing the role of
Sixtus Beckmesser – the comic villain in Richard Wagner's *Die Meistersinger von Nürnberg* – the following Wednesday.

A mastersinger, Meistersinger, was a townsman in Germany who
belonged to a guild of singers. In the case of Wagner's opera, the guild
was placed in Nürnberg in the mid-sixteenth century. Most of its members practiced a trade and delighted in singing and creating songs of
love and adventure. After setting very strict and narrow rules, they held
contests to honor the most distinguished compositions.

Wagner, in an attempt to vent his anger, fashioned the character of
Beckmesser after Eduard Hanslick, the Viennese music critic who had
written derogatorily about his work. Beckmesser was, in a sense, a pe-
dantic critic. He was the mastersingers' marker, scratching the contestants' errors with chalk on a slate, forever skeptical of everything new,
especially when it was the work of one of his adversaries in a competition, in this case, a young knight named Walther von Stolzing. The

prize of the contest: matrimonial bliss with one of the mastersingers' daughters, Eva.

After a somewhat lengthy prelude (overture), the curtain opened to the interior of a church. Eva was sitting in the first row of pews during the afternoon service when Walther walked in and spotted her, the two instantaneously beginning to flirt. Later when the two became better acquainted, Walther, who wasn't a mastersinger, quickly endeavored to become one when Eva explained that she was the prize in the upcoming contest. She was quite pretty in a peasant-type dress with a long full skirt, a V-shaped cross-laced bodice with wide sleeves, and a shawl.

Not long after Eva departed from the stage, Beckmesser made his entrance with Eva's father, Veit Pogner. Beckmesser (Franz) looked sinister from the very start, Franziska thought, laughing to herself. He was dressed in all black. His breeches and shirt were almost completely hidden by a three-quarter-length jacket over a long waistcoat.

Beckmesser was a role Franz loved to play because he could really be a ham. It was not a part that allowed him to show his true resonant voice, however; in fact, he disguised and lightened his voice to make it sound more baritonal than it really was.

"Beckmesser should not sound like Hans Sachs," Franz had told Franziska many times. "If he does, then he's a bad Beckmesser."

Hans Sachs, patterned by Wagner after the real Hans Sachs, filed onstage after the other mastersingers. A respected cobbler in the town, he was admired for his fairness and integrity, and for his expertise in creating poetry and music.

Hans Sachs watched on as Veit Pogner introduced the group to Walther, who was anxious to take the mastersingers' test so that he could vie for Eva's hand in marriage. Before Beckmesser (Franz) barricaded himself inside the marker's booth, he pulled out a piece of chalk from his coat pocket and held it tauntingly in front of Walther's eyes.

"*Sixtus Beckmesser Merker ist,*" he sang, enunciating the syllables of his name.

He reached into the booth and showed Walther the slate on which he would mark the errors. More than seven, and Walther would be eliminated.

Franziska loved watching Franz; he was so evil. His hair was parted in the center and pasted down on his scalp; and he was wearing heavy pancake makeup, with shadows to give his cheeks a sunken look and penciling to make his face look more villainous.

"*Fanget an!*" he sang loudly after he stepped into the booth and pulled the curtains around himself. "Begin!"

Walther sat in the singer's chair and proceeded. He could soon hear the scratching of chalk on the slate, but the noise really sounded more like a gigantic spoon being propelled up and down a washboard. Finally Beckmesser marched out of the booth and displayed his chalkboard. There wasn't any more room on the slate. Walther had failed to become a mastersinger as the first act came to an end and the curtain fell. But he was not about to give up.

Within minutes, the church was history, and the stage crew pushed the lower parts of houses onto the stage and flew in rooftops from the grid above to connect with them. The pieces fit together like a jigsaw puzzle. The quaint Nürnberg street – with Hans Sachs's house on one side and Veit Pogner's house on the other – was ready for action, the peak of the action occurring at the end of the second act when Beckmesser (Franz) entered to serenade Eva. He was dressed suavely in another long black coat, this one adorned with a cloak. And even though he was the only mastersinger who didn't practice a craft – he was the town clerk – he wore an artisan's beret atop his head. Again, Franziska couldn't help but laugh when he started to play his lute, which served as a cue for Hans Sachs to sing his shoemaker's song and make a racket with his hammer. Beckmesser tried to serenade Eva but was always interrupted by Hans Sachs, who finally agreed to act as his marker. After plucking and strumming his lute – Franz only pretended to play the instrument since the music really came from the orchestra – Beckmesser sang and Hans Sachs struck the sole of one of his shoes to indicate each error. As Beckmesser attempted to complete his song, the faults mounted and the continuous clamoring woke up the neighbors, including David, Hans Sachs's apprentice, who looked out of the window and saw Beckmesser serenading not Eva, but his girlfriend Magdalene, who worked as Eva's nursemaid and was standing by her window. As David jumped down and started attacking Beckmesser, the townspeople hurried to the scene in their sleeping attire and eagerly joined in what soon became a free-for-all. But at the sound of the night-watchman's horn, everyone dispersed. And when the make-believe street was finally quiet and bare, Beckmesser limped offstage defeated and bedraggled.

In the next act, Walther created a new song for the contest while Hans Sachs coached him and wrote down the words. After the two left Sachs's workshop, Beckmesser (Franz) peeped through the window and swung the door open. Still in pain from the brawl the previous evening, he limped into the vacant room. And as he snooped around, many of his movements were synchronized with some of the orchestral sounds. He seemed to make certain defined motions on specific beats: he held his aching back; he rubbed his knee, accidentally sitting on a hammer; he grabbed the hammer and walked to the window at the other side of the room; he struck the sole of one of Hans Sachs's shoes with it and then held both objects over his ears as if to drown out the clanging noises embedded in his memory from the previous night; he raced across the room swinging his arm back, dropping the shoe and reaching for his spine; he traveled back to the window, this time mimicking a sword fight; he slammed the window shut and propped himself up against a table which had something on it. He thought that he'd found a courting song by Sachs. He took the piece of paper that he'd found and hid it in his pocket.

Franziska was simply amazed at Franz's acting ability. She'd always appreciated his voice; but in this role, he'd proved that he could move agilely onstage while communicating the personality traits and emotions of his character to the audience. Only now Franziska realized how talented Franz really was.

As the act progressed, Hans Sachs discovered Beckmesser in his workshop. When he learned that the town clerk had stolen the words to Walther's song, he told him to keep the poetry as a present. Thrilled, Beckmesser ran out the door anxious to choose a melody and memorize the verses before the contest.

Later, behind the closed curtain, the stage crew quickly pushed away Hans Sachs's house and turned the setting into a festival meadow, by flying in tree flats covered with net and painted muslin, and by rolling out a burlap carpet of fake grass and leaves.

After revealing the set to the audience, merrymakers began arriving from all around: tradesmen with the banners of their guilds, apprentices, journeymen, women, and children. Then, dressed in black robes with their distinguishing medallions hanging from their necks, the mastersingers entered in a grand procession, among them: Hans Sachs, Beckmesser, Veit Pogner, and of course, Eva.

Called upon to compete first, Beckmesser approached the contestants' platform appearing outwardly nervous. Before standing on it, he complained that it was wobbly.

After the apprentices attempted to secure the platform in place, Beckmesser (Franz) stood on it and pulled out a handkerchief to wipe the perspiration from his brow. Next he bowed to the mastersingers and to Eva; he played a prelude on his lute and sang. His memory was failing him.

The townspeople couldn't understand what he was singing; the words didn't make any sense to them so they whispered among themselves (by vocalizing, of course). Beckmesser began to sing again after peering at the words on the ruffled sheet of paper he'd hidden under his mastersinger's gown. The words didn't fit his melody, and the crowd continued to ridicule him until he stepped off the platform in a rage, announcing that the song was not his, but was given to him by Hans Sachs.

Sachs defended himself by explaining that he had not written the piece, and he asked any witness to step forward who could verify his statement. Walther, the true author, then appeared, and Sachs asked the mastersingers to listen to him perform the verses correctly.

Everyone was dumbfounded by the knight's impassioned delivery, including the defeated-looking Beckmesser. Walther was declared the victor, and Eva crowned him with a floral garland. However when Veit Pogner attempted to place the mastersingers' medallion around his neck, he refused to accept it, remembering how he'd been treated the day before.

Hans Sachs responded to his actions by singing an aria entreating him not to scorn the masters, but to honor their art, which remained

German and true. If anything were to happen to the Germans under foreign rule, Sachs sang that the mastersingers' contribution would assure the longevity of holy German art.

Hans Sachs took the medallion from Pogner and placed it around Walther's neck, this time without rejection. As the townspeople echoed Sachs's last phrases in praise of holy German art, Hans Sachs approached Beckmesser and graciously shook his hand to make amends. Then as the mastersingers pointed to Sachs with outstretched hands as if hailing to their leader, the cobbler marched upstage and off while they sang "*Heil Sachs*" until the curtain fell.

Even though it was a dress rehearsal, there was an audience, and everyone applauded generously. But when the bass-baritone who played Hans Sachs took his curtain call alone, he received a standing ovation. Then the conductor walked onto the apron of the stage with the entire cast. Franziska was standing with everyone else, applauding and looking all around. Then it happened: three young men a few rows behind her extended their arms and shouted, "*Heil Hitler!*" The applause suddenly ceased. This was Czechoslovakia, not Austria or Germany, and everyone seemed legitimately surprised. A little frightened, some elderly people began to applaud half-heartedly again as if nothing had occurred. The curtain calls came to a halt, and the audience members anxiously filed out of the theater, including the group of rabble-rousers.

Franziska rushed out of the theater as well, re-entering through the artists' entrance. Franz had told her to meet him backstage after the performance, but she didn't know which dressing room was his. She asked a musician who pointed her in the right direction. She knocked on the door, heard the words "Come in," and entered. Franz was sharing the room with two other singers. They were all still in their costumes.

"Did you see what happened?" Franziska asked, bolting in toward Franz. The other singers weren't Jewish, so Franz didn't want to have the conversation that he was anticipating.

"Yes, I did," he said. "Why don't you let me get out of my costume and makeup so that we can leave, and then we'll talk."

Franziska suddenly looked around and seemed to see the other singers for the first time. "Oh, hello," she said, trying to calm down. "I really enjoyed your performances."

"And how about mine?" Franz questioned.

"Oh, you . . . you were so deliciously nasty, but we'll talk about it later. . . . Change fast. I'll be right outside your door." And Franziska left.

About fifteen minutes later, she was standing in the wings watching the stage crew disassemble the set when Franz approached from behind and wrapped his arms around her waist. She didn't even jump; she knew the touch.

"Well, hello," she said turning around. "Would you like to go home with me?"

They talked about the performance as they walked home. First Franziska complimented Franz enough to last until her next visit. But then her face grew serious as she described how she felt about the Nazis in the audience.

"I was scared," she said. "They were so close to me that I started to tremble. I wanted to be like an ostrich and hide my head in the ground. I have dark hair and wear eye makeup, red lipstick, and rouge – hardly Aryan traits. I thought they might pick me out of the audience and intimidate me. You don't know how relieved I was when they didn't."

"I'm so sorry that you were alarmed. If I'd known that they were going to be here, I wouldn't have let you come to this performance. They just probably wanted to see *Meistersinger* simply because it's an opera that promotes German nationalism. That's why Hitler likes it so much."

"I understand that, but I'm not in Austria. I didn't expect that what happened would have happened here, and certainly, not after a rehearsal."

"But this is the German Theater, Franziska. Unlike the other theaters in Prague, everything here is performed in German."

"But who were those people?"

"That's hard to say. Maybe they were members of the Sudeten German Party headed by Konrad Henlein. Maybe they were visiting here from Germany. I don't know. I don't want to worry about it. I sing in Aussig. If I agonized every day about the political beliefs of the people in the audience, I wouldn't be able to walk onstage. I have a contract to sing opera, and that's all I try to think about."

"But what if there had been more of them and they'd started a riot? Those Nazis timed their little outburst perfectly; they knew that the management of the theater wouldn't oust them during the curtain calls."

"Okay, Franziska. Would it help if I told you that I'm worried? Well, I am. But it doesn't do me any good to talk about it. I'm safer here than I would be in Vienna."

As soon as Franz uttered the sentence, he knew that he'd made a mistake. Franziska stopped walking and started to cry.

"But I live in Vienna. I have to stay there, and I don't know what's going to happen."

Franz held Franziska close. "We won't be apart forever, my darling. Just give me time to prove myself."

Neither spoke anymore until they'd reached Petrská Twenty-Four. Once inside, they released their pent-up emotions with some affectionate cuddling and tenderness. Franz wanted to protect Franziska, and she so much wanted to feel cared for; but she'd soon be back home in Vienna where she'd have to face the world alone.

Franziska was becoming accustomed to waking up with Franz beside her every morning. The thought of having to say good-bye to him the next day seemed more than she could bear. She imagined herself sleeping in her tiny room back in Vienna and waking up all alone. And then, of course, she started to cry. As always, Franz tried to comfort her, but her last night in Prague was definitely not a happy one.

The next morning she put a smile on her face, determined not to repeat the same teary farewell she'd forced Franz to endure when he left Vienna for Prague. This time when they were on the loading platform and it was time for her to board the train, she kissed Franz blithefully as if she was coming to visit him instead of going home. He pulled open the door of her passenger car and placed her bag inside. She kissed him again, this time more intensely, then broke away and boarded the train. But when she was seated safely in her compartment and could see him waving to her from the outside, the tears began streaming down her cheeks as the train rolled its way out of the train station.

Franz Schubert.
(By Joseph Kriehuber.)

Giuseppe Verdi.
(*By Etienne Carjat.*)

CHAPTER FIFTEEN
Henlein and the King

Prague and Aussig, Czechoslovakia
February 1938

1 February 1938

Franziska:

> *Oh dearest art, how often in dark hours of sadness,*
> *When life's cruelties have encircled me,*
> *Have you inspired a warm new love in my heart,*
> *And brought me into a far better world!*

Schubert's "An die Musik" may be a hymn to music, but every time I sing it, I turn it into a serenade to you, my sweet Franziska. I sang it in Aussig at Sunday's matinée in commemoration of Franz Schubert's birthday. And at that performance, I really did feel as if life had caught me in its cruel trap, and I needed to envision your gleaming onyx eyes in order to quell my nervousness. Of all the male singers at the Stadttheater in Aussig, the general manager selected me to sing when the guest of honor was Nazi leader Konrad Henlein. I simply didn't want to be there; I certainly didn't want to meet him; and I was glad that I didn't know his whereabouts in the audience. Fortunately I was only called upon to sing three Lieder since

175

there were other musicians and soloists performing. When I sang "Heidenröslein," you could have heard a pin drop. Schubert's music is so lyrical and melodic that I sang Goethe's poetic story of the poor rose being picked from the hedge as delicately as possible, coloring my voice with ample pianissimos. I concluded with a very mournful "Am Meer" ("By the Sea"). The melancholy quality that I always integrate into my voice throughout the Lied was very difficult for me to sustain since I kept wondering how many Nazis were sitting in the audience and how many of them had contemplated my Jewishness. But by the time the accompanist's chords had urged me on to sing "From your loving eyes, the tears fell," I was already focused into the mood of Heine's foreboding love story. And at the end, a hush fell over the audience before the applause began.

I didn't want to stay until the end of the performance because I was afraid that the general manager, Alfred Huttig, would introduce me to Konrad Henlein. I'm not sure if Huttig was aware that I'm Jewish; he could have selected me to sing unknowingly. On the other hand, he opposes the Nazi doctrine, and might have deliberately chosen me so that he could play a private joke on Henlein and laugh to himself when the Nazi leader complimented my talents. But because I didn't want to stay around to confirm my assumptions, I left.

I was so anxious and apprehensive that morning that I couldn't decide what to wear. I'd just had a tuxedo and tail coat made and had purchased one pair of trousers with silk braided side seams for both. Neither was really appropriate. I should have worn something in between a tuxedo and a suit, so I must have looked quite over-dressed in my tails in the middle of the afternoon. I hope that my singing made up for my lack of savoir-faire.

Can you imagine what one of the other singers told me before the performance? Since we knew that Konrad Henlein was going to be in the audience, we started talking about politics. Hermann Göring, Hitler's right-hand man, came up, and I made fun of the array of his made-to-order decorated uniforms. The singer, a German soprano, defended him and announced that she was a friend of Hermann Göring's wife. "They're such lovely people," she said.

Now, my little Franziska, I must reflect on the conversation we had just a month ago when those Nazis attended my performance of Meistersinger. *I'm sorry if I was somewhat curt with you. I realize now that I can no longer block the Nazis from my mind. I shudder to think of the future, yet I must try to be optimistic.*

Write soon, my darling! And please start planning another trip! I miss you so!

Love,

Franz

Shortly thereafter, very unexpectedly, Franz received a telephone call from the general manager. He needed a one-evening replacement for the King in Verdi's *Aïda*. The incident happened either in Prague or Aussig.

Most of the performance information on the New German Theater has been lost or destroyed, although a history of the theater with some dates has been published.

According to the archival records in Aussig, Aïda *was performed five times in February. However, the German Theater produced a new production of* Aïda *in December 1936, with subsequent performances in March 1937, so it is possible that* Aïda *was also produced at the German Theater during the 1937-1938 season.*

Therefore, Franz performed the King in one theater or the other. And if he was in Aïda *in Aussig, it was for a performance in February.*

That said: the general manager had attempted to replace the role by calling neighboring opera companies without any luck. The scheduled bass had come down with influenza, and the performance was in just two days. When the general manager telephoned Franz, Franz explained that he had learned the role but was unfamiliar with the staging. "Never mind," the general manager said. "We'll work it out."

So Franz reported to the opera house the next morning and was assigned an accompanist. They worked all day, and at noon on the day of the performance, Franz felt ready. Then he went into the costume department, where he was fitted in the typical costume of an ancient Egyptian king, with a few additional accessories to make him look taller. He was put into a long tunic-type garment which covered his feet, a royal apron and cape ornamented with semiprecious stones and gold, a lofty headdress that peaked as high as the Great Pyramid, elevated shoes instead of the customary sandals, and lavish jewelry held tight around his wrists.

At six o'clock, a makeup artist applied heavy Egyptian makeup to his face, arms and neck, and helped him into his costume. Then he sat in his dressing room waiting. At seven, he could hear the overture and then Radamès' famous aria, "Heavenly Aïda." A young captain, Radamès had hoped to lead the Egyptian forces to victory against the Ethiopians and then to share the glory with his beloved Aïda, the Ethiopian princess who had become a slave to Amneris, the King's daughter. But Amneris had designs on Radamès as well.

It was almost time for Franz to make his entrance. He was somewhat nervous because he had never sung the part of the King with an orchestra and was still somewhat insecure with the staging. He was supposed to be carried onstage while sitting on a chair-like throne. In the wings, four bearers were to lift the chair into the air while Franz was to climb an adjacent ladder and then manipulate his body onto it. The maneuver began as planned. The chair had been elevated into the air by the four bearers, and Franz was standing on the highest step of the ladder studying his score. The stage manager told him to get on the chair. "I will," he said.

"You must get on it now," the stage manager said firmly.

"I will in a second," Franz repeated, still glancing at his score.

Hearing his musical cue, the stage manager said, "Go." And the four bearers began to walk.

Franz quickly dropped his score on the floor and reached for the chair with one of his legs. He navigated more than half of his body onto the moving object, being forced to release the other leg from the ladder. Partially seated on the left side of the chair with one leg in the front and the other hanging over the side, Franz lifted himself up with his hands and slid into a more centralized position, quickly bending the hanging leg under his behind. And as the bearers proceeded on the stage, Franz propelled his constricted leg into its desired position. *Thank heavens I have on a long skirt. I hope no one noticed,* Franz thought. But he wasn't out of the woods yet.

The bearers set the chair down on the stage. Franz stood and then didn't know what to do. The singer who was playing Ramfis turned his back to the audience and whispered to Franz, motioning with his head: "Go up there."

Another more stationary chair-like throne was sitting on top of a platform. Franz walked toward it, took his first step up and couldn't move. Then the mezzo-soprano who was playing Amneris pointed to the bottom of Franz's skirt, motioning him to lift it. He couldn't because he was standing on it. Finally he freed himself and walked up to the throne, turned, faced the audience, and sang. He was watching the conductor's every move.

As the King, he asked the Egyptians to hasten to the banks of the Nile, declared war on the Ethiopians, and proclaimed Radamès commander of the army. Now Franz could rest until the second scene in Act Two.

Fortunately for him, when the curtain rose this time, he was already seated on his throne as the victorious Egyptian soldiers paraded in – to the flourish of trumpets and waving banners. Franz enjoyed the fanfare at the beginning of this scene: hearing the vibrant "Triumphal March" and watching the ballet. The theater and stage were too small to produce the spectacle that was often created in larger houses, so the victorious Radamès did not enter on a horse-drawn chariot, but by foot instead. The King (Franz) rose to greet him.

Then as the Ethiopian prisoners were shepherded in, Franz walked down a few steps from the throne to the main level of the stage and felt himself stepping on his skirt again, so he lifted it coolly and continued on. He listened to Radamès' request to free the prisoners and to the high priest Ramfis' resistance and later compromise to at least retain Aïda and her father as hostages. Then he gave Radamès his daughter's hand in marriage, adding that one day Radamès would reign with her.

The melodic edict created quite different sentiments from all of the main characters who articulated them clearly in a musical climax.

Franz was grateful that during the curtain call at the conclusion of the act, when all of the principal singers lined up on the apron of the stage to take their bows together, he was the one standing closest to the wings.

For the King, the performance was over. Franz had been a little clumsy, but he'd sung well. It was time to go home.

CHAPTER SIXTEEN

Annexation

Vienna, Austria
Prague, Czechoslovakia
March 1938

9 March 1938

Dear Franz,

I am very frightened. In February, Chancellor Schuschnigg went to Berchtesgaden to meet with Hitler. When he came back to Vienna, he appointed a number of known Nazis to key positions in the Austrian cabinet: among them, Artur Seyss-Inquart who was named minister of the interior. Soon later, he gave a speech affirming his determination to maintain Austria's autonomy. And then tonight, he announced that in three days we would be called upon to vote whether or not we favor a free, independent Austria.

The number of Nazi street demonstrations has increased drastically, and the police don't do anything to deter them. I'm afraid that Hitler and his troops are going to move into Austria at any moment; then the Nürnberg Laws will take effect, and the Jews here will be treated just as harshly as those in Germany. I won't be able to work; I won't have enough money for food. What am I going to do?

You're so lucky to be in Prague! Sometimes I worry that I'll never see you again. I love you so very much, Franz! Pray for me!

Franziska

On the eleventh of March, the plebiscite was called off. And on that fateful Friday evening, all ears were glued to the radio as Chancellor Schuschnigg resigned. Franziska was sitting on her bed and then ran into the living room to be with the Grünwalds.

"We are yielding to force," Schuschnigg's voice echoed over the radio waves. "Since we are not prepared – not even in this grave hour – to shed blood, we have ordered our armed forces, in case the invasion takes place, to withdraw without offering substantial resistance and to await the decisions of the next hours. . . . God protect Austria."

Franziska sat frozen in disbelief as the radio network played Schubert's "Unfinished" Symphony at the conclusion of Schuschnigg's address. Magda Grünwald started to cry. "We are too old to leave Vienna and find a new home," she uttered. "What will become of us?"

"*Mein Liebchen*," her husband said, placing his arms around her comfortingly. "We are two old people; they are not going to harm us."

Soon later, shouts of "*Heil Hitler!*" and "*Sau Jud!*" could be heard from the neighboring streets. Since the Grünwalds' apartment was near the commercial Mariahilferstrasse, Franziska could hear the shattering of glass as windows were smashed and Jewish-owned businesses ransacked.

The drapes and shades in the apartment were closed, but Franziska peered through one of the windows and was appalled to see youths with swastikas around their arms marching along the street, laughing joyously and yelling the familiar Nazi slogans, including: "Jews, go back to Palestine!"

In addition, she could already see swastikas and portraits of Hitler in many of her neighbors' windows. These were people to whom she had cordially said hello when walking to and from the Grünwalds' apartment, never suspecting that any of them might be Nazi sympathizers and most probably anti-Semitic.

After she had some hot milk and pastry with the Grünwalds, she retired into her bedroom, hoping to get a few hours of sleep. But she was afraid to change out of her clothes in fear that Nazi hoodlums might barge into the apartment. She sat up against the headboard of her bed and turned on her radio so that the volume was barely audible. It was official: Artur Seyss-Inquart had been appointed Schuschnigg's successor. It was also reported that there were crowds of people celebrating in the city center and in front of the government headquarters among local uniformed members of the Nazi storm troopers (SA) and protective squads (SS).

Franziska didn't know what to do or to whom to turn. She didn't know if a phone call to Prague would even get through, so she didn't try. Besides, how could Franz help her now? Then there were the members of her family. No, she wouldn't call them either. They'd treated her so coldly that she rarely spoke to them. Besides, they were probably desperate themselves. As she contemplated her fate, she became somewhat drowsy. But whenever she reached her much desired state of repose, her head jerked her awake as she heard low-flying airplanes droning above like a swarm of honeybees en route to a foreign hive.

In the morning, she knew that she had to do something. She was really afraid to venture out of the apartment but decided that she had to muster the courage to visit Franz's mother. She didn't bathe or change clothes. She went into the bathroom, took her blouse off, washed her face, and cleaned her teeth. Then she reapplied her makeup very sparingly without rouge or red lipstick. She combed her hair out of her face and made it look shorter than it really was by rolling it under and pinning it into place. She slipped back into her blouse, buttoning and tucking it in her skirt while walking back to her bedroom. She threw on a coat and placed a soft-brimmed hat in the center of her head, then pushed it forward over her right eye so that her hair and a portion of her face were almost completely covered. Her goal was to walk down the street unnoticed.

Since it was early, she left a note for the Grünwalds so that they wouldn't be worried. As she walked out into the morning air, she knew that she was in a different Vienna; it was no longer the city she loved. She walked briskly along Mariahilferstrasse, keeping her head down as she paced. She tried to avoid stepping on the fragments of glass that glazed parts of the sidewalk, often without success. A few times she glanced up at broken windows, then quickly ducked her head and continued on. She walked around torn-down store signs and passed vendors selling swastika badges. Because it was so early, there were very few people on the street, so it was relatively quiet; yet she could still hear the low buzzing sounds of the German aircraft circling above.

When she reached the Ringstrasse, she boarded a tram and sat on one of the benches inside, intentionally slouching. When the conductor approached her for her ticket, she lifted her head up slightly to exhibit her pass, then observed that he was wearing a swastika armlet. "*Danke*," he said moving on. She quickly lowered her eyes, placed the pass back in her purse, and reassumed her bent-over posture.

When she reached Schottentor, she changed to another tram, this one already flaunting a swastika banner that was affixed to the outside. Again she sat hunched over like Richard III, but she couldn't fool this conductor. When he asked her for her ticket, she handed him her pass. Sensing that she was Jewish, he looked at the picture on it, nodded his head up and down, and then tossed it next to her feet on the floor. At first she was somewhat startled as he walked away; then she reached down quickly, grabbed it, and threw it back into her purse.

Upon reaching the terminal in Pötzleinsdorf, she observed some brown-shirted SA men strutting around authoritatively. She stepped down from the tram and slithered by them seemingly unseen. She walked so swiftly up Pötzleinsdorfer Strasse that she stumbled over her own feet a couple of times. It was as if she were rushing to a family reunion after many long years. Only this reunion wasn't with a blood relative; it was with a woman Franziska had grown to care for simply because the woman had been giving and understanding, and had been able to transfer the love she felt for her own son, to the other woman who made him so happy. Olga Jung did indeed have a special place in Franziska's heart. So when Franziska reached the front of the house, she stood very still for a moment and then looked directly at what seemed to be her salvation.

She opened the gate, walked down the pathway on the side, and knocked on the door. Nobody answered. She went to the back entrance and knocked again. Still nobody answered. Finally she heard Vinzi's voice calling out: "Who is it?" When Franziska replied with her name, Vinzi opened the door and shouted to Olga to come into the kitchen. "It's Franziska," she said. "It's safe to come down."

Vinzi was Czech, and she wasn't Jewish. She was plump, fair-skinned and blond, and she was extremely anti-Nazi.

When Olga entered, she immediately went over to Franziska and hugged her. "*Mein Kind*," she said. "How are you?"

"I came because I'm so frightened. Tell me what to do, Frau Jung."

"Come. Sit down."

At this point, Vinzi left to allow the two women some privacy.

"You know, Franziska, I'm in a quandary myself. I don't want to leave the house, yet I wonder what has happened to my *Putzerei*. I assume I'll lose everything there, and I still have outstanding bills. I'll send Vinzi to see what has happened."

"I can't go back to work either. I'm sure that Appenzeller will be one of the first stores hit, if it hasn't been wiped out already. . . . And this is only the beginning. Hitler and his army haven't even arrived yet. Everything that's been done here has been done by Austrians: the people I grew up with, the people I thought were my friends."

"You have to forget all of that now, Franziska."

"And even if we have money, the local stores may not sell to us. . . . Franz is so lucky to be in Czechoslovakia."

"Yes, Franzi! Thank God he's safe!"

"Tell me, Frau Jung, what should I do?"

"I can't give you any answers. I can only make a few suggestions. First, you are welcome to stay here with me if you like. I have more than enough room."

"Oh, Frau Jung, how kind of you. . . ."

"But I think I have a better suggestion," Olga continued. "You are a Czech citizen and you have a Czech passport."

"Yes. . . ."

"And you love my son."

"Yes. . . ."

"So what are you doing here? You must go to Prague to be with him."

"That sounds wonderful in theory," Franziska answered. "But I don't know if I can get out. And even if I could, I don't think I have the money for the train fare. Herr Appenzeller owes me a paycheck, and my spring coat is being altered at the tailor shop."

Olga made a direct beeline to the telephone. She learned that the trains were still running and that everyone was being allowed through. But she was told that the situation would probably change once the Germans arrived.

"You must go today," she told Franziska. "You cannot wait. You must go home, pack, and get out."

"But . . ."

"I will give you the money for the fare, and I will pick up your paycheck if the store still exists. But you'll have to call the tailor. Here's the phone."

Franziska looked up the number in her address book and dialed. Then: "*Guten Morgen*, Herr Schmidt. This is Franziska Perger. . . . Yes, I'm fine. I'm calling because I plan to leave Vienna this afternoon. . . . I'm leaving from Franz-Josefs-Bahnhof. . . . No, I'm not coming back for a while. I want to be with Franz. . . . I wish you the best too, Herr Schmidt. Now about my coat: I would really like to take it with me, but I don't have time to pick it up. You understand. . . . So could you please give it to Ilona the next time she visits you? . . . *Danke*, Herr Schmidt. You've done such fine work for me. *Auf Wiedersehen*, Herr Schmidt. . . . *Auf Wiedersehen*."

Franziska hung up the phone and sighed. She'd miss Emil Schmidt. He'd always come to the rescue when she needed something altered in the last minute and didn't have the time or inclination to do the job herself. He was employed by Knize, a highly respected tailoring establishment where all of the clothes sold were made-to-order. But he also worked privately for selected clients at reduced rates. He'd always liked Franziska because she labored in the same business as he did. And

Franziska appreciated him as well, for she believed that he was a decent human being. And even now, as the Germans were taking over Vienna, he still treated her as kindly as always, just as she had known that he would.

"I'll be back in a minute," Olga told Franziska. "I'm going to get your train fare."

Franziska sat in the kitchen as Franz's mother went up into the attic where her family's World War I hiding place in the ceiling still endured. She removed the piece of wood covering the small compartment and withdrew the money she needed along with some jewelry. She placed the wood back carefully and returned downstairs to the kitchen.

"Here you are, my dear. Here is the train fare plus a little extra, and some jewelry. I'm afraid to keep it here in the house."

"Oh, thank you, Frau Jung. You are so good to me. I'll accept everything now; but one day, I'll give the jewelry back to you."

"No, no! It's for you and Franz. Maybe you'll need to sell it."

"Well, I'm going to try not to," Franziska said.

She took the money and laid it in her shoe. Then she placed the jewelry in the bottom of her purse.

"Go now. . . ."

"But what about you, Frau Jung? Are you thinking of leaving Vienna?"

"I don't know what the future will bring, Franziska. Ilona and Hans are here, and Hans would never leave his dying father. For the time being, I plan to stay. . . . But you must go now, *mein Kind*. May God keep you safe."

Franziska stood up, placed her hands on Olga Jung's shoulders and kissed her on the cheek. Then Olga opened the door, and Franziska began her journey back to the Grünwalds' apartment.

The streets were more crowded now; the trams, much more busy. When Franziska reached Schottentor and then rode the tram along the Ring, she noticed that policemen in front of the Rathaus were now sporting swastikas and saluting the SA and SS men all around. If she were harassed, she feared that the police would do nothing to protect her.

When she managed to get off the tram without incident, she hurriedly half-walked, half-ran to the Grünwalds' apartment. It was just past
noon when she arrived home, explained her plans to the Grünwalds,
and quickly packed her clothes and belongings into one large-sized suitcase, leaving the items she didn't absolutely need behind. She packed
the jewelry inside some of her shoes, put the money she needed in her
purse, and sewed the extra money Franz's mother had given her into
the lining of her coat. When she was completely packed, she decided to
call her mother to say good-bye.

"Hello, Mutti. How are you? . . . Yes, I know you're frightened, and
I know that I haven't called you in months, but I never know how I'm
going to be received. . . . Yes, I'm aware that it will be hard for anyone to
work now; that if I'd move home, I wouldn't have to pay outside rent; and
that what little money I do have would help the family. But I called to
tell you that I'm leaving Vienna this afternoon. I'm going to Prague. . . .
Thank you for understanding, Mama. . . . Yes, I'll be with Franz. He's
still singing there. . . . Yes, maybe we will get married one day. . . .
Don't cry, Mutti. You'll be all right. You're with Lilly, Fritz, and Paul;
they won't abandon you. . . . Yes, I promise to write. But I really have
to go now, Mama. Take care of yourself, and try not to worry. And say
hello to the others for me. . . . Good-bye, Mama."

After finishing the telephone conversation, Franziska called for a
taxi, took her suitcase into the living room, and waited. She heard on
the radio that SS chief Heinrich Himmler had arrived at the airport,
and the German military had already moved into the western portion
of Austria. She wanted to be out of the country before the armed forces
actually reached Vienna.

Just before the taxi arrived, the Grünwalds told Franziska how much
they'd miss her, thus giving her a very warm farewell. The taxi driver
carried her luggage into his car while she held on to a coat and hatbox, and they proceeded north toward the railway station. As Franziska
looked out of the window, she suddenly developed a sinking feeling in
the pit of her stomach. She was leaving the city where she'd grown up,
the only place she'd ever really known, and she might never return.
She started to get nauseous and quickly grabbed the top of her hatbox

and threw up into it. The taxi driver didn't say anything but looked a little pale. Once at the railway station, Franziska paid him, discarded the saturated lid, and asked a porter to help her with her suitcase. She felt a little warm because she was dressed in the same coat and soft-brimmed hat she'd worn that morning. Holding an additional coat and the uncovered hatbox, she walked up to a window and purchased a one-way ticket to Prague. The train was leaving at four o'clock. It was only three-fifteen.

The terminal seemed quite busy. There were a number of people who looked as shaken as Franziska, bundled in heavy coats when the weather didn't really call for them. Walking toward the display monitor, Franziska spotted vendors who were selling swastika badges and newspapers headlining the Nazi takeover. As she looked up, she saw her train and destination listed, and walked with her porter to the designated track on the platform. She decided that she couldn't expect the porter to stand next to her for more than half an hour just so that he could carry her luggage onto the train, so she gave him a tip, and he left.

Every minute seemed like an hour to Franziska. She kept thinking that Hitler would issue a mandate disallowing anyone to cross the Austrian border. She stood for so long with her weight on her right leg that it became perfectly stiff and she thought she'd never be able to bend it again. She quickly tried to balance herself and shook the taut leg back to its normal flexibility. She looked around at the other people waiting, trying to decipher which ones were pro-Nazi and which were not. Her task was simplified considerably when a group of SA men strutted by, and some of the bystanders waved and cheered. At that very moment, Franziska realized that she could no longer trust another fellow-Viennese again unless she'd grown to know the person well or was aware that the individual was Jewish. It was good that she was going to Prague, she thought, but the experience of leaving her home was still a little daunting.

She stood facing the tracks, watching the trains come and go until she heard her name being called. She turned around, and to her surprise, Emil Schmidt was walking swiftly toward her. "Franziska,

Franziska," he was shouting somewhat out of breath. "I've come to bring you your coat."

So much anxiety and tension had amassed in Franziska's body that when she saw the tailor's familiar face, she didn't know whether to smile or cry. "Oh, how kind of you, Herr Schmidt," she said as he handed her the garment. "It's the only spring coat I own, and I really need it. Oh, thank you, Herr Schmidt."

"Well, it was finished, so I wanted you to have it."

"But how did you know where to find me?"

"You told me that you were leaving from Franz-Josefs-Bahnhof this afternoon, so I called and got the schedule, and here I am."

"I feel so much better now. It's almost like having a member of my own family sending me off," Franziska said as she searched in her purse for her wallet."

"No, no, I couldn't accept anything. Think of it as a farewell gift," the tailor commented.

"I'm so very grateful. I wish that there was some way I could pay you back."

"Please, Franzi, don't give it another thought. There is so much evil in the world. I'm just trying to even things out a little."

Franziska felt such warmth for the kindhearted man that she reached around him and gave him a daughterly hug. It was a strange, awkward kind of embrace since she now had two coats draped over one arm, and the hatbox dangling from the other.

The train chugged in promptly at four o'clock, and Herr Schmidt insisted on carrying Franziska's luggage all the way into the train and to her compartment. "Now you will have a bright future," he told her. "Don't ever look back!"

She was so touched that she hugged him one more time. "I'll never forget you," she said. He nodded and smiled, and then he quickly left the train.

Franziska sat down and placed her coats and hatbox next to her. She tried to get comfortable, but the seats were hard – she wasn't traveling first-class – and she was extremely nervous. She felt that she couldn't re-lax until she was safely over the border. When the train started moving, she still felt quite anxious; but after about an hour, the steady motion seemed to hypnotize her into a more tranquil state as she looked out of the window at the fertile scenery: an abundance of lush vegetation spotted with the architecture of suburban towns. She was glad that no one joined her in her humble compartment because she didn't want to have to indulge in either small talk or the more pressing topic of the day: the Nazi takeover.

At about half past four, a conductor asked to see her ticket and then continued on. There were no scheduled train stops in Austria except one in Hohenau, right next to the northeast segment of the Austrian border. At about five, just a few minutes before the train was set to reach Hohenau, an Austrian immigration officer and a man in an SA uniform entered her compartment.

"May I see your passport?" the governmental official asked.

Franziska produced it quickly, her hand visibly shaking.

"So you're a Czech citizen," he said, showing the passport to the Nazi.

"Yes," Franziska uttered.

"What is your destination?"

"Prague," she answered.

"Do you plan on returning to Vienna?"

Franziska didn't know what to say. If she said "no," the two men would realize that she was fleeing. So she replied: "Probably."

Then the man in the SA uniform spoke. "I see that you are not wearing a swastika yet," he said. "In your hurry to get to the train station, you must not have had time to purchase one."

Franziska looked up at the Nazi but didn't say anything.

"My colleague needs to go through your luggage," the immigration officer said. "Please open it."

Franziska pulled her suitcase toward her and unlocked it.

"Oh, I'm so sorry," the Nazi said. "My hands are not very clean. I was just eating some *Mozartkugeln*, and some of the chocolate must have melted."

The Nazi then rummaged through Franziska's things, rubbing his hands into everything, including her personal effects. "Oh, I'm so sorry," he said again. "I've soiled this lovely satin slip. You must have looked enchanting in it."

The Nazi held up the hand-embroidered slip, now completely ruined, and then he continued examining Franziska's belongings. "You understand that we have to search for items we do not want taken out of the country," he said, taking out a pocket knife and slashing the lining of Franziska's suitcase. "Of course, I realize that no one like you would transport anything illegal."

Then he started unraveling the tissue paper around Franziska's shoes. He reached into one of her pumps. "Oh, what have we here? This is quite exquisite."

He'd found the gold and ruby bracelet that Olga Jung had given Franziska. "This piece looks like it might have been stolen. I'll have to keep it in my custody," he said.

Franziska felt completely victimized. She wanted to cry out but was too afraid of the consequences to do so.

"Oh, this emerald and sapphire cocktail ring is equally magnificent," the Nazi said. "I can't believe that it could be yours." And within a few minutes, he had also accumulated a strand of pearls and a brooch.

"Well, I think we've done a thorough job here," the Nazi told his colleague. He looked Franziska squarely in the eyes and wished her a good evening. The immigration officer stamped Franziska's passport, handed it back to her, and then the two immoral cockroaches walked out.

Franziska was devastated. She'd left so many things behind, only packing what she absolutely needed, and now many of those items would be unsalvable. And the jewelry: it meant so much to her. Oh, how she'd wished to return it one day to Franz's mother. Franziska just sat there looking in disbelief at the demolished open suitcase. How would she ever get the chocolate out of her clothes? What would she wear? She couldn't afford to buy a new wardrobe. How could human beings be so vindictive?

Franziska began to cry just as the train stopped in Hohenau. She could see from the window that a number of immigration officers and SA men had gotten off. She lifted her suitcase onto one of the empty seats across from her and appraised the damage done to her clothes, holding certain items up, and then neatly folding and placing them back into her suitcase. The flow of her tears would not subside, their salty taste lingering on her lips.

The train began moving again. Franziska closed her suitcase and left it on the seat. Her crying had ceased and she was looking out of the window now. "Just a few more minutes. . . . Just a few more minutes," she kept saying to herself.

More vegetation. A river. And less than half an hour later, the train was stopping in Břeclav. Franziska had arrived safely in Czechoslovakia. She'd crossed the border. Within moments, she began to feel exhilarated. Soon she'd be with Franz again, and there would no longer be any sad good-byes.

The train rolled out of the Břeclav station past flat fields of wheat; and about half an hour later, a Czech official entered her compartment. "May I see your passport?" he asked politely in Czech.

Franziska didn't understand him, but she knew that almost everyone in Czechoslovakia spoke German. "*Deutsch, bitte,*" she said. So he repeated his question in German.

Franziska suddenly tensed up. Through all of the excitement, she was sure she'd misplaced her passport; she couldn't remember putting it back into her purse. She looked all around and uttered a sigh of relief when she found it sitting on top of her coats. "Here it is," she told the official.

"Are you going to Prague?" he asked as he stamped it.

"Yes, indeed I am," she answered gleaming.

Her sparkle made him laugh. "Have a good trip," he said returning the passport, and then he left without any mention of perusing her luggage.

She could breathe again. She could finally breathe. But when she stopped thinking about her good fortune, she began worrying about Franz's family and her own. What was Hitler going to do next? What was he capable of?

The brakes brought the train to a halt once more in Brünn where two nice young women joined Franziska in her compartment for the duration of the trip. Franziska placed her suitcase back on the floor, and the two neatly-dressed women sat across from her. They'd brought some food to eat, which they generously shared with her, and the three talked about everything under the sun except the news of the day.

The train continued gliding past towns, hills, and forests, until it grew dark and the scenery became barely discernible. A ride through a tunnel here and there, a stop in the industrial city of Kolín, and the train moved on to Prague.

It was after eleven o'clock when Franziska arrived at the main train station. The two young women vacated the compartment, and Franziska opened the window and called to a porter outside. The porter entered her compartment and carried her baggage out while she followed with her coats and hatbox. She couldn't decide whether to telephone Franz or to take a taxi directly to his apartment. But she didn't have a key. What if he'd sung that night? What if he wasn't home? She still had some Czech money left from the last time she'd been in Prague, so she asked the porter to set her luggage down while she called. The telephone was ringing. He was home; he picked up the phone.

"Hello, Franz; it's me."

"Where are you calling from, Franziska? I've been worried sick about you."

"I'm here, Franz. I'm here in Prague . . . at the train station. Your mother gave me the money for the fare."

"Oh, thank God. . . . I didn't have to sing today, so I haven't budged from the radio. Hitler is in Linz, and the German army has already moved into Vienna. I'm so glad that you're out."

"So am I, Franz. So am I."

"How are my mother and sister?"

"I haven't talked to Ilona, but your mother is frightened, yet strong."

"Don't let's talk on the phone, Franzi. How much luggage do you have?"

"I have one big suitcase."

"Don't move. Wait by the entrance on Wilsonova, and I'll be right down."

"Are you sure you don't want me to just take a taxi?"

"No. I'm coming right now. I'm already half out the door."

"I'll see you in a few minutes, Franz. I love you."

"I love you too, Franziska. Good-bye."

"Good-bye, Franz."

When Franziska hung up the phone, she noticed that the porter had waited like a faithful pet for her to complete the telephone call, so when they reached the terminal entrance, she gave him a generous tip. Within fifteen minutes, the doors opened and Franz was standing in front of her. The two hugged as if they were locked together. Then Franz released Franziska, tenderly held her face between his hands and kissed her. "Are you all right?" he asked.

"Now I am," she answered, nodding her head up and down.

"Come on," he said. "Let's go home."

Franziska's coats were laying over her suitcase, and her hatbox was standing beside them.

"What happened to the top?" Franz asked, pointing to the coverless case.

"I'll tell you later," Franziska answered, grasping it with one hand and lifting up her coats with the other.

Franz then grabbed her suitcase, and they took the same taxi back to his apartment that had whisked him to the station a few minutes before.

Once inside Petrská Twenty-Four, Franz listened sympathetically as Franziska told him all about her experience on the train. When she opened her suitcase and showed him all the damage inside, his face became serious and sad. And when she cried as she described how the man in the SA uniform had confiscated his mother's jewelry, he held her close and told her that what mattered most was that she was safe, and that from then on, they would confront all of life's challenges together.

Franziska spent the night sleeping soundly, feeling Franz's arms wrapped around her like an impregnable fortress. And when they awoke, they made love with a keen, unwavering, deep-rooted sense of connection. But Franziska still felt insecure.

"I'll bet you didn't expect a permanent house guest," she whispered, skimming Franz's chest delicately with the tips of her fingers.

"You're not my house guest, silly," he replied. "This is your home now, as modest as it may be. I only wish you'd come much sooner."

Franziska smiled – she'd heard what she'd wanted to hear – and Franz rolled on top of her and disappeared under the covers.

Later, after they'd dressed and eaten, Franziska disengaged the money in the lining of her coat and gave it to Franz, explaining that it was a gift from his mother. Franz immediately handed a portion back to her, clarifying that it was meant for both of them, that they were now beginning their lives together and should share everything equally. "Whatever is mine is yours," Franz told Franziska. "And that's the way it will always be."

Later, Franziska attempted to strip the chocolate stains from her clothing with some ammonia and water, achieving a much more favorable outcome than she had anticipated. Hopefully a *Putzerei* would be more successful with the items that remained slightly damaged. As for the few pieces which were ruined, Franziska decided to slowly replace them when the money could be spared, if at all.

The radio was turned on all the time for the next few days. A broadcaster reported that Hitler had arrived in Vienna to throngs of cheering people and streets bedecked with flowers and swastikas. He said that Hitler was expected to deliver a speech from the balcony of the imperial palace overlooking the *Heldenplatz* (Heroes' Square).

Later, another commentator described the crowds as "jubilant" and reported that the Viennese were filling the *Heldenplatz* in anticipation of the arrival of their new leader. They had even climbed onto the statue of the much-revered Prince Eugene of Savoy, who had defeated the Turks in the seventeenth century. However, the new Austrian hero was Adolf Hitler, and when the people saw him, their shouts became deafening.

Hearing the brouhaha on the radio, Franz and Franziska stopped what they were doing. Franz sat on the armchair in the living room with Franzi then sitting on his lap. Hitler had already begun speaking. The approving crowd was cheering him on.

"As Führer and Chancellor of the German nation, I report now, before history, the entry of my native land into the German Reich," Hitler declared.

Franz and Franzi looked at each other with grave sadness in their eyes. Then Franziska laid her head on Franz's shoulder. The annexation of Austria was complete. Franz Jung had undeniably and officially become a German.

Gioacchino Rossini.
(*By Félix Nadar.*)

CHAPTER SEVENTEEN
Dr. Bartolo

Vienna, formerly Austria
Czechoslovakia: Aussig and Prague
March 1938 to 1 May 1938

*C*he radio was flooding the airwaves with reports relating to the *Anschluss*, the annexation of Austria. The newspapers were jetting forth headlines and stories. German leaders were declaring that within a few years, Vienna would be *Judenrein* (free of Jews).

The Nazis were harassing Jews, taking over their homes and businesses, and marking the word *Aryanized* on store signs and windows. Many of the terrorized Jews attempted to emigrate with barely enough funds to survive after their possessions and assets had been confiscated. For a while, no one was allowed to cross the border. Then it became difficult to attain the required documentation for the journey. Most Jews ascertained that they couldn't leave legally, if at all; and even if they were willing to attempt the feat, they couldn't find any countries that would grant them visas.

Frightened – Olga Jung moved into an apartment in Sievering, then moved again to be near her business on Esslinggasse. She soon closed her *Putzerei*, delivered her clients' items back to them, sold her rotary presser, and paid her outstanding debts. Most of her customers fulfilled their monetary obligations. However there were a few who took advantage of the situation and refused to render what was due.

Ilona's husband, Hans Beck, tried to continue working at his office near Schottentor; however he ended each day a few hours early so that he could visit his sick father in the hospital. When he was walking along Wipplingerstrasse one afternoon, five armed storm troopers surrounded him, shoved and pushed him to the *Börseplatz* and rammed him to his knees, forcing him to scrub the pavement with a group of other men. Their utensils: toothbrushes and lye. Their audience: storm troopers and citizens taunting and spitting at them. When the Nazis finally marched off, Hans's hands were red and burnt from the sharp solution. And by the time he arrived home, they were covered with blisters. Ilona quickly applied a soothing salve and wrapped his hands in gauze to shut out the air. She desperately wanted to get out of Vienna, but Hans refused to leave his father.

Franz and Franziska moved into another apartment on the other side of the river in Smíchov. It was slightly larger and more economical, and Franz moved the upright piano with him.

The communication between them in Prague and their families in Vienna had almost completely broken off. Every time Franz received a letter, the details were always eliminated, as was the return address on the envelope. The short notes were always in generalities like: "*We're all fine. We're happy that you're well. Hans's father is very sick.*" Franziska's cards were even worse: "*The weather is beautiful. Wish you were here.*" Yet Franz and Franziska were grateful for the messages they did receive. The Nazis were herding Jews off; at least they knew that the members of their immediate families were still alive and in Vienna.

They soon discovered that the security they'd originally felt in Prague was waning. It had become quite evident that Hitler wanted much more than Austria. At the very least, the Czechs were led to believe that he wanted the Sudetenland, the mountainous region along the northern border of Czechoslovakia. Egged on by Konrad Henlein, the German-speaking inhabitants there maintained that they were being discriminated against by the Czechs. Henlein rejected proposals made by the Czech government to mitigate the tensions and countered them with a much more far-reaching Nazi program – the Karlsbad Program – to establish an autonomous German province within the state. When the Czechs declined the plan, the Nazis increased their propaganda efforts, creating outrageous stories of abuse against the Sudeten Germans which later led to reports of shooting incidents. Nazi leader Wilhelm Keitel met with Hitler on the twenty-first of April, and they sketched out Operation Green in private: the invasion of Czechoslovakia.

During this time of crisis, Franz was scheduled to sing at the Stadttheater in Aussig at the end of April. The morning before the performance, he left Franziska in his rented room while he went to a rehearsal. She was looking forward to seeing him play Dr. Bartolo in Rossini's *Der Barbier von Sevilla* (*The Barber of Seville*). She loved seeing him in basso buffo character roles because he was such a good actor that he could pull off anything a director asked of him.

Much like Mozart's *The Marriage of Figaro,* because both operas are based on the same Beaumarchais comedy, the Count in this opera is the same Count Almaviva Franz shared the stage with in Mozart's opera. Only in *The Marriage of Figaro*, Almaviva is married to the Countess – Rosina – and Figaro is in his employ. In *The Barber of Seville*, the Count isn't married to Rosina yet; he's courting her. However Rosina's guardian, Dr. Bartolo, wants to marry her, too. But Bartolo doesn't trust Rosina; he suspects she has eyes for the Count and that Figaro – a barber – has been acting as their liaison. After the Count disguises himself and after some hemming and hawing from Dr. Bartolo, Rosina and the Count are finally married, and Dr. Bartolo has no choice but to congratulate the happy couple.

Franz liked the role. All of the movement and blocking enabled him to really act. When Franz arrived home after rehearsal, Franziska was reading contently on the bed, where he promptly joined her.

The next morning, the dog in the house woke the couple up with a few loud barks. "I wish I could turn him off with Papageno's magic bells," Franz said jokingly, referring to one of his favorite roles: Papageno in *The Magic Flute*. But the spell of sleep had been broken; it was just as well though. Franz had just the right amount of time to get ready for the late matinée.

They were at the theater early. Since the performance wasn't set to begin for a couple of hours, Franziska decided to walk around the downtown area of Aussig before taking her seat in the auditorium. She wished Franz good luck at the artists' entrance and then continued strolling in the square in front of the theater. That's when she heard some people talking about rushing right home because the Germans could march in at any moment. Their troops could be seen at the border in Saxony, someone said. Franziska continued walking until she reached a nearby museum and heard another story which was quite similar.

"Some friends of mine told me that troops have been moving through Pirna," she heard one man telling another. "It appears that Henlein might break off negotiations. He'll probably meet with Hitler, so you figure it out."

Franziska dashed to the theater, back to the artists' entrance, and directly to Franz's dressing room. She knocked on the door and the makeup artist opened it a shade. "Is Franz Jung there?" she asked.

"Yes, he is."

"I assume the singers are getting into their costumes, so could you please ask him to come to the door? It's important."

Franz came out into the backstage corridor, already in full costume. He was wearing a seventeenth century shirt, cravat, waistcoat, breeches, white stockings and pumps, plus a periwig. In spite of the tension, Franziska couldn't help but smile.

"You didn't come to gawk at me, did you?" Franz asked.

"No, no. I came to tell you that there seems to be a rumor circulating," she said.

"I've heard one too," Franz responded. "What have you heard?"

"When I was walking around Aussig, some people said that there is terrible friction between the Czechs and Germans here. German troops may be stationed at the border, and if they aren't, they will be soon. They said the Germans could march in at any time."

"That's exactly what I've been hearing inside the theater."

"But Hitler must realize that he can't just walk into Czechoslovakia like he did in Austria without any opposition. He must be aware that other countries like France and England and Russia would stand behind the Czechs, and he'd be starting a war."

Franz and Franziska stood silently looking at each other – thinking. "I want to make a quick telephone call to verify some of this," Franz said. "I'm going to ask the Weinraubs what they think."

Arnold and Klara Weinraub had come backstage after one of Franz's initial performances in Aussig. Arnold was a Hungarian Jew, and he and his wife owned a fabric store in the center of the city. Franz immediately felt comfortable with the couple, and the three became close friends even before Franziska moved to Czechoslovakia. The Weinraubs had a spacious home on top of a hill, and Franz and Franziska were invited there often.

Franz walked to a nearby telephone and dialed. "Hello, Arnold. This is Franz Jung. . . . Oh, I'm sorry. I don't want to keep you. . . . That's what I'm calling about. So you believe there's some validity to the rumor. . . . You're leaving Aussig? . . . For good? . . . They've been boycotting your business? . . . Yes, yes. Call us in Prague. Talk to you soon."

Franz hung up the phone and walked back toward Franziska feeling somewhat numb. He could see that she was nervous because she couldn't stand still; she was kind of bobbing up and down, her knees bending a little and straightening, bending and straightening. When he reached her, he put both of his hands on her shoulders to ground her. "I just talked to Arnold, and I've decided that I want you to leave Aussig right away and go back to Prague."

"What? Alone?"

"Yes."

"But I want to see the performance."

"You can see me as Dr. Bartolo here another time, or in Prague."

"But what about you? When are you going back?"

"I'd like to get on a train right now; but I have a contract, and I'm going to get through this performance. If I'd leave now, without a replacement, I would never get another engagement in Europe."

"But I'll worry. . . . No. . . . I'm going to stay, and then we'll go back together."

"Oh, no, you're not! You are going to leave right now!" Franz blurted out, suppressing the volume to his voice.

Franziska was stunned. For the first time in all of their years together, Franz had actually ordered her to do something. He'd enunciated each word succinctly, and he'd gripped both of her arms so athletically that she felt fixed to the ground. For a moment, she was at a loss for words. Then:

"All right. If you feel that strongly about it, I'll go," she said meekly.

As Franz released her, he realized how firm he'd been and was inwardly sorry. But he refrained from revealing his true feelings because he wanted her to leave at once.

"Go back to the house, pack, and leave," he said much more amiably. "There's some money in the pocket of my robe in the closet. Take enough for the train fare and a taxi. After I finish the performance, I'll do exactly what you're doing. I should be just a few hours behind you."

"Okay. . . . But you never told me . . . what did Arnold say?"

"He said that he and Klara are moving to Prague."

"They're giving everything up?"

"Yes, I think so. . . . Some Sudeten Germans have been boycotting their business. Arnold didn't tell me the specifics. . . . They'll call us as soon as they're settled."

"Oh, how awful," Franziska uttered, a worried look crossing her face.

"But now, it's time for you to take care of yourself," Franz said, softening and placing his arms around her. "You must go, and I must perform. I'll see you much later."

"Try to concentrate on your singing," Franziska said. "That's all that you can really do. . . . And let me do most of the worrying."

Franz exuded a short laugh of sarcasm, kissed her, and went back into his dressing room. She left the theater, took a taxicab back to the house, and packed the few things that she'd brought with her.

By this time, Franz was waiting nervously in the wings. The Count was serenading Rosina in German, even though *Barber* was then usually sung in Italian. Figaro then described the joys of being a barber and how indispensable he was while singing the aria, "Platz dem Faktotum" ("Largo al factotum"). And then Franz entered as Dr. Bartolo to check up on Rosina because he'd locked her in under house arrest with orders that no one was to be admitted. Then he took a series of quick short steps to exit and plan their wedding.

Another lyrical serenade followed with the Count masquerading as the poor student, Lindoro. Then Rosina wrote a love letter to him and sang one of the most glittering coloratura arias in all of opera: "Eine Stimme hört' ich eben," or in Italian: "Una voce poco fa." Don Basilio, the music teacher, hammed it up while advising Dr. Bartolo to spread malicious rumors about the Count to put a halt to his amorous intentions toward Rosina, but Bartolo simply wanted to marry her, so after a long pause, he responded with a "No" that made the audience laugh.

Then he sang "To a doctor of my standing," threatening Rosina for being distrustful and for deceiving him by corresponding with someone else.

The audience was engrossed. Franz as Dr. Bartolo sang quicker and quicker, and every syllable was understandable. It was as if he was on a race track. Well, he kind of was. He wanted to get out of the theater, catch a train, and go back to Prague.

At about that time, Franziska was taking a taxi to the train station. She was sitting anxiously in the back seat, trying to remain calm by imagining Franz as Dr. Bartolo.

But the Count's disguise as a drunken soldier with a painted moustache and patch on his eye drew all the attention. Chaos ensued when the soldier was arrested, having to privately reveal his true identity.

The curtain closed on the first act, and the cast filed onto the apron of the stage. The applause was gratifying. However, as Franz looked out at the tastefully-designed ivory auditorium, accented in gold and red with fastidiously-placed decorative sconces, masks, and figurines, he had a feeling that this could be his last performance in the theater. He went back to his dressing room for the duration of the intermission, hoping that Franziska was well on her way back to Prague.

She wasn't. She had just reached the small dilapidated train station in Aussig. To get to the terminal building, she had to walk on some dried-up soil and on a few boards that served as flimsy bridges over some sludgy mud. She purchased her ticket, then went outside and sat on a bench by the tracks to wait for her train. There were people all around, but she still felt terribly alone.

Franz was thinking about her while he was in the wings waiting for his next entrance.

More chaos was brewing. The Count was disguised as a music teacher. It was time for Franz as Dr. Bartolo to sing another aria. He didn't like the music Rosina was singing, so he sang her an old-fashioned song of his own choosing, inserting her name into the tune as an endearment, which was just before Figaro was about to shave him.

Rosina and the Count were making plans to elope then. They were married by a notary, and all Dr. Bartolo could do was congratulate them.

Franziska was still waiting for the train. It finally arrived. All of the people who were standing and sitting, including Franziska, ran or walked quickly over some tracks and through the dried-up soil to board the train. They all seemed to fear that it would leave without them. They had dispersed into different cars, so once Franziska was in her compartment, she was all alone again. As usual, she was carrying a coat, which she placed next to her. She laid her suitcase by her feet, feeling a little dizzy, since her body was curved downward when the train moved out of the station. Trying to capture her equilibrium, she jolted her body to an erect position, which only served to make her feel more unstable. She took a deep breath and then sat very still. Then she suddenly smiled.

She could imagine Franz on the apron of the stage taking his final curtain call and receiving a warm applause.

But as Franz glanced out into the house, he could see that it wasn't full. Some people with tickets must have decided to forgo the performance in light of the political developments.

At that very moment, Franziska was traveling through a tunnel. She felt like everything was closing in on her, probably because the walls of the tunnel seemed extremely close to the train. But it was dark, so maybe they really weren't so near, but then again, maybe they were. . . . Ah, light.

Franz didn't stick around. He changed back into his civilian clothes and was out of the theater before the others had even reached the dressing room. He did exactly what Franziska had done a few hours before. While riding in the train back to Prague, he kept trying to evaluate the situation. Yes, he wanted to leave Czechoslovkia and go to a country where his life wouldn't always be threatened. But he knew his options were limited with a German passport. And then, of course, he only wanted to move to a country where he could earn a living. Singing was his only way out. He needed to find an opera company in a safe country that would offer him a contract. He needed to proceed in that direction immediately, he thought.

When he arrived home, Franziska was cuddled up in a warm robe and slippers, drinking a cup of hot cocoa.

"Well, don't you look comfortable," Franz said as he opened the door and set down his suitcase. "Are you all right?"

"I'm fine," Franziska replied. "How about you?"

"I don't know yet. I haven't had time to think about it. . . . So . . . were we overreacting to a rumor or what?"

"I don't know. I haven't heard anything about troop movement on the radio, just the usual news about tensions between the Czechs and the Sudeten Germans."

"Well, we didn't make the whole thing up. We'll see what's in the paper tomorrow."

"By the way, Franz, how did you sing?"

"I'm not sure. All the tones came out of my mouth. . . . I stayed with the orchestra and we both ended at the same time, so I guess that I made it through okay. I know that I was on the stage today, yet part of me can't remember a thing. . . . However I do recall what I was thinking about on the train."

"What was that?"

"I want both of us to get out of Prague," Franz said, sitting down on the sofa next to Franziska. "I'm going to write Wilhelm Stein tomorrow. I want him to try to get me a contract in a country where we'll be out of danger. . . . And I'm also going to write André Mertens. He has his own agency, and he's the general European representative of the Columbia Concerts Corporation. He heard me sing in Vienna and wanted to try to place me, but Wilhelm Stein had already come through. Maybe he'll be able to get me an engagement."

"Come on, Franz. Let's call it a day."

"André Mertens really liked my voice. I'm sure he'll be interested in helping me."

"Franz, I said let's call it a day," Franziska repeated, unbuttoning Franz's raincoat. It wasn't raining, but Franz had decided to wear the coat over his pants and shirt rather than pack or carry it. Franziska slipped her arms under the coat and around Franz's ribcage, bending and lifting her legs onto the sofa. "Come on . . . relax," she said, placing the side of her face on Franz's chest. "I'm tired."

"So am I," he responded, kissing the top of her head. "So . . . am . . . I."

CHAPTER EIGHTEEN

Mobilization Day

Prague, Czechoslovakia
1 May to 21 May 1938

$\mathcal{F}$ranz mailed the letters promptly after his ordeal in Aussig. Then strangely within a few days, probably by coincidence, he received a letter from Wilhelm Stein. Stein was attempting to secure him a contract for the following season with the Palestine Opera, a fledgling company with a new soon-to-be director, Walter Eberhard, who was based in Rome. The letter said that Franz would be engaged to sing sixteen performances each month in the cities of Jerusalem, Tel Aviv, and Haifa; and in the summer, there would be open-air performances in Egypt and Greece. He didn't know which roles or operas he'd be performing, only that the summer repertoire would be *Salome*, *Aïda,* and *Samson et Dalila*, and he'd be asked to sing some of the roles in French or Italian. Although the work ahead of him would be demanding, he wanted the contract, for it would be his ticket out of Prague.

They were on their way to the Uruguayan Embassy, although they weren't exactly sure why they were going there. Franz's uncle, Doktor Walter Werner, had gone to school with the consul general when both of them were young boys growing up in Moravia. Franz's mother had told Franz to pay Uncle Walter's old friend a visit, but Franz had never gotten around to it. Now Franz thought that the gentleman could possibly offer him some sound advice about moving to another country.

On the way there, Franz and Franziska stopped at the café in the Koruna Palace, which had never been the residence of sovereignty, but rather, the home of an insurance company. The bottom portion of the building was structurally simple with large glass panels and windows, while the upper part was much more elaborate; and, as one might expect, atop the domed tower, there rested a *koruna* (a crown). Franz and Franziska often went to the café at the street level – actually it was much more informal than a café – because they loved the potato pancakes. On this Monday, Franz was paying the woman behind the counter with four Czechoslovak korun when someone tapped him on the shoulder.

"Franz! Franz! Is it really you?" the person said.

Franz turned around, and low and behold, it was his old childhood friend, Fritz Sachsel. "Fritz," he said smiling, reaching out to shake his chum's hand. But instead of reciprocating, Fritz grasped both of Franz's arms in a momentary strong masculine hug, and then he kissed Franziska's hand jovially.

"We're going to sit right over there," Franz said, pointing. "When you get your food, why don't you join us?"

Franz hadn't seen his friend in many years, but he knew that Fritz was a Czech citizen. They sat and talked for a while. Franz told him about his singing career, and Fritz told Franz about his job as the representative of a fine line of men's shoes. They reminisced about the five o'clock tea so many years before when Franz had first met Franziska. And they exchanged addresses and telephone numbers, vowing to rekindle their lost friendship.

After they said good-bye and walked out onto Wenceslas Square, they separated, and Franz and Franziska continued on their way to the Uruguayan Embassy. It wasn't at all what they'd expected. It was in a residential area of Prague, and it was located in a two-story house. Once inside, they observed that the building was indeed reserved for business matters.

"I would like to meet with the consul general . . . Herr Walter Landsmann," Franz told the secretary, fumbling in his pocket for the small piece of paper with the consul general's name on it. "Would you be kind enough to tell him that my name is Franz Jung and that I'm Walter Werner's nephew?"

"Of course," the secretary answered. "Please take a seat."

A few minutes later, an extremely well-dressed gentleman with graying hair approached.

"*Guten Tag!* I'm Walter Landsmann," he said, shaking Franz's hand. "It's so nice to meet you. Won't you please come with me?"

Franz and Franziska nodded and followed the consul general into a modest-sized well-appointed office with pictures of Uruguay hanging from the texturized walls. He motioned them to sit down while he positioned himself behind his desk. "So how is your uncle?" he asked. "I haven't talked to him in months."

"Well actually, I haven't spoken to him for a while either," Franz said. "I've been in Prague since last August singing at the German Theater."

That little tidbit of information sparked an intense discussion about opera between the two while Franziska sat silently listening. "And who is this lovely lady you are with?" the consul general finally asked.

"Oh, I'm so sorry for not having introduced you to her earlier," Franz said. "This is Franziska Perger. She means everything to me."

"So how can I help you both?"

"I'm really not sure," Franz answered, explaining his situation: that he wanted to leave Prague and hoped to secure a contract in a more politically-desirable country.

"I assume that you both have passports."

"Yes," Franz responded. "Franziska has a Czech passport, so she'll be able to go anywhere. But because of the *Anschluss*, I have to exchange my Austrian passport for one that's German, and I know it will be very hard for me to get a visa. That's why I want to secure a singing contract in another country. Then I'd only need a work permit."

"It sounds like you've thought everything through . . . except the most pessimistic eventuality: what if you don't get the contract?"

Franz didn't say anything. He couldn't think of an answer. "I don't know," he finally said.

"The only thing I can do is offer you both visas to Uruguay."

"That's very generous of you," Franz responded. "But I simply have to wait to determine if we'd need them."

"I understand," Walter Landsmann said. "But you should plan for the worst possible outcome. Apply for visas. That's the only way to secure your safety."

"Thank you for your advice. I'm going to give it a lot of thought," Franz remarked.

"And one more thing . . . you know that you're going to be traveling, don't you?"

"Yes."

"Possibly on a boat?"

"Yes."

"Well, I don't mean to pry into your personal affairs, but you said that Franziska means everything to you; is that correct?"

"Yes, of course," Franz replied, looking at Franziska with deep affection in his eyes.

"Then let me suggest that if indeed you do love each other, you might consider getting married. Maybe I'm a bit stuffy and old-fashioned, but it just doesn't look appropriate for two young people to travel together unless they're joined in holy matrimony."

Franz and Franziska looked at each other with a strange smile on their faces as if marriage had never even entered their minds. Every young girl dreams of her wedding day, and Franziska was no exception. But the only time she really ever thought about it was when her mother asked. And as for Franz, somewhere just outside of his deep subconscious, he'd planned to wed Franziska when he could adequately support her. But most of the time, his thoughts were elsewhere. In his eyes, they were already married, and they didn't need a piece of paper to prove it. As for Franziska, she felt much the same.

"Thank you again for your advice," Franz said rising from his seat, followed by Franziska. "This just might be the right time to make our union legal."

"I'm pleased," Walter Landsmann said, standing and walking the couple out of his office and back into the waiting area. "And if you change your mind about the visa, don't hesitate to let me know."

"Thank you," Franz said. And the two left the embassy with a new outlook for the future.

That evening, Franz and Franziska decided to get married. There was no romantic overture that culminated in a grand proposal. The decision was simply the natural outcome of a rational discussion.

The next day they went to the magistrate's office in Smíchov with their birth certificates and citizenship papers. They filled out a few forms and were told to bring two witnesses on the day of the wedding, which was scheduled for Saturday, the twenty-first of May.

That Tuesday evening before the wedding, Franz phoned his mother with the good news. She was surprised to hear from him by telephone because he hadn't called since the *Anschluss*. She was very happy for the two of them, but sorry that she couldn't attend. Unlike Franz, Franziska refrained from calling her family. She'd simply write her mother a letter after the wedding was over.

As for the witnesses, Franz wanted to ask the Weinraubs, but he didn't know how to reach them. However he did know how to get in touch with Fritz Sachsel. Fritz immediately accepted the invitation and told Franz that he'd be there at noon.

But the wedding was not the foremost issue on the couple's minds. On Wednesday, Franz and Franziska went to the United States Embassy to apply for visas. They were told that each of their names would be registered with a quota number, and that the number would be honored by any U.S. embassy or consulate in the world. Franz realized that it could take years to attain an American visa, but he wanted a place on the list.

On the Thursday before the wedding, Klara Weinraub called with her family's new address and telephone number. After Franziska told her about the wedding, Klara explained that she and her husband were going through a period of turmoil, trying to get settled after abandoning their home and business, but she said that she would send her sister, who was the wife of a cantor, so that her family would be represented. She told Franziska that she'd heard a radio commentator report that a newspaper in Leipzig had confirmed the deployment of German troops along the border.

Although dismayed, Franz and Franziska spent the next day preparing for the wedding. In the morning, the bride and groom-to-be went to a jewelry store, where Franz rented a simple gold wedding ring for himself, and purchased one for Franziska. He never wore jewelry, so why waste the money? When they arrived home, Franziska made some last-minute alterations on the dressy ivory crepe suit she planned to wear, while Franz opened the letter that he'd just received from his mother. He read it out loud:

> *My dearest children,*
>
> *I am so very happy for both of you because I have known for a very long time that you are meant to be together always. Marriage is a very sacred union, and you must treat it so. You must never take each other for granted, but must always be responsive to each other's needs and desires. There must always be peace and understanding between you. If one of you is weak or in pain, the other must be strong. You must be willing to go through thick and thin together. And now, my children, a mother's word to each of you.*
>
> *My dear Franziska, I greet you now as my third child. You will receive from me the same love from my heart that I give to Ilona and Franz. I believe that I know my son, and can honestly say that you are getting a husband with good character, heart, and spirit: a man who will always support and love you.*
>
> *You, Franziska, I do not know so well. Therefore I beg you to be a kind, selfless partner. Before you left Vienna, you told me that you loved my Franz. Make him a home that is untroubled and serene, for life has many obstacles, and if your home is tranquil, he will have the strength to protect the both of you and overcome the hurdles. I know that it is hard to be the wife of an artist. If there is harmony in your home life, my Franz will always be in top form. You are, Franziska, a very capable person. You are beautiful, cultured and adept at all of the social graces. Use your talents well to help him, and he will be yours for the rest of your lives.*

And now, my dear Franz, I must remind you as well to be loving and tolerant. I know that you are a kind, giving person with a full heart, but I also know that you can be mischievous and sometimes a little quarrelsome. Do not allow that side of you to spring forth, for you will only be sorry. Try always to be the caring, sensitive person that you are. You will now have a lovely and gracious partner with whom to share life. You must be grateful for your good fortune – always.

And now, my children, I ask both of you to live modestly. You see now how difficult life can be when you have little, so you must create a basis from which to start. And remember that your finances should never intrude into the spirituality of your union. You must trust each other with your hearts and souls, and no person or thing will ever have the power to draw you asunder.

Congratulations, my children!

Your loving Mama

Franz folded the letter and sat on the sofa next to Franziska. She had stopped sewing and was listening intently. "How moving," she said. "I really feel like I'm part of the family."

"That's because you are," Franz said, placing the letter back in the envelope. "And there are telegrams here from Mama, Hans, and Ilona."

"Everyone has made me feel so welcome," Franziska said, then went back to her sewing as Franz turned the knob on the radio.

"The Czech government has reason to believe that there is German troop movement at the border. After an emergency cabinet meeting, the government is calling for an immediate partial mobilization."

Franz and Franziska stared into each other's eyes. No words could describe the anguished expressions on their faces. They listened to the radio for a while and then decided to go outside to see how the public was reacting. They walked all the way to Wenceslas Square. There were taxis everywhere, and reservists were running in the streets to get to them so that they could report to their stations. The city was in a state of chaos.

Franz and Franziska watched the action like disturbed spectators at the scene of a fire. They stopped at a small market on the way back to pick up some cold meats and vegetables. The events of the next few days seemed uncertain, and their icebox was almost completely empty. When they reached the check-out counter and began talking to the cashier in German, she responded with: "*Nerozumím.*"

"What? She doesn't understand?" Franziska said to Franz. "She seemed to comprehend what I was saying just perfectly the other day."

"Yes, but you have to remember, my dearest, we're Germans to her and we represent the enemy." So Franz paid the bill and they walked out of the store.

When they arrived home, they turned on the radio again. A government spokesman was talking: "Tonight, the Czech government asks that all of your windows remain covered, all drapes and shades drawn, so that our glorious city of Prague seemingly disappears into the darkness. The government does not want to alarm you. This is only a precautionary measure. If there is any military action, and we seriously hope that there will not be, the activity would most likely take place in the Sudetenland. We assure you that our defenses are strong in the border regions along our Czech Maginot Line. And although we cannot guarantee your safety, you can rest assured that your protection is our primary mission."

Franz pulled down all of the shades and drew the drapes. Just a few hours before, Franziska had finally started to feel a little fluttery about the wedding. But now, she wasn't even sure that there would be one.

The radio was on all night. Neither was able to sleep. By morning, all of the army units had been mobilized. Should they go through with the wedding, or shouldn't they? What if the magistrate's office was closed? They decided to go ahead with their plans. At eleven o'clock, they were dressed: Franz, in a charcoal-gray suit; and Franziska, in her ivory-colored two-piece crepe bridal ensemble. One last touch: a matching crepe hat with a short, sheer tulle veil, and Franziska was ready to be a bride.

They walked to the magistrate's office. Fritz Sachsel was waiting in front, but then ran toward them until he reached them. There were very few people to be seen, and most of the stores appeared closed. They walked on some cobblestones, but Franziska's heel was suddenly lodged between two of them. Franz had been holding his arm in hers and continued walking until he felt her pulling. He helped her out of her momentary, yet familiar dilemma, and the three proceeded up a few stairs and into a small sitting room where another couple was already waiting. Franziska asked the bride what time her wedding was scheduled for. One o'clock: The couple had come early. Franziska began to feel nervous. *Where was Klara Weinraub's sister? Where was their second witness?*

Then a woman in a lovely pink dress approached from a doorway. She called their names and asked them to come with their witnesses into the adjoining room. They entered it. *Where was the second witness?*

The woman asked them to sit down. She took some information and then described the ceremony.

Then all three people in the wedding party were told to stand and proceed to another portion of the room, which was really not much larger than a spacious office. Fritz Sachsel and the nicely dressed woman began walking toward the magistrate. But as Franziska started to rise, Franz held her back for a moment.

"This is your last chance to change your mind," he said softly. "Now you have a Czech passport; nothing will happen to you. But if you marry me, you'll be forced to renounce your Czech citizenship. You'll be considered German with a German passport."

"I know, Franz. I want to marry you," Franziska said.

"Shouldn't we wait? Nothing would change between us. Something might happen to me . . . but as long as you have your Czech passport, you'll be able to find a safe haven."

Franziska's eyes started to fill with tears. "No!" she said, firmly. "If something happens to you, I want it to happen to me, too. I don't want to be alone. I want to be with you always."

Franz took out a handkerchief and wiped the tears from her eyes. "It's going to be all right," he whispered. "I'll marry you. I just wanted you to know the risks."

Franziska sniffled and nodded her head up and down attempting to break a smile. Franz helped her up, and as they walked toward the others, he began to realize how much she loved him. She was actually willing to sacrifice her life so that they could be together. Franz would never forget what she had said to him.

Once in front of the magistrate, the couple's composure returned, and Klara Weinraub's sister Ida came rushing through the door excusing herself. She was promptly directed to stand to the right of the bride and groom, next to Fritz Sachsel. Franz and Franziska looked at each other and smiled as the wedding ceremony commenced, with the magistrate speaking in Czech, and the nicely dressed woman acting as an interpreter.

"We are assembled here today to unite in matrimony Franz Jung and Franziska Perger," the magistrate said in Czech, and the interpreter repeated in German.

"The contract of marriage must be taken extremely seriously, with full realization of the responsibilities and obligations inherent within it," they continued.

"Do you, Franz Jung, voluntarily take this woman, Franziska Perger, to be your lawfully wedded wife? . . ."

Franz and Franziska said their wedding vows, placed wedding rings on each other's fingers, and were pronounced husband and wife. Franz kissed his bride tenderly. They signed their wedding certificate, followed by their two witnesses, and the group walked in a short procession out of the room, through the little waiting area, down the few steps, and out. The street had been so quiet before, but suddenly some photographers lunged forward to take their wedding pictures. "No, no!" Franz said, holding one of his arms up in front while wrapping the other around Franziska's waist and walking briskly in the sunlight. But the photographers were like paparazzi deluging a dignitary. "No, no!" Franz repeated. The wedding party then jumped into a taxi and was whisked off to a nearby café.

The Café Mánes was one of Franz and Franziska's favorite spots because of its lovely view of the Moldau River. The two-story white Functionalist building was unlike any other in Prague. It was much simpler and more modern, creatively constructed to bridge a channel of the river from the embankment to the Slovanský Island. The building was situated on the site of the city's ancient waterworks, and only the old medieval tank tower still remained, fitting incongruously into the setting. What made the building even more interesting to Franz and Franziska was the group of people who frequented inside its unconventional walls: some, belonging to the artists' association on the premises, displaying their works in the exhibition gallery; some, part of Prague's literary, cultural or political intelligentsia; and some, simply looking for a good time.

Franz and Franziska usually came to the café in the evenings because a singer performed popular songs on the café's diminutive stage, often in English. The atmosphere was lively, and for Franz, the music was quite a diversion from Mozart and Strauss.

On this, their wedding day – the afternoon of the mobilization – the café was relatively empty. Seated at a table with a view of the Moldau and the island, they tried to be personable hosts to their two guests, but no one really felt much like celebrating. Everyone just wanted to go home and turn on the radio. They perked up slightly when Günther Maher, the choral director and conductor, arrived with a bouquet of flowers and a card with congratulatory wishes from all of the regulars at the New German Theater and the Stadttheater in Aussig. But the topic of discussion soon pivoted back to the mobilization, if there would be a war, and how much they all really wanted to emigrate from Prague.

The party – if you could call it that – broke up at half past three. When Franz and Franziska arrived back at their apartment, they found an uplifting congratulatory letter from Ilona and Hans. They changed into some comfortable clothes, and that evening they sat on the sofa listening to the radio.

The French and the British governments had exerted pressure on the Germans. Their ambassadors had warned the Germans that military action against Czechoslovakia would undoubtedly lead to a European war.

"You see," Franziska said. "I told you that Hitler's troops wouldn't be able to march into Czechoslovakia without opposition. I hope that all of this diplomatic support frightens him. . . . Oh, Franz, I don't want to be here if there's going to be a war."

"Let's go to sleep, Franziska. I don't want to worry about it anymore tonight."

"Do you feel any different, Franz?"

"What do you mean?"

"Well, now that we're married."

"No, I feel exactly the same."

"Me, too. . . . I couldn't have loved you any more before, and I couldn't possibly love you any more now."

"That's my old Franziska," Franz said, starting to smooch with his bride on the couch.

"This is our wedding night, Frau Franziska Jung. Why don't you escort me into the bedroom and show me just exactly how much you really *do* love me."

And for a few hours that night, they completely forgot the difficult, trying day that they'd spent. It was the twenty-first of May in 1938. It was a beautiful day. It was the day that they became husband and wife.

CHAPTER NINETEEN

Broken Glass and a Café

Prague, Czechoslovakia
May to December 1938

A week after Franz and Franziska's wedding, life in Prague was back to normal. The German government had resolutely denied any buildup of troops along the border and had assured the Czechs that there was no hostile intent to militarily occupy any part of Czechoslovakia.

The season at the Stadttheater in Aussig was finished. The season at the New German Theater in Prague lasted until the end of June. However judging from the anti-German feeling displayed in the city by the Czechs – as was evident when Franz and Franziska had tried to speak German to the cashier in the market – Franz approached each performance as if it could be his last.

One afternoon he was standing by the piano with his score of Wagner's *Das Rheingold* on the piano's music stand. He was practicing the role of Alberich – singing the passage which occurs when Wotan, the ruler of the gods, sets Alberich free after seizing the powerful "Rhinegold ring" from him, the ring which Alberich forged after promising to renounce love.

"W*ie durch Fluch er mir geriet, verflucht sei dieser Ring!*" Franz was singing. "As through a curse it became mine, cursed be this ring!"

There was a knock at the door. Franziska came out of the kitchen.

221

She looked at Franz and they shrugged their shoulders. The knock subsequently turned into more of a pounding sound.

"*Policie! Policie!*" a man said.

Franziska suddenly grew pale. What had they done?

Franz opened the door. "*Nerozumím,*" he said in Czech. Then in German: "*Ich spreche nur Deutsch.*"

The man wasn't wearing a uniform; he must have been a plainclothes man. He apparently realized that if he didn't speak German, he wasn't going to have a conversation. So he was suddenly able to speak Franz's language.

"*Sie konnen nicht in Deutsch singen,*" he said. "You cannot sing in German. If you do, I will have to arrest you."

Franz appeared outwardly composed, although seething inside. His neighbors must have called the police.

"I am an opera singer here in Prague," he explained. "I don't agree with what the Germans are trying to do to Czechoslovakia. But I am rehearsing the role of Alberich, and Wagner is always sung in German."

Franz seemed to have appeased the police detective because he nodded and said, "Try not to sing in German any more than you have to, and try to keep your voice down." Then he turned around and left.

Franz was incensed. So far in his life he'd only had to deal with anti-Semitism. Now he was being discriminated against, not because he was Jewish, but because he spoke German. It was too much. He had to get out. He hoped that the contract with the Palestine Opera would materialize.

The preliminary agreement arrived in the mail almost immediately thereafter. The pay was eighteen pounds per month and included travel expenses from Trieste to Franz's destination. The exact length of the season would be specified in the final contract, which Walter Eberhard wrote would be forwarded in July. But there was no stipend for Franziska, and Franz didn't know what would be required for her to enter Palestine. Yet he had to be satisfied. Wilhelm Stein was doing his utmost, and Franz was grateful.

But he was worried: worried about the future and worried about his family in Vienna. Hans Beck's father had died, and Hans was making plans to leave Vienna with Ilona; his mother, Else; and Olga Jung. Ilona wrote Franz a letter which she hoped he'd understand. There was no return address.

9 June 1938

Dear Franz,

Expect a package of Else's Sachertorte on Tuesday, the four-teenth of June. Else will be visiting her relatives, and she will deliver it to you personally, probably in the early afternoon. She told me that she has all of the ingredients; and a wealthy, valuable friend is helping her to refine the recipe, from beginning to end.

Else knows how much singing means to you, so she's shipping some props to your friends at the Metropolitan Opera. I think that Hans will do the same.

Else will see you soon!

Love,

Ilona

Franz read the letter to Franziska. "That's tomorrow," he said. "They're going to be here tomorrow."

"What did Ilona mean by '*relatives*'?" Franziska asked.

"Oh, Hans has an aunt in Prague."

"And who is this '*wealthy, valuable friend*'?"

"He's probably the person Hans is paying to lead them across the border; and I guess they're shipping all of their furniture to America, probably to New York."

"I'd better clean up the apartment because it looks like we're about to have overnight guests."

"It's just going to be for a couple of days until we can help them find another place. Of course that might be difficult since they won't be here legally. I don't think that Else and my mother even have passports, let alone visas."

"I think your mother should stay with us," Franziska said. "She might feel more comfortable here. And Else can stay with Ilona and Hans."

"That's a good idea. Thanks for being so thoughtful."

Franz didn't sleep that night. At about five o'clock in the morning, he tried to picture what his mother and the Becks were doing. He imagined that they were probably already assembled together with a scant amount of luggage. Later, when he was dressed and sitting on the sofa, he visualized that they were being driven to a secluded, unguarded area along the border. Then their *"friend"* was walking them across. He kept on fantasizing. Someone was taking them to a railway station. They were boarding a train in Brünn. He fell asleep on the sofa.

"Hey, what are you doing?" Franziska said, nudging him awake.

"Oh, I must have dozed off. . . . Are they here?"

"No, not yet. But they could be. It's already half past twelve."

"Don't let's eat until they get here," Franz said. "They might be hungry."

At one o'clock, they still hadn't arrived. At two o'clock, Franziska brought Franz a roll with *Schinken*. He only ate part of it.

"Where could they be? Maybe something horrible has happened to them," he said with an alarmed tone in his voice.

"Don't jump to conclusions this early. Try to stay calm."

"I can't. . . . If they've been caught, they could be on their way to a concentration camp."

"Why don't we listen to some music?" Franziska said, turning on the radio.

"I can't listen to lullabies now. Can't you see that I'm excited?"

Franz switched off the radio and paced around the room. . . . It was three o'clock. He tried to study some music. . . . It was four. He read the newspaper. . . . It was five o'clock. Then six. Then seven. Finally the phone rang. He grabbed it.

"Hello, Mother? . . . Oh, Ilona! It's so good to hear your voice. Where are you? . . . At home? What happened? . . . I see. . . . But you're all right. You didn't catch cold. . . . Good. . . . Please write soon. . . . Yes, I will. . . . Yes. . . . And don't forget to tell her that I send my love too. . . . Good-bye, Ilona."

Franz hung up the receiver.

"So they're all right?" Franziska asked.

"I think so. Ilona said that they left and it was raining, so they went back. . . . She said she'd send more details by mail. But judging from her letters, I think I'll have to wait until I see her to get the true story."

And Franz was right. The letter came a few days later.

15 June 1938

Dear Franz and Franzi,

Else couldn't visit her relatives after all. Just as well. She didn't really have the best ingredients for the Sachertorte. Her wealthy friend wasn't very valuable because his recipe produced a bitter dessert, so Else gave it to him as a sample. Then they left, and just as Else thought that they were traveling on the right path to her relatives, her friend bumped into some of his acquaintances. And then there was so much thunder and lightning that Else grew very frightened and walked all the way home. Else hopes to find a friend with a more foolproof recipe next time. And then she'll bring you her Sachertorte personally.

We plan to take very good care of ourselves and hope that you do the same.

Love,

Ilona

"Look at this," Franz said to Franzi, giving her the letter. "What do you think it means?"

"It's perfectly clear to me," Franziska said after reading it. "The person who was supposed to take them over the border handed them over to the Germans, and they were forced to walk back. But I don't know what the '*thunder and lightning*' means. There must have been some shooting."

"That's how I see it, too. But Ilona said that everyone's all right.

Oh, I don't know. . . . But can you imagine? They must have walked for hours. And my mother isn't so young anymore. She's almost sixty-two."

"Well, let's just hope that they're more successful the next time."

In July, Walter Eberhard sent the final contract to Wilhelm Stein; and as Franz's representative, Stein signed it. But because of subsequent letters, Franz began to have reservations about the whole project. As more and more Jews were fleeing the Nazis and immigrating to Palestine, the Arabs there were becoming increasingly antagonistic, stepping up their attacks to deter the area from becoming a Jewish national home; and the British government, which ruled the territory, appeared ready to capitulate to some of the Arabs' demands.

Wilhelm Stein had written Franz that the Palestine Opera was being funded by a worldwide Jewish organization. Eberhard was still in negotiations in August, and Franz wondered if the company's season would ever truly come to fruition. Then Eberhard wrote him that he could only afford to pay fourteen pounds per month, and that as a requirement of entry into Palestine, Franziska would need to bring in thirty. However in spite of the amendments, Franz didn't write or say anything to either Stein or Eberhard. He just wanted to sit tight.

Franzi was unhappy in their apartment and wanted to be more centrally located. Some singers had moved out of Petrská Twenty-Four, so Franz and Franziska moved back.

That September, violence again intensified in the Sudetenland. Franz and Franzi listened as speeches were broadcast from a rally in Nürnberg.

"A petty segment of Europe is harassing the human race," espoused Hermann Göring. "This miserable pygmy race [the Czechs] is oppressing a cultured people, and behind it is Moscow and the eternal mask of the Jew devil."

Later Hitler demanded justice. "The Germans in Czechoslovakia are neither defenseless nor abandoned," he shouted. "Of that you can rest assured."

The speeches triggered more rebellion in the Sudetenland, thus compelling the Czech government to declare martial law. British Prime Minister Neville Chamberlain met with Hitler twice, then tried each time to convince the French and Czech governments that the Führer's demands should be satisfied. But a European war seemed imminent.

Franz and Franziska were desperate. The Palestine Opera season still wasn't confirmed. The atmosphere was frightening, and the fear of death was in the air.

But it was more pronounced in the minds of the victims in Vienna. Nazi leader Karl Adolf Eichmann had set up an office for Jewish emigration, relieving Jews of their assets and issuing them exit permits and passports. But the assembly-line hothouse actually placed the Jews in a precarious pressure-cooker-like situation. Although they wanted to leave Vienna, the entrance doors to most other countries were closed. So Eichmann's office often led them directly to a concentration camp instead.

Convinced that they would succeed in escaping the foreseeable doom, Olga Jung and the Becks secured what they needed and firmly decided that they would immigrate to the United States. Just as Franz and Franziska had done in Prague, they registered their names at the United States Consulate. After talking to numerous people, Hans finally believed that he knew the way out. It was so simple. Their timing was perfect. They boarded a train and went directly to Budapest. They didn't even need visas. Hans represented companies in different countries; so when he arrived there, he collected what was due him, and the group of four stayed in a fine hotel.

When they telephoned Franz with the news of their whereabouts, Franz was elated. Of course they didn't know which route they would take to enter the United States. But they had some time now. They were free.

Franz knew then that he wanted to be with his family. The United States would be his only destination. He notified Wilhelm Stein and André Mertens of his decision and then spent all of his time trying to map out a course of direction for himself and Franziska.

But the threat of war was still hovering over Czechoslovakia like a soaring, voracious eagle spreading its broad and sweeping wings over a target. Czech, British, and French troops were being readily mobilized in anticipation of the probable German onslaught. There seemed to be no turning back. Finally one last attempt for peace: Hitler agreed to a conference in Munich with the heads of state of England, France, and Italy. They gave him everything they thought he wanted. Having been abandoned, the Czech government was forced to yield. The Czechs had lost the Sudetenland and all of their fortifications along the German border. They were left defenseless.

Walter Eberhard wrote Franz that he was unable to ease the financial demands to secure Franziska's entry into Palestine, and Franz would not leave without her. The United States would be his destination.

But there was more. When Franz rang his sister one afternoon at the Hotel Astoria, he was told that the Beck party had already checked out.

"Where did they go?" he exclaimed excitedly to Franziska. "They would have called us if they could. Something horrible must have happened."

Then a couple of days later, another telephone conversation: "We're in Milano," Ilona said to Franz. "We've been through quite an ordeal, but I guess we're closer to America now than we were before."

"What happened?" Franz asked.

"Two Hungarian police officers came to arrest us."

"Why?"

"They said that we were in Budapest illegally."

"Well, were you?"

"Yes, in fact, we were."

"But you said that you didn't even need visas."

"That's true. But when we crossed the border and stopped in Hegye-shalom, the immigration officer stamped our passports and told us to register in the government office when we arrived in Budapest."

"Did you?"

"Yes. . . . At first we were told that we could stay for a week. Then we went back and were granted two more. But the last time we tried, an official stamped our passports and wrote that there wouldn't be any more extensions and that we'd have to leave Budapest no later than the twenty-fifth of October. That only gave us one more week. Now where do you think we were going to go?"

"So?"

"So after the week was up, the authorities came and said that they were taking us back to the border. So Hans made a quick phone call to the owner of one of the companies he represents, and then we were *escorted* to the railway station."

"And . . ."

"When we got there, Hans's business friend was graciously waiting for us. He shook hands with Hans and passed him a large sum of money. Feeling exhausted and helpless, we boarded the train with one of the police officers, and then Hans did something quite inventive. Well maybe it wasn't so inventive. It was quite logical actually, but it was also a gamble."

"What did he do, Ilona?"

"He walked with the officer into the corridor of the train and offered him all of the money if he'd take us to a safe destination. Apparently the man didn't have a family because he agreed."

"How do you know that he didn't have a family?"

"He led us off the train and onto one that went through Yugoslavia into Trieste and to Milano. And then he decided not to go back. Anyway, we're here. We don't need visas and we're staying in a pensione."

"I'm very relieved," Franz said. "I was really worried."

"So were we. . . . Now tell me, little brother, what are your plans?"

"At the moment, we'll stay here in Prague. I don't want to leave until I have a strategy that will lead us to the United States. Milano just might be a way out for us too, but I want to go to Switzerland first."

"Yes, you must."

"So enjoy Milano and don't spend too much money at La Scala."

"We wouldn't dream of it, at least not until you're on the program."

"Maybe one day. . . . Franzi and I send our love to all of you."

"And the same from us to you."

"Good-bye, Ilona."

"Good-bye, little brother."

Franz hung up the receiver and told the whole story to Franziska.

"But why do you want to go to Switzerland?" she asked. Franz explained to her that his father had opened a bank account in Zürich before he died. And when Ilona married someone of substantial means, Franz's mother had given him the account. It didn't contain a vast sum of money, but enough to be extremely beneficial for a short duration. Olga had told Franz the secret account number, and he needed to go to the bank personally to withdraw or transfer the money. But he didn't want to make any plans yet. He wasn't ready.

On the eighth of November, the newspapers were filled with stories about the murder of Ernst vom Rath, a secretary in the German Embassy in Paris. The assassination was an act of protest by Polish student Herschel Grynszpan for the mistreatment of his parents, who were among thousands of Polish Jews who had been transported by the Nazis into labor camps.

Retaliation by the Nazis was swift. There were brutal attacks throughout Germany against the Jews. Synagogues, homes, and businesses were destroyed, the streets littered with shattered glass. Jews were killed; Jewish women, raped; and thousands were herded off to concentration camps.

Franziska cried when she heard the radio reports. "Can you imagine those poor women who were raped by those Nazi thugs," she said to Franz, "forcing themselves on those girls who were so helpless and exposed? The Nürnberg Laws forbade Aryans to have sex with Jews. Hitler's own people violated his orders, and I'll bet their filthy acts won't even be punished. Thank God my family is out of Vienna."

When Franziska had written her mother about her marriage, her mother had continued to correspond. Fritz had escaped to Paris. Paul found a way to travel along the Danube River via the Black Sea to the Mediterranean so that he crossed into Palestine.

Franziska's sister Lilly had placed an advertisement in an Australian newspaper requesting work as a housekeeper. Someone responded to the ad, and Lilly was on a boat to Australia just a few weeks after Franziska's wedding. Lilly met a gentleman on the boat who helped her find sponsors for the whole family, and all of the Pergers were in Australia.

But as Franz and Franziska listened to radio broadcasts during the weeks following the pogrom – *"Kristallnacht,"* it was called, "the Night of Broken Glass" – they feared for the lives of all of their relatives still remaining in Vienna. Even though they were no longer in close contact with these blood relations, their hearts ached when they learned how Jews were being discriminated against in every facet of society: barred from entering theaters, cinemas, libraries, and parks; prohibited from sitting on public benches; segregated into separate compartments on trains; and forced to give up the compensation they'd received from insurance companies for damages to their personal property.

Franz wanted to run or fly, if he had to, from any place that even remotely had the possibility of becoming another Vienna, and he believed that Prague could be next on the list. He received an agreement from Nelly Walter, André Mertens' associate, to sing two performances as Melot in *Tristan und Isolde* at the Grand-Théâtre in Bordeaux, and two as Masetto in *Don Giovanni*, one in Antwerp and one in Brussels. The engagements were spread between February and May. By that time, Hitler could occupy Czechoslovakia, he thought. No, he had to find a better way out than that.

He did a great deal of thinking and walking with Franziska the beginning of that cold December month. They went to cafés almost every night to hear what people were saying, hoping to learn the slightest bit of information which would be the key to opening a lock that would ultimately lead them safely out of Europe and to America. To Café Arco, to Café Slavia, to Café Continental – always listening, always looking; never caring if the coffee was stale or the service unfriendly – they just kept moving.

It was a Sunday night. The room was smoky, noisy, and crowded. They often went to this café located on the second floor of the Kolovrat Palace on Na příkopě. It was near Wenceslas Square, and it was the second home of many German-speaking Jewish immigrants. On this particular evening, the Café Continental was buzzing as usual. All of the small round tables and slightly larger booths were taken. It felt good to come in from the cold. Franz and Franziska were both bundled in warm woolen overcoats with their hands still plunged deep inside their pockets. Where were they going to sit? One of the waiters they knew greeted them.

"Come this way," the waiter said. "I think I see a table in the corner."

They followed him, unable to really discern the vacant table until they were almost in front of it. Franz helped Franziska off with her coat and placed it on a nearby coat rack, then hooked his coat right next to hers. They couldn't have been seated for more than a few minutes when the waiter approached them with another gentleman.

"You see how crowded it is," the waiter said to Franz. "Would you mind if this gentleman sits on the same table with you? He's been coming here for years."

Franz looked at Franziska. They really didn't want to have to indulge in a conversation with a stranger, but they agreed.

The gentleman sat down and introduced himself: Gottfried Holländer, he said his name was. He was a tall man of about fifty. He had a receding hairline and wore glasses, and from the curious glare in his eyes, Franz and Franziska couldn't decide whether he was suspicious-looking or trustworthy.

The waiter brought them each *eine Tasse Kaffee*. He knew them all so well that they didn't need to order. Then . . .

"The lust for power can be a terrible thing," the man said from out of nowhere.

"Yes," Franz agreed.

"Hitler and Franco. . . ."

"Yes, but no one is revolting against Hitler," Franz said. "He's seizing everything without the use of military force. At least in Spain, they're fighting 'til the finish."

"Oh, don't talk that way," Franziska said. "I wouldn't want to live in all of the upheaval, but apparently your cousin does."

"You have a cousin fighting in the Spanish Civil War?" Herr Holländer asked.

"Yes," Franz responded. "He's from Vienna and he's fighting against Franco on the side of the Loyalists."

"Fredl Gold?" the man said.

"Yes," Franz answered somewhat stunned.

"I know him. He's a very nice fellow . . . about five years older than you . . . speaks excellent Spanish. Seems his mother died when he was a child, and he was raised by his father and aunt. He has a brother and two sisters, I believe."

Maybe it was just a coincidence, Franz thought, but the table was suddenly much too small for the three of them.

"Fredl's father was a lawyer," the man continued. "He has an uncle and a number of aunts, I seem to recall. . . . Oh, you must be the opera singer."

That was enough. Franz's face grew flushed. He didn't say anything but quickly rose, grabbed the two coats from the coat rack, swung them over his arm, threw some coins on the table to pay for the *Kaffee*, and said: "We really must be going. A pleasure to have met you." He pulled Franziska's chair out as she stood, and they hastened out of the café and down the stairs. Franz threw Franziska's coat over her shoulders, and she slid her arms into the sleeves while trying to keep up with him as he left the building and began walking swiftly in the direction of their apartment. Her nose was cold, her ears were cold, and she was out of breath. She stopped to rest, leaning against the front of one of the bank buildings along Na příkopě. Franz turned around expecting her to be right behind him. When he discovered that she wasn't, he backtracked until he reached her.

"When I turned around, you weren't there," he said. "Are you all right?"

"You're the track runner, not me. . . . I'm out of breath and I have a side ache."

Franz put his arm around her waist, and they proceeded back to the apartment at a much slower pace. "You know . . . once you left the café, Herr Holländer wasn't about to follow you."

"You're right," Franz said as they were walking. "I was just so upset. How did he know so much about my family? We were set up. He must be in cahoots with the waiter. Maybe he's a Nazi spy. Maybe he would have forced us back to Vienna and then into a labor camp."

Once inside their apartment, Franz grew excited again. "I can't go around wondering who's looking over my shoulder. I refuse to become paranoid," he said. "Maybe we should try to leave Prague now, even if we don't know exactly where we're going."

"Don't be so rash about the situation. You have to think everything through logically."

"But how can I be logical when strangers know my life story better than I do," he said almost yelling.

"Franz, you're working yourself up so much that either you'll lose your voice or you'll get a heart attack."

"I'm too young to have a heart attack," Franz shouted.

"Oh no you're not," Franziska screamed back. And then both of them looked at each other and started to laugh. They laughed hysterically until the tears rolled down their cheeks. And when they were through laughing, they hugged and held on to each other.

"Oh, how I love you," Franz said. "Somehow, we're going to get through this."

She made him a cup of hot cocoa, and they cuddled up on the sofa. "Did anyone ever tell you that you have profoundly expressive onyx-colored almond-shaped eyes . . . and irresistible lips?" Franz asked alluringly.

"It seems that I might have heard that before."

Franz kissed her deeply. The telephone rang.

"Not now," he said. "I'm not going to answer it."

"Maybe you'd better," Franziska said, moving away.

Franz picked up the phone. "Hello," he said somewhat angrily. "Oh, Ilona, I'm sorry. I didn't know that it was you." Then there were a lot of "uh-huhs," and he set down the receiver.

"They're leaving Milano," he told Franziska. "They got visas to the United States. They're embarking on a boat from Genova tomorrow, and they're going to New York."

Franz was flabbergasted, and a little bit jealous. "That does it," he said abruptly. "Your family is out. My family is out. And we're just sitting here trying to play it safe. Maybe it's time to gamble while we still have the chance. I swear to you, Franziska, before this month is up, we'll be out, too!"

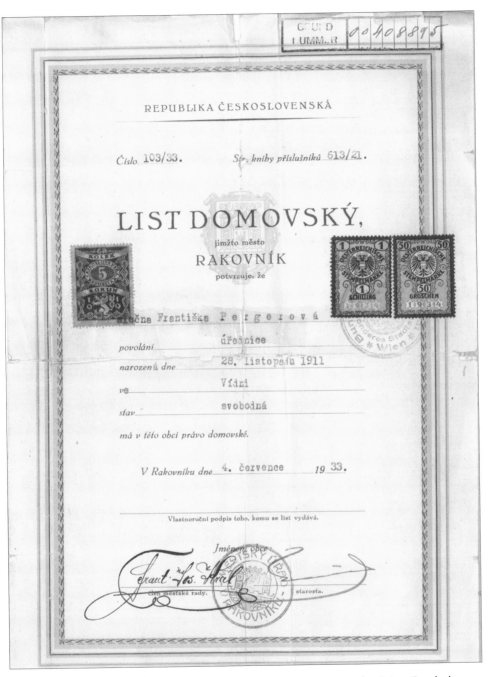

REPUBLIKA ČESKOSLOVENSKÁ

Číslo 103/33.   Str. knihy příslušníků 613/21.

LIST DOMOVSKÝ,

jimžto město

RAKOVNÍK

potvrzuje, že

slečna Františka P e r g e r o v á

povolání _____ úřednice

narozená dne _____ 28. listopadu 1911

ve _____ Vídni

stav _____ svobodná

má v této obci právo domovské.

V Rakovníku dne 4. července 19 33.

Vlastnoruční podpis toho, komu se list vydává.

Jménem obce:

_____ člen městské rady.   _____ starosta.

My mother's *List Domovský* (certificate of domicile) in 1933. Note that it is a Czech document since she had dual citizenship. Information regarding her Austrian citizenship and residence is written on the back. Note that her Czech name was "Františka Pergerová."

NEUES WIENER KONSERVATORIUM
I, MUSIKVEREINSGEBÄUDE WIEN I, HIMMELPFORTGASSE 11

BESTÄTIGUNG

daß *Herr Franz Jung*

die *Gesangs* Klasse *u Opernschule*

VII Semester ·

frequentiert hat.

Wien, den *4 / 4.* 193*6*

Hauptfachlehrer(in):

Die Direktion:

Franz Jung's Diploma (*Bestätigung*) from the Neues Wiener Konservatorium, 4 April 1936.

The faculty of the Neues Wiener Konservatorium, and others. Second row left: Thomas Philipp Martin (née Fleischer), the son of my father's voice teacher, later to become a conductor with the New York City Opera and the Met; front row second from left, my father's voice teacher Arthur Fleischer next to Josef Reitler on the right, director of the Konservatorium and a highly esteemed classical music critic. (*Courtesy of Mary-Anne Martin.*)

The Grosser Saal (Grand Hall) in the Musikverein. (© *Andreas Pessenlehner/epa/Corbis*)

Franz Jung's certification as an official opera singer in the Austrian theater artists association, dated 6 May 1936.

The Wiener Staatsoper in 1937. (*Photo by Philip Gendreau;*
© Bettmann/CORBIS)

The *Opernball* with the debutantes and flowers decorating the Wiener Staatsoper.
(*© Raymond Reuter/Sygma/Corbis*)

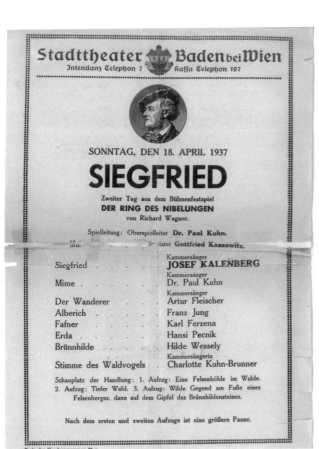

Stadttheater Baden
bei Wien playbill
notice with my father's
name on it as singing
Alberich in Richard
Wagner's *Siegfried*,
dated 18 April 1937.

Renowned baritone
Arthur Fleischer,
my father's voice
teacher, as the
Wanderer in Richard
Wagner's *Siegfried*.
Note, he wrote some
encouraging words
to my father on the
photo.

REPUBLIKA ČESKOSLOVENSKÁ.

Čís. 1/316.-

OSVĚDČENÍ

O STATNÍM OBČANSTVÍ REPUBLIKY ČESKOSLOVENSKÉ.

Okresní úřad v ____Rakovníku____ osvědčuje podle získaných

úředních zpráv, že

(jméno a příjmení) ____Františka Pergerová,____

zaměstnáním (povoláním) ____úřednice____

narozený (den, měsíc, rok, místo a pol. okres narození) ____29.listopadu 1911 ve Vídni____

____polit. okres Vídeň-Rakousko____

z domovské obce ____Rakovníka____ , pol. okres ____Rakovník____

bytem v obci ____Vídeň,III,Blüthengasse 9____ , pol. okres ____Vídeň v Rakousku____

jest podle (zákonný důvod státního občanství) § 1, bodu 1. _____ ústavního

zákona ze dne 9. dubna 1920, čís. 236 Sb. zák. a nař.,

státním občanem republiky Československé.

Ve státním občanství sledují ho manželka

narozená dne _____ roku ____ v _____ pol. okres

a nezletilé dítky

Toto osvědčení pozbývá platnosti 10 let ode dne jeho vystavení.

Dáno dne ____15. června____ 19 37.-

Okresní hejtman:
vrchní rada polit.spr:

Státní tiskárna v Praze. — 6141-36. Čís. skl. 3.

My mother's *Osvědčení O Statním Občanství Republiky Československé* (her Czech certificate or proof of citizenship) in 1937. Pertinent information regarding her dual citizenship is written on the back.

The New German Theater, now the Prague State Opera. (*Photo by Andreas Praefcke.*)

The Stadttheater in Aussig before 1937. (*Ústecké Divadlo / Tisk Herazet Děčín*)

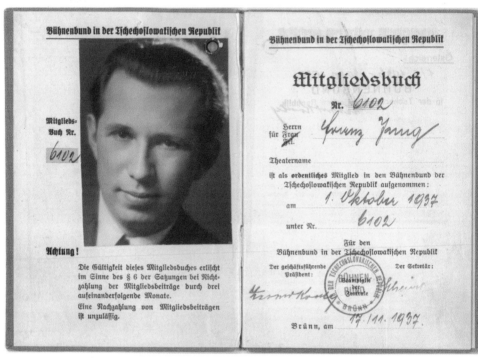

My father received a *Bühnenbund in der Tschechoslowakischen Republik* book with a page titled "Mitgliedsbuch" in October 1937. This little booklet meant that he was a member of the German theater and dramatic artists' trade association in Czechoslovakia when he began singing there.

Photo of my father in 1937.

Photo of my father singing the Holzhacker (Woodcutter) in Engelbert Humperdinck's *Königskinder* at the Stadttheater in Aussig in January 1938.

Photo of my father singing Baron Douphol in Verdi's *La Traviata* at the Stadttheater in Aussig in 1937.

My father singing Dr. Bartolo in Rossini's *Barber of Seville* at the Stadttheater in Aussig in April 1938. (*Photo by Alexander Erdmann.*)

My father as Dr. Bartolo with his Rosina in *Barber* in Aussig. (*Photo by Alexander Erdmann.*)

INTERNATIONALE KONZERTDIREKTION / THEATERAGENTUR UND GASTSPIELZENTRALE

DR. ARTUR HOHENBERG

POSTSPARKASSA-KONTO: C-85-996 — KONTO: BANKHAUS LANGER & CO., WIEN I, BÖSENDORFERSTRASSE NR. 2

WIEN III, LOTHRINGERSTRASSE 20 (KONZERTHAUS), TEL. U-16-1-79, U-16-1-80

TELEGRAMMADRESSE: HOHENBERG KONZERTHAUS WIEN

Ws/Ws   WIEN, am _____ 4.Mai 1938.

Abteilung Wilhelm S t e i n.

Herrn
Franz J u n g
bei Fried
P r a g - Smichov
Na Brezelega 22

Lieber Herr Jung !

    Von Ihrer Frau Mutter bekam ich Ihre Adresse und hoffe, dass es Ihnen gut geht.

    Ich habe eine ganz interessante Sache für Sie und Ihren Kollegen Walter Herbert, dessen Adresse ich leider nicht kenne und dem ich Sie das Gleiche, was ich Ihnen mitteile, zu sagen oder zu schreiben bitte:

    Die Gründung der Palästina Oper, die seit vielen Jahren vorbereitet wird, steht jetzt bevor und die Vorstellungen sollen im Oktober mit Vorproben am 15. September ihren Anfang nehmen. Die Saison dauert bis zum 1.Mai, im Sommer sollen dann grosse Freilichtfestspiele mit den Opern Aida, Königin von Saba, Salome und Samson stattfinden. Es sollen ungefähr 15 Vorstellungen im Monat stattfinden, und zwar abwechselnd in Jerusalem, in Tel Aviv und Haifa.

    Wenn Sie die Sache interessiert, schicken Sie bitte Herrn Direktor Walter E b e r h a r d in Rom, Albergo Nettuno unter Bezugnahme auf mich Kritiken- und Photomaterial sowie vor allem die genauen Personaldaten ein. Das Gleiche möge auch Herr Herbert tun. Ich habe Sie beide sehr warm empfohlen und man interessiert sich sehr für Sie. Tun Sie es auf jeden Fall, welche Pläne Sie auch sonst immer haben mögen. Bestätigen Sie mir bitte die Durchführung und seien Sie bestens gegrüsst von

                    Ihrem

4 May 1938 letter from Wilhelm Stein, my father's agent, to my father in Prague, with the agency's letterhead -- one of the top agencies for opera singers in Vienna at the time, simply called "Dr. Artur Hohenberg." It was housed in the Konzerthaus.

Překlad - Uebersetzung.

x-x-x-x-x-x-x-x-x-x-x-x-x-x-x-x

Trauungsschein.

GZ. Sm.39061/38.

Der Magistrat der Hauptstadt Prag, Amtsstelle in Smichov, bestätigt hiemit, dass in seinem Amtsbuche der Trauungen, Band 10, Seite 73, Nr. 164 eingetragen erscheint:

Jahr, Monat und Tag der Trauung: eintausendneunhundertachtunddreissig, am einundzwanzigsten Mai - 21.V.1938.

	Bräutigam:	Braut:
Vor- und Zuname:	Franz Jung	Franziska Perger
Geburtsort:	Wien-Deutschland	Wien-Deutschland
Heimatszuständig:	Wien-Deutschland	Rakovník
Beschäftigung:	Opernsänger	
Wohnort:	Prag-Smichov Nr. 1101	Prag-Smichov Nr. 1101
Alter:	24.Oktober 1909	28.November 1911
Stand:	ledig	ledig
Religion:	jüdisch	jüdisch
Vor- u.Zuname, Beschäftigung der Eltern:	Jakob Jung,Kaufmann, Olga geb.Werner	Heinrich Perger,Kaufmann, Stefanie geb.Popper
Name und Rang der Standesbeamten:	Dr.jur. Alois Mayer, Magistratsrat	
Vor- u.Zuname u.Wohnort der Zeugen:	Zdenka Vitková, Revidentin des Hilfsdienstes	Friedrich Sachs,Geschäftsvertreter,Prag I., Ida Grünbaum,Ob.Kantorsgattin, Smichov
Beseitigung der Ehehindernisse:	Dispens von allen Aufgeboten und vom zweiwöchentlichen Aufenthalte erteilt für beide Brautleute durch das Landesamt in Prag am 17.V.1938.Nr.8348 ex 1938 Ab.9 Ehefähigkeitszeugnis des Bräutigams von besonderen Stadtamte I im staatl.Urkundenbereiche in Wien vom 10.V.1938, Nr.B.St.A.I/1-J 14/1938.	

Bemerkung: GZ. m. 39061/38.
L.S.

Prag, am 21./ai 1938.

Für den Primator:
Unterschrift unleserlich.

ODDACÍ LIST.

MAGISTRÁT HLAVNÍHO MĚSTA PRAHY
úřadovna na Smíchově

referát populační potvrzuje, že v jeho úřední knize oddavek svazek 10 na str. 73 už.řád. 164 jest zapsáno:

Rok, měsíc a den sňatku: Jeden tisíc devět set třicet osm dne dvacátého prvního května . 21. V. 1938.

	ženich	nevěsta
Jméno a příjmení	František Jung	Františka Pergerová
Rodiště	Vídeň - Německo	Vídeň - Německo
Příslušnost	Vídeň - Německo	Rakovník
Zaměstnání	operní zpěvák	-:-:-
Bydliště	Praha-Smíchov čp.1101	Praha - Smíchov čp.1101
Věk	24. října 1909	28. listopadu 1911
Svobodný,ovdovělý,rozvedený čili neženatý	svobodný	svobodná
Náboženství	židovské	židovské
Jméno, příjmení a zaměstnání rodičů	Jakub Jung,obchodník Olga rodem Wernerová	Jindřich Perger, obchodník Štěpánka roz. Popperová
Jméno, příjmení a bydliště svědků	Bedřich Sachs, obchodní zástupce, Praha I.Hradební 1 Ida Grünbaumová,manželka vrch.kantora,Smíchov	
Jméno a hodnost oddávajících úředníků	JUDr Alois Mayer , magistrátní rada Zdeňka Vitková, revident pomoc.služby správní	
Odstranění překážek sňatku	Dispens ode všech ohlášek a od 6ti nedělního pobytu uděleno oběma snoubencům zemským úřadem v Praze dne 17.V.1938 čj.8348 z r.1938 odd.9. Osvědčení o způsobilosti ke sňatku uděleno ženichovi měst.úřadem I.v státi.oboru úředním ve Vídni dne 10.V.1938 č.B.St.A.I/1-J 14/1938.	
Poznámka	Č.j. Sm. 39.061/38.	

V Praze dne 21. května 1938.

Za primátora:
vrchní mag. rada.

My parents' marriage certificates in Czech and German. They married in Prague. The Czech certificate names my mother as "Františka Pergerová" and my father as "František Jung."

Café Mánes. (*Courtesy of Jan Binar. Photo by Vaclav Čermák.*)

My mother's *Heimatschein* after she married my father. She no longer had dual citizenship. She gave up her Czech citizenship to marry my father.

Agreement in German dated 31 May 1938 from Walter Eberhard, director of the Palestine Opera, to Wilhelm Stein, my father's agent, to my father.

Post card dated 11 September 1938 from Walter Eberhard in Tel-Aviv to my father in Prague, stamped "Censured."

Sehr geehrter Herr Jung!

Für Ihre W. Fattin sehe ich keine
Möglichkeit Ihr Amreise zu erlangen.

Somit beschliesse ich hiermit unsere
Korrespondenz. Erstätten Ihnen bei
dem amerik. Nachlass 1 wünsche
Ihnen gute Überfahrt mit Nah 1
Musikad.

Besten Gruss
Walter Eberhard

WALTER EBERHARD

Letter from Walter Eberhard in October 1938 from Palestine. Note the Hebrew
letterhead.

ANDRÉ ME TENS & Co.

General European Representatives of COLUMBIA C.CERTS CORPORATION of Columbia Broadcasting System
New York - City, 113, West 57th Street
Cable address: Merwie Newyork

Metropolitan Musical Bureau, Inc. · Evans and Salter, Inc.
Concert Management Arthur Judson, Inc.
Haensel and Jones · Wafsohn Musical Bureau of N.Y., Inc.
Community Concert Service.

Paris (VIII•), le **22. November** 19 38

252, Rue du Faubourg Saint-Honoré (Salle Pleyel) - Adr. Télégr.: MERCONCERT-Paris - Téléphone: Carnot 700

Herrn
Franz J u n g
c/o. Koopmann
Petrska 24
P r a g   II.

Sehr geehrter Herr Jung !

Herr Mertens schickt mir Thr Schreiben vom 22. Oktober wieder ei
beauftragt mich, :Sie zu ▪   tändigen, dass er Ihnen nur helfen könnte, wenn Sie es einrichte.   nnten, auf eigenes Risiko nach Ameri z
kommen. Bei dem grossen Andra ng ist nur für den etwas zu errei   en
der zur persönlichen Verhar   ng zur Verfügung steht, und von desse.
Stimme die Interessenten se.   t einen Eindruck gewinnen können. Leid-
kann Ihnen aber Herr Mertens it einem Scheinvertrag nicht behilf·
sein, da diese Schritte stren gstens von der Columbia untersagt wur
und er hofft, dass Ihrer Ein· ichung um ein Visum auch ohnehin statt
geben wird.

Falls Sie noch in Europa bleiben, möchte ich fragen, ob Sie für fol-
gende Angelegenheiten Interesse hätten: Diese Angebote sind allerding
für Sänger gedacht, die sich in Paris oder zumindest Frankreich auf-
halten und dadurch wenig Reisespesen und Zeitverlust hätten. Es würde
sich um Uebernahme des "Melo "in zwei "Tristan" - Aufführungen am Gr
Théatre in B o r d e a u x am 22. und 26. Februar unter der Leit ng
von Hoesslins handeln. Gesamthonorar für beide Abende franz.Francs.
4.000.-, wovon unser Büro lo Provision bekäme. Ich würde in Ihrem
Fall zu erreichen versuchen, dass Ihnen das Kostüm des "Melot" in Bordeaux zur Verfügung gestellt würde.

Ferner: Uebernahme des "Maseto in italienischer Sprache (1
loser Aussprache vorzubereitn) in unseren Aufführungen von
vanni" am 29. April in Antwe.en und am 6. Mai in Brüssel, G.
rar belg. Francs 4.000.-. In diesem Fall müssten Sie sich Ihr
selbst versorgen. - In Erwa ung Ihrer baldgefl. Verständ·
bleibe ich

                    it besten Grüssen

                    Nelly Walter

Letter dated 22 November 1938 from Nelly Walter on behalf of my father's second agent,
André Mertens. Walter was his assistant. He was the European representative of Columbia
Concerts Corporation of Columbia Broadcasting. Both became vice presidents of Columbia
Artists Management Incorporated, or CAMI, one of the largest agencies for performing artists
and opera singers in the world, guiding the careers of Plácido Domingo and many other great
singers.

CHAPTER TWENTY

Christmas Eve

Prague, Czechoslovakia
Zürich, Switzerland
December 1938

$\mathcal{F}$ranz and Franziska were issued new passports: German passports – each stamped with a big red "J" on the front page to label their Jewishness. They didn't know if they'd be able to secure visas to Switzerland or not. The policies of most countries seemed to change from day to day. But on the twentieth of December, they obtained transit visas; however they did not know where they would go from Zürich. They hoped Milano. If the route had worked for Ilona and Hans, maybe it would work for them. They telephoned the Italian Embassy. No visas required. It was a go! They purchased airline tickets for Saturday, the twenty-fourth of December: Christmas Eve. They were leaving in just two days.

They bought a huge trunk and Franziska began avidly packing. She filled it with their belongings, including most of Franz's music and shoes, which took up a sizable portion of it. None of Franz's costumes belonged to him, but he always liked to wear his own custom-made shoes because they fit and because they were slightly elevated to make him look taller onstage. The trunk would be routed directly to Milano, so they packed an overnight bag for their brief stay in Zürich. They didn't think much about leaving Prague. They liked the city, but Vienna had been their real home: imperial Vienna with all of its sophistication and culture. What had happened to it? Where had it gone? The Viennese made them feel like unwanted foreigners. They doubted that they'd ever go back.

It was Christmas Eve and they were sitting on a plane to Zürich. They were extremely nervous because it was the first time that they'd flown on an aircraft. In addition, an incident which had occurred the day before served to exacerbate their agitation.

"Well, we're on our way!" Franz said as the plane glided down the runway, increasing speed and then taking off.

"I feel kind of strange," Franziska complained as the plane began climbing. "It's sort of like being in an elevator."

Once the aircraft reached its cruising altitude, the ride became smoother. "I hope that we made the right decision to fly today," Franz said. "We could end up like the Jews on that flight that was forced to make an emergency landing in Germany yesterday. The Nazis took them off the airplane, and we'll probably never hear from them again."

"I wonder if their plane really did have engine trouble."

"I guess we'll never know."

Franziska looked out of the window, but all she could see was clouds.

"Please fasten your seat belts." The pilot's voice could be heard through the loudspeaker. "We're experiencing some turbulence."

"Oh, no," Franziska said as the plane began rocking.

After the stewardess walked down the aisle to make sure that everyone's seat belt was fastened, she sat down and secured her own.

"What if we have to land in Germany?" Franziska said, sounding somewhat alarmed.

"Just sit back. I'm sure there's nothing wrong with the plane, and the bad weather will pass."

"I hope you're right. I feel so helpless in here. There's so little between us and the atmosphere."

"These airplanes are much stronger than you realize."

Awhile later, the pilot's voice could be heard once again resonating through the cabin. "We're flying over Munich now and will continue over Germany and into Switzerland without further interruptions."

Franz and Franziska were relieved. As they approached Zürich, they thought they'd made it home free. The plane was descending, the landing gear lowered. The wheels struck the ground with a jolt.

"Ohhhhhh," everyone moaned. Landing was a new experience for almost all of them.

The pilot taxied the plane to the unloading ramp. And after a secure halt, the passengers were directed to the exit door, down a long stairway outside, through a gate, and into the terminal building.

They were standing in a sectioned-off area. An immigration officer collected their passports and left to evaluate and stamp them. Franz and Franziska were apprehensive again. They possessed the required documentation to travel through Switzerland, but they didn't have visas to any other country. As they sat on some scantly upholstered bench-like adjoining chairs, Franz grasped Franziska's hand, meshing his fingers with hers so intensely that she thought their appendages were permanently locked. They stood up again when the officer returned, began calling out names, and handed the passports back to their rightful owners. There had been less than twenty passengers on the flight, so the process was swift. The others were allowed to claim their baggage. "You have to wait," the official said to Franz and Franziska. And he walked away again, probably to consult with his colleagues.

"The authorities aren't going to let us through," Franziska remarked anxiously. "What are they going to do with us? Are they going to fly us back to Prague? Oh, my God! Since we have German passports, they might take us back to Germany."

"But we have transit visas. They're obliged to let us through."

"They're not obliged to do anything. Maybe they think that we want to stay. If we'd secured visas to some other country, we wouldn't be in this situation."

"That's the problem, Franziska. Most other countries aren't issuing visas."

"Some Latin American countries are."

"But . . ."

"When Walter Landsmann offered us visas to Uruguay, you should have accepted them."

"But I didn't want to go to Uruguay."

"That isn't the point. . . . The Swiss would have seen the stamps in our passports and would have let us through."

"It's almost dark. Maybe they'll be more lenient since it's Christmas Eve. They probably want to go home to their families."

Franz and Franziska separated. She stood in front of the window looking at the ramps and runways while he paced within the large cubical, then joined her when the floodlights were glaring and her view became brightly illuminated. He held her hand again. "Are you glad you married me now?" he asked softly.

She looked into his eyes without speaking. She'd given him her answer. He nodded his head with a peaceful look on his face and then stroked her cheek with the tips of his fingers. No matter what the future would bring, they were together for the duration. They didn't know how long they'd been waiting. It seemed like hours. Finally the officer returned with their passports.

"You have no visas," he said in German, "and you cannot stay here."

"We don't plan to stay," Franz explained. "We're going to Italy . . . to Milano, and we don't need visas there."

"When are you leaving?"

"Today."

"Please wait just a few more minutes," he said walking away again.

"This is awful," Franziska uttered. "This could be the most pivotal moment in our lives. He and his cohorts could be determining whether we live or die."

"Well that would depend on whether they're planning to take us back to Prague or to Germany."

"What? You don't think they're going to let us through?"

"I don't know, Franziska."

"The authorities in Prague most probably wouldn't admit us. We'd be returning under completely different circumstances than when we first arrived. You came as an opera singer, and I entered with a Czech passport. Our situation is quite different now. I see everything much more clearly. . . . They are definitely considering whether or not to transport us to Germany."

The immigration officer returned. He opened Franz's passport to the page stamped with the transit visa. "You see that the portion which says '*mit Aufenthalt von zwei Tagen*' has been crossed out," he said. "You cannot stay here for even as long as two days."

"We understand," Franz answered. "We are definitely leaving today."

The official didn't say anything for a moment. He looked at the passport and then stared at Franz and Franziska contemplatively.

"All right," he finally said, stamping and handing them back their passports. "But make sure that you do leave today."

They said that they would, but they couldn't. They faced two nights in Zürich illegally.

A hideout: an inconspicuous hotel. The banks would be closed until Monday.

Hotel Krone. (*Photo by author.*)

The Hideaway

Zürich, Switzerland
Chiasso, Italy and Southward
26 December 1938

$\mathcal{T}$he Hotel Krone was the perfect Swiss hideaway for Franz and Franziska. Located in the Old Town section of Zürich on the right bank of the Limmat River, it seemed sequestered from the hustle and bustle of the main commercial and banking boulevard, Bahnhofstrasse, which was on the other side. A modest hotel, the Hotel Krone was squeezed between two higher buildings which failed to conceal its somewhat dilapidated beige façade. The humble interior matched its neglected exterior in unpretentiousness; yet the quaint lobby and dining room overlooking the river bestowed upon the lodging a semblance of charm. Unfortunately, the rooms lacked most of the amenities of comfort and convenience, thus necessitating the guests to acquaint themselves with each other as they frequented the bathroom facilities at the end of the hall.

Franz and Franziska stayed nestled in the hotel from the time they arrived on Christmas Eve until the following afternoon. Then Franziska couldn't bear the seclusion anymore and literally dragged Franz down the narrow lift, into the lobby, and out onto Limmatquai. The air was

243

fresh, the temperature cold, and the two walked freely, though somewhat paranoid that a police officer would suddenly appear in front of them, hold out his arms and bar them from stepping any farther. They passed Grossmünster, the Romanesque cathedral with majestic twin Gothic towers that rose above the landscape of the city. And they viewed the renowned Opernhaus as they approached the juncture of the Limmat River emptying into the icy, shimmering Lake Zürich. If Franz hadn't been engaged to sing in Prague in the fall of 1937, he would have accepted the contract offered to him by Karl Schmid-Bloss to perform in Zürich, and this lovely picturesque city would have been his and Franziska's home. There would have been no reason for them to leave neutral Switzerland; however Franz knew that he would have always been fearful and apprehensive. Yes, it was good that they were immigrating – disconcerting but good.

Franziska was freezing so they reversed their steps; and once back in their hotel room, she sat warming her feet by the furnace. It was a quiet Christmas: no fanfare, a tranquil dinner in the dining room. And the next morning, the two checked out early and embarked on their journey to retrieve the money from Jakob Jung's bank account.

Walking over the Rudolf-Brun-Brücke (Bridge) to Uraniastrasse, the street name instantly sparked memories of their early meeting place in Vienna: the Urania. Those were the happy, naïve days in their lives when they discovered their passion for life and for each other. They turned briskly left onto Bahnhofstrasse and were immediately thrust into the tempo of a gust of businessmen who were rapidly pacing toward their mercantile destinations. Zürich had been branded with an international reputation as the city of high finance, and the numerous people on display in their svelte business suits only served as an attestation to that international conception.

Franz and Franziska passed the Volksbank, which was fronted by multiple stories of beige stone, then a similarly attributed Schweizerische Bankgesellschaft. All they could see were the odd numbers. The even numbers were across the street.

When they reached the bank they were looking for, they were astounded at the architectural magnificence of the neo-Gothic-style structure, with its ornate triangular roof and sculptures distinguishing it from the other edifices along the boulevard. As they walked into the imposing loggia, they approached the arched entryway with cautious reserve. After being greeted by a uniformed security guard in the lavish foyer, they proceeded through the arched wrought-iron entrance into the luxurious main room which, almost void of customers, conveyed an intrinsic essence that was not unlike a religious shrine to be regarded with supreme reverence. It was said that Empress Maria Theresa of Austria had been one of the financial institution's initial clients.

Somewhat intimidated by their surroundings, Franz and Franziska found themselves almost tiptoeing on the exquisite marble floor mosaic. They sensed that even a whisper would have echoed throughout the chamber, which was cloaked by an ornamental curved ceiling with crystal chandeliers, and was partitioned with Italian Renaissance-style marble columns. Franz was jarred into reality when he turned around and recognized a gentleman in a rumpled suit standing in the foyer. The gentleman was Franz's former neighbor on Pötzleinsdorfer Strasse, Egon Eisenstadt, and Franz had never seen him in anything *rumpled* before. He was standing next to a tall, Aryan-looking fellow who could have been Nordic as well. The two nodded, shook hands, and then the stranger exited from the bank. Egon Eisenstadt looked dazed and visibly frazzled.

"Egon . . ." Franz called out just above a whisper. Franz grasped Franziska's hand and walked briskly back into the foyer, but he was greeted with a blank stare. "Egon, are you all right?" he asked.

"Yes . . . uh . . . I think so," his former neighbor responded. "They have my children. They have my children," Egon repeated distraughtly.

Attempting to conceal his emotions from the security guard, Egon placed his hand on Franz's shoulder and led Franz with Franziska outside into the open air. Then he broke down completely. "They have my wife. They have my children," he cried. He was openly weeping.

Franz didn't know how to react. Egon Eisenstadt was really no more than an acquaintance. He was an art dealer and fifteen years Franz's senior. Yet Franz wanted to comfort him, so he placed his arm around his former neighbor's shoulders, and then the horrific story was steadily disclosed.

"The Nazis ransacked my business and home, took my wife's jewelry, our artwork, and then detained us. I was forced to divulge all of my financial holdings, and then they separated me from my family and threatened me. . . . I thought that I would lose my mind. I didn't know if my wife and children were safe or not, and I didn't know what was being done to them. The Nazis told me that my family's fate was in my hands. So I finally confessed my secret Swiss bank account; and they told me that if I willingly handed over the funds, I would be given my freedom. They said that when the money arrived safely in Vienna, they would release my wife and children, and would send them back to me."

"So you were with their agent," Franz said.

"Yes," Egon responded. "He treated me like I was a criminal. He referred to Jews as *vermin* that should be *exterminated*. I shook when I heard his comments on the train ride here. He guarded me in our compartment like I was a prisoner. If I wouldn't have been aware that he had orders to escort me to this bank in Zürich and then to return to Vienna, I would have feared for my life."

"Terrible," Franz remarked. "But you are free of him now."

"Yes," Egon laughed somewhat piteously. "I have a visa, but I don't have enough money to go anywhere. And I still believe that I might never see my family again. They could already be in a concentration camp . . . or worse."

After hearing the story, Franziska felt compelled to speak. She had never actually been introduced to Egon Eisenstadt, but she had seen him a few times when visiting Franz in Pötzleinsdorf.

"I'm Franz's wife," she said. "You have to try to be more optimistic. I have faith that you will soon be reunited with your family."

"Faith? What is faith?" Egon Eisenstadt said. "I don't think that I have any of that anymore."

"You must," Franziska answered.

"I have to go now," Egon uttered. "I need to find someplace to stay, and then I must spend time at the railway station. Maybe someday soon

I'll see my two sons running toward me . . . and my wife . . . but I doubt it somehow. . . . I somehow doubt it."

Franz and Franziska didn't know what to say. Egon Eisenstadt seemed so lost.

"I know that the next time we meet, it will be under much happier circumstances," Franz said, attempting to sound somewhat uplifting.

"Yes. You'll be with your family," Franziska added.

But Egon Eisenstadt just stood there as if all of the energy had been drained from his body. He was moving his head negatively from left to right. "Good-bye," he said limply. "Good-bye." And as his voice trailed off, he ploddingly proceeded down Bahnhofstrasse between the stores and the leafless linden trees, which, much like himself, looked vulnerable and defenseless.

His demeanor had affected both Franz and Franziska deeply. They were spent. They had problems of their own, but now theirs seemed slight. They were so grateful to have each other that they wanted to embrace right there in front of the bank, but they didn't. They walked back inside instead, through the foyer into the main room, and directly to one of the bank clerks.

"I would like to speak to a financial officer," Franz requested.

A few minutes later he was greeted by one of the vice presidents of the bank. He explained that he wanted to close his deceased father's secret bank account by transferring the majority of the funds to the Chase National Bank in New York – the main branch was near Wall Street – and by withdrawing the remainder.

The bank officer was very cordial and escorted Franz and Franziska back through the foyer and upstairs into an exclusive office. The executive board of the bank prided itself on its cultured private banking philosophy, which focused on meeting its clients' needs with prestige and committed professionalism. The offices upstairs were utilized for those customers with secret bank account numbers, and Franz received the service the board prescribed. He produced the required documentation, including a copy of his father's death certificate, wrote down the account number, and the bank official completed the transaction swiftly and painlessly. Back down the stairs and out along the cobblestoned

Bahnhofstrasse, and Franz and Franziska were on their way to the railway station.

Zürich's Hauptbahnhof was immense. When Franz and Franziska entered it from the Bahnhofplatz side, they felt like they were being engulfed into a winding maze of echoing noise and activity. The station's high vaulted ceiling only contributed to the effect, which fostered a cold atmosphere and aloof attitude among the bystanders. Franz walked swiftly with the velocity of a sudden gust of wind, while Franziska attempted to keep up behind him. But Franz had learned his lesson back in Prague when he had raced ahead of her after fleeing from the Café Continental. He knew that she didn't have his stamina, so he continually looked over his shoulder to assure himself that she was close at hand.

He discovered the ticket lines and purchased two tickets. Then the two of them were obliged to find their departure track. "Which way is Track Nine?" Franz asked the closest person to him. But the young man, who was only an arm's length away, refrained from responding and kept on moving. "Track Nine?" Franziska said questioningly to the woman on her left. No response. The attitudes could have caused an ice storm.

Franz and Franziska finally migrated to an information station where they found numerous people who were similarly frustrated. But Franz was the impatient-type. The train was scheduled to leave for Milano in twenty minutes; he and Franziska didn't have time to wait their turn. The line moved quickly and they were given directions. They found the track and train, and boarded their designated passenger car with five minutes to spare. It was one o'clock and they were sitting across from each other in their compartment.

As the train pulled away from the station, the ride seemed remarkably smooth, yet Franziska still felt somewhat off-balance. Her back was facing the front of the train; so even though the locomotive was moving forward, as she watched the scenery from her window, she had the feeling that she was traveling in the reverse direction. She'd heard that the countryside was breathtaking in the spring, especially around

Lake Zugersee. She'd seen a painting once that expressively depicted the houses in the foreground, the yellow flowers hugging the mossy grass, and the white-blooming cherry trees spread picturesquely around the lake amid the mint green-leaved lindens – both species portrayed in such fragile and graceful shapes that Franziska had always wanted to travel to the area to determine if such vegetation did in fact exist, or if the artist had sculpted the setting from his imagination. The trees on the canvas were so lifelike: one had the frail physical attributes of an old man all twisted and curved; another was weeping. And the entire scene was set before a backdrop of the snowcapped Alps. But it was winter, so as the train passed Lake Zugersee, Franziska could only catch a glimpse of what the artist had captured; yet her creative mind filled in the gaps, and she was convinced that what he'd rendered from his palette was real.

Next: a brief stop in Rigi, some cows grazing, and the conductor collected the tickets just before the train rolled through the St. Gotthard Tunnel, a fifteen-kilometer (ten-mile) passageway through the Alps. Another stop in Bellinzona, and then the train seemed to transform itself into an aircraft gliding high above the scenery and yielding a panoramic view of land and water patches from above.

However the climax of the train ride was yet to come. Franz still feared that he and Franziska were in jeopardy of being sent back to Czechoslovakia or Germany, but he didn't want to worry Franziska. Maybe he had been misinformed and they really did need visas to stay in Italy; they couldn't remain in Switzerland either. So while Franziska was looking out of the window at the terrain, Franz was feigning sleep.

He kept up his pretense as the train passed through Chiasso and a governmental officer entered their compartment. "May I see your passports, please?" the officer asked in Italian.

"*Deutsch, bitte*," Franziska said. The official then repeated the question in German.

The dialogue reminded Franziska of her intimidating train ride from Vienna to Prague.

"Franz, Franz, wake up!" she said shuddering a bit, nudging Franz gently on the arm.

Franz opened his eyes, yawned and appeared dazed.

"Your passports, please," the officer requested again.

Franz reached into the inside pocket of his jacket, fumbled, and then produced what was requested.

The official examined the documents. "No visas," he said matter-of-factly.

Franz's heart seemed to stop. A trickle of perspiration eased down his cheek, culminating its journey in the minuscule crevice at the corner of his mouth. The officer stamped the passports after a brief pause and handed them back to Franz. "*Guten Abend* (Good evening)," he said and walked out of the compartment.

The masquerade was over. Franz was wide awake again just as instantaneously as if he'd been struck by lightning.

"Were you really asleep?" Franziska asked.

Franz began laughing and laughing. "No, of course not," he answered, wrapping his arms around Franziska and kissing and kissing her.

"We're out of danger now. We're finally out of danger," he declared ecstatically. "We are in Italy!"

The train ride was indeed nerve-wracking for my father. He told me that he was very relieved to arrive in Italy. I took the ride myself so that I could describe the route and beautiful scenery.

CHAPTER TWENTY-TWO
Good-Bye . . .

Italy: Milano and Genova
26 December 1938 to 17 January 1939

$\mathcal{M}$ilano! Fashion, industry, and opera! Franz and Franziska's aim was to enjoy the city thoroughly and then to forsake it for the United States. But they had no idea how much longer they would have to wait to attain their American visas. They checked with the United States Consulate. Nothing yet. So they tried to entertain themselves in their surroundings.

Once again they were staying at a modest hotel, the Casa Svizzera – actually it was more like a *locanda* (inn) – which was located on Via San Raffaele just a few steps from Milano's foremost Gothic cathedral, the Duomo. The Duomo was truly a grandiose structure, but Franz and Franziska were accustomed to monumental architecture. After all, Vienna had Stephansdom. The similarities between the two Gothic churches – each was situated in a square at the core of its city – served to remind Franz and Franziska that they wanted to journey as far away from Europe as possible. If Adolf Hitler could turn the serenity of Stephansplatz into anarchy, he could do the same to the Piazza del Duomo, which was often the site of religious and political events as well as a gathering place for the Milanese and their visitors from around the world. Franz and Franziska went there every day, hoping to hear about some faraway locale that would serve as a haven for them until they could immigrate to America. Then they always wandered through the cross-shaped neo-Renaissance-style Galleria to the Piazza della Scala, another square where opera enthusiasts often congregated for a glimpse of the highly revered Teatro alla Scala, simply known throughout the world as La Scala. Franz hoped to perform at the theater after he became a well-established singer in the United States and had a place that he could once again call home.

A few days after their arrival in Milano, Franz and Franziska crossed the street in front of the piazza to examine the framed glass-enclosed playbills hanging on the neoclassical golden façade of La Scala. They stopped in front of the one which displayed the cast and dates when Giuseppe Verdi's *La Traviata* would be performed, each wanting to be in the audience. Franziska was always saddened by the ill-fated love story of Alfredo Germont and Violetta Valery, the latter succumbing to an untimely death from consumption. And Franz felt a need to evaluate the baritone who would be portraying Alfredo's father, a role which he had sung before and was looking forward to singing again. But *La Traviata* wasn't being performed until February. They would be long gone by then.

Next, they stopped in front of the playbill that listed the cast and dates for Giacomo Puccini's *La Bohème,* another bittersweet love story between the poet, Rodolfo, and the flower maker, Mimi, who also succumbs to an untimely death from consumption. *La Bohème* was being performed in a little over a week.

Suddenly Franz heard a familiar voice but couldn't discern who it was.

"Dreaming, are you?" the voice said.

Franz turned around.

"Bing," he said, matching the voice to the face. "What are you doing here?"

The Slavic-looking silhouette belonged to Bing Lemberger, one of Franz's colleagues from Vienna. Bing had studied privately with Arthur Fleischer, and Franz hadn't seen him in more than a year.

After hugging Franziska warmly, Bing explained that he had been singing in Reichenberg, which was part of the Sudetenland, and when the theater was closed there, he immediately fled to Milano with his wife, Marie.

"So you finally got married," Franz remarked. "Congratulations!"

"Thank you," Bing responded. "Now maybe I'm being a little presumptuous in asking, but what about you and Franzi?"

"We're married too," Franz replied. "I was singing in Czechoslovakia much like you, only in Prague and Aussig, and we've been in Milano for a week. But our final destination is really the United States."

"Ours too," Bing said. "We just got visas. We'll be leaving for America in less than two weeks."

Franz felt a streak of jealousy darting through him, but he instantly attempted to conceal any semblance of it from reaching his face. "How wonderful!" he said. "We've registered with the United States Embassy in Prague, but our numbers haven't come up yet."

"They will; they will," Bing said optimistically. "You've got to have patience."

"But we don't really want to stay in Europe while we're waiting," Franz said.

"Where do you want to go?"

"Almost any place that's safe," Franz responded, looking at Franziska and stroking her forearm, not to keep her warm but to show his affection for her. "Do you have any suggestions?"

"Right now, the only countries that are accepting Jewish immigrants are those where you would probably not choose to go," Bing said.

"We plan to go to America. Anyplace else would simply act as a stopover," Franz responded.

"Well, I've been talking to people, and I believe that you can still go by boat from Trieste to Shanghai."

"That's so far. Anywhere else?"

"Bolivia . . . the Dominican Republic. How about Cuba?"

"Cuba: idyllic sandy beaches . . . azure waters . . . palm trees. And just hours from the United States. . . . Cuba just might be our solution," Franz said. "Are you sure that we'll be able to get visas?"

"Well, let's say I'm confident that you can. But I'm not absolutely positive."

"Hmm . . . I wonder where the consulate is. We'll have to go there tomorrow."

"But while Marie and I are still here, why don't we all go to *La Bohème* together?"

"We'd love to," Franz answered, "but our minds are on other things right now."

"Come on . . . the performance will do wonders for your morale," Bing said. "Let's go to the box office right now and purchase tickets for the eleventh of January."

"Oh . . . I don't know," Franziska said meekly.

"All right then. . . . I've made the decision that Marie and I will definitely be in the audience a week from Wednesday, and we'd really enjoy your company."

Franziska looked into Franz's eyes questioningly. A pause and then: "Okay! We'll meet you here before the performance," Franz said. And he and Bing purchased gallery-seat tickets from the box office.

Much like Zürich's Hauptbahnhof, Milano's Stazione Centrale was another colossal, frigid railway station with a high steel-vaulted ceiling. Franz and Franziska hadn't anticipated another train ride so soon, but the Cuban Consulate was in Genova, a two-hour ride south of Milano. They shared their compartment with three young people who talked loudly and incessantly in Italian, causing them to arrive at the Stazione Porta Principe in Genova with headaches. After leaving the train, they walked and walked in the direction of what they thought was the exit, finally stopping to ask someone, who pointed them toward some stairs. One long flight down, and they steered themselves to the sunlight of the city.

"Piazza della Vittoria," Franz told a taxicab driver. And within minutes, Franz and Franziska were viewing the sights of Genova: Centro Storico (Old City), the historical section reminiscent of a quaint medieval town of seafarers; the Piazza de Ferrari, which was edged with ancient stone civic buildings and banks; and Via Venti Settembre, the long, arcaded commercial boulevard flanked with Genova's most exclusive shops, restaurants, and hotels. The taxi driver was so proud of this bustling seaport city, the birthplace of Christopher Columbus, that he was intent on serving as a friendly guide; however Franz and Franziska wanted to go only to the Cuban Consulate. But the driver could not be dissuaded and was in his element upon approaching Piazza della Vittoria, which he described as the home of Genova's miniature Arc de Triomphe, erected to commemorate the local soldiers lost in World War I. He stopped in front of the consulate, was graciously paid by his passengers and then drove off, probably back to the train station or to the seaport in search of some other weary travelers.

Upon his departure, Franz and Franziska looked into each other's eyes and walked hand in hand into the stately beige-colored stone building in front of them. They proceeded up a narrow stairway, the railing decorated with wrought-iron balusters, until they reached a black wooden ornately-carved door with a contrasting white sign attached. The name of the consulate was written in Spanish: "*Consolado General de la República de Cuba*," Franz read. He rang the buzzer and someone opened the door a crack. "We would like visas," Franz said in German. The door was pulled ajar so that he and Franziska could see the small but ample waiting area filled with people, as well as the adjoining office, which was staffed with an inadequate number of consular agents to service everyone's needs in a timely manner. After Franz wrote his and Franziska's names on a substantial list, they joined the waiting, surveying the room in an attempt to determine the nationalities represented. Some Italians, mostly Cubans: Franz and Franziska could only differentiate by listening to the languages spoken.

Their names were finally called. Franz was a little apprehensive. Was Bing Lemberger's information accurate? Was the Cuban government really allowing European refugees to enter its autocratically-run country – to remain indefinitely? When they reached the counter, Franziska pulled out an array of papers from her oversized handbag: their marriage and birth certificates, citizenship papers, and, of course, their passports. Franz pretended to be very secure, attempting to display a calm matter-of-fact attitude.

"We would like to travel to Cuba as soon as possible," he told the consular agent. "I believe that everything is in order."

The agent perused the papers, looked up at Franz and Franziska while stroking his dark, bristly mustache, handed them some forms to fill out, and then re-examined their records. "How long do you plan to stay?" he asked.

"We've applied for visas to the United States," Franz answered. "We plan to leave as soon as they're issued to us."

The applications complete, the agent asked them to remain at the counter for a few minutes. He seized their passports and disappeared through a doorway behind him. Franz and Franziska breathed deeply, turned around and noticed that the waiting room had thinned out, then completed their revolution, each inhaling another whiff of oxygen.

The consular agent returned and slapped their open passports down in front of them, each signed by the consul general and stamped with the official governmental seal.

"Here is the address of a travel agency," he said, handing Franz a slip of paper. "You can walk there and book either a luxury liner or a passenger-cargo ship. . . . Enjoy your stay in Cuba."

The agency was on Via Garibaldi, a narrow street in Centro Storico lined with historical *palazzi* (palaces) and mansions that were converted into museums, art galleries, banks, and offices, still retaining their original ornamental façades, frescoes, and gardened courtyards. Before locating this noble street, Franz and Franziska wandered through the nearby curving alleyways, savoring the scents of perfume, dried fruits, and pesto sauce, which were emanating from the secluded shops and restaurants.

When they reached the agency, their olfactory senses and salivary glands sufficiently stimulated, they blocked out their immediate tendency to satiate their ravenous appetites in favor of allaying a more long-lived hunger for safety and freedom.

"I can book you on a freighter to Panama," the travel agent said, peering over the counter. He was a heavyset man wearing elastic suspenders to hold up his trousers, a shirt with rolled-up sleeves, and no jacket. Although cold outside, the temperature in the office was soaring.

"I'm sorry but there's something wrong with our furnace, so please be so kind as to bear with the insufferable heat," he continued, shaking out an immense white handkerchief and wiping the perspiration from his forehead.

"But we want to go to Cuba," Franz said oblivious to the temperature, nevertheless removing his overcoat. "Franziska! Please show the gentleman our passports."

Franziska, unscathed by the heat, went rummaging through her handbag, a few moments later withdrawing the passports. Franz grasped one and opened it to the page which displayed the Cuban visa. "You see," he said, showing the travel agent the stamped documentation.

"But, sir, all of the ships that are going directly to Cuba are completely booked for the next few months. The *Rialto* is the only one I can offer you that's departing in that direction in the immediate future. She leaves Genova on the seventeenth of January and will arrive in Panama on the ninth of February, that is if she stays on schedule."

"But the *Rialto* is a freighter. Is she equipped to carry passengers?" Franz asked.

"Absolutely, only not as many as you'd find on a luxury liner. She's really a combination passenger-cargo ship."

"But then how do we get to Cuba?"

"I only have access to two liners that are going from Panama to Cuba at that time, and they are both fully booked, so you'll have to make arrangements after you dock at the port in Cristóbal."

"Hmm . . . just our luck," Franz said, throwing his coat on the counter. "Is there any chance that you could be mistaken? Maybe there'll be a cancellation."

"I'll keep tabs on the situation, and I'll notify you if there's any change."

"And what about visas?"

"You'll have to go to the consulate in Milano. The only thing I can do is sell you the tickets."

So even though Franz was insecure and agitated, he gave the travel agent the required amount of lire and was given his certificates of passage.

"You need to be at the Stazione Marittima two hours before departure. The *Rialto* will begin boarding from the Ponte Andrea Doria embarkation pier at four o'clock in the afternoon. She's scheduled to leave at six."

The travel agent gave Franz a small map of the Porto di Genova and placed an arrow on the *Rialto's* designated embarkation pier. Franz thanked him for his service and handed Franziska the tickets, map, and passport, which she immediately deposited into her purse. He grabbed his overcoat, swinging it around his shoulders, and the two scurried out of the office, back to the train station, and to the Casa Svizzera in Milano.

Franz couldn't sleep at all for three nights, waiting for Monday to come. Would they be able to secure visas to Panama? And would they be able to find a vessel that would transport them from Panama to Cuba?

The Consulado de la República de Panamá was located a short distance from their hotel on the narrow cobblestoned Via Bagutta, in an apropos-style Milanese-looking stone building with Latin American accents: the lowest story, a natural light brown; the upper two painted gold with dark brown-shuttered windows; and a roof of terra cotta-colored tile. Franz and Franziska were standing in front of the building at nine o'clock in the morning, expecting a long wait. But after they climbed the stairs, walked down a long brown carpet to the entry door of the office and rang the buzzer, they soon determined that the consulate was almost empty: quite a contrast from what they'd experienced the day before. A secretary welcomed them inside, leading them past an imaginatively-decorated waiting room with a festive "*Discover Panama*" painting hanging from the wall and a curio cabinet filled with some of the country's distinctive dolls and artifacts. A few steps farther and they were in a one-desk office which displayed a large-scale picture-framed map of Panama.

The secretary, who could have passed for either Italian or Panamanian, was an attractive young woman with shoulder-length brown hair turned under at the ends into a pageboy. When she sat down behind the desk and answered the telephone, she spoke fluent Spanish; when it rang again, she spoke Italian. And for Franz and Franziska, she communicated in German.

"Don't worry," she told Franz after he'd explained their situation. "We're here to help you."

After asking them to sit down, she knocked on a door a few steps away from her desk and advanced into a private office, reappearing a few minutes later with a distinguished-looking older man in a well-tailored charcoal gray suit.

"We would like to accommodate you," the consul said to them in Italian, the secretary translating his words into German. "May I see your passports, please?"

Franz and Franziska rose, Franziska producing the documents. And while the consul was examining them, Franz explained that they would be leaving Genova on the seventeenth of January for Panama, and that upon their arrival, they would immediately attempt to book a liner for Cuba.

"But while you are in Panama, wouldn't you like to see our beautiful country?" the consul questioned. "I always call it the 'Great Connector' because it links North and South America."

"Yes, of course," Franz responded to be polite. "The Panama Canal is such a monumental accomplishment. I would definitely like to see it."

"And you will have that opportunity when you take the train from Colón to Panama City to have your passport stamped at the Department of Immigration. Just think, before the canal was built, ships had to travel more than twelve thousand kilometers (seven thousand miles) around the tip of South America to pass from the Atlantic to the Pacific. Now the trip is only about eighty kilometers (fifty miles)."

"Yes, it's miraculous," Franz said while wondering why they would have to go to the Department of Immigration. Maybe the consul wasn't going to issue them visas."

"There are many immigrants in Panama right now," the consul said. "How can you be sure that you will be leaving?"

"We have visas to Cuba," Franz answered.

"Yes, I see them here. . . ."

"And then we plan to go to the United States to be with my family."

"But you don't have passage tickets."

"Surely there must be many liners that depart from the port in Panama for Cuba," Franz interjected quickly.

"Yes, there are," the consul said pausing, then continued scrutinizing their passports. "I see that you are an opera singer."

"Yes," Franz replied proudly. "I studied at the Neues Wiener Konservatorium at the Musikverein in Vienna, and I just completed a season in Prague."

"Good! So you've been working?"

"Yes," Franz responded, realizing that the consul was attempting to determine if he had the financial resources to pay for the voyage to Cuba and to subsist in Panama until the journey's commencement. "Some of the top agents in Vienna were lining up engagements for me until I informed them that I wanted to immigrate to the United States. Their American representatives will immediately begin working on my behalf when I arrive, hopefully in New York. In fact, Franziska and I just spent a few days in Zürich attending to some banking matters which pertain to our change of residence."

All at once, a gleaming spark flickered in the consul's eyes. Franz had apparently told him exactly what he'd wanted to hear.

"I am giving you transit visas," he said, standing over his secretary's desk while stamping the passports and signing them. "And I'm writing that your destination is Cuba. If you're unable to leave Panama the day of your arrival, you must have the visas extended at the Department of Immigration. I wish you much luck in your travels and in your career."

After the consul's final phrases had been translated, he gave the passports to Franziska, shook Franz's hand again, and returned to his office.

The consul's secretary then continued conversing, introducing herself for the first time as Luciana Ferretti. She explained that her younger brother, Enrico, was an aspiring opera singer studying at the Conservatorio. "He dreams of singing at La Scala, and then maybe one day at the Metropolitan Opera," she said. "He has *una voce tenorile magnifica*, and when he sings 'Nessun dorma,' he makes our mama cry."

Luciana was such a warm-hearted, compassionate person that after fifteen minutes of talking, Franz and Franziska felt as if they'd known her for years. And by the time she accompanied them back toward the door, they knew they'd made a very special friend. Yet a well-wisher just didn't seem to be enough. Yes, they had their visas on the third of January. But how were they going to get to Havana, Cuba?

"I don't want to be stranded in Panama," Franz kept on saying. "I don't want to be stranded in Panama."

Franz and Franziska's daily ritual continued for another week. A walk from the hotel to the Piazza del Duomo, through the Galleria to La Scala, along Via Manzoni past the luxurious Grand Hotel et de Milano, and then down Via Montenapoleone for a glimpse of the stylish boutiques of fashion, furniture, and jewelry. Franziska was trying to imagine that she didn't have a care in the world. However: "I don't want to be stranded in Panama. I don't want to be stranded in Panama" was constantly being drummed into her ears.

"Oh, stop it!" she finally said sharply to Franz, coming to a halt in front of an elegant jewelry store. "Can't you just try to enjoy yourself for the few days we have left in Milano?"

"How can I enjoy myself when I'm so worried?"

"Just pretend you're not . . . for me, please."

On the eleventh of January, Franziska looked lovely as usual as she proceeded with Franz to La Scala. They had picked up their trunk from the airport, so they had all of their belongings with them. Franziska was wearing a navy taffeta skirt and matching jacket, both bordered in a slightly darker velvet, and the outfit was accented with a grape-colored chiffon blouse. But she didn't feel nearly as elegant as she appeared. She had spent very little time applying her makeup and fixing her hair, for all of the traveling and insecurities had drained the vitality from her. But she knew how to put up a poised front, and this was one of those evenings when her acting ability would soon be tested.

Franz on the other hand only summoned his acting skills when he was onstage. Although matching Franziska in color – he was wearing a dark blue suit – his face appeared drawn and fatigued. But in spite of how they actually felt, at seven o'clock, Franz and Franziska were standing under the colonnade by the entrance of La Scala, cloaked in heavy woolen coats to shut out the rain.

After being greeted by Bing and Marie, whose spirits were considerably higher, they all walked into the aristocratic marble-columned, crystal-chandeliered foyer of La Scala, checked in their wraps, and then proceeded to the top gallery, where they were seated in the center of the front row. The horseshoe-shaped auditorium with plush red-upholstered chairs and tiers of ivory and gold filigree-faced boxes was quite exquisite, impressing even these four, who had frequented the best. Yet although Bing and Marie had tried to focus Franz and Franziska's attentions on music, the only thought on their minds was immigration, and their demeanors remained stilted and stiff. So during the minutes preceding the beginning of the performance, Bing and Marie sat quietly whispering to each other while Franz and Franziska stared down at the stage.

The conductor finally approached the podium and raised his baton. There was a hush in the audience as the orchestra began playing. By the time Franziska heard Rodolfo sing "Che gelida Manina," telling Mimi his romantic dreams; Mimi's "Mi chiamano Mimi"; and their duet, "O soave fanciulla" – she was in heaven and very much in love with Franz. She placed her hand in his. He smiled slightly and ever so gently stroked the side of her face.

There was joy in their eyes while Musetta was singing her alluring "Quando me'n vo," trying to attract Marcello. Then sorrow returned as Mimi and Rudolfo sang their "Addios," unable to part. A poignant duet sparked Franz's desire to portray Marcello. And when Rudolfo cried out to his lifeless Mimi, the tears rolled down Franziska's cheeks, and Franz brushed them away with his handkerchief.

After the curtain calls, the two couples remained in their seats thoughtfully discussing the performance. Franziska liked Marie. She was tall and had an interesting, classical-looking face with straight pointed features, and she was quiet-spoken and had a soothing voice. But Franziska didn't have much opportunity to converse with her that evening since Bing and Franz were seated in the center, with the two ladies on either side. Franziska noticed that Bing was doing a great deal of talking. At first she thought that he was comparing notes with Franz since the role of Marcello was also in his repertoire. But as she eavesdropped, she came to the conclusion that they were trying to figure out how Franz could get from Panama to Cuba. Franziska wasn't worried, though. She was glad they had gone to the opera.

Most of the audience had already cleared the theater, and Franz knew that the auditorium would soon be dark. So the couples meandered leisurely downstairs – the two gentlemen retrieving the wraps – and they said good-bye in the foyer before dashing out beyond the portico, their launched umbrellas navigating them on the rain-saturated cobblestones to separate taxicabs.

Back in their hotel room, Franziska had to contend with: "I don't want to be stranded in Panama. What will we do if we can't find a boat to Cuba? Maybe the authorities will send us back to Genova."

Then at eight o'clock the next morning, there was a knock at the door. "*Telefono! Telefono!*" a woman was saying. They were still in bed.

Franz scrambled for his clothes while Franziska pulled the blanket over herself, burnt sienna bedspread and all. "*Uno momento! Uno momento!*" Franz called out. He ventured from the room and down the stairs to an unobtrusive lobby, where the gentleman who owned the hotel . . . or inn . . . or pensione . . . set the telephone down on the wood-paneled counter in front of him. "*Per te,*" the hotelier said. And then the conversation commenced:

"Hallo. . . . Oh, Signorina Ferretti. . . . All right – Luciana. . . . Yes, of course we still want to go to Cuba, desperately. . . . You have? How thoughtful of you. Franziska and I never anticipated that you would go out of your way like that. . . . You have?"

Franz was in awe. He listened to Luciana for a few minutes. Then: "So this company in Panama is reserving a cabin for us on a ship that transports its bananas? . . . Please hold on while I get a pencil."

Franz motioned to the hotelier who handed him what he needed. Then as Luciana conveyed the information, he repeated what she said as he wrote it down: "Hallo—Luciana? Now what's the name of the company? . . . The United Fruit Company. . . . Oh, the ship's part of the Great White Fleet. Do you know the name of the liner? . . . Could you spell that for me, please? . . . *C-H-I-R-I-Q-U-Í*. And when does she leave? . . . At noon on the thirteenth of February. . . . Uh-huh. So I can pick up the tickets at the steamship office near the port of Cristóbal in the Canal Zone, near Calle Once (Eleven) and Avenida del Frente. By the way, how much are they? . . . Yes, that seems reasonable. . . . Yes, I think I've got it all now. Thank you, Luciana. I am so very grateful to you. . . . Yes, Luciana, we are leaving tomorrow, and we really do want to keep in touch with you. Please give me your address, Luciana. . . . Uh-huh. . . . Uh-huh. And when we're settled in America, I hope that you'll come and visit us. Maybe your brother and I will sing together one day. . . . Yes! Maybe at the Met. Good-bye, Luciana. And thank you so very much again. . . . Good-bye."

As planned, Franz and Franziska were at the Stazione Marittima at four o'clock on the seventeenth of January. Franziska was wearing a double-breasted wool overcoat with a beaver collar, a pillbox hat seated on the crown of her head, and leather gloves. Similarly, Franz was also attired in a double-breasted coat and hat and gloves. They looked almost like twins, except Franz's collar was furless, and he was sporting the tan-colored cashmere scarf that Franziska had given him the year before.

As they made their way through the terminal – the inside of the building appeared quite dismal and cold to them – Franz was pushing their oversized trunk laboriously, and Franziska was carrying their small overnight bag. After stopping at an information counter in search of the Ponte Andrea Doria embarkation pier, they were directed to a window on the other side of the terminal, where an official stamped the last page of their passports and showed them where to exit to get onto the pier.

They had never seen anything like the Porto di Genova before. They'd grown up around vast rivers and lakes. But the expanse of the sea – that was something altogether different. They'd heard that this port was the largest and busiest in Italy. And judging from the panoramic vision before them, they gathered that the assessment was undoubtedly true: a voluminous sheltered harbor; vessels of all conceivable shapes and sizes cruising to and fro; piers jutting into the hollow gulf with moored ships loading and unloading cargo, boarding and disembarking passengers; and the scenic seafaring town of pastel-colored buildings framing the spectacle and sweeping outward and upward into the hills.

It was windy and foggy on the wharf as they caught their first glimpse of the vessel that would carry them to Central America. It seemed relatively small when compared with some of the other liners in the port. The hull was black, the upperworks white, and the name "*Rialto*" was written on the bow and stern. The longshoremen had just completed lowering the cargo into the holds, and they were sealing the hatches. Franz and Franziska walked along the dock until they reached some port officials and crew members, who asked them to go aboard upon examining their passports and tickets. Franz was told to leave the trunk with them, as it was too cumbersome to keep in their cabin and would be stored in a separate compartment. However Franziska was still carrying their overnight bag, which contained some of Franz's music. So Franz took it from her, and the two walked up the accommodation ladder and along the gangway until they reached the main deck. They deposited the luggage inside their assigned cabin in the afterhouse just behind the midships line, and then they sat down on one of the beds to rest. The wood-paneled stateroom contained a bathroom and a closet, two mahogany chests of drawers with a lowboy between them, and a couple of chairs. The somewhat cramped space would act as Franz and Franziska's home for the next three weeks, and they were committed to making the best of it.

"This isn't going to be so bad," Franziska said jokingly. "I think we're really going to get to know each other much better in here."

Franz placed a quick kiss on the tip of her nose, and they were up and out in pursuit of the dining room, galley, and social hall. As they wandered into the forehouse amidships near the bridge, they noticed some other passengers who, like themselves, were drifting around like migratory birds, among them: an American couple, two nuns, and some refugees. But they didn't stop to get acquainted; they had plenty of time for that later. Instead they went back outside. It was getting dark and the crew was casting off the lines. The lights from the surrounding buildings and vessels were hurling luminous reflections onto the misty waters. The *Rialto* was beginning to inch away from the wharf. A little tug was towing her out of the harbor.

"I'm somewhat frightened," Franziska said, snuggling up close to Franz on the deck, his arms held tightly around her waist.

"Of what?" he asked.

"The unknown, I guess . . . leaving Europe . . . being exposed to different countries and people and customs . . . having to speak another language."

"Don't worry, my darling. We're together. That's all that really matters."

So as the little tugboat broke away from the larger sister freighter to return to her customary dock in the harbor, the *Rialto* was destined to discover new, unfamiliar territories – much like Franz and Franziska – and to leave her anchorage behind.

"Good-bye," Franziska said, waving and looking back at the seaport. "Good-bye Vienna and Italy and Europe. I may never see you again."

"Oh, don't be so nostalgic," Franz said. "We're ending a chapter in our lives that has been filled with unkindness and evil, and we're beginning one that is imbued with hope and freedom."

They stood on the deck clinging to each other, sailing optimistically toward a replenished future, their senses engulfed with the mingling sights, smells, and sounds of the whispering wind and the swells of the effervescent sea.

CHAPTER TWENTY-THREE

On the *Rialto*

The Mediterranean Sea
Marseille, France
The Atlantic Ocean
17 January to 1 February 1939

*O*h was Franz sick!

Franz and Franziska had eaten their induction meal in the dining room in the forehouse that evening. Fittingly, the entrée was fish. They'd had the opportunity to meet some of the forty-three passengers there, although no more than half of the guests had ventured in. The "dining salon," as it was called, was a cozy room with twelve circular tables: some with four wood-framed chairs and some with six. There was a chandelier; curtains were draped over the portholes; and as in all finer European dining establishments, there were tablecloths.

Franz and Franziska had been sitting with an amiable fellow from Vienna when Franz began feeling woozy. The gentleman's name was Heinz Hilgermann, and he seemed somehow oddly risqué. He talked at length about his famous composer-brother in Hollywood. "And when I arrive there," he said proudly, "my brother is going to welcome me with a live band at the pier, and then I'm going to meet some movie stars and see how films are made."

Heinz Hilgermann was so animated about his future intentions that

Franz and Franziska had to conceal their urges to laugh. That is until Franz got sick. Then they had to excuse themselves from the table as Franz raced in front of Franziska, from the forehouse to the afterhouse, just barely making it to the sink in their cabin in time. Then Franz moaned and groaned as he fell like a shooting star onto the bed, and then he moaned and groaned some more.

Franziska actually found the whole turn of events quite amusing. Both grown men had seemed somewhat childlike to her: one for the naïve type of inflated significance he bestowed to a somewhat fantastical illusion; the other for his immature, exaggerated reaction to a common, harmless, almost predictable illness.

"I'm so sick; I'm so sick," Franz kept uttering as he lay flat on his back on the bed, staring at the whitewashed walls. "It must have been the fish. The fish must have been spoiled."

"Just rest, Franz. It wasn't the fish; it's the movement of the ship. You're simply seasick."

"But I'm so nauseous and dizzy. Everything is whirling around. . . . Oh, I'm going to faint."

"Come on," Franziska said. "Maybe you'll feel better if you take off some of your clothing."

Franz barely moved as Franziska removed his shirt and then unbuttoned and pulled down his trousers. The scene would have really been quite comical, except Franz was s-o-o-o sick.

But he survived, and early the next morning, they discovered that the *Rialto* was docked at the port in Marseille, the largest seaport in France and the most important in the Mediterranean, so it was only natural for the ship to stop there. But what were they going to do for the two hours onshore while she loaded?

They were told that the Rue de la République would lead them to the Vieux Port (Old Port), which no longer was the hub of the harbor's mercantile activity where the *Rialto* had docked, but the home of hundreds of fishing vessels that had spawned the flavors, scents and tones for which the port was famous. From the Place de la Joliette, they began walking. But they soon discovered that they were on the wrong street – on the Rue de l'Evêché – and they had no idea where they were going except that it was in the right direction. They walked down the narrow streets and hilly passageways unaware that they were frequenting the Panier, a quarter recognized for its old-fashioned picturesque, somewhat Neapolitan charm, since many of the inhabitants were either fishermen and their families, or refugees from Italy. The houses were wedged together closely, with lines of multicolored laundry blowing in the tempered winds above. A baker was opening his doors, waiters were serving their first customers café, and some artisans were beginning a game of *belote* (cards).

By then they were walking on the Rue des Moulins, then the Montée des Accoules. Smells of fried fish and garlic were already infiltrating the streets. Shutters were flying open: A woman was shouting to her friend on the neighboring balcony.

Franz and Franziska were approaching the Vieux Port now. They'd reached the palatial Hôtel de Ville (City Hall) on the Quai du Port, then continued to the Quai des Belges, where some fishermen were unloading their catches, others unfurling their nets to dry. The view was stupendous: hundreds of fishing vessels with their masts and sails held high.

"Oh, look!" Franziska said. "They're eating the fish right out of the shells. Do you want some? Those women are selling them."

"No, I don't think so," Franz said. "I was so sick last night that the sight of those slimy things makes me nauseous. . . . Besides, we should really start heading back if we don't want the *Rialto* to leave without us."

"What? No time for the Canebière? I've heard about that street for years."

"No, Franzi. There's only time for the Rue de la République. We're right next to it now, and I think that it will take us directly back."

They arrived at the dock in time to see the booms swinging the cargo onto the *Rialto*, where it was loaded through the central hatch. They weren't really that interested though, so they went straight up to their cabin. Franziska took out a needle and some thread; Franz, his pitchpipe; and they both proceeded to do what made them feel the most comfortable. She sewed, he sang, and the *Rialto* sailed.

It was a gloomy day. But then, maybe they were all gloomy on a ship, Franziska thought. Nothing but fog and water and sky, all blurred together into an endless hue of murky gray, broken only by the undulating ripples created by the sustained motion of the vessel and the propeller. And as the evening turned the gray into black, Franz and Franziska moved from the deck to the dining room to the social hall. The social hall, which resembled a large comfortable living room, was a place to make lasting friendships, they were told. But everyone's final destination was different. The American couple was going home to California after their annual voyage to and from Europe. The two Italian nuns had been missioned to Argentina. A Polish family was immigrating to Costa Rica. And the list of the final landing places was as diverse as the nationalities represented.

The *Rialto's* course was from Italy to Cristóbal, through the Panama Canal, and up the Pacific coast to Canada. Franz and Franziska couldn't help but envy those who would continue on from Cristóbal to the United States. One of them was Helene Reinhardt. She'd attained an American visa; and after Franz and Franziska had spent some time talking to her that evening, they learned that she was the girlfriend of one of Franz's boyhood chums from Vienna: Felix Sklar. She seemed heartbroken after having been forced to say good-bye to him the afternoon before.

"You mean Felix was at the pier yesterday to see you off?" Franz asked.

"Yes. And he gave me this flower," Helene said whimpering, pulling out a very wilted gardenia.

"Gee . . . I haven't seen Felix in ten years. . . . How is he? What is he doing now?"

"He represents a vacuum cleaner company and he's been transferred to Shanghai."

"Oh. . . . Well at least he's getting out of Europe."

"Yes, but I may never see him again."

Helene looked so dejected that Franziska felt sorry for her. She was a pretty girl, taller than Franziska with lighter-colored hair, and she had a youthful, coquettish personality that was evident even in her current state of heavy-heartedness.

"Life is strange," Franziska said. "Maybe one day the two of you will meet again in America."

Just then, their conversation was interrupted by one of the ship's officers. "As you all know, we are traveling past Spain where a civil war is deep in progress," he said, standing in the middle of the social room. "We'll be passing through the Strait of Gibraltar in the middle of the night, and the captain has ordered a blackout." The officer made the announcement in Italian, then repeated it in German and English.

"What does that mean?" one of the passengers shouted without giving the officer an opportunity to continue.

"We're going to be very close to shore, and we want to sail through invisibly to ensure your safety," the officer said. "All of the ship's running lights will be extinguished."

"We're in danger. . . . I know that we're in danger," a woman cried out.

"That is not at all evident," the officer continued. "I must repeat that the blackout is simply a precautionary measure to ensure your safety. So when you return to your cabins, please close all of the curtains over your portholes and turn off some of your lights."

"We *are* in trouble," another man bellowed in English. "This is an Italian ship, and the Italians have been aiding General Franco. As soon as the Loyalists see the name *Rialto* on this ship, they're going to attack."

"Now be realistic," another man responded. "How are they going to identify this ship in the dark? And even if they could, it's quite obvious that this isn't exactly a battleship."

The officer didn't want to get involved, so he left the passengers alone to continue their heated discussion. They stayed together in the social hall until well after midnight; some were frightened, while those who were fleeing from Hitler's evil grip remained unaffected. Then most, including Franz and Franziska, walked back to their cabins to adhere to the officer's blackout instructions, some pledging to return to the social hall to spend the sleepless night with others.

Franz and Franziska remained in their stateroom, Franz thinking of his cousin, Fredl, fighting on the side of the Loyalists. Helene went back to the social hall, worrying about being all alone without Felix. And at three o'clock in the morning, the industrious *Rialto* sailed through the narrow Strait of Gibraltar. Spain was on the North, the North African country of Morocco on the South, and there were only fifteen kilometers (nine miles) between them at one point. No shooting! No fireworks! And when they'd traveled through the fifty-six kilometer (thirty-five mile) east-to-west passageway, they were frequenting the Atlantic Ocean.

The trip was quite enjoyable. Franz and Franziska thought so, and so did Helene Reinhardt. She'd recuperated from her bout of brokenheartedness and was flirting with all of the single men on the *Rialto*. Franz and Franzi tried not to notice. However as the weather improved, they spent hours on the deck chairs near Helene, who was invariably modeling her bathing suit around the collapsible pool.

"Oh, you're so lovely," Franz heard one of her suitors say. And before long, Helene and the suitor had disappeared into the afterhouse, never to be seen again for the remainder of the day.

"Oh, you're so accomplished. . . . Oh, you're so irresistible." The array of compliments was never-ending, and the play on words was almost as phenomenal as the text in an imaginative libretto; for by then, the passengers were in need of some stimulating entertainment.

So . . . Franz had the voice; Austrian-born Rudolf Friedler, the fingers; and the social hall harbored the keyboard.

It was a Wednesday afternoon on the first of February. The captain announced the concert over the loudspeaker, and almost everyone attended that evening: the passengers, the officers, and even part of the crew. They sat on the sofas, the chairs, the tables; and some were standing.

It was all so professional. Franz stood in front of the piano and nodded his head when ready. From the simple introductory chords, he immediately perceived that Rudolf Friedler was an able accompanist who could play with sensitivity. Franz opened with "An die Musik." Franz *always* opened with "An die Musik." The passengers seemed amazed. Apparently they'd expected mediocrity. Franz was just warming up.

Schubert's "Der Wegweiser" was next. How apropos! "The Signpost." Wilhelm Müller's text paralleled Franz and Franziska's journey almost perfectly, and some of the other passengers' voyages as well: Why were they being forced to avoid the roads that others were allowed to travel? They had done nothing wrong, but were compelled to wander in search of peace.

For many on the *Rialto*, the road to such repose would ultimately end in the United States. Yet it was the final phrases of the *Lied* which had the most significance for everyone. They addressed the road from which no one ever returned.

Journeying on that road was inevitable, but many on the voyage had feared facing it prematurely, and some envisioned those of their relatives who had already been forced to traverse it. The passengers who could understand German were moved by Franz's interpretation, and those who couldn't were still affected, affected by the emotion he displayed both vocally and visually.

In an attempt to lighten the mood and provide some contrast, Franz chose a lively aria to sing next, an aria which allowed him to demonstrate his showmanship. As he pantomimed a toast to the audience, he began singing the "Toreador Song" from Georges Bizet's *Carmen*. He'd never studied the entire role of the bullfighter Escamillo before; however he'd learned the torero's aria – in French. The rhythm of the music was so invigorating that some of the passengers were tapping their toes. Franz was waving an imaginary cloak in front of an invisible bull, then giving the ferocious animal a blow with a sharp banderilla. The audience loved him.

He closed with one of his old favorites, "Der Erlkönig." He'd come a long way since having heard it sung by Alexander Kipnis some three years before. And although Kipnis had remained his role model – especially in *Lieder* – Franz's voice was more baritonal, and his characterized interpretation was his own. He sang the *Lied* with unsettling urgency, the Erl King claiming the life of the man's son. And when the narrative ended with the definitive, "In his arms, the child lies *tot* (dead)," the audience seemed spellbound. There was silence, then applause; and some of the people called out, "Beautiful! Beautiful!"

The crew complimented him. The captain complimented him. And after that evening, Franz was the most popular passenger on the *Rialto*.

CHAPTER TWENTY-FOUR
Cine General Salom

Puerto Cabello, Venezuela
6 February 1939

*P*uerto Cabello was originally a sleepy port town on the Caribbean coast of Venezuela. Rumor had it that centuries ago the town was named after a fisherman, Antonio Cabello, who aided smugglers in the illegal importation of cacao to the nearby Dutch colony of Curaçao. But rumor also had it that the town's name simply stemmed from the calmness of the harbor, whose waters were incapable of disturbing even a strand of hair (*cabello*) atop a young lady's regal crown. But over the years, the port became one of the busiest in Venezuela.

It was a Monday morning. The crew was tossing the heaving line over to the dock where the fellows there were putting tension on it until they could grab the heavy line and tie it to the cleats. The *Rialto* was scheduled to remain at the wharf for twenty-four hours so that the crew could unload and load the ship's cargo; hence the passengers were permitted to disembark.

They walked past a long line of refugees who seemed tired, frazzled, and disoriented, and who were unlikely to proceed to a further destination. The people's clothes looked worn; their luggage, meager; and their dispositions, defeated. Those at the head of the line were showing their papers and passports to the authorities. Franz and Franziska concluded that some of the fortunate ones would eventually move on, possibly to the United States, while others would either be sent back to their homelands – a death knell – or would remain for the rest of their lives in Venezuela: not a bad fate, but one which was uncertain.

Suddenly Franz stopped walking. He was staring at a short, round man of about sixty who was clothed in a wrinkled gray suit and fedora. Franz tugged on Franziska's arm, bringing her to a halt, and then went over to the man, who was unaware of Franz's presence.

"You're dressed rather warmly for this climate," Franz said casually, attempting to be somewhat buoyant.

The man then turned so that he was facing his inquisitor. "Ah, Franz," he said with immediate recognition. "*Guten Morgen.*" But there was no zest in his voice, not even a hint of surprise. The gentleman placed his arm around the woman next to him – she was his wife – and said: "Look who is here, my darling. It's Franz. . . . You remember Franz."

For a second, a faint smile appeared on the woman's face. No more words were exchanged. Franz stroked the man on the shoulder – they both seemed to understand the circumstances – and Franz and Franziska continued walking on toward the town.

The man had been Franz's pharmacist in Vienna. Franz didn't even know his name. But seeing the man and his wife there in a line with refugees in a strange locale, Franz couldn't help but feel a kinship with them. Yet what could he do? So he just walked on.

Although the day had started off on a somewhat nostalgic note, the latter portion proved to be much more rewarding, thanks to Boleslav Manowski, an influential Polish businessman who resided in Puerto Cabello and owned the local theater. At a quarter past four in the afternoon, Franz was performing for a packed house.

How did it happen? The answer was simple. A few minutes after Franz was finished talking to his pharmacist, he heard a robust man's voice calling from behind.

"Franz Jung," the man was calling repeatedly, walking swiftly along the pier and glancing hesitantly at each one of the travelers as he passed them by.

When Franz finally identified himself, the man paused and placed a relieved smile on his face. He introduced himself and explained to Franz that the captain and some of the passengers on the *Rialto* had told him about the gifted opera singer aboard. "I knew that I wanted to meet you," he said to Franz in broken German, since his native tongue was Polish. "Would you like to show the people of Puerto Cabello what a beautiful voice really sounds like?"

Within the next few minutes, Boleslav Manowski had asked Franz to give a concert that afternoon at his theater. However after Franz agreed to the proposal, Manowski must have had some misgivings because he wanted to hear Franz's voice first. So Franz and Franziska were given a quick walking tour of Puerto Cabello as they proceeded toward the theater: along the seaside Malecón; down Calle Comercio to the plaza named after Venezuelan liberator Simón Bolívar; a brief repose to look at the patriot's statue and the coral-rock walls of the Iglesia de San José; and then down Avenida Anzoátegui to the theater. Along the way, Franz told Boleslav Manowski a little about his background and how much he wanted to sing in the United States. The streets were narrow and cobblestoned; the buildings, colonial; and the façades were painted in vivid colors. But the theater was not at all what Franz had expected: It was an open-air movie theater with a screen and no stage. But Franz didn't say anything. He'd consented to sing that afternoon at the Cine General Salom; and if Boleslav Manowski approved of his voice, he would keep his commitment. He just hoped that there would be some sort of monetary compensation, because he was worried about his and Franziska's sustenance.

"Wonderful," Boleslav Manowski said after Franz sang a few bars of the "Toreador Song." It was immediately evident to him that Franz had a great voice. "The performance will begin at four. I'm sure that the audience would like to hear some lighter music mixed in with the opera. I must rush now to get the word out."

Boleslav Manowski left Franz and Franziska to wander around the town. But they walked back to the *Rialto* instead, where Franz sang a few scales, changed into a dark blue suit, and gathered some sheet music. When they returned to the theater at half past three, it was completely filled with people. Boleslav Manowski had distributed flyers, he said. But where did all of the people come from? Everyone in the town must have been there, including some from the nearby city of Valencia.

As Franz walked into the theater with Franziska, he wondered who would be accompanying him and from where he would be singing. He looked at the cinema much more closely now. The rows of seats in the front section were in the open air. The people were facing the screen. They were dressed casually and a few had even brought their pets from home. (Franz had never sung for an animal before.) But the seats in the back of the theater were covered by a roof, and there were boxes.

Boleslav Manowski found a seat for Franziska in the front. Then he went back to Franz, who was still standing behind the last row. He escorted Franz up some steps on the left and down a passage which led to the front left side of the cinema. A dividing wall made the elevated walkway invisible to the audience, so Franz had the familiar feeling of being backstage in the wings.

"I will introduce you, and then you will sing from this platform. It is the closest semblance of a stage that I have to offer you," Boleslav Manowski said.

Franz looked out into the house. He was going to be singing from a ledge on the side. The people would have to strain their necks to see him. Well, at least he didn't have to worry about moving. *Maybe I shouldn't sing the "Toreador Song,"* he thought. *I wouldn't be able to dance around with my cloak very much, and I wouldn't be able to give that bull much of a blow with my banderilla. One such lunge and I'd be down in the audience.*

At least Franz had a sense of humor about the situation. But who was going to accompany him? He didn't even see a piano.

"Oh, I thought that you could sing a cappella," Boleslav Manowski said when Franz confronted him.

"Well, I suppose I could. I always carry my pitchpipe," Franz responded. "But you must have a piano around here somewhere . . . for silent films."

"We usually play talkies," Manowski said. "But there is a piano in the building."

"Good!"

"But I don't have an accompanist for you."

"Maybe there's someone in the audience."

"There are some people here from the Teatro Municipal, but . . ."

Boleslav Manowski then directed some employees to move the piano to what would become Franz's stage. And he found an accompanist as well: a music teacher from a nearby school.

Franz sang his opening aria – Tonio's "Prologue" from *Pagliacci* – at a quarter past four, a little later than planned. This was one of the few times that he did not begin with "An die Musik." He didn't know if this audience would appreciate German *Lieder*, so he decided to show off his voice from the onset with opera. The audience responded favorably. The people seemed legitimately taken by the volume of his voice. He hadn't planned a long program: just one aria, a few Italian folk songs, and some American standards.

To Franz's surprise, the accompanist had brought a guitar onto the makeshift stage, and he began strumming some introductory chords before Franz sang "Santa Lucia."

"Sul mare luccica l'astro d'argento. . . ."

Franz had become a sailor on the ocean, singing about the silvery star sparkling on the sea and the soft winds setting the waves in motion. He had selected wisely. Most of the people who lived in Puerto Cabello either belonged to fishermen's families, worked at the port, or were in some way connected to the harbor's mercantile activity. The sea was in their veins. And although they spoke Spanish and no Italian, the two Latin languages were similar enough for them to somehow comprehend what Franz was singing. And as practicing Roman Catholics, their eyes shown of enthusiasm when he sang of Santa Lucia: the saint whose light would lead the sailor agilely across the sea, and whose vision would lead all of them safely through life's unforeseeable journeys. Franz had won his audience's attention and approval. The applause was warmly gratifying to him.

Next, another song with an allusion to the sea: this one, a Neapolitan love song by Ernesto and Giambattista de Curtis.

"*Vide 'o mare quant'è bello, spira tanto sentimento. . . .*"

Franz was singing of the passionate sighs of the ocean and of the anguish he would feel if his lover left him and never returned.

"*Torna a Surriento – famme campà,*" he sang. "Come back to Sorrento – don't let me die."

And even if the Venezuelans didn't understand Italian – the song was written in a Neapolitan dialect – they were moved by the emotion that Franz communicated through his voice, and they applauded heartily.

Just at that moment, Franz looked down at Franziska. Their eyes met briefly, and they smiled in unison. This concert was a very unique experience for Franz. He was not singing much opera or *Lieder*, and he wasn't performing in front of his usual sophisticated audience. Yet he was really entertaining these people; they appreciated him, and he felt genuinely rewarded.

The songs "Because" and "I'll Be Seeing You" were next.

Franz charmed everyone – even if they didn't understand any English – and they loved him. They applauded and applauded. He extended his arm to acknowledge his accompanist, who rose and bowed his head modestly.

"All right! One more song," Franz said, although no one probably understood his German except Boleslav Manowski and Franziska. "Rodgers' and Hart's 'With A Song In My Heart,' " he announced in English as the accompanist fumbled through Franz's music to find the song.

Franz looked down at Franziska, and once again their eyes met as he started to sing to her.

The audience could see that he was serenading the very special woman in his life. For Franz and Franziska, it was as if nobody else was in the theater except the two of them. Franz always knew that he would live life through with a song in his heart for Franziska.

There was silence. Some of the women sighed. Then the applause started up again. Franz smiled and bowed as the people continued to clap. It was extremely warm, and some of the men and women were wiping their foreheads with handkerchiefs. A dog let out a bellowing bark. But the applause remained constant.

"Say *muchos gracias*," Boleslav Manowski shouted from the end of the pathway which led to the stage. So Franz did what he suggested, and the applause became even more thunderous.

"*Muchos gracias! Muchos gracias!*" Franz said repeatedly. He really didn't want to sing anymore; so since there was no curtain, he simply walked offstage toward Boleslav Manowski, with the accompanist following him and returning his music.

The applause finally dwindled. It started to fade . . . and then it stopped. The audience began leaving. And Franz, the accompanist, and his host proceeded back through the pathway, down the steps, and into the house, where Franz graciously thanked the music teacher for his help and said good-bye. As Franz and Boleslav Manowski made their way toward Franziska, many of the people smiled at Franz, gave him a friendly pat on the shoulder and congratulated him. "*Su voz es bella*," some of them said. "*Muchos gracias*," Franz always replied.

Then Franz really received the surprise of his life. A young man with light-brown hair and fair skin stopped him to echo the other people's sentiments: "*Sie haben eine sehr schöne Stimme*," the young man said.

Franz couldn't believe his ears. The lad, who surely was no more than eighteen years of age, explained to Franz that he was German and lived with his family in Valencia. Attempting not to stimulate any further conversation, Franz refrained from asking any questions. "*Danke*," he simply said and continued walking toward Franziska.

She was standing when Franz reached the front row. She was putting on the bolero jacket that matched her print crepe dress. Franz helped her into it and kissed her lightly on the cheek. Then she smiled and complimented him on his performance. They were both glad to be back together again.

The audience was thinning out. Most of the people had already left. Franz placed his arm around Franziska's waist and was about to lead her toward the exit when Boleslav Manowski took an envelope out of his coat pocket.

"I've really enjoyed meeting and hearing you," he said. "Thank you for performing on such short notice. You've given the people in this town something that they will talk about for a long time."

"It was my pleasure," Franz said.

"You will be very famous one day, and I hope that you'll remember us here in Puerto Cabello. Please accept this as a token of my gratitude."

Boleslav Manowski handed Franz the envelope, which Franz assumed was a small remuneration. "You're very generous," Franz said without opening the envelope. "I assure you that this day will remain in my mind forever."

The three walked to the exit at the back of the theater. Franz shook Boleslav Manowski's hand, and he and Franziska made their departure from the cinema. A few steps up Avenida Anzoátegui, and Franz stopped to glance back at the theater. From the outside, it looked like a stately two-story stone building with a flat roof, balconies with ornamental balustrades, and three tall entrances with wrought-iron gateways. Franz would have never guessed that part of the interior of the building was outdoors. He opened the envelope.

"Three hundred American dollars," he said in awe to Franziska. "I'm stunned. Many well-established opera singers perform for far less. I don't even know if the audience had to pay to hear me sing. I wonder why Boleslav Manowski has been so generous."

"Maybe he concluded that we could use the money since we were forced to leave Vienna," Franziska said. "Maybe he wanted to help us."

"Yes, maybe it's because we come from Europe like he does. . . . Maybe it's because I'm an opera singer."

"Don't try to figure him out, Franz. Just be happy. We have a lot to be grateful for."

When I went to Puerto Cabello in 1999, a guide and local official led me to where the theater had been. I stood there for many minutes reflecting and imagining the concert that had taken place on that spot. No one could remember the name of the generous gentleman who had arranged for the concert, so the name in this chapter is not really his. He gave my father a photograph of the Cine General Salom on a postcard and signed it, but his signature is not legible. My father never forgot his generosity. Maybe one day I will learn who he was.

A building in Colón in 1998. (*Photo by author.*)

CHAPTER TWENTY-FIVE

Panama Gold

Port of Cristóbal/Colón and Panama City
9 February to 13 February 1939

"*I* don't think this trunk is going to survive until we reach the United States," Franziska said as she and Franz were checking into the Hotel Internacional in Colón. When they'd docked in Cristóbal, a crane had offloaded their trunk with such force that the trunk had split open at the bottom, and one of the longshoremen had to nail on a board to give it a new base.

"It'll be just fine," Franz responded. "Even though it's not as cosmetically pleasing, it's just as strong as ever now."

Yet it was Franz and Franziska who were beginning to feel a little weary, so they went to the Hotel Internacional, which was the closest hotel they could find. It was an acceptable place. Although far from luxurious, it had four floors of rooms – some with balconies – and it had a presentable lobby with an adjoining cafetería. More important, however, it was near the office of the United Fruit Company, where they would purchase tickets the next day to depart on the *Chiriquí* for Cuba.

After receiving the key to their room – the key had been hanging on one of many hooks mounted on a massive piece of walnut behind the reception counter – Franziska grabbed their overnight bag and walked toward the elevator while Franz pushed the afflicted trunk after her.

"Once you get that trunk in here, I don't think there's going to be any room for you," Franziska said as she entered the narrow lift and backed up against one of the side walls.

"Sure there is," Franz responded emphatically as he propelled the overburdened case into the elevator, squeezing himself into the lift afterwards. "But you're going to have to push the button. Push three . . . please."

The Hotel Internacional was located on Avenida Bolívar near Calle Once. The office of the United Fruit Company was just a few blocks away. But before going there the next morning, Franz and Franziska wanted to get something to eat – not in their hotel though, because the cafetería had a bar, and the environment somehow seemed inappropriate that early in the morning. So they walked down Calle Once toward the steamship office. At the corner of Calle Once and Avenida Balboa, Franz thought that he saw a restaurant in the distance. So they turned left onto Avenida Balboa and continued on until they saw the Restaurante Cristóbal across the street. Once inside, they determined that the restaurant was no more than a small café with about eight tables and a lot of smoke. It was probably more undesirable than the cafetería in their own hotel, but they weren't about to go back. In addition, everyone spoke Spanish except for them, and they didn't know how to communicate. So when the waiter asked what they wanted, Franz pointed to the table next to them, where a man was eating some sort of heavy soup: not exactly their first choice for a morning meal. Nevertheless, a few minutes later, that's exactly what they were consuming. Franz took a spoonful and swallowed hard. Then he grabbed a glass of water. "This is spicy," he said, his face turning somewhat reddish, perspiration appearing in the creases of his forehead.

"What's in it?" Franziska asked, examining the bowl in front of her, gliding her forefinger around the circular edge.

"Beans and rice, and maybe this is chicken or pork," Franz answered.

"And what's that?"

"It's sort of a cross between sour cream and custard," Franz said, tasting it.

"I think the custard is about all that I'm going to ingest," Franziska remarked, beginning to eat very precautiously.

About half an hour later, Franz wanted to pay the bill, but the waiter wouldn't accept any money. "Since we don't speak Spanish, he probably thinks that we're poor immigrants," Franz told Franziska. "Maybe he feels sorry for us."

Then the man at the next table explained: "They serve the soup for nothing," he said in broken English. "People get thirsty from it and buy more drinks, especially when they serve *bocas* . . . uh . . . other side dishes as well."

Franz and Franziska got the gist of what the man was attempting to say because they could still remember some of the English that they'd learned in school.

"Come on, Franzi. We've done enough eating," Franz declared, standing. "Let's go and get our tickets." So they were out the door a few minutes later, walking back to Calle Once, turning left, and almost running toward the port until they reached the steamship office. "Here it is," Franz said. " 'United Fruit Company.' I sure hope that our places are still reserved on the *Chiriquí*."

United Fruit was on the ground floor of a two-story Colonial-style office building near Calle Once and the street closest to the harbor, Avenida del Frente. A sign with its name was visible above the entrance. There were just a couple of desks inside, so Franz and Franziska approached the agent sitting behind the one closest to the door. Not expecting to make himself clearly understood, Franz showed the agent the Panamanian transit visa that was stamped in his passport, and then he said in English: "Luciana Ferretti . . . reservations on the *Chiriquí*."

The agent looked through a list of names and responded: "You're not here."

"No? We must be," Franz replied, becoming excited. "Can we still get on?"

"The *Chiriquí* is filled, sir."

Franz started speaking very agitatedly in German to Franziska.

"Since you are not leaving Panama yet, you need to go to the Department of Immigration in Panama City to extend your visa," the agent said.

Franz's earlier fears of being stranded in Panama were becoming a reality. "I'm feeling rather light-headed and strange," Franz suddenly announced to Franziska. "I think that I'm going to faint."

"Faint . . . faint . . ." Franziska uttered in English. And a few seconds later, she and the agent were leading Franz to the sofa against the wall.

"Lie back," Franziska said, gently guiding Franz in the right direction and then removing his shoes.

"I feel better. . . . I feel much better now," he said a few minutes later.

"Just stay there for a while. Don't get up too soon."

"I'm all right. Really I am," Franz asserted assuredly.

However Franziska wasn't convinced. It was her turn to take the initiative: "Now Mister . . . Mister . . ."

"Alvarez," the agent said.

"Mister Alvarez," Franziska proceeded in English, her ability to speak the language far surpassing Franz's. "The secretary at the Panamanian Consulate in Milano has definitely booked us on the *Chiriquí*. . . ."

"But your name is not here, señora."

"That is impossible," Franziska said firmly. "Let me see the list, please."

"There is no Luciana Ferretti on it," the agent reiterated.

"But I am not Luciana Ferretti. Luciana Ferretti made the reservations for us."

"Who are you then?" the agent asked heatedly.

"I am Franziska Jung. . . . Here is my passport with my picture and name in it. . . . My husband's name is Franz Jung."

"Oh, señora, I am so sorry. There has been a terrible misunderstanding. You *are* on the list."

So after a lot of apologizing, Franz and Franziska purchased the tickets and decided to immediately venture to Panama City to extend their visas. The railroad station was almost next door. Franziska knew that the train ride would be interesting because it followed the route of the Panama Canal.

After departing from the Caribbean and Atlantic side of the Canal Zone that Friday afternoon, the train passed the Gatún Locks, which were known for raising vessels from sea level to the height of the Gatún Lake. But Franz and Franziska were unable to actually see very much there. Through tropical rainforest, swampland, and along a bridge over the Chagres River, the tracks led them to the Pedro Miguel Locks, where they had a much better view of a ship moving into a lock and being lowered to the level of the Miraflores Lake. The mechanics really fascinated Franziska: the gates closing around the ship and the locomotives guiding her through. However while the train was stopped at the terminal there, Franz only watched the goings-on with passive interest: He cared solely about reaching the Department of Immigration before it closed. One more set of locks, the Miraflores Locks, finalized the process of lowering vessels to the Pacific Ocean's tidewater level. And the trip was almost complete. They'd been traveling for nearly two hours. They'd seen long ropes of green vines, Spanish moss, air plants, and orchids. And they'd also seen cows lazily grazing in the grasslands. It was three o'clock. The train was rolling into the Estación del Tren de Ancón. They were in Panama City.

There were *cucarachas* everywhere – well, not everywhere – but along the the main street that Franz and Franziska were traversing. Mister Alvarez had told them to simply say "Avenida Central" to anyone at the train station, and they'd be pointed in the right direction. The street was easy to find, but the *cucarachas* . . .

They entered a main shopping area – a marketplace really – where stores were located on the bottom floors of apartment buildings, and salespeople were bargaining out in front to attract customers. Some of the goods were displayed right on the sidewalks. And there was food for sale: fruits and vegetables and drinks.

"I'm thirsty," Franz said, "probably because I ate all of that spicy food this morning. I'm going to buy some soda water. Do you want anything?"

"No, thank you, Franz. I'm glad now that I restrained myself from eating before. Maybe I'll have some fruit later."

But Franz couldn't find anything familiar to drink – at least nothing that he'd ever seen in Vienna – so he bought a cup of what looked like cold coffee. "Oh, this doesn't taste like *Kaffee* at all," he said to Franziska. "What is it?"

The vendor saw the perplexed look on their faces. "Coca-Cola," he said. "From the United States."

It didn't seem odd at all to Franz that the Panamanians were patronizing U.S. products. After all, Americans had built and were controlling the canal. But that didn't mean Franz had to like their commodities. "I hope that other American foods are better than this," he said. "If not, I'm going to starve."

"I doubt that," Franziska remarked tauntingly. "Let's just hope that you have that problem soon."

The next blunder of the afternoon came just a few minutes later when Franz tried to get directions to the Department of Immigration. "Take a streetcar that way," one of the merchants said. "I want to go with feet" was Franz's response. It would be a long time before he could really converse in English.

So . . . they went with their feet along Avenida Central into the colonial part of Panama City – Casco Viejo – looking for the immigration office. Their path led them by pastel-colored Spanish, French, and neoclassical-style façades with ironclad balconies; through Plaza de la Independencia, where the Panamanians had avowed their autonomy; past the luxurious high society-oriented Hotel Central; and near the statuesque neoclassically-designed Teatro Nacional. They'd reached the Department of Immigration, which was housed in a distinctive governmental building with a grandiose main entrance and staircase. They found the correct office, which was crowded with people who apparently wanted to remain in Panama for a while. However, unlike Franz and Franziska, most of the people spoke Spanish. The wait was sure to be endless, they thought. All of the seats were taken. Then: "*Wo sind Sie von?*"

Who was that? Who wanted to know where they were from? Whomever this man was, he must have heard them speaking in German. Or maybe they simply looked out of place: Franz was wearing a gray wool suit that was much too heavy for the hot, humid climate of Panama. Now this man – this man who seemed to have appeared from out of nowhere – he certainly didn't look like anyone else in the room either. He was dressed in a well-fitted lightweight beige-colored gabardine suit, a suit which only someone wealthy could have afforded. He was German or formerly Austrian, Franz surmised. *"Von Wien. Wir sind von Wien,"* Franz responded.

The man, Hubert Schüler, explained that he had come to the immigration office with two of his relatives. He had made it possible for thirty relatives and friends, with their families, to enter Panama. He pointed to those who were seated in the waiting area: "I've come to help them extend their visas," he said, "and to fill out the necessary forms so that they can work for me. I am a clothes manufacturer. I'm happy here, but many of my relatives would like to immigrate to the United States."

After Franz introduced Hubert Schüler to Franziska and explained their reason for being in Panama, Hubert Schüler responded with an invitation. "You still have two days here until you leave for Cuba," he said, writing his address on a piece of paper and handing it to Franz. "You're staying in Colón, and I live and work there. Please come and visit me tomorrow. You should be able to walk from your hotel."

"Oh, how lovely!" Franziska replied. "We feel so lost here."

"I can make you feel much more at home," Hubert Schüler said. "You're from Vienna. Maybe we know some of the same people."

"I doubt that," Franziska said. "Vienna is a big city."

"Do you know the Ullmanns or the Hornsteins?"

"No," Franziska answered.

"Maybe you'll remember some of my relatives.... Uhhh ... Marianne Weiss?"

"No."

"The Rosens?"

"No."

"How about Doktor Peter Gottesmann?"

"Yes!" Franz blurted out with surprised recollection. "We were Boy Scouts together. I haven't seen him since *Realgymnasium*. . . . 'Doktor Peter Gottesmann' – that sounds pretty impressive. What is he doing now?"

"He's a lawyer. . . . Would you like to see him?"

"Yes, of course, I would!"

"Well, then you will . . . when you come to visit me tomorrow. . . . It's been very nice chatting with you, but I must go back to my relatives now. . . . Until tomorrow, *auf Wiedersehen!*" And Hubert Schüler retreated back into the crowd.

At half past four, Franz and Franziska's last name was finally called. Hubert Schüler and his relatives had left an hour before. The procedure was simple this time. The transit visas they'd been issued in Milano clearly stated that their destination was Cuba, and they had their tickets to prove it; so an immigration manager stamped each of their passports with their date of departure, and they were allowed to remain legally in Panama until the thirteenth of February.

It was late. The governmental office was just about to close. They had another train ride ahead of them, and they were exhausted and starved. At least they had the next two days to relax and unwind.

The following morning, Franz and Franziska showed Hubert Schüler's address to the clerk at the reservation desk in their hotel. He told them to walk down Calle Once, turn right onto Avenida del Frente, and continue north. He said the address was near the Hotel Washington on Calle Dos.

Franz and Franziska walked and walked. It was warm and humid again. Only on this day, Franz was wearing a lightweight linen suit with a Panama straw hat, and Franziska was in a thin silk blouse and skirt. They'd found the hotel. Its Spanish Colonial elegance was matched with lush green grounds and sedate palms. Then they found the address Hubert Schüler had scribbled on the piece of paper.

The house was large and looked quite different from those in Vienna or Prague. It was two stories high and had a modern, airy look about it. A hipped roof supported by columns covered a generous front porch and garden, while another similarly styled larger one protected the main dwelling behind. They walked up the steps in the front and knocked on the door. A woman who was about the age of Franz's mother answered it.

"Hubert Schüler invited us," Franz explained in German.

"Just a minute, sir. Please wait here," the woman said, disappearing into the house.

A few minutes later, Hubert Schüler greeted and welcomed them. "Come this way," he said, leading them through a lovely living room toward the back of the house. He opened a door, and there were at least thirty people – mostly women – sitting and working on sewing machines. "These are some of the people that I was able to rescue from Europe," he said. "I help them, and they help me."

Franziska noticed that one woman was sewing a hem; another, a seam; and one woman was carefully fitting gatherings to a waistband. "I've worked for two dress shops in Vienna," Franziska explained to Hubert Schüler. "I've made patterns and shopped for materials, and a few of my designs have even been manufactured. . . . Do you mind if I walk around?"

So while Franziska was observing, Franz continued talking to Hubert Schüler. "I enjoy this house," Schüler said. "The floor plan allows me to both live and work here. My relatives come in every morning through the rear entrance. They have access to the adjacent bathroom and kitchen while they're on the job. They know that the bedrooms are upstairs, and they respect my privacy."

After a few more minutes of discussion: "So Peter Gottesmann . . . is he here?" Franz asked. "You don't have him sewing, do you?"

"No, not quite," Hubert Schüler responded. "Come with me."

So as Franz was walking toward the back of the room, he tapped Franziska on the shoulder, and she immediately joined him. They walked out the rear door into the backyard, and there he was, dressed in a printed sports shirt, cotton pants, a straw hat, and boots. And he was firing a rifle.

"Oh!" Franziska called out startled, jumping up at the sound of the gunshot. Until that moment, Doktor Gottesmann had been unaware that anyone was watching him. He'd been aiming at a target. He looked over and smiled.

"Franzl," he said, placing the gun down and walking toward them with open arms. "I haven't seen you in years. What are you doing here?"

Many of Franz's childhood friends had added the letter "l" to the end of his name because it made his name sound more informal. "I might ask you the same question," Franz responded, the two giving each other a bearhug.

Franz explained his circumstances and introduced Doktor Gottesmann to Franziska.

"Franziska! Such a stern name for such a little girl," Doktor Gottesmann said. "Franzi . . . Franzi – now that's much more like it."

Franziska was amused. She smiled and even let out a laugh. She could tell right away that Doktor Peter Gottesmann was a character. After all, he was Franz's age, and he'd grown a mustache.

"I'm learning to shoot because I'm going to need to be able to defend myself when I go out into the jungle."

"Into the jungle?" Franz questioned. "What are you going to do there?"

"Oh, not the jungle in Africa," Doktor Gottesmann explained, "the jungle in Panama."

"All right," Franz continued. "I must repeat – what are you going to do there?"

"Well, search for gold, of course. I'm going to make my fortune here in Panama."

"How can you be so sure?"

"Riches are part of Panama's history. The Inca Indians brought gold from Peru, and the conquistadors transported it along the isthmus and shipped it to Spain."

"So . . ."

"And the Panama Railroad was built after the California gold rush, to profit from wealthy Americans traveling from the eastern United States to the West."

"But that doesn't mean that gold is a natural resource of Panama."

"Oh, but gold *has* been found all over Panama: in the central provinces, in Darién, and in the province of Panama. The town of Las Minas was named after the mines that were excavated there. And both the Spanish and the English have toiled in the mines of Cana. That's where I'd like to go. I've heard that the gold that washes down from the mines there can easily be found in the riverbeds. But Cana is so very far away."

Franz was listening somewhat astounded. Peter Gottesmann had done a great deal of research. But Franz thought that his old friend was surely dreaming.

"I could go to Natá. . . . I could go to Taboga . . . or maybe I'll just go to the northern part of Veraguas."

Doktor Gottesmann looked like he was in deep contemplation. "I must continue my target practicing. I don't have much time. Very nice seeing you again," he said, then rushed into the yard, picked up his rifle and aimed it.

"Let's go inside," Franziska said. "I don't think that I care much for the noise."

On Monday morning, Franz and Franziska were ready to go to Cuba. They'd checked out of the Hotel Internacional and were taking a taxi to the port. They would have walked the few blocks, but Franz's trunk was just too heavy to push that far.

"Stop! Stop!" Franz said excitedly, opening the door before the driver barely had a chance to step on the brakes.

"Franz! Are you crazy? You're going to get killed!" Franziska shouted.

The taxicab driver had slammed on the brakes right next to the entrance of the port, near Calle Once and Avenida del Frente. And there *HE* was again, in a plaid cotton-flannel shirt, solid-colored flannel pants, the same brown boots and a straw hat. Doktor Peter Gottesmann was coming toward them. He was walking down Avenida del Frente. Only he wasn't alone. He was leading a mule. And the mule was hauling a wagon.

"Franzl . . . Franzi," Doktor Gottesmann shouted, waving. A few minutes later, he and Franz were standing face-to-face in the middle of

Avenida del Frente. And a few seconds after that, Franziska abandoned the taxi and joined them.

"I'm off. . . . I'm finally off to the jungle. I have food and supplies and a rifle. And my friend here will transport my treasures."

"Do you know where you're going?" Franz asked.

"There are so many places to look, so I've decided to start close to Colón in the area where the Chagres River meets Gatún."

"And what if you don't have any luck?"

"I'll move on to some of the places I mentioned to you the other day. I recently met an old Englishman who came across some ancient maps that were found in Portobelo, where treasures were stored hundreds of years ago before they were shipped to Spain. He gave me a couple of the maps. They're a bit ragged and torn, and I can barely make out what's written on them, but they will eventually lead me to those old mines."

"But there might not be any gold there anymore."

"I'll find it. If there's gold to be found, I'll find it."

"Peter, I don't want to discourage you," Franz said. "I . . ."

"Then *Don't!*" Doktor Gottesmann interrupted firmly, immediately sweetening again. "Bon voyage Franzl and Franzi. When we meet next, I will be rich."

Franz opened his mouth to speak, but Peter Gottesmann placed his hand in front of it. *"Auf Wiedersehen,"* he said. And as he and his mule began walking down Avenida del Frente, Franz shouted after him: "The jungle can be a dangerous place. At least try to stay healthy and safe."

Doktor Gottesmann waved his hand while nodding his head in acknowledgment, but he didn't even turn around to look back. He just kept moving.

Hubert Schüler was a real person, but my father could not remember his name. I feel it is important that I make mention of that fact because the man I call Hubert Schüler made a difference during his life: he saved the lives of at least thirty people and made it possible for them to work for him and survive. Oh, and, yes, Doktor Gottesmann existed, too. And his name was indeed, Doktor Gottesmann.

CHAPTER TWENTY-SIX

Triscornia

Havana, Cuba
16 February to 3 March 1939

I went to Havana legally from Miami in 1999, and when I arrived there, I met with Jeffrey DeLaurentis, who was, at the time, the First Secretary of Politics and Economics in the U.S. Interests Section. He was extremely cordial and provided me with a guide. I met various people along the way and was given some pertinent information about Triscornia, which I have tried to describe to the best of my ability in this chapter, and in the chapter notes at the end of this book. I went to the location of the former internment camp, which, at the time, had become a maritime business of sorts. I spoke to the vice director and was able to walk on the grounds. I was asked not to take photographs, but I managed to snap a few anyhow. Although I learned in 2012 that the site was the home of a military facility, I have written this chapter based on what I saw in 1999, along with my documentation. Even ten years later, little was written or known about Triscornia, sometimes called "Tiscornia." I saw that a few people had posted requests on the Internet to communicate with anyone who might have known immigrants who were sequestered there. They were searching for information about their families. When I visited the synagogue and Jewish community center in Havana – the Gran Sinagoga de la Comunidad Hebrea de Cuba, known as "El Patronato" – the people I spoke to did know about Triscornia. I believe that even this short chapter will make the public more aware of its historical existence as part of the Holocaust experience.

𝒯he *Chiriquí* was steaming into Havana Bay. Much larger than the *Rialto*, she accommodated a hundred passengers and was more luxurious, Franziska thought. Four decks with a glass-enclosed promenade; a lounge with a mural and skylight, piano and dance floor; a handsomely paneled Tudor-style library and smoking room; an elegant Spanish-decorated dining room; a multipurpose café which alternated as a romantically moonlit ballroom; and a permanent swimming pool. But the *Chiriquí* was much more than a cruise ship. She didn't simply cater to wealthy Americans and Europeans who were only interested in traveling from port to port. She had four main refrigerated holds which stored fifty thousand stems of bananas. And she had booms positioned at her two masts to facilitate their loading and discharge, as well as strategically placed wing hatches to expedite their movement through her conveyor belts.

The accommodations on the *Chiriquí* were adequate, although a little cumbersome for Franziska, even though Franz didn't seem to mind. The larger cabins with private facilities were rather expensive, so Luciana Ferretti had reserved one with only a sink, necessitating Franz and Franziska to share a complete bathroom with the couple in the quarters next to them. Their cabin had two beds with a bureau and mirror in-between, an ample wardrobe, and real windows – not portholes – with curtains, shades, storm shutters, and mosquito screens.

Because the duration of their journey on the *Chiriquí* lasted for only a few days, they had very little time to partake in the activities on board. But then, how could they? Normally they would have gravitated to the ballroom, but they intentionally stayed away. They didn't want to hear music; they didn't want to dance; they simply had the desire to dock in Cuba. They were very insecure about their future. How long would they be forced to remain in this new, strange country before being allowed to immigrate to America? Where would they stay? Would they have enough money? How well would they be able to adapt to a place where everything was foreign to them? They spent a great deal of time holding on to each other. They were closer now than ever before. Yet on some occasions, not even Franz could quell Franziska's frustrations. She began smoking. She'd smoked a little when she was twenty, just after moving out of Blütengasse Neun. The sport had made her feel mature. But as soon as Franz began singing, she quit: She didn't want to harm his voice. But now she suddenly missed those small white cigarettes with the little red mouthpieces. Yet she still didn't want to harm Franz's voice, so while on the *Chiriquí*, the smoking room became her special hideaway.

"We're going to dock soon," Franz said, entering her retreat. "I've got the overnight bag. Come out on deck with me."

Franziska was the only one in the cypress-paneled smoking room. She was sitting on a leather-upholstered chair, glaring at the beamed ceiling above, her half-smoked cigarette diagonally positioned in the ashtray on the table in front of her. "You mean we're in Havana?" she asked.

"Havana Bay, my sweet. La Habana is waiting for us."

Franziska crushed her cigarette, swiveling it back and forth in her ashtray. Then she stood up and walked toward Franz. He kissed her on the forehead; she placed her arm around his waist; and they walked out onto the promenade deck, which was completely fringed with people looking out at the bay, which resembled a large tranquil lake bordered with long intrusive quays and edged with various sized edifices that seemed to expand up into the hills on one side, like the irregularly-shaped pieces of a jigsaw puzzle, and on the other perimeter, seemed to mesh into a vast metropolis. A blast of the whistle could soon be heard emanating from the bridge, and a tug pulled up alongside the snow-white turbo-electric-propelled steamship and began nudging her toward the dock.

The man standing next to Franziska was speaking French to the woman beside him. Since Franziska could converse in the language, she explained to him that she'd be remaining in Cuba until she could immigrate to America, and she asked him if he was aware of a reasonably priced hotel.

"*Regardez là-haut,*" he said, pointing up into the hills. "*Çela est El Morro; l'autre, La Cabaña. Et là-bas – là où vous resterez.*"

"What did he say?" Franz asked.

"He said that we would be staying up there, next to those two fortresses, " Franziska pointed.

"In that impressive white building?"

"I guess so. It must be a very stylish hotel."

"It looks like a Baroque castle. It sort of resembles the Karlskirche in Vienna with that big dome on top. . . . Do you recall that awful experience I had there, when the Nazis held a demonstration and Bruno Eichler spit into my face?"

"Yes, I remember when you told me about it."

"I sure hope this hotel leaves me with better memories than the Karlskirche did."

Two immigration officers soon boarded the *Chiriquí*, and the purser pointed them toward Franz and Franziska. After examining their passports, the officers directed them to disembark from the side port. They climbed down some steps into the motorboat that was tied there, and the officers whisked them off across the bay.

As Franziska sat in the battered, weathered motorboat listening to the sloshing of the water and breathing in the scents of the sea, she looked into Franz's eyes, and the two communicated without speaking. Where were they being taken? They were out of Europe. There were no concentration camps in Cuba. Should they be frightened?

After their brief ride in the motorboat, they were led along a small, winding road. One officer was in front of them, one behind. Their trunk was still on the *Chiriquí*, but Franz was carrying their overnight bag. It was uphill all the way and there were numerous steps to climb. Franziska was out of breath. Ever since her bout with rheumatic fever, she'd never been able to develop much stamina. Her face had turned red and she was bracing herself against a tree. Franz was worried and went over to comfort her. The officers let them rest for a few minutes, and then they were told to continue moving. But where were they going? And why?

They reached a large gate that opened from the center, the type used to herd cattle into a corral. After the guard assessed their passports, the gate was unlocked, and they were led inside. There was barbed wire all around. The Frenchman had been right. They *were* going to stay in the hills above Havana Bay, however not in the beautiful Baroque castle with a dome, but in what seemed to be a prison.

"You're going to have to remain here," a young soldier told them in English. He probably wasn't a soldier at all, but he looked like one in his khaki dust-colored uniform and badge.

"But why?" Franziska questioned. "We're here legally. We have Cuban visas."

"All of the immigrants stay here. That's all I know. Those are my orders."

"Is this a detention camp? An immigration camp?" But the soldier refrained from answering.

The surroundings were somewhat gloomy. There was a dirt road with low buildings on either side that had the cold essence of military barracks; and the overgrown dying grass and shrubbery resembled the brush in a neglected burial ground.

The soldier took Franz and Franziska to a stark-looking building on the left, announced that cohabitation was prohibited, and declared that this dormitory was where Franziska would sleep. "No! No! I will not be separated from my husband," Franziska cried out, throwing her arms around Franz.

"Sweetheart, I'm sure it won't be for long," Franz uttered, trying to calm her. "There must be a way out of here."

"But how are you going to . . ."

"I don't know. But if there's a way out, I'll find it. . . . Here . . . you take the overnight bag."

"But . . ."

Franz touched Franziska's lips. "Don't worry, my sweet. I'll get us out of here."

So Franziska walked slowly and grievously through some grass and up some steps into the dormitory. And then Franz was led a little farther along the road to a dorm on the right.

That night seemed unbearable to Franziska. There were twenty-four other women in the dorm, all of them refugees, some with Cuban visas and some without. The facilities were totally inadequate. Most of the twenty-five cots only had one bedsheet. Luckily the weather was warm because some of the women had to go without blankets. And none of the linens seemed clean. In fact, Franziska detected bedbugs. "Oh, no," she uttered. Since moving out of her mother's apartment, she'd been able to avoid the pests. Now all of her memories were recurring, and she knew that as long as she was forced to remain in this prison, she would not be able to sleep. There was absolutely no privacy. The spaces between the beds were so narrow that not even the bedbugs had enough room to roam. So even when the shades of night and dimmed lights created a misty cloud which only sleep could overcome, the disheartened women in the dorm found relief only through their camaraderie. They were Polish, Czech, French, Yugoslavian, German, and Austrian; and at least five of them were over the age of seventy-five.

"I've been in this camp for almost two months," an elderly Austrian woman told Franziska. "I spend most of my time in here because there aren't enough chairs and benches around, and I need to rest. My heart is so very weak . . . so weak."

"Be careful of the food," a younger German woman warned. "A lot of people have dysentery or the grippe."

"What do you mean 'be careful'?" another woman offered sarcastically. "We don't have much choice. All of the food here is tasteless."

"Yes, but I just want to warn her about the meat and fish. It's usually spoiled."

"Thank you," Franziska said, cutting off the discourse. "By the way, are we allowed to go outside and wander around this . . . this facility whenever we like? I really want to be with my husband."

"Yes, yes! We can go anywhere," the German woman answered, "as long as we remain in Triscornia."

"Triscornia?"

"That's the name of this camp, my dear. Welcome to Triscornia."

"But why are we here? I don't fully understand."

"I'm afraid none of us do," the German said. "Ask President Brú and Batista."

"But what does the government gain from all of this?"

"Money."

"What do you mean?"

"Oh, you don't know yet. . . . Each of us has to pay thirty dollars a month for room and board, and we're permitted to buy extra items from the canteen, but it's terribly expensive."

"Is there any way out?"

" 'Is there any way out?' she asks," the German woman mimicked. "Money is the answer . . . Are you Jewish?"

"Yes," Franziska replied.

"Then when the representative from the Jewish relief organization comes, go and talk to him."

"Do you know when that will be?"

"He comes every morning, but he's not allowed inside. If you follow the dirt road past the men's dorms, you'll see a vacant area on the right. Just walk through it, and you'll find him waiting on the other side of the fence."

"Thank you. Thank you so much," Franziska responded. Her heart was beating so aggressively that she feared her chest would burst. She wanted to rush right out to tell Franz; but of course, she couldn't. Instead she lay dressed on her cot until daybreak, staring at the sterile ceiling and smudged walls, and swishing the bedbugs away from her.

The next day, Franziska went to the men's dorms, but she couldn't find Franz in any of them. She suddenly became panic-stricken and began pacing up and down the road in a frenzy: *"Where could he be? What could have happened to him?"*

She could see a few of the women from her dorm walking toward her. Upon making contact, they tried to coax her into joining them in the communal mess hall. "Oh, I couldn't eat a thing," Franziska explained. "My husband must be looking for me. I want to be as visible for him as possible."

"Maybe he's inside eating," the German woman said. "Come on . . . why don't you join us?"

"I really don't think that my husband would have gone in there without me."

"But if you have any doubts . . ."

"All right. I'll just stay for a few minutes to have a look around. I don't want to reproach myself later for failing to explore every possibility."

The large room truly was a communal mess hall. It was filled with people: some in long lines waiting for servers to fill their empty bowls with soup ladled from humongous vats; and others sitting on long benches in front of large wooden tables, eating and talking obsessively.

Franziska didn't stay with the women. She wandered around instead. And then she saw Franz sitting at the end of one of the tables, sulking. She wanted to run to him, but she approached him with reserve instead. "May I join you?" she asked.

"Oh, Franziska . . ."

"Here you are eating. I thought that you'd be out looking for me."

"I had a terrible night. I wanted to regain my composure because I didn't want to depress you."

"My night wasn't exactly fun and games either. Don't you realize that we're better together than apart?"

"Yes, of course, I do. But I couldn't think of a plan to get us out of here."

"Well, I think that I might have the answer."

Franziska told Franz about the man from the Jewish relief organization. She cheered him up a little, then got herself some soup and bread, and the two stayed awhile to get a better perspective from some of the others around them. They learned that Triscornia housed about four hundred fifty refugees. Not all of them were Jewish. Some had been placed in concentration camps when the Nazis learned of their abhorrence to Hitler's policies. Once freed, they'd never expected to be placed in an internment camp. But here they were. And "Why?" was always their question.

The children didn't understand either. The little two-year-old sitting across from Franziska refused to eat the soup his mother was feeding him. He kept on turning his face from side to side. Keeping his jaw clenched tight, his mother tried to force some nourishment into him, but the soup kept dribbling from his mouth to his chin onto his unwashed clothes. The mother explained to Franziska that fruit juice and milk were unattainable, except from the canteen which was too expensive. She hoped that the relief organization would ship in some bananas and oranges before her son became ill. "I can't afford to take him to the clinic here," she said. "An injection would simply be too costly."

Franziska sympathized, but she had her own problems. She wanted to bathe, she wanted to change her clothes, and she wanted to find a way out. The wooden table in front of her was rough to the touch. "Ouch!" she cried, sucking her finger. "I've got a splinter in it. Now where am I going to find a needle to pull it out?"

"Don't you have one in the overnight bag?" Franz suggested.

"Oh, yes, of course. I guess I wasn't thinking."

They finished eating, said good-bye to the mess hall, and proceeded along the road toward Havana Bay. To the right through some grass and mud, and they could see a man standing behind the barbed-wire fence: an American gentleman wearing a linen suit and straw hat.

"Hello," Franz said.

"Hello," the gentleman reciprocated, tipping his hat. "I'm a representative from HIAS, and I'm doing what I can to help the people who are detained here."

"What is HIAS?" Franziska asked.

"Hebrew Immigrant Aid Society," the gentleman answered. "The organization is based in New York."

"We were told that you could help us find a way out of here," Franziska told him.

"Yes, that's true. But it's really *you* who has the power to get yourself out."

"But how?"

"It's simple: five hundred dollars apiece, and then some."

"That's a lot of money," Franz murmured.

"Yes, but it's the key to your freedom."

"Isn't there any way to attain the key to our freedom for less?" Franziska asked.

"You can try. . . . If it's any consolation, the five hundred dollars apiece will be returned to you when you leave Havana. The Cubans don't want you to stay. The money serves as a security deposit and ensures them that you're going to leave. But the additional money will be lost. That money is not required by the Cuban government; however you'll have to pay it in order to get out of Triscornia. That sum is negotiable."

"To whom do we give the money?" Franziska asked.

"To one of the immigration officers in the guardhouse by the gate."

"We won't have practically anything left to live on," Franz then told Franziska in German.

"Why don't you think about it?" the gentleman suggested. "But if you do decide to pay, make sure that you get a receipt stipulating that the thousand-dollar deposit will be returned to you upon your departure from Cuba. If you need any more advice, you know where to find me."

They'd been in Triscornia for almost two weeks. Franz was losing weight, and Franziska had developed stomach pains. The physician in the clinic had told her that he suspected appendicitis, which was of course impossible: She no longer had her appendix.

Hoping to invigorate themselves, Franz and Franziska purchased some items from the canteen: some hard-boiled eggs, milk, butter, fruit . . . and some chocolate. They later debated about their fate under what appeared to be the remnants of a gazebo that overlooked the harbor. The sporadic brownish-green grass in their view looked burnt; the sea, slate; and the harbor and city beyond seemed devastatingly unreachable.

"This isn't a concentration camp," Franziska said, "but it's torturous enough for me. I feel dirty and sick, and we can't even send mail out."

"Or receive it," Franz added.

"If we needed money, we wouldn't even be able to write to our bank to forward it," Franziska continued, her voice crescendoing. "And if someone sent us a check or money order, we'd never receive it. We're truly in prison here, and we could buy our way out. So what are we waiting for?"

"Calm down, Franzi. I'll tell you what we're waiting for. I've heard a rumor that the immigration chief here is helping Jewish refugees."

"But why?"

"He deplores Hitler. I've heard that when someone approaches him with a heartrending story, he sometimes allows the person to leave for less than the customary amount."

"So what's *our* story going to be?"

"That's what I've been trying to devise."

"We don't appear to be terribly poor or terribly sick, and we don't have any children."

"I know."

"Maybe you'd like to give a recital. Maybe the immigration chief will give us our freedom as a remuneration," Franziska quipped.

"Very funny. I'm sure he's an opera buff."

"It's good that we can still joke about our predicament. But I don't want to spend too many more nights in that dorm. Look at all of these bites. They're starting to make me sick. I thought you were going to take care of me. Money isn't everything. You're going to be a famous opera singer. You're going to make lots of money. But as long as we're in here, we won't even know when our American visas come through."

"All right. I promise to do something about our situation tomorrow."

"They could deport us."

"That's highly unlikely. We're out of Europe."

"Just *do* something."

"All right! I said I would, and I will!"

⁘

Franz stood in front of the guardhouse the next morning for almost five minutes without going in. He was trying to gather enough self-confidence to be convincing. But how would he be able to pull this off in English? His English was getting better, but still . . .

Once inside the hut-like guardhouse, he explained to the immigration chief that he and Franziska did in fact have Cuban visas and should probably have never been brought to Triscornia at all.

"A mistake there must have been," he said, feigning innocence. "Any day now our American visas. Have to get to New York. My agent . . . engagements arranging at the Met."

"The Met?" the immigration chief questioned unknowingly.

"The Metropolitan Opera," Franz declared, "Grandest opera house in America where lives one of the greatest opera companies in the world."

"Oh, yes, of course," the immigration chief said, acting as if the name had simply slipped his mind. Then after some contemplation: "I'm in a powerful position, and I try to make my decisions wisely," he said. "Although your story is quite singular, I cannot enable everyone in Triscornia to leave. I therefore try to reserve my energies for only those who display dire need, either due to their families' circumstances or to their own. I'm sure that you will find a way to meet your commitments; but unfortunately, I will personally be unable to assist you."

Franz waited a few seconds without responding, attempting to dream up a rebuttal. "I understand," he finally said, discouraged. "For listening . . . thank you."

Franziska did not react very sympathetically. "You should have just paid him the thousand dollars on the spot," she said angrily when he told her what had occurred. "And then you could have negotiated with him about the extra amount. Every day we spend in Triscornia is one day too much." With that edict, she marched into her dorm and didn't come out for the rest of the day.

So the next morning, Franz went to the guardhouse with the money. And that afternoon, they were free.

CHAPTER TWENTY-SEVEN
Good and Bad

Havana, Cuba
4 March to July 1939

$\mathscr{F}$ranziska was standing next to the front desk in the Hotel Luz while Franz was dozing in their room upstairs. She was puffing a cigarette in one hand and flicking the consequential ashes into the small glass ash-tray she held in the other. The hotel was utterly dilapidated. It was true they hadn't wanted to spend much money, but this establishment was so neglected that even the dorm in Triscornia looked admirable. At least they were together again. They'd only be staying at the Hotel Luz for a few days, maybe a week at the most, just long enough to find an apart-ment. The hotel was centrally located, near the harbor in La Habana Vieja on the street after which it was named: Calle Luz. Characteristic of Old Havana, it had a lime-green colonial façade with large French doors that opened onto balconies with ornate wrought-iron balustrades. But even from the outside, the building was run-down, with blotches of white where lime-green had once adhered. The lobby was nonexistent. And the walls of Franz and Franziska's room upstairs flaunted smudges of gray nimbus clouds over a peeling white background. The bed linens were worn; the sink, stained; and the wood on the bureau was chipped bare. The bathroom down the hall was at least clean, although the anti-septic smell was somewhat pungent.

Franziska spent as little time up there as possible, her smoking habit increasing by the hour. She'd barely spoken to the clerk behind the counter, yet he knew precisely who she was. Those unmistakably beautiful onyx eyes and hair: No other guest at the hotel could compete with her.

She was standing near the front desk, not really thinking about anything in particular, when two uniformed men walked in and approached the clerk behind it. One had dark bushy hair; the other, a coif pasted down with the essence of tonic. She heard the men talking to the clerk, but couldn't make out what they were saying. She really didn't care. She knew that she was in Cuba legally. She knew that she was free. Then she heard one of the men pronounce her name: "Jung," he said. "Franz and Franziska Jung."

She froze. She started to get the chills and wished that she could stick her head in the ground like an ostrich. *These men must be immigration officers,* she thought. She was certain that the clerk would immediately point her out. She wanted to escape from the scene and quickly walk upstairs, but then she would draw attention to herself. So she stayed where she was, smashing her cigarette into her ashtray.

The desk clerk opened the registration book. "No . . . they're not here," he said to the men in Spanish.

"But everyone from Triscornia stays here," the bushy-haired officer commented.

"No," maintained the clerk, "they must be at another hotel."

"No" was the only word that Franziska could understand. Yet she realized that the desk clerk had not betrayed her.

The uniformed men left the premises.

"*Gracias,*" she told the desk clerk timidly. Their eyes met briefly for a moment. She set the ashtray on the counter and scurried upstairs.

"Franz! Franz!" Franziska shouted, jiggling the key, trying to slide it into the keyhole.

"Shhh . . ." Franz said, opening the door. "Everyone in the hallway can hear you."

"Some men . . . some men . . ."

"Slow down. Take a deep breath. Now . . ."

"Some men were downstairs next to the reception desk. They were wearing uniforms; they must have been immigration officers."

"And . . ."

"They said our names. They were looking for us."

"Go on."

"The desk clerk said that we weren't here. But those men are looking for us. They're going to find us, and they're going to take us back up to Triscornia. What are we going to do?"

"Calm down! They're not going to find us. They only came here because this is where almost everyone from Triscornia stays."

"But why would they want to take us back? We paid."

"Yes, but they want more money. They would have probably taken us up there and told us that we had to pay another five hundred apiece to get out."

"Can they do that?"

"Why not? This is Cuba."

"*Aduana.*"

Franz looked the word up in his dictionary. "This must be the customs office," he told Franziska.

When they were taken away to Triscornia, they'd been forced to leave their trunk behind on the *Chiriquí*. After checking in at the Hotel Luz, they'd gone to the harbor office of United Fruit to retrieve it. But they were told to go to customs. They waited almost a week before journeying there, however, because they wanted to be settled in an apartment first in order to curtail transporting the cumbersome trunk from place to place.

They'd moved into the apartment the day before, on the ninth of March, just six days after they'd been freed from Triscornia. It was located in the fashionable Vedado section of La Habana, on Calle Cinco entre Cuatro y Seis. The apartment was unfurnished. But that was something they'd worry about another day. On this day, they simply wanted to recover their belongings.

The customs office was in one of the large beige, turquoise-trimmed terminal buildings that bordered the port, the building's half-moon-shaped stained-glass French windows in a row across it like a line of tin soldiers at attention. From the street side, the massive edifices seemed to barricade the port like a fortress. When standing in front of them, it was almost impossible to conceive of the maritime activity and sea behind.

Franz and Franziska went up the steps, into the office ahead of them, and directly to the counter. "We'd like the luggage to pick up," Franz said. "Was on the *Chiriquí*."

Luckily, the customs official spoke English. His skin was tan; his dark hair and mustache, full; and his voice and laugh, devious. "Let me see your passports," he said matter-of-factly. "Is your luggage labeled?"

"Yes," Franz answered.

"How many pieces do you have?"

"*Einen* trunk."

A few minutes later, the customs official dragged the trunk in. Too big to lift onto the counter, he left it on the floor beside him. "I need to go through this," he said. "Could you please give me the key?"

Franziska pulled the key out of her purse and reluctantly handed it to the official.

He seemed to enjoy rummaging through everything. Then to Franz and Franziska's amazement, he pulled out a brand new billfold that Franz had recently purchased in Prague. "Oh, this is *n-i-c-e*," he said with an insidious smile on his face.

Franz and Franziska didn't know what to think. They wanted to leave the customs office as quickly as possible without any fees, and they wanted to keep all of their belongings – well at least, most of their belongings.

"Would you like the billfold?" Franz asked the customs official.

"Yes," he said with a cunning grin on his face.

"Then keep it," Franz said.

The official nodded his head affirmatively and dropped the billfold into a bag that was conveniently attached behind the counter.

"Oh, this is *n-i-c-e*," the official said again, this time referring to a bottle of French perfume. "My girlfriend would *r-e-a-l-l-y* like it."

"Then it's yours," Franz conveyed.

"Oh . . . and this tie – my brother would like this."

And so the items that Franz graciously forfeited to the official kept mounting.

The trunk was sitting in the middle of their living room as a coffee table. They'd purchased a small sofa, two beds, a few lamps, an icebox, and a music stand. The stove was already there. They hoped that their stay in the apartment would be brief. But at least the apartment was passable.

It was in a very rectangular, boxy-looking three-story Colonial building with just enough balconies and columns to bestow upon it a hint of the complexion of Italian Baroque. It was a ground-floor apartment with a convenient separate entrance, which was one of the reasons Franz and Franziska rented it – the other apartments were accessible from the main doorway on the left – and it had a lovely patio in front, amply shaded by the graceful fan-like leaves of a palm tree and numerous plants. Upon entering the apartment, there was a long hallway on the left with a cement floor and more greenery – thanks to the previous tenants. The hallway resembled a covered patio or hothouse that culminated with the entrance to the dining area and kitchen. A wall on the right divided it from the other main rooms, which were placed one behind the other like a stack of dishes: the living room, two bedrooms, and a bathroom in-between. Franz and Franziska didn't need the second bedroom, but they were tired of looking for apartments, and the price was reasonable.

"Let's go to the American Embassy soon," Franziska told Franz the day after they'd brought home their trunk.

"What? You want to leave Cuba already?"

The following week, the front page of every newspaper was blanketed with stories about the German takeover of Czechoslovakia. The eastern portion, Slovakia, had seceded, and the remainder had become a German protectorate. President Emil Hacha had surrendered the country without a fight. And to Hitler's delight, the Slovakian government thereafter asked for German protection as well.

"Thank God we left Czechoslovakia when we did," Franz said one evening just before turning in.

"I think the world is going to wake up now," Franziska added. "When the Nazi troops marched into Austria, the people welcomed them. And when the Sudetenland was handed over to Hitler, he took it with the guise of rescuing the victimized Germans there. But now he's done something different. The Czechs didn't want his intervention. Now he's taken a foreign country."

"I wonder where he's going to strike next."

"So do I."

And Franz turned out the light.

Franz and Franziska were on their way to the United States Embassy. They'd taken a bus along Havana's coastal highway, the Malecón, where all of La Habana seemed to extend on either side of them. They passed the eastern end of Vedado and contemplated getting off at the Prado and walking the rest of the way, but they opted to continue past Centro Habana into La Habana Vieja instead. They'd promenade along the handsome Paseo del Prado when they had more time. So the bus continued down Avenida del Puerto, and they got off just a few steps from the Plaza de Armas.

But which building in the square was the American Embassy? There was El Templete, a small Doric temple where the first mass was held; the Palacio de los Capitanes Generales, a majestic Baroque building, once the presidential palace, later converted to City Hall; El Castillo de la Real Fuerza, the first fortress built in Cuba by Spain; the Palacio del Segundo Cabo; the Palacio de los Condes de Santovenia: But where was the U.S. Embassy?

"That must be it over there?" Franziska said questioningly, walking toward the massive three-story arcaded edifice at the southern portion of the square.

Once inside, they found the appropriate office, where Franziska, who was by now quite fluent in English, did most of the talking. "We've registered for immigration visas in Prague," she told the consular agent. "We were told that the number assigned to each of our names would be honored all over the world. We're here to check on the status of our applications."

After examining their passports and reviewing a long list of names, the agent declared that there were no visa applications on file for either Franz or Franziska Jung.

"There must be," Franz retorted, the pigment on his face becoming somewhat scarlet.

"Do you know what your quota numbers are?" the consular agent asked.

"No, I didn't know that we were privy to that information," Franziska responded.

"I'm sorry, but I cannot help you," the agent said. "I don't advise re-applying right now either. You'd have a long wait in Cuba, maybe years. It would be in your best interests to try to determine what happened to your records."

"I will contact the lawyer right away," Franz said.

T E L E G R A M

23 MARCH 1939

DOKTOR IVAN REIDL
OPLETALOVA 37 PRAHA 1 =

LA HABANA =

NO RECORDS OF AMERICAN VISA APPLICATIONS IN CUBA
NO NUMBERS LISTED FRANTIC FOR EXPLANATION PLEASE
CLEAR UP MISTAKE WITH AMERICAN EMBASSY IN PRAGUE
= FRANZ AND FRANZISKA JUNG +

Franz and Franziska were terribly disillusioned. Maybe they'd never get to America at all. The days following the transmittal of their telegram were difficult ones. Why wasn't their lawyer responding? Each day seemed to blend into the next. They tried to mingle with other refugees to make the foreignness of their surroundings less intimidating. Some of the refugees were opening kitchens – that's what Franz liked to call them. They weren't really kitchens though; they were family-run restaurants in private homes and apartments.

Franz and Franziska were eating many of their evening meals at Pensión Friedländer. Located on Calle Doce entre Tres y Cinco, the kitchen wasn't far from where they lived. Since their apartment was on Calle Cinco, they simply had to walk west along that street to Calle Doce, then turn right until they reached a peach-colored three-story building with a tiled roof and balconies. The kitchen was in the spacious second-floor apartment of the Friedländer family. Originally from Berlin, the Friedländers were renting two of their four bedrooms out to other German immigrants; thus, the name "Pensión Friedländer" evolved. *Mutti* did the cooking and her husband, Alex, did everything else – that is, with the assistance of their three children: Dorrit, Albert, and Charles. Franziska always wondered what *Mutti's* first name really was, for to everyone who ate at the establishment, she was simply *Mutti*, the name Franziska affectionately often called her mother.

In actuality, the restaurant/kitchen was really more like a dining room. There were six tables set with white linen tablecloths, attractive china, crystal glassware, and candles as centerpieces. It was quite evident to Franz and Franziska that a family lived in the apartment, because whenever they left the dining room, they undoubtedly stumbled across an open door, with a bedroom, bathroom, or sitting room in view.

On this occasion, Franz and Franziska were seated with Max Schenirer and his girlfriend, Dora. They'd met the couple a few days before. Max had looked so familiar to Franz, but he couldn't decipher why. After conversing, Franz had learned that Max Schenirer was from Vienna, loved music, and had attended a number of his performances. Max spoke German and English, and was working as an interpreter for the American Jewish Joint Distribution Committee. He and Franz became immediate friends. As for Dora, she was also an interpreter. But she was from Poland and spoke English, Polish, some Yiddish, and a marginal amount of German. She'd been studying at the New York University on a student visa, didn't want to go back to Poland, and accepted the job in Cuba until she could attain an immigrant visa to the United States. The two couples were busily guzzling some beefy Rostbraten while they were conversing.

"Mmm . . . this is delicious," Max said. "It's good to have some homemade cooking."

"I agree," Franz echoed.

"Is that a hint?" Franziska asked. "Are you trying to tell me that I don't cook enough for you?"

"No, not at all," Franz answered. "We have a lot on our minds right now."

"I'll cook for everyone some night soon," Dora said. "Then we'll be poisoned."

The group laughed and ate and then laughed some more.

"You know about these things, Max. Have you ever heard of immigration applications being lost?" Franziska asked, changing the tone of the conversation.

"No, not here in Cuba. But I have heard of quota numbers being sold, mostly in other countries though."

"That's corrupt," Franz uttered.

"You know . . . that kind of makes sense," Franziska reasoned. "A lot of people are probably trying to get out of Prague now that the Germans have taken over. Many are probably attempting to buy their way out, and some of the consular agents just might be willing to accommodate them."

"But if our numbers were sold, we'll have to reapply. And we may never get to America," Franz said.

"Maybe our lawyer will have some success."

"But if our numbers were sold, they're gone."

"Yes! But our lawyer could probably buy some new ones – with our money, of course – or he could simply scare the appropriate consular official into finding some."

"But then two other unknowing people would be robbed."

"Why don't you wait until you hear from your lawyer. Maybe there's a logical explanation," Max suggested. "I shouldn't have insinuated . . ."

"That's all right," Franz said. And they changed the subject.

TELEGRAM

5 APRIL 1939

FRANZ JUNG
CALLE 5 #604
VEDADO LA HABANA =

PRAHA =

EVERYTHING STRAIGHTENED OUT GO TO AMERICAN
EMBASSY IN CUBA TO VERIFY = IVAN REIDL +

"We've got quota numbers," Franz told Max Schenirer a few days after receiving his lawyer's telegram, sitting down to another homemade meal at Pensión Friedländer. "We went to the American Embassy, and the consular agent confirmed that our visa applications are on file now. And we've got numbers."

"Congratulations!" Max said. "By the way . . . did you find out what happened?"

"No, actually we didn't."

"Oh . . . so then you don't know if your numbers were actually sold or not."

"No."

"Did your lawyer have to buy you new ones?"

"I doubt it, because he didn't ask us for any money."

"Then maybe he scared some guilty soul into miraculously finding some numbers which may or may not have been connected to anyone."

"That's possible. Exposing a guilty party could mean the end of that party's livelihood."

"Precisely . . . as well as other parties' livelihoods in the same office."

"You two are awful," Dora said. "Maybe there was some sort of mix-up. Maybe the files were simply misplaced."

"Or maybe there was some glitch in the transmission," Franziska added. "At any rate, everything is straightened out now."

Franz was learning *The Marriage of Figaro* in Italian. One day he was sitting with Franziska at an outdoor café on Calle Obispo in La Habana Vieja. The couple went to various cafés almost every afternoon, always ordering one large Pepsi-Cola with two glasses, and splitting it. The price of a large Pepsi was the same as a small Coke, they'd discovered, so Pepsi-Cola became their beverage of choice. On this afternoon, Paul Csonka was sitting at the table next to them. He was a wealthy impresario from Vienna, the son of an oil magnet and financier. Csonka had worked in his father's company, and he and his father had been business partners with one of Franz's uncles. After the two caught up on old times, Franz learned that Csonka was trying to organize a Mozart tour in the United States. Franz realized that he was going to have to learn many of the operas in his repertoire in Italian if he wanted to be successful, so he decided to begin with *The Marriage of Figaro*.

He was standing in his living room with one foot propped on top of his unpacked trunk. There was no piano – he only had a pitchpipe – and his operatic score was resting on the music stand in front of him. He was practicing Figaro's first aria.

"Se vuol ballare, signor Contino . . . il chitarrino le suonerò, sì, le suonerò, sì, le suonerò."

There was something wrong with his voice. He couldn't put his finger on it. Technically, he felt very relaxed and secure: He wasn't straining, his tones were placed correctly, and he was singing with support. But there was something wrong. His voice lacked some of its luster. Nevertheless, he continued working, trying to ignore the doubts that were invading his mind. The next day would be better, he thought.

The problem would resolve itself. But the next day, his voice hadn't improved. And a week later, it still had a different quality. Franz was beginning to worry.

"Franzi," he called out one Thursday afternoon, the end of April. "Would you please come in here for a minute?"

Franziska wiped her hands on a dishtowel in the kitchen and walked into the living room.

"Sit down on the sofa," Franz said. "I want you to listen to me sing a Schubert *Lied*."

"All right," Franziska answered, trying to figure out what was wrong. So Franz sang:

> *Rauschender Strom,*
> *Brausender Wald,*
> *Starrender Fels,*
> *Mein Aufenthalt. . . .*

Franz, as the character in the *Lied*, was likening his rolling tears to the waves of the sea, his unremitting heartbeats to treetops swaying ferociously in the wind, and his everlasting grief to the enduring solidity of a rock formation.

Something was missing in Franz's delivery. It never dawned on Franziska that there was anything wrong with his voice. She thought that he simply wasn't conveying much emotion. He wasn't singing with enough feeling, she thought. But after all, he was performing in their living room without an audience, hardly the surroundings to stimulate one's adrenal glands.

"What do you think?" Franz asked.

"I don't know what you want me to say."

"Did you hear anything different?"

"No."

"Come on. . . . Be critical. Don't try to spare my feelings."

"Well . . ."

"Go on."

"You didn't sing with as much heart as you usually do."

"That's all?"

"Uh-huh."

"My voice sounded the same?"

"I think so."

"Did you ever wonder what we'd do if I lost my voice?"

"Oh, Franz, don't talk that way."

"All right . . . I'll tell you."

"Tell me what?"

"When I sing lately, I feel as if there's something missing in my voice. The timbre is different. And it's the quality of my voice that has always set me apart from all the others."

"Maybe you're just imagining . . ."

"No, I don't think so."

But a week later, nothing had changed. And two weeks later, Franz sang the same *Lied* for Franziska again:

> *Rauschender Strom,*
> *Brausender Wald,*
> *Starrender Fels,*
> *Mein Aufenthalt. . . .*

"You hear a difference now, don't you?" Franz questioned.

"Well . . . yes. But it's not a great difference."

"Tell me . . . what do you hear?"

"I . . . I think that . . ."

"Go on."

"I think that . . . your voice . . . it doesn't sound as full."

"You mean that it isn't as mellow."

"Yes. And it's hard to evaluate in this room, but . . ."

"But what?"

"But I'm not sure if . . ."

"If what?"

"If your voice has as much strength as it did."

"It's all right, Franzi. I don't want to kid myself. I know that some of the power is gone. I won't be able to sing over an orchestra soon. My career is over."

"Please don't say that."

Franziska rose from the sofa she'd been sitting on and went over to Franz. She faced him and placed both of her hands squarely on his shoulders. "This is only temporary," she said. "The climate is different here. You've always suffered from allergies and hay fever in the spring. I know that your voice is going to come back better than ever."

"Oh, what am I going to do?" Franz said, sitting on his trunk, Franziska descending along with him. "Paul Csonka is setting up an audition for me with Alberto Erede. Csonka wants Erede to conduct the Mozart tour, and he'll be in Havana soon. What am I going to do?"

"You'll audition. That's what you're going to do. You have to be optimistic. Continue learning *The Marriage of Figaro* in Italian, continue practicing, and maybe your indisposition will clear up."

"But I don't have an indisposition. Can't you see that my voice is leaving me? All of those years of studying down the drain. And I'm not prepared to do anything else but sing opera. And what's worse, I don't want to do anything else but sing opera. Singing is my life."

Franz was getting hysterical. Franziska had the urge to slap him across the face to shock him out of his frenzy, but she put her arms around him instead.

"Now I'm hurt; I thought that *I* was your life," she said.

"Well, you are," Franz answered guiltily. "But . . ."

"You don't have to explain. We have each other, and we're free. That's all that really matters."

"But all of my dreams . . . all of my hopes . . ."

"You really don't know anything for sure yet, so hold on to all of your hopes and dreams."

"But . . ."

"I don't want to hear anymore about this," Franziska said, kissing Franz on the lips trying to divert his attention. She began to unbutton his shirt and kiss his chest, but he wasn't responding. He was just sitting on his trunk as motionless as the statue of Johann Strauss in the Stadtpark.

"I can't, Franziska. I feel as grief-stricken as the poet in the *Lied* I just sang you."

"Now you're making me sad," Franziska said. "It's far too early for that. I'm sure that Doktor Witte would have been able to cure you."

"Maybe . . . but I don't have access to Doktor Witte here. I won't be able to get help until we're in the United States."

"Then be optimistic. Maybe your voice will be back to normal in a few weeks. But if it isn't, that still doesn't mean that it's disappearing for good. A doctor in the United States will most certainly be able to revive it."

"I don't know if that's true."

"Well, I do."

"I want to believe you."

"Then you must."

But Franz continued to sit on the trunk staring straight ahead in a stupor. He would not find relief for a very long time, he believed, if ever. Oh, what had happened to his voice? What had happened to it? *There must be an explanation*, he repeated over and over again in his mind. *There must be an explanation.*

Even though Franziska tried to manifest a cheerful attitude, a cloud was floating over the Jung household. Leaving Cuba was of primary importance if Franz was to ever snap out of his depression.

Two days before their anniversary, Franz and Franziska went to the German Embassy: the Embassy of the Third Reich. Max Schenirer had told them about one of Hitler's latest decrees, and they wanted to be assured that their passports were in order.

The embassy was near Calles H y Diecisiete in Vedado. The building was shielded with a high wrought-iron fence in the front, and Franz had to explain their business to the guard before being allowed entry. The swastika above the doorway certainly looked familiar. Then more ornamental wrought iron adorned the staircase which led them to the consulate.

The office was empty and quiet. They'd been in so many governmental buildings lately. This one seemed no different, except in this one, they somehow had the urge to tiptoe. They felt the need to be cautious of everything they said and did. After all, this place represented the enemy.

The consul examined the Cuban visa in Franz's passport and didn't say anything. Then he looked back at the first page, the large red "J" stamped bountifully to the left of the word, "*Reisepass*." Wasn't that enough of a delineation?

The consul wrote something above Franz's first name, dated, and signed the amendment. Then he did exactly the same thing to Franziska's passport. No pleasantries; no conversation – he simply closed the passports, handed them back to Franz, and walked away.

"Max was right. I now have '*Israel*' written above my first name, between my first name and last name like a middle name," Franz whispered. "Here, look at yours."

"Mine says '*Sara*.' Sara was . . ."

"Don't let's talk about this in here. Come on; let's go."

Once back outside, Franziska continued: "Sara was the wife of Abraham in the Bible, and the mother of Isaac."

"Yes, and Israel was Isaac's son and Sara and Abraham's grandson. The twelve tribes that became the Jewish people were made up of the descendants of Israel's sons."

"So what's so terrible about being named Israel or Sara? I don't understand. They sound like noble names to me."

"Not to the Germans. The Nazis laugh when they hear those names. They find the names degrading."

"Your father's name was Jakob; that was Israel's real name. Why didn't the Nazis rename all Jewish men, 'Jakob'?"

"They could have. You know my mother often called my father 'Jacques' in public. She didn't want to draw any attention to his religion in order to avoid the possibility of anti-Semitism. Now it's quite evident that she had cause to worry."

"For the people still being victimized in Europe, these names on their passports could be devastating. But for us, they really don't mean anything. We aren't going to be deported, and no one here or in the United States cares what our religion is. We're free."

⚶

"We're always one step ahead of disaster," Franziska told Franz a little over a week after they'd received the additions to their first names. They were sitting on their sofa in the living room, with two demitasses of café cubana on the trunk in front of them.

"I don't know that I can agree with you," Franz said. "Losing my voice – that's the biggest disaster I could have ever imagined, and it's actually happening."

"First of all, you don't know if that's really true. Second of all, we're out of Hitler's reign. There is no danger that we'll ever be placed in a concentration camp. We have our lives."

"I used to think like you, Franziska, but I don't anymore. Without my voice, I don't really have a life."

"You should be ashamed of yourself," Franziska said, taking a sip from her demitasse. "Look at those poor people who are stranded in Havana Bay right now. More than nine hundred of them boarded the *St. Louis* in Hamburg with barely any money, hoping to find refuge in Havana, and the Cuban government won't let them in. . . . We could have been on that boat. Some of those people are probably from Vienna, and I'll bet that the ship is going to be turned back."

"You're probably right. But I'm sure that most of them don't have Cuban visas."

"But I heard that they do have some sort of landing permits that were issued to them by a top ranking Cuban immigration official, but apparently, the permits have been invalidated."

"Look . . . I don't know anything about the legalities of the situation. But I don't believe that the Cuban government would have the means to shelter all of them . . . not even in Triscornia."

Franziska was right. Immigration official Manuel Benitez had issued landing certificates to the passengers on the *St. Louis* as if they had been tourists, not refugees, thus profiting from the sales. Cuban President Federico Larado Brú learned of his profiteering and issued Decree 937, which invalidated the landing certificates before the *St. Louis* embarked and established strict new immigration laws. A massive demonstration of forty thousand Cubans against Jewish immigration followed.

Because of high unemployment, many Cubans felt that the immigrants were competing with them for jobs; thus Cubans were ripe to embrace anti-Semitism, which was encouraged by the Cuban Nazi Party there.

Unaware of Decree 937, passengers on the *St. Louis* set sail on the thirteenth of May, arriving in Havana on the twenty-seventh.

The powerful armed forces chief, Fulgencio Batista y Zaldívar, did not interfere. The ship's captain, and representatives from the American Jewish Joint Distribution Committee of New York and the Joint Relief Committee in Havana, held negotiations with Brú to no avail. The *St. Louis* was turned back after spending six days in the port of Havana, on the second of June. Then she headed north, floating between Havana and Miami, but the U.S. government would not grant her passengers asylum. So with very little optimism, those on board began their journey back across the Atlantic Ocean to Europe, many believing that their fates had been sealed. Finally several European countries agreed to take the refugees in, including Great Britain, Belgium, France, and the Netherlands.

Although Franz was extremely unhappy about his voice and the anti-Semitism and corruptness in Cuba, he and Franziska still felt blessed to be out of Triscornia and in Havana.

Then Paul Csonka came through with his promise. An audition was scheduled for Franz with Alberto Erede. Franz was very nervous because he hadn't informed anyone about the problems he was having with his voice. He only hoped that he could sing with so much expression that the change in timbre and reduced volume would be unnoticeable. But he was singing Mozart, not German *Lieder,* so he wouldn't have the opportunity to be overly dramatic in order to disguise his vocal quality. But who was he trying to fool? A renowned conductor like Maestro Erede would surely be able to detect the lack of brilliance in his voice immediately.

On the way to his audition, he and Franziska took a bus ride along the Malecón, then walked down the Prado. Ordinarily Franziska would have never gone with Franz, but she felt that he needed her support. In reality, she didn't plan to go inside, but would wait for him in the shady Parque Central or in the outdoor café of the Hotel Inglaterra.

She walked with Franz past the hotel, which was one of Havana's finest, and they kissed good-bye. Then she went into the park, and Franz stood waiting for Paul Csonka in the loggia of the Teatro Nacional. It was a grand theater in every sense of the word, the outside comparable in architectural beauty to the magnificent theaters of Vienna, Franz thought, but more ornately wrapped with columns, statues, balconies, balustrades, lantern turrets, and shuttered windows.

First Paul Csonka arrived with an accompanist, then Alberto Erede. Csonka introduced Franz to Erede, and then they walked through the lobby and upstairs into a rehearsal hall, conversing very minimally. Franz told the maestro about his singing background and then handed his music to the accompanist, who was already seated at the piano. Csonka and Erede stood at the back of the room, Csonka telling the conductor about Franz's rave reviews and about the top agents who were working on his behalf.

"Start whenever you like," Erede told Franz, who was standing next to the accompanist.

A few moments later, Franz nodded his head, and with very little introduction, he began singing Figaro's aria at the end of the first act of Mozart's *Marriage of Figaro*, when Figaro frolicsomely explains to Cherubino the rigors of military life. Franz had sung the aria so many times before in German, always receiving a resounding applause at its completion. But for this audition, he sang in Italian, and he knew that there was something very wrong with his voice. He tried to show Erede his acting prowess by moving around as if he were on a stage, and by gesturing to an imaginary Cherubino. But he knew that he wasn't fooling anybody.

When Figaro describes to Cherubino that he'd be among soldiers with a gun on his shoulder and a sword at his side, Franz's voice should have been full and robust, but it wasn't. And when Franz concluded the aria, saluting Cherubino on to victory and military glory, the elation of the moment was lost. He hadn't felt this much coldness since his first audition in Prague for Paul Eger. Yet even then, he was able to redeem himself. But not this time. Nothing could help him now.

"Thank you for coming," Maestro Erede said.

"I need to speak to Alberto about a number of things concerning the Mozart tour," Csonka told Franz in a booming voice. "Say hello to Franziska for me."

"Yes, I will," Franz responded downheartedly. The accompanist handed him his music, and he slowly walked back toward Alberto Erede and Csonka, forcing a vague, rigid smile across his lips as he exited the rehearsal hall.

He couldn't think straight. He was in a blur, hanging onto the balustrade as he ploddingly walked down the stairs, his senses quite numb. Once outside, he walked toward the Hotel Inglaterra, crossed Calle San Rafael, and stood there immobile. Franziska, who was wandering around Parque Central keeping an eye out for him, came running, but she slowed down as she made her approach.

"Oh, surely it couldn't have been that bad," she said softly.

At first Franz didn't answer. Then: "It was humiliating."

"Come on. We can't stay here. Let's walk."

But Franz remained stationary.

"Darling," Franziska said, placing her hand on Franz's shoulder. "This was only one audition."

"No doubt, my last."

"Don't be so hard on yourself, Franz. All singers have problems with their voices at one time or another. With you, it really could be the climate, or it could be all of the excitement you've undergone. As soon as we get to America, everything will change."

Finally Franziska was successful in getting Franz to move. The air was balmy as they walked along the Prado toward the bay. Then they turned left at Calle Colón and right at Calle Crespo. Now why had they done that? They were lost.

The street was narrow, and the buildings were lined up one adjacent to the other, only the array of pastel colors serving to disjoin them. People were sitting on the balconies above, watching, while the street below remained mystifyingly almost vacant. One tall recessed French window or door next to the other – many open, with dark mesh screens hiding the unlit interiors behind: What was going on in there?

"Psst . . . Psst," Franz and Franziska heard emanating from one of the dwellings. "Psst . . . Psst!"

A young man spruced up in a white linen suit and Panama straw hat was trailing behind them. Franziska turned around and detected him withdrawing the flower from his lapel and throwing it toward one of the windows. "Psst . . . Psst!" Apparently someone inside was trying to attract his attention. He smiled and kept on walking.

Soon later, a much rounder man, wearing simply a shirt and trousers, was walking toward them. "Psst . . . Psst! Psst . . . Psst!" That same coaxing endearment was now emerging from another window.

The portly man rolled down his shirt-sleeves and then buttoned them. "Psst . . . Psst! Psst . . . Psst!" He licked his fingers and smoothed the sides of his hair. "Psst . . . Psst! Psst . . . Psst!" And then he disappeared inside.

"Let's get out of here," Franz said. "I'm depressed enough, and here we are, walking in Havana's red-light district."

Franziska started to laugh. "I was only trying to raise your spirits. I couldn't have found a better place in which to do it."

For one brief moment, Franz began to crack a smile.

"Anyhow . . . my keen sense of direction tells me that if we keep walking in this direction, we'll reach the Malecón, and then we can catch a bus back to our apartment."

Yet by the time they'd reached Vedado, Franz's somber mood had returned. "You know, if I could have told them that I was sick, they might have understood," he said as they were getting off the bus. "Then Alberto Erede would have known that I wasn't in good voice and normally sing much better. But since I didn't feel that I could say anything, he thought that what I delivered was all that I had."

When they were at the corner of Paseo and Calle Cinco: "I'm sure that Paul Csonka told Erede what kind of a reputation I have, and Erede probably couldn't understand it."

And when they were in front of their apartment: "If I could have secured a contract for the Mozart tour, we would have been able to go to the United States, and then maybe . . . maybe we could have stayed there.

"I've made a mess of things all the way around, Franziska. I'm sorry. I'm so very sorry," Franz said as he opened the door to their apartment.

And when he walked inside, he fell onto the sofa . . . and cried.

Saving Face

Havana, Cuba
August to 8 October 1939

*E*ven though Franz had told André Mertens and Wilhelm Stein that he intended to immigrate to the United States and couldn't commit to any engagements until he arrived there, he did send them his address in Havana. André Mertens subsequently notified him about a possible engagement in Australia. Mertens wrote Franz that he was currently in Hollywood, California, and would soon be driving east, to the Columbia Concerts Corporation office in New York.

"Not everybody has a prestigious international agency working for them like I do," Franz told Franziska one morning while she was dusting around him in the living room. "I'm going to have to write André Mertens and tell him the truth about my voice, and then he'll never work for me again, even if it does come back."

"Be smart," Franziska said. "Wait!"

"But . . ."

"You have time to tell him when he offers you something. And by then, your voice might be just fine."

"Maybe you're right. My voice could come back when we get to the

United States, and then André Mertens could possibly . . . eventually . . . arrange something for me at the Met."

"A wise decision."

" It's very difficult to find opera singers in America who can sing Wagner in German, roles like Beckmesser and Alberich. And for those parts, my height even works in my favor."

"That's very true."

"Oh, stop it," Franz said, abruptly changing the tone in his voice. "You're just humoring me. I know that I'll never sing at the Met, or anywhere else for that matter, and so do you."

"I don't know anything of the sort, Franz! If *you* want to be a pessimist, go right ahead. But please do not include me."

"But I can't take the pressure anymore!" Franz began screaming.

"Now that's incredibly good for your voice. That should make it come back real soon."

"But you don't understand."

"Oh, yes, I do."

"You don't understand how devastated I feel. I want to get up and throw every piece of music I have around this room."

"Then do it."

"But then I might be sorry when I can't put everything back in order again."

"Ah-ha! So I *do* detect a smidgen of hope in your voice."

"Well, maybe."

"I thought so."

Franz had learned from Paul Csonka that Giuseppe Verdi's *Rigoletto* would be performed at the Teatro Nacional with Walter Herbert portraying the baritone lead of Rigoletto. He was very interested in attending this particular performance because Walter Herbert had been one of his best friends when the two were students at the Konservatorium; however Franz had always thought that his own voice was quite superior. Nevertheless, Herbert was a baritone, not really a bass-baritone, and he was taller than Franz; so he learned the standard baritone roles, while Franz was studying those for character baritones and comic basso buffos. The engagement at the Teatro Nacional had been arranged for Herbert by one of Paul Csonka's friends, an agent who had learned that the singer was living in Havana while awaiting an American visa.

Franz hadn't been back to the theater since his audition the month before, and he hadn't seen Csonka since then either. When they met on this warm, humid evening in the lobby, not a word was spoken about either Alberto Erede or the Mozart tour. Franz realized that Csonka was being friendly, not because he was interested in Franz as a singer, but rather, in deference to the relationship that had existed between Franz's uncle and Csonka's father. This made Franz extremely melancholy because it meant that Csonka didn't think much of his voice, and therefore wouldn't respect his opinion as a vocal critic either. So how could they have an intelligent verbal discourse about the performance they were about to see? Franz felt belittled even though Csonka had done nothing to diminish his self-esteem. Franz realized that until his voice returned, attending this opera performance, or any other, would simply hurt him too much to be in his best interests. Nevertheless, he had to get through this evening somehow.

Their seats were excellent: in the eighth row, yet somewhat on the side. The inside of the auditorium was quite lovely, although different from the more ornate, neo-Renaissance and Baroque-style theaters in Vienna and Prague. With little knowledge of architecture, Franz surmised that the décor was more in keeping with the Spanish tradition. Paul Csonka was sitting the closest to the aisle, then Franz and Franziska.

First there was a dramatic prelude; then the curtain opened to a magnificent ball scene in the palace of the Duke of Mantua. The Argentinian tenor sang the Duke's first aria – "Questa o quella" – alluringly with spicy zest and gusto, the Duke confessing his devil-may-care attitude toward women.

"Well, we're off to a glorious start," Paul Csonka said while everyone was applauding the tenor.

Later it was Herbert's opportunity to prove himself with "Pari siamo!"

"We are equals! I have a tongue; he has a dagger. I am the man who mocks; he is the one who kills," Herbert sang as the hunchbacked Rigoletto, comparing his life as a court jester to that of the assassin he had just encountered, then reflecting on his life as a deformed buffoon.

Next, a poignant duet with his daughter, Gilda, singing of the compassion he felt for her departed mother. And another discourse with Gilda's nurse, entreating the woman to watch over his innocent daughter.

"Hmmm," Paul Csonka uttered, nothing else.

The act continued with the Duke vowing his love to Gilda and Gilda dreaming on with "Caro nome."

"Hmmm," uttered Csonka again. "She shows promise, but . . . the *fioriture* . . . not delicate enough . . . not free."

At intermission, Csonka, Franz, and Franziska walked out of the theater to inhale some fresh air. "So what do you think?" Franz asked Csonka while they were standing under the arcaded loggia.

"Hmmm" again. Then: "The tenor is quite accomplished; the soprano – not bad but technically a little wobbly; and Herbert – a competent delivery . . . that's all."

Paul Csonka hadn't even asked Franz for *his* opinion, yet Franz had studied voice for years at the Konservatorium. Franz knew so much more about vocal matters than he did.

"I wanted to hear Herbert to consider him for future engagements," Csonka said. "But well . . ."

Franz had a beseeching urge to say: "We studied together, but I always seemed to get more acclaim than he did." However Franz knew that he couldn't verbalize those thoughts, because Herbert's voice was now much larger than his own, and far superior.

"I'll bet he's considering Herbert for the Mozart tour," Franz whispered to Franziska as they were walking back to their seats. "He's already eliminated me."

"Not if you get your voice back," Franziska whispered in return.

Csonka seemed to enjoy the beginning of the next act, probably because the Argentinian tenor did such an agreeable job with his first aria. But when Rigoletto came looking for his daughter, denouncing the courtiers for having abducted her, his "Cortigiani, vil razza dannata" didn't seem to please the impresario, because at the end of the act, Csonka told Franz that he'd had enough, and he walked out.

Franz and Franziska were startled. Csonka hadn't even stayed to hear the tenor's "La donna è mobile," or to watch Gilda die at the hands of the assassin, Sparafucile.

"I didn't think the performance was *that* bad," Franz said as the curtain fell. "Judging from the applause, the audience seems to approve.

"Even though Herbert's characterization was quite commendable, if *I* had played Rigoletto, Csonka would have never left," Franz said . . . then remembering. "Of course, that will never happen now."

Franziska pretended that she didn't hear him. "Do you want to go back to say hello?" she asked after the last curtain call.

"No, I don't think so. I'm in a precarious situation now. I know that I have a better voice than he does, yet I don't really have it anymore. I don't want to congratulate him. I can't talk to him about my future while he boasts lavishly about his. And I can't explain to him what's wrong with me either. I wouldn't want his pity."

"But . . ."

"Do you think it was easy for me to sit next to Csonka tonight without having some sort of outburst? I have . . . *had* a beautiful voice, and Csonka treated me as if I wasn't even an opera singer, as if I only had the illusion that I was."

"Maybe you should have told him."

"I couldn't . . . not yet . . . because maybe, just maybe my voice will come back. *Then* I'll tell him. And as for Herbert, I just don't want to be around him tonight. I don't want to go to any more performances, Franziska, not until I'm *in* one, even if I never go to another performance again."

"But you can't live this way, Franz."

"Opera makes me sad now. I can't look at the singers on the stage because I'm supposed to be there. I can't watch them perform the roles that I've learned, because in many instances, I sang them better. I've worked so hard, Franzi. I've worked so very hard, and for what?"

"Please, Franz . . . please, let's go home."

"Home . . . where's that?"

"Come on, Franz; come on," Franziska said coaxingly. "The theater is emptying out."

"Yes, let's go," Franz said, rising from his seat. "Let's go."

On the first of September, Hitler invaded Poland. In the months before, Hitler, who had been intent on seizing the country, engineered the signing of the Pact of Steel between Germany and Italy, both powers pledging reciprocal military assistance in the event of war, and the signing of the Nazi-Soviet Nonaggression Pact, whereby the German and Soviet governments promised not to attack each other and formed an agreement regarding the division of Poland. Thereafter, Great Britain and France declared war on Germany, and the United States proclaimed its neutrality. It was the beginning of World War II.

"I knew this was going to happen," Franz said while he and Franziska were drinking their afternoon Pepsi at an outdoor café in La Habana Vieja. "Hitler wants to control Europe."

"But what if he wins?" Franziska asked. "Germany's military forces are stronger and better prepared than those of the other countries."

"Yes, but I don't think the rest of the world is going to stand back and let him take over."

"At least we're out of Europe," Franziska added. "Like I've told you before – we're always one step ahead of disaster."

They'd been notified that their quota numbers had come up, and they went to the consulate in the American Embassy the following day.

"Congratulations!" the vice-consul said. "Pack your bags. You're on your way to America."

He handed Franz and Franziska their passports, opened to the page stamped with their United States immigrant visas. They looked at the visas silently for a moment, then thanked the vice-consul and shook his hand. Franz was so excited that Franziska thought he'd never let go of the vice-consul's hand. He just kept shaking it and shaking it and shaking it.

Upon standing at the entrance to the American Embassy building – or in their case, the exit to the building – they looked at each other, smiled, and then began laughing. They hadn't been this happy since their wedding day. And then, right in the middle of the Plaza de Armas, they hugged and hugged and kissed each other.

That was Friday, the fifteenth of September. On Monday, the day after the Soviets followed Germany's lead and attacked Poland, Franz and Franziska were already packing their trunk. They'd purchased tickets to sail for Miami on Thursday. Nothing could hold them back now, they thought. Only one more thing to do: get their thousand dollars back.

"The money will be returned to you on the ship," the officer told them the next day in the immigration office.

Franz didn't believe him. "We're not leaving Cuba until the thousand dollars we get back," he retorted in English. "You've seen the American visas and travel tickets. You know we will not stay here, so we want our money to have."

"I'm sorry, sir. I cannot oblige you. I must follow the rules."

"Let me speak zu Herrn director," Franz demanded.

"I'm sorry, sir. He isn't here now."

"Tell him we come back tomorrow for our thousand dollars."

But the next day nothing had changed. The immigration officer refused to give Franz and Franziska their money.

"We are going to postpone the trip now. We will exchange the tickets for others. We are not leaving Cuba without our money," Franz said definitively. And he and Franziska marched out.

On Friday: "Here are the new tickets," Franz said, exhibiting them to the immigration officer. "We have two weeks now, and we stay in Cuba until you give us what is due."

The officer left Franz and Franziska waiting for a few minutes and then returned. "You are in luck," he announced. "I have just spoken to the director, and he is willing to make an exception in your case. Here is your money."

They were on a ship again in Havana Bay, again looking up at the impressive white building that looked like a Baroque castle with a dome: only this time, they weren't saying hello to it, but good-bye. They had no illusions anymore; they were aware of the realities up there on the hill, and they were happy to be leaving.

Their trunk was already on its way to New York, whereas their next stop on the *S.S. Florida* was Miami. Once again, with only an overnight bag – the voyage was merely fourteen hours long – they set sail on the *Florida* as scheduled, at six o'clock in the evening on the second Sunday in October.

She was a true cruise ship if ever there was one: no cargo, no holds, no hatches; just cabins along the decks, from the bow to the stern. They could have dined; they could have danced; but they settled for a quick meal and a good night of sleep in their cabin.

"I can't wait to get to New York," Franz said while they were resting: she in one small bed, he in the other. "I didn't have a chance to write Ilona and Mama. Boy are they going to be surprised." Then almost mournfully: "But they don't know about the loss of my voice. How am I going to explain that to them?"

"Don't think about it now, Franz. We'll find a good doctor there for you. Everything is going to be all right. We're finally going to reach the end of our journey and make a new home for ourselves."

Franziska then gracefully floated over to Franz, setting herself girlishly on the edge of his bed. He drew her down toward him, and they kissed. Then he stroked her face with the cushiony tips of his fingers, ever so gently feeling the soft texture of her skin.

"Without you . . . without you, I would be lost," he said, fixing his warm brown eyes on hers.

"Me too," she answered.

"You help me in everything we do. You give me the strength to want to protect you. And you'll give me the strength to survive without my voice."

But then, totally involuntarily, the tears began to fill his eyes.

"Oh . . . oh . . . no – you mustn't," Franziska said, tenderly wiping away the moisture.

"It seems like we're switching roles now," Franz uttered. "But I can't help myself. I just can't help myself."

"It's all right, sweetheart. That's what love is all about," Franziska said soothingly. "Now it's your turn to lean on me."

And the next morning, they were in Miami.

My father's passport with the big "J" on the first page and "Israel"
above his name.

My father's passport photo page.

My mother's passport with the "J" on it and "Sara" above her
name as a middle name.

My mother's passport photo page.

Stamp of *"Transitvisum"* to Switzerland in my mother's passport, issued 20 December 1938. Also, the stamp in my mother's passport on 24 December 1938, the day my parents left Prague and entered Zürich, Switzerland.

The page in my mother's passport stamped in Genova with a Cuban visa.

No. **139**

CONSULADO DE LA REPÚBLICA

DE PANAMÀ EN MILAN.

VISTO BUENO PARA EL TRANSITO.

MILAN, 2 de Enero DE 193~~2~~ 1936

DERECHOS B. 5.— (cinco)

EL CONSUL DE PANAMÀ

para 30 (treinta) días.

El interesado ha efectuado en este Consulado el Deposito de Repatriación por este visto de transito para que se dirige a Cuba.

EL CÒNSUL DE LA REPÙBLICA DE PANAMÀ

9

The visa stamped in my father's passport in Milano for Panama.

The *S.S. Rialto*. Note that the *Rialto* really was a freighter or passenger-cargo ship. (*Courtesy of The Steamship Historical Society Archives, sshsa.org. Photo by A. Duncan: The Uhle Collection.*)

Photo of the Cine General Salom theater in Puerto Cabello, Venezuela on the postcard given to my father with a greeting on it from the generous gentleman who sponsored a concert for him.

My father's passport stamped on 10 February 1939 in Panama, entering on the *S.S. Rialto*. Also, note the stamp on my father's passport dated 13 February 1939 on board the *S.S. Chiriquí* for Cuba.

The *S.S. Chiriquí*. More luxurious than the *Rialto*, she still transported bananas. (*Photo courtesy of The Steamship Historical Society Archives, sshsa.org: The Uhle Collection.*)

Author's photo taken in 1999 at the site of the entrance to the former Triscornia immigration camp in Cuba.

Photo taken by the author in 1999 of the grounds inside the former Triscornia detention camp.

ANDRÉ MERTENS & Co.

General European Representatives of COLUMBIA CONCERTS CORPORATION of Columbia Broadcasting System

New York, N. Y., 113, West 57th Street
Cable address: Merwie Newyork

Metropolitan Musical Bureau, Inc. • Evans and Salter, Inc.
Concert Management Arthur Judson, Inc.
Haensel and Jones • Wolfsohn Musical Bureau of N. Y., Inc.
Community Concert Service.

Paris (VIIIe), 252, Rue du Faubourg Saint-Honoré (Salle Pleyel) - Adr. Télégr.: MERCONCERT-Paris - Téléphone: Carnot 7002

c/o Columbia Management of California
Columbia Square
Hollywood, California

Hollywood, California
August 14, 1939

Mr. Jung
Calle 5 No. 604
HABANA-VEDADO, Cuba

Dear Mr. Jung:

Miss Walter informed me about your letter of July 8. She has talked to Professor
Reitler concerning the Australian matter in which you seem to be still very
interested. When are you coming to the States? I am in Hollywood right now
and I shall be here until the opening of the San Francisco season August 25.
Then I will drive back to New York.

    I shall be pleased to hear from you and Mr. Sconka, to whom I want to
send my best regards. With best wishes, I am

                                        Sincerely yours,

                                        ANDRE MERTENS

AM:GM

A letter from André Mertens to my father in Cuba in August 1939.

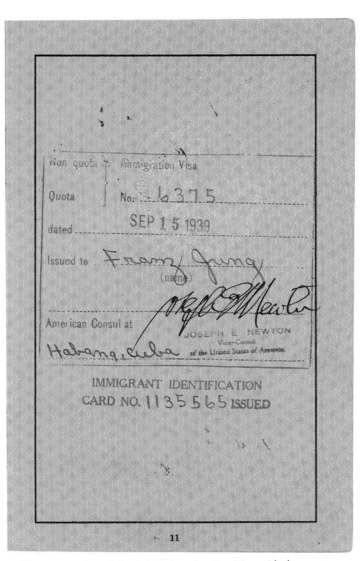

Non quota or Immigration Visa

Quota   No. 6375

dated   SEP 1 5 1939

Issued to   Franz Jung
(name)

American Consul at

JOSEPH E. NEWTON
Vice-Consul
Habana, Cuba   of the United States of America

IMMIGRANT IDENTIFICATION
CARD NO. 1135565 ISSUED

11

The stamp of my father's U.S. Immigration Visa with the quota number on it in his passport, dated September 15, 1939 in Havana.

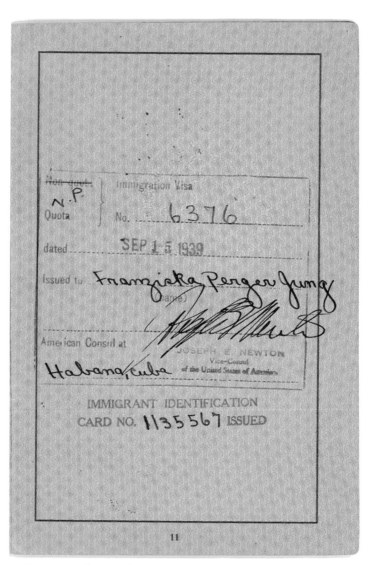

Non-quot. Immigration Visa
N. P.
Quota   No. 6376

dated   SEP 15 1939

Issued to   Franziska Penger Jung
              (name)

American Consul at   JOSEPH E. NEWTON
                       Vice-Consul
Habana, Cuba   of the United States of America

IMMIGRANT IDENTIFICATION
CARD NO. 1135567 ISSUED

11

The stamp of my mother's U.S. Immigration Visa with the quota
number on it in her passport, dated September 15, 1939.

Florida East Coast Railway Station, 1940.
(*Photo by Liddle & Kohn; Courtesy of HistoryMiami.*)

CHAPTER TWENTY-NINE
The Park

Miami, Florida
October 9, 1939

*E*very port has its own personality – that's what Franz and Franziska discovered in Europe. But the Port of Miami was different: It was in the United States.

From the first moment they stepped onto the pier, they felt free. There seemed to be so much space: water all around and a sprawling young metropolis. Even the air seemed different. However they felt lost. No familiar buildings, no familiar people – everything was new to them.

They walked and walked down Biscayne Boulevard, hoping to find the railway station, and they stopped to eat something at a diner. Franziska had continued to have stomach problems in Cuba, and a doctor there had recommended cornflakes. Whatever they were, Franziska saw them on the menu and ordered them.

A waitress placed a carton of cornflakes in front of her, a small pitcher of cream, and a bowl. Franziska looked perplexed.

"You're supposed to throw them into the bowl, put cream and sugar on top of them, and then eat them with a spoon," Franz educated her.

"Oh," she answered. "So this is American food."

Next stop: Bayfront Park. They couldn't help themselves. It was Miami's answer to the Stadtpark. Shrubs, palms and flowers, and even an afternoon concert. But it wasn't a Johann Strauss waltz that they were hearing. The sound was distinctly American: it was rhythmical and danceable. The instrumentalists of a small band were performing on the platform in a corner of the park. There were only a few spectators since it was a weekday.

"Oh, my gosh!" Franziska said. A vocalist was singing in German.

"*Bei mir bist du schön*," the chanteuse was singing. But all of the other lyrics were in English.

"Fascinating Rhythm," "The Continental," "Lullaby of Broadway": None of the melodies were familiar to them. They wanted to hear more though, yet they wanted to sit down. There were only a few benches, and they were taken.

"Why isn't anyone sitting on this one over here?" Franz questioned.

"Because it says 'For Colored Only,' " Franziska responded.

"How awful!" Franz said. "We were forced to leave Vienna because of Hitler's discrimination. I thought that America would be different."

"And what's so ironic," Franziska added, "is that *we* are not allowed to sit on this bench, and I want to sit down."

Then Franz wanted a drink of water. "You aren't going to believe this," he said softly into her ear. "The drinking fountains are labeled, too."

"Oh, dear," Franziska uttered. "The immigrants on the *St. Louis* weren't allowed in, and the colored people can't sit with the whites."

"At least we're not the ones being discriminated against now. . . . But then, that's what the Viennese said. And if they had done something to help us, Hitler wouldn't be taking over Europe right now."

"You're absolutely right, Franz. But since we don't have the power to change anything, let's just hope that this doesn't happen in New York."

It happened again. They'd purchased their tickets at the Florida East Coast Railway Station, and Franz had wanted to use the public restroom. "For Colored," "For Whites" – the concept was extremely distressing to him.

The station was much like those in Europe, except it wasn't as elaborate as many in the larger European cities. The terminal building looked like a giant two-story wooden cabin with a rustic shingle roof, and the train tracks were just beyond it outside, with all of downtown Miami in view. There were people everywhere, most of them extremely well-attired in dresses, suits and hats, some carrying coats and luggage. And many of them seemed to know each other, for they were conversing in a very cordial manner.

The train was scheduled to leave at four o'clock. Franz and Franziska still had a fifteen-minute wait.

"I'm in the mood for a piece of chocolate," Franz said. "I saw a candy machine close by. I'll be right back."

"You better be," Franziska answered, "because if you're not, I'll get on the train without you."

"You can't," Franz said, smiling and walking away. He was holding something up in the air. "*I've* got the tickets."

The train rolled in a few minutes later, and almost everyone hustled toward the passenger cars. Franziska was anxious to get on, but Franz still hadn't returned. "If we miss this train, I'll never forgive him," she whispered to herself.

Although there were numerous people milling around the station and waiting along other tracks, there were now only a few in Franziska's immediate proximity. She was getting nervous. *He can't be far. There must be a way to communicate with him*, she thought. *Ahhh* . . . Then:

"Psst . . . Psst," she uttered somewhat timidly. "Psst . . . Psst."

But *No* Franz. Where was he?

"Psst . . . Psst!" she enunciated again much louder. "Psst . . . Psst!"

He heard her calling. He was rushing toward her.

"I knew it was you," he said out of breath. "We're not in Cuba anymore, so I knew it was you."

"Where have you been?" Franziska asked. "Everyone has already boarded the train."

"I had some chocolate, and . . ."

"Come on!" Franziska interrupted.

And a few minutes later, they were comfortably settled in their compartment. And a few minutes after that, they were finally on their way to New York City.

CHAPTER THIRTY

The Voice of Freedom

15 West 82nd Street
New York City
October 22, 1939

*I believe that this is one of the most significant chapters in the book.
MY FATHER'S VOICE HAD PROBABLY SAVED HIS LIFE, and possibly
my mother's as well.*

They were all together at last, together under a single roof in New
York City. It was their reunion celebration: the Jungs' and the Becks'.
Franziska was serving them a sumptuous meal in the modest one-bed-
room apartment she and Franz had rented at Fifteen West Eighty-second Street. The furnished ground-floor apartment was located in a typical three-story brownstone with large bay windows and stairs leading
up to the building's entrance. The diminutive parlor had a coffee table
and couch, and there was a dining room table next to the Lilliputian
kitchenette near the entry door. There was a piano as well, but it wasn't
provided by the management. Franz had discovered it at a moving and
storage company in Greenwich Village. He'd had his choice of three
uprights that had been abandoned there. The owner of the facility was
so glad to get rid of one of the old pianos that he delivered it free of

charge to Franz and Franziska's apartment. It was placed at the far end of the living room, next to the adjoining undersized bedroom and bathroom. Yet in spite of the apartment's shortcomings, it did have a strong selling point: It was just a short block away from Central Park. And for Franz and Franziska, a walk in Central Park in October was a little like taking a stroll along the *Hauptallee* during an autumn in Vienna. The air was crisp; the tree branches cloaked the walking paths; and the falling leaves provided a soft carpet on which to tread. If only all of Franz's relatives could have been in New York to breathe in this newfound fresh air of freedom.

"We are so lucky to be here, finally all together," Olga Jung said, "eating a good meal and sipping wine."

"We are truly the fortunate ones," Ilona continued. "The Nazis and Soviets have divided up Poland already. They're taking over more and more of Europe."

"And the evacuation of Jews is beginning, forced labor in concentration camps, the outlook is bleak," Hans added.

"Terrible," Franziska said with a grim expression on her face.

"Oh, my poor sisters," Olga cried.

"Now we must stop this type of conversation at once," Ilona said. "We are celebrating our good fate this afternoon. The future is bright. Hans has met someone who wants to go into business with him – manufacturing clothes. She has the knowledge, and he has the assets."

"But isn't that risky?" Franz questioned.

"I am a businessman," Hans declared. "I have a sense of what is profitable. This woman knows what she is talking about. We'll be selling to Saks Fifth Avenue and Macy's inside of a year."

"And Franz, you'll be singing at the Met soon," Ilona said. "Why don't you give us a little preview performance?"

Franz looked at Franziska, who was sitting across from him at the table. Their eyes met in a locked stare. There was a pause. Then: "I make it a practice never to sing on a full stomach," Franz jested.

"I'm going to clear the table," Franziska cut in quickly. "Why don't you sit on the couch or move your chairs into the middle of the living room, and I'll serve dessert in there."

"Speaking of dessert, do you remember when I sent you that letter to Prague about a year and a half ago, informing you that Else would be gifting you with a *Sachertorte*?" Ilona asked.

"Yes," Franz responded. "Your hieroglyphics were brilliant."

"And when I wrote you in my own inimitable way that we had been handed over to the Nazis at the border, where they ridiculed us, fired gunshots into the air, and forced us to walk back to Vienna in the rain?"

"Yes."

"Well, now we are all together at last, and we can finally savor some of Else's *Sachertorte*."

Then everyone laughed, especially Else.

"Yes!" she exclaimed. "I've baked a large *Sachertorte* especially for this occasion, and we're going to have it *mit Schlagobers*."

The group moved into the living room, ate their whipped cream-covered chocolate delicacy, and talked and talked over numerous cups of *Kaffee*. (Or maybe the cups were simply filled with coffee. After all, the Jungs and the Becks were in America now, even if they were indeed still speaking German.)

"Now Franz, *mein Sohn der Opernsänger*," Olga said proudly. "Sing for us. I haven't heard your beautiful voice in so long. Sing 'Vier ernste Gesänge.' Oh, how I love your interpretation of the 'Four Serious Songs' by Brahms. When I die, I want you to sing them for me at my funeral."

Franz didn't say anything at first. He simply wore a somber expression on his face. Franziska had been washing the dishes in the kitchenette, but she must have heard the conversation because she walked into the living room, drying her hands on a dishtowel. There was silence for a couple of minutes, and everyone seemed to be eyeing one another.

"I can't," Franz said almost inaudibly. "I can't sing."

More silence.

Finally: "Franz has some sort of catarrh," Franziska explained. "And it's affecting his voice."

"How long have you had it?" Ilona asked.

"Since the last few months in Cuba," Franziska answered.

"Oh, it's probably just an allergy," Ilona said. Then, as if Franz wasn't even in the room: "Franz has always had hay fever in the spring; only it isn't spring now – it's October."

"I have to be honest with all of you," Franz said haltingly. "I don't believe that I have an indisposition. I believe that I'm losing my voice."

Ilona's face instantly displayed an alarmed look, and Olga's eyes filled with tears.

"Naturally, we do not know if that is true yet," Franziska said. "We are trying to find a doctor . . . a specialist . . . who will be able to help us."

"Maybe the climatic changes have harmed your vocal cords . . . maybe you've had too much excitement," Ilona concluded. "Your voice will come back; I know that your voice will come back."

"I do not believe this," Olga insisted. "Sing for me, *mein Sohn*. Sing for me now."

"No, Mama!"

"Please! I want to hear for myself."

So Franz reluctantly went to the piano and played a beginning tone. Then he started to sing the first of the "Four Serious Songs," the words taken directly from the Old Testament (Ecclesiastes 3, 19-22):

"*Denn es gehet dem Menschen wie dem Vieh. . . .*" he sang. "For that which befalleth man befalleth beasts. . . ."

He described that as one dies, so dies the other, and that man has no eminence over a beast, for all is vanity.

Then Franz picked up the tempo: "*Es fährt alles an einen Ort. . . .*" he sang, explaining that we all go to one place; we are of dust and return to dust again.

Then he suddenly stopped singing. "I can't!" he shouted, half crying. "I feel like I'm singing my own funeral march. I can't sing of rejoicing about my own works, because I was going to make my mark in life with my voice. But now I'm not. So who am I? I'm nothing now."

Franziska rushed over to Franz and wrapped her arms around him. "That's not true," she said. "You are my husband. And if you would have continued singing, you would have felt uplifted when you reached the final *Lied*, which you know affirms the power of love; for my dear

Franz, you must know by now that you have all of my love, just as I know that I have yours."

"But love will not get me through this."

"How can you say that, Franz? Love can get you through anything."

"Not this."

"Franz," Ilona said. "You do still have a voice. I just heard it. It may not be the voice you once had, but I believe that you'll find a doctor who will revive it to its full splendor. You must always remember, Franz, that your voice has been a blessing. Without it, you might have remained in Vienna and been apprehended by the Nazis."

"Yes, *mein Sohn*," Olga added. "Ilona is right. I never told you this, but soon after Hitler took over Austria, some Nazis came snooping around, looking for you. Yes, your voice probably saved your life."

Franz was suddenly stunned out of his tantrum. He didn't know how to respond.

"And if you would have stayed in Vienna, I would have never fled to Czechoslovakia. I would have never left you," Franziska said. "So your voice might have saved my life, too."

There seemed to be a lull in the conversation. There was really nothing more to say.

"Well, I think it's time for us to go now," Ilona announced. "You need your rest."

So within a few minutes, the Becks and Olga Jung were standing by the door with their coats. "We had a lovely time," Olga said, hugging Franz. "And you *will* sing the 'Four Serious Songs' at my funeral."

"*Guten Tag*, little brother . . . or maybe I should say *guten Abend*," Ilona said. "It's already getting dark."

"Thank you for a lovely meal," Else Beck complimented Franziska, then quipped: "Of course, it wouldn't have been nearly as good without my dessert."

"*Auf Wiedersehen*," Hans said, giving Franziska a kiss on the cheek and then shaking Franz's hand. "It's good to be back together as a family again. Yes, it feels good."

"*Auf Wiedersehen*," they all said in unison.

And a few minutes later, Franz and Franziska were alone once again in the quietness of their apartment, suddenly embracing each other as if they'd never let go.

My father had suddenly realized that his voice had served a purpose in freeing him so that he could pursue a better life with my mother in America.

CHAPTER THIRTY-ONE

Encounters

New York City
November 3, 1939 to December 5, 1939

$\mathcal{T}$here was Broadway and then there was Broadway. One was the street, and the other was the theater district. Yet if one walked along the street, Broadway, between roughly Fortieth and Fifty-seventh streets, that person would technically also be walking on Broadway, in the theater district, which is exactly what Franz and Franziska did on many an afternoon and evening, amazed at all of the lights and glitter emanating from all of the buildings and theaters. In fact, Franz and Franziska often bumped into people that they knew from Vienna – then always conversing in their native tongue.

"Hatschek! I don't believe it," Franz found himself saying one late Friday afternoon in early November, when strolling with Franziska on, *yes*, that street. Hatschek had been one of Franz's accompanists at the Konservatorium. For just a moment, Franz was back in Vienna – a promising student with a splendrous voice – but then he snapped out of his reverie and remembered where he actually was. He didn't really want to say anything to Hatschek about his vocal problems. Hatschek was probably accompanying some singers from the Met. The Metropolitan Opera House was just a few blocks away between Thirty-ninth and Fortieth streets. Hatschek was coming from that direction.

"Let me know when you need my services," the accompanist said.

"Soon . . . soon," Franz responded.

"Where did you sing after you left the Konservatorium?" Hatschek asked.

"Oh . . . the German Theater," Franz answered. "Franziska and I were married in Prague."

"Congratulations."

"Yes, well that seems so long ago."

" I know what you mean. But I don't think that we look much older. Do you?"

"No, not at all. . . . So . . . are you accompanying some of the singers from the Met?"

"Yes . . . some."

It seemed that both men were trying to hide something.

"I want to work, but my allergies have been plaguing me," Franz finally admitted.

"I can identify with your thinking," Hatschek said. "Obstacles often stand in the way of progress. I hope that you won't think that I'm being too presumptuous, but I have a suggestion. Along with my regular accompanying chores, I'm involved in an educational program aimed at cultivating an appreciation for opera and classical music among the young people in New York City. Singers are needed to perform at various schools throughout the public school system.

"How rewarding," Franz said.

"I realize that you are probably speaking to agents and setting up engagements, and I know that you've set your sights on something much more prestigious. But would you consider participating in such a program?"

Hatschek was right. Franz would have ordinarily been speaking to André Mertens about singing Wagner at the Met, performing a more varied repertoire in San Francisco, or at the least, about setting up some engagements for him in Australia. But now, in Franz's precarious situation, singing for children in the New York City public schools was just about as much as he could hope for. "Yes, I would be interested," Franz replied.

"Good," Hatschek said. "Let's exchange telephone numbers." So he pulled a piece of paper from his coat pocket, wrote his telephone number on the top, and then handed the paper and a pen to Franz. "Why don't you write yours on the bottom and tear it off?"

"Okay," Franz said, doing what he was asked. "Here it is."

"Thank you," Hatschek said. "I'll be talking to you real soon, and I'll give you all of the details."

"Excellent," Franz said. "And since you've been so helpful already, I'd like to ask you if you happen to know the name of a throat specialist who treats singers, maybe some from the Met."

"Actually, I don't know of a doctor offhand. But I'll look into the matter."

"Wonderful," Franz said. "Well, I guess that we'd better be moving along. It's getting chilly, and I don't want Franziska to catch a cold. What am I saying – I don't want to catch a cold either."

"Good-bye," the accompanist said. "I'll talk to you soon."

Franz and Franziska continued walking along Broadway, watching the hottest news story of the day unfold in illuminated letters that were revolving around the building at Forty-second Street and Broadway. They stopped at the Horn & Hardart in Times Square. The restaurant had introduced them to a new, distinct way of eating. The dishes displayed behind small windows were retrievable by placing the appropriate coinage into the slots next to them. "It's kind of like playing the slot machines in a casino, only food comes out instead of money," Franziska said the first time that they'd encountered the automat.

The Horn & Hardart waiterless restaurants were located all over New York City. They were quick, convenient, and inexpensive. And once again, Franz and Franziska met someone they knew.

They had each played their favorite slot machines: Franziska recouping soup and a turkey sandwich, and Franz claiming a chicken pot pie and chocolate cake. They were sitting down at one of the tables. The noise of the chair legs scraping the floor as they pulled out the chairs was noticeably raspy.

"Give me your coat. I'll put it over this vacant chair," Franz said to Franziska while surveying the room.

"Okay," she responded, handing Franz her coat.

"Why look who's sitting over there," Franz said.

"Who?"

"Oh, I feel terrible. He's all alone. I'll bet he was never reunited with his family."

"What are you talking about?"

"It's Egon . . . Egon Eisenstadt . . . from Zürich."

Franziska turned around. "Oh," she said, echoing Franz's sentiments. "You're right. He looks so forlorn."

"I'm going to ask him to join us," Franz said.

"Yes . . . Good," Franziska responded.

Egon Eisenstadt's lips curled up ever so slightly into a vague smile when Franz reached his table. Franziska could see the two men shaking hands. Then Egon nodded his head affirmatively, stood up, and the two walked toward Franziska, with Egon Eisenstadt carrying his plate of half-eaten meatloaf.

"It's so good to see you again, Franziska," he said, setting his food down at the table, then taking Franziska's hand and kissing it. Franz quickly grabbed Franziska's coat and placed it around her shoulders as Egon Eisenstadt descended onto the empty chair. Franz was afraid to ask Egon about his wife and children, but the words began streaming out of Egon's mouth like a cascading waterfall.

"I am all alone in the world now," he said. "The Nazis never sent my wife and sons to me in Zürich. After I met you there almost a year ago, I went to the railroad station every day, faithfully reading the display monitor to determine where all of the trains from Austria would arrive, and then waiting for my family at the designated tracks. I spent hours at the station every day for more than a month, but my wife and children never appeared."

"I'm so sorry," Franziska said.

"No doubt they are in a concentration camp; or even worse, they may have been killed. . . . The Nazis lied to me, but then what could I have expected from them? They took my money."

"Isn't there anyone you could contact to learn the truth?" Franz said.

"No, that would be too dangerous. . . . I have given up hope."

"How long have you been in New York?"

"Since last spring."

"Have you been able to earn a living?"

"The Hebrew Immigrant Aid Society has helped me greatly, and I work part time at the Metropolitan Museum of Art."

"That sounds good," Franziska said.

"I have so much trouble concentrating though, especially when I am at work. I keep on seeing my wife, Erna, with our two sons, playing and having a wonderful time in our garden in Vienna. And then I imagine them separated from each other and starving in a filthy concentration camp. I envision my wife being beaten by SS guards; then I see a Nazi sexually abusing and ridiculing her – making fun of her skeletal body, telling her that she is unappealing, that not even her husband would want her now, so she must be with him in order to learn how to please a man. He is rough and insensitive. Her eyes are glassy with desperation as she succumbs to him. And when he is through with her, he laughs, shoves her clothes into her arms and pushes her away. She has forgotten the person she once was. He has stripped away her feelings of self-worth. . . ."

"Stop it! Stop it!" Franziska cried out, interrupting. "I can't listen to this kind of talk anymore. You're recalling a nightmare which you yourself have invented. None of it is true."

"And then I fantasize that this Nazi has passed her on to his brutish colleagues."

"Stop it now! The Nazi would have never done this. Hitler has forbidden Aryans to have such relations with Jews. If a Nazi had disobeyed the decree, he would be fearful to boast about it."

"You are right," Egon Eisenstadt said. "It's all a fantasy. But I must face the reality that I will never see my wife and children again. I feel such pain inside. Without my wife, I really don't want to live, yet I wake up every morning to see the light of day. Why is this? Can you tell me why this is?"

Egon Eisenstadt always made Franziska feel so helpless and sad. "Time has a way of healing. Give yourself some time," she said.

"Nothing will make me feel better."

"Why don't you give us your telephone number? I would like nothing more than to invite you over to our apartment for a home-cooked meal."

"That would be very kind of you. I would enjoy it," Egon Eisenstadt said. "But I do not have a telephone. Perhaps you could call me at the Metropolitan Museum of Art."

"Yes, of course," Franziska said.

They had finished eating and conversing. They were tired. "We really must be going," Franz said, rising from his chair and helping Franziska on with her coat. "It has been so very nice seeing you again."

"Likewise," Egon Eisenstadt said. "Likewise."

"You see," Franziska whispered to Franz as they were leaving the restaurant, "everyone who is faced with leaving his homeland has a story to tell. I think I'd rather be in our shoes than his. At least we have each other."

"You're right," Franz agreed, locking his arm around Franziska's waist. "Now we have a home again, as small as it may be. So let's go home."

Hatschek telephoned Franz a few days later; and a few days after that, Franz was auditioning in the auditorium of an elementary school on the Upper East Side. He sang King Philip's soliloquy from *Don Carlos*. The audition examiners – a few were retired singers who had performed at the Met – couldn't understand why Franz was singing an aria for a bass. The answer was simple: Franz was losing his voice, and the aria was written in a comfortable range for him; it wasn't too low or too high. But he was reluctant to tell the appraisers his rationale. He feared that if he told them that he was losing his voice, he would be passed over. So when one of them interrogated him with, "You're singing a role for a bass," Franz simply responded, "I know."

Well, he got the job. He began singing at New York City public schools approximately twice a week, and he received five dollars each time he performed. But there was a catch. One of the examiners had sensed Franz's vocal impairment. "I would like you to come to my apartment," she said. "I know that I'll be able to help you improve your technique."

That's not exactly what Franz had wanted to hear. But in order to retain his new job, he went to the woman's apartment. He'd felt humiliated: He knew how to sing, probably better than she did. His technique was not the problem; he could probably teach her a thing or two.

She had him singing scales. "Sing over there," she said, "way out in front of yourself." Her approach was valid, although different from his. However he was not in a position to debate, or to explain that his problem was a physical one. He didn't need a voice teacher – he needed a doctor. But he lived through the ordeal, even though his self-confidence was wavering.

Then Hatschek came through again. He told Franz about a Dr. Wilhelm Mayer-Hermann, a refugee from Berlin who treated famous singers. Some performed on Broadway; others sang at the Met. Franz felt encouraged. He hoped that Dr. Mayer-Hermann could help him.

The doctor did help Franz at the beginning, mentally at least, because he gave Franz some hope. He never told Franz exactly what was wrong with him, but he gave Franz injections at least twice a week, and he never charged anything. Dr. Mayer-Hermann was known for being a bit of a bon vivant. He'd even posed for a painting by the renowned Expressionist artist, Otto Dix. But Franz believed that he was a kind person, and very empathetic.

His office was on Seventy-second Street between Park Avenue and Madison Avenue on the ground floor of a brownstone. The waiting room was cozy and looked like a salon or living room with autographed photographs on the walls of well-known singers, actors, and movie stars. With such a famous patient clientele, Franz hoped that maybe Dr. Mayer-Hermann could help him.

The weather was gloomy that day. It was the beginning of December, and it had been raining for hours. Not even Central Park looked appealing now. A nurse led Franz into one of the patient rooms. He took off his raincoat and draped it around a chair. "The doctor will be in to see you shortly," the nurse said, leaving the room and closing the door behind her.

A few minutes later, Dr. Mayer-Hermann entered. He was a short man: a little heavyset with graying hair. "So have you noticed any changes?" he asked.

"No," Franz responded. "My voice is about the same. It's there, but it has no luster."

"When you were in Cuba last spring, how were your allergies?"

"No worse than usual; in fact, they were probably better than in Vienna. But I've noticed lately that I have a constant postnasal drip, and it might have started in Cuba. I just didn't really pay any attention to it there. I really didn't notice it."

"So it's gotten worse?"

"I don't know. I only know that I'm conscious of it here, and it doesn't go away."

"I don't think that could cause you to lose your voice, but if you're clearing your throat a great deal or coughing, that could cause trauma to your larynx."

"I haven't really been coughing though."

Then Dr. Mayer-Hermann examined Franz's nose and throat. "Well, I think that we should watch this," he said. "But at the present time, I'd just like to continue with the shots."

"But so far, they aren't doing any good," Franz responded. "Isn't there something else that I could try? I'm emotionally distraught because my voice is my life. I'm not prepared to do anything else but sing, and my wife depends on me."

"I understand," Dr. Mayer-Hermann said. "You are a refugee like me, in a strange, new country, trying to become proficient in a foreign language. Even the mental strain could be affecting your vocal cords."

"Please try to help me, Herr Doktor. Please try!"

Dr. Mayer-Hermann didn't know how to respond to such an appeal.

"I'm doing everything I can," he said. "But I will be consulting my colleagues, and if there is anything new that I can suggest, I will."

"Thank you," Franz said. "You have been so generous to me."

"Right now, why don't you prepare for the shot."

But as Franz was lowering his trousers, the electricity in the building went out. So Dr. Mayer-Hermann opened the door and asked for a nurse to bring in some candles.

A few minutes later, Franz lay on the table with his buttocks exposed. He saw the glare of the candles and felt the sting of the needle as Dr. Mayer-Hermann gave him the injection.

"How romantic!" a woman said.

Could that have been the nurse? Franz wondered. *That certainly wasn't the type of comment a nurse would make.*

So he turned around and saw that it was Hildegarde: Hildegarde, the famous chanteuse. She was one of Dr. Mayer-Hermann's patients.

Franz quickly jumped off the table and pulled up his pants. Dr. Mayer-Hermann was laughing. So what else could Franz do? He felt quite awkward and embarrassed, but he laughed, too.

Conductor Thomas Philipp Martin.
(*Courtesy of Mary-Anne Martin.*)

CHAPTER THIRTY-TWO
Trials and Tribulations

New York City
January 1940 to August 1940

"*M*mm ... Mmmm ... "

Franz was moaning in his sleep and it woke Franziska up. *He must be dreaming*, she thought. But she didn't want to wake him.

"Mmm ... Mmmm," he moaned. "Ahhhhh!" He sat up suddenly. His eyes were wide open and he looked stunned.

"Are you all right? You must have had a nightmare," Franziska said, putting her arms around him.

"Oh ... oh, it was terrible," Franz said. "I was in a concentration camp.... They'd cut out my tongue, and I couldn't speak. My voice was gone. I couldn't sing."

"It didn't happen, Franz. It didn't happen. Calm down, and let's go back to sleep."

"Pretty soon I won't be able to sing. I won't be able to sing at all."

"That's not true. You're shaken up. Come on ... lie down," Franziska said soothingly, gently propelling Franz back into a prone position, then reclining and resting her cheek on his chest. "Let's sleep; let's sleep."

363

Bzzzzzzz . . .

"Oh, no! I don't want to get up," Franz said. "I hate that alarm clock."

"So do I," Franziska echoed groggily. "But you have to get up. You're supposed to be at a school in Brooklyn at eight-thirty. If you're not out of the apartment in half an hour, you'll never make it."

"I don't want to get up," Franz repeated.

"Well, you're going to," Franziska joshed, rolling Franz off the side of the bed.

"Oh . . . you have no sympathy," he responded.

"I have to get up too. I have to work at the tailor shop, remember?"

"Yes, but you don't have to be there until nine, and you just have to walk down the street."

"You're right. But since we have a miniscule bathroom and can't get ready at the same time, you better go in there now; otherwise I'm the one who's going to be late, and then Sebastian, the tailor, won't pay me my eight dollars a week for doing all of those elaborate alterations."

"All right! You've made your point," Franz said. "You don't have to make me breakfast. I'll just grab some juice on the way out."

So Franz showered and shaved, dressed and drank his juice. He warmed up his voice by the piano, then grabbed his music, threw some impromptu costuming into a canvas bag, kissed Franziska good-bye, and ran out the door.

It was half past seven, and he knew that he was running late on this January morning. It wasn't raining or snowing, but it was cold. Franz was wearing a woolen suit, a scarf around his neck, and an overcoat. He was walking briskly to the subway station at Eighty-sixth Street and Central Park West. Even though he was out of breath and felt the need to open his mouth and pant, he refrained, because breathing in the cold air could be detrimental to his voice. Besides, he didn't want to get sick.

He walked rapidly down some steps into the station, which was like a separate city beneath the real city. Franz felt as if he were being whirled into a hurricane as he stormed through one of the turnstiles to the platform along with hundreds of others who were doing exactly the same thing on their way to work on this dreary rush-hour morning.

He just barely stepped into the train when the doors slammed shut. He couldn't find a place to sit, so he stood, holding on to one of the metal posts, fearing that if he let go, he'd be thrown – thrown like a matador being flung by a bull into the arena. Of course, that could never happen, he realized, because people were standing all around him, jammed together tightly as if they were canned sardines.

The train moved swiftly. Franz hoped that he'd know when to get off and transfer. There were so many people all around that he couldn't see the signs outside the train. He hoped that he'd be able to hear the conductor.

"I'm going to West Fourth Street – Washington Square," he told the man crammed next to him. "Could you tell me when to get off?"

"I'm going there too," the man responded. "Just get off with me."

When they arrived, Franz really wanted to leave the station to see the marble arch outside: the arch which commemorated George Washington's first inauguration. It was supposed to look like the Arc de Triomphe – Franz had already seen one duplicate in Genova – but Franz simply didn't have enough time.

"I have to catch the train to Brooklyn. Where should I go?" he asked a friendly woman at the information counter. Then once again, he felt as if he was being herded in. But this time, he did find a place to sit on the train. However, when he arrived at the station on Seventh Avenue and Ninth Street, there were people standing in every discernible corner. First he wasn't sure if he'd reached his destination. Then by the time he was certain, he couldn't maneuver his body through all of the people in order to get off on time.

"Oh, no!" he said as the train continued on. "I've missed my stop. Now I'm going to be late."

So he got off at the next station and took another train back. The school wasn't far, but it was already half past eight. He walked along Seventh Avenue to the John Jay High School, which was located between Fourth and Fifth streets. It was a large school, and although mostly brick, its elaborate entrance – with ornate pediment, pilasters, and friezes – contributed to its classically Grecian style.

Franz hastened into the office and explained the nature of his visit.

An office clerk led him to the auditorium, which resembled a small theater equipped with a stage and numerous rows of chairs. The accompanist was already playing the introductory bars to the aria Franz planned to sing. Franz raced onto the stage, positioning himself in front of the piano, and then he began the recitative to Figaro's first aria from *The Marriage of Figaro.*

He (as Figaro) was singing in German to an invisible Count Almaviva, explaining that he understood the Count's designs on his fiancée, Susanna, but would not allow the Count to proceed. Franz wondered if the children had read a synopsis of the opera. Were they mature enough to understand the theme?

When he was finished singing, they applauded politely. There was a microphone on the side of the stage, and a student began explaining the story behind his next aria. Franz then realized that this same student had probably made some opening remarks before his first selection as well.

He would have ordinarily sung the second aria from *The Marriage of Figaro*, when Figaro describes to Cherubino what it's like to be a soldier. But after having used the aria as an audition piece for Alberto Erede in Cuba, Franz could no longer bear to perform it – maybe one day when his voice came back, hopefully one day soon.

So instead, he sang the "Toreador Song" from *Carmen*, pantomiming the actions of the torero, Escamillo: swinging his imaginary cloak gallantly and piercing the invisible bull with his banderilla. By the time he sang the words "*Toréador, en garde! Toréador! Toréador!*" the children were smiling, and some of them were moving their hands in time to the music as if they were the young protégés of Arturo Toscanini, discovering at long last that they wanted to become conductors. Franz was glad, because even though his voice lacked brilliance and power, he was serving a viable purpose. The children were enjoying opera – most of them for the very first time – and maybe, just maybe, he'd sparked some of them to learn a little more about it.

But it was his final aria that brought the house down. He selected it because even though his voice was far from brilliant, he could act his way through this one, but he had to make some preparations. So while the plot of the opera was being explained to the audience, he walked offstage into the wings.

A student explained to the young audience the difference between Rosina and Count Almaviva in *The Marriage of Figaro* and the same two characters in *The Barber of Seville* – how the Count was courting Rosina in *The Barber of Seville*, and how Dr. Bartolo interfered because he wanted her for himself.

"In this aria, Dr. Bartolo explains to Rosina in no uncertain terms that she cannot pull the wool over his eyes," the student said, moving away from the microphone.

When Franz walked back onstage, the children roared. He had taken his suit jacket off and was wearing a seventeenth century waistcoat, cravat, and periwig, just as he had worn in Aussig. And then when the children were just about finished laughing, he pulled out a pair of spectacles and set them on his nose.

"I cannot sing the aria until I have a Rosina to sing to," he said loudly in English to the audience. "Would someone volunteer, please?"

Most of the girls in the audience were laughing and nodding their heads negatively as if to say, "No! Not me!" while some of the boys were pointing at them hintingly, as if to say, "Her! Choose her!" But then one girl about half way back in the auditorium stood up, raised her hand and said, "I volunteer. I'll be your Rosina." She was in the first row behind the horizontal aisle which divided the auditorium into two parts and marked the beginning of the seats that were gradated upward like those layered in a stadium. As she walked toward Franz and then up the stairs onto the stage, the students were making all kinds of noises like "Yea" and "Boo." Then the assistant principal dragged a chair out and left it just a little left of center stage.

"What is your name?" Franz asked the girl, a pretty brunette with long curly hair.

"Rose," the girl said. "That's the reason I volunteered."

So Franz chivalrously kissed the girl's hand as she sat down, and everyone laughed. "Shall we begin?" he said to cue the accompanist behind them. And then:

"To a doctor of my station – such excuses, young lady," Franz (as Dr.

Bartolo) sang very sternly in German, looking directly at his Rosina. He advised her to deceive a little better, then continued to berate Rosina, alternating between placing his hands on this waist and shaking his finger at her. She was embarrassed and smiling. Then he softened, circled and sang to her that he would forgive her if she confessed.

Of course, she didn't, so Franz held up a pair of keys. And then the music started moving very quickly, so quickly, in fact, that even if he had been singing in English, the children in the audience would have been unable to understand the words. However, he was telling Rosina that in the future, whenever he had to leave the house, he would lock her in her room, and the servants would be watching.

Everyone was laughing hysterically, including Franz's Rosina. He was singing faster and faster, making numerous gestures and facial expressions. At one point when he was singing feverishly, he even held his heart in anguish as if he were having a heart attack, then popped a pill into his mouth – a pill that he had plucked from the pillbox concealed inside his pocket – and as soon as the tablet reached his lips, the grin on his face was indescribable.

The children were having such a good time that when Franz completed singing the aria, they laughed and applauded, and most of them even stood up to give him a standing ovation. He didn't need to have a great voice to win their approval; he simply needed to be a marvelous performer, which of course, he was.

Franz was walking up the steps that led to the entrance of his apartment building. There was someone behind him. He felt a tap on his shoulder and then turned around. He saw a man running along the sidewalk and into the neighboring building. Then he looked down. There was an envelope on the ground. He picked it up and opened it. It was a summons to appear in court. His neighbor was charging that he was disturbing the peace with his singing.

"How were the children?" Franziska asked when he walked in the door.

"They don't understand anything about opera, so they loved me," Franz said. "But look! You aren't going to believe this."

"What?"

"It's a summons. I'm being charged with disturbing the peace by some neighbor that I don't even know. He doesn't like my singing. . . . Well, for that matter, neither do I."

They were sitting in the courtroom: Franz and the super's wife. Franziska was at work; she didn't want to take the chance of losing her job. Pearl, the super's wife, had offered to go with Franz so that he wouldn't get lost. They took the El – elevated railroad – to the Civic Center area, and then they walked to the courthouse. Pearl was afraid that Franz wouldn't understand the proceedings, and she didn't want to lose him as a tenant. If he was told that he could no longer sing in his apartment, Pearl knew that he would move out.

The courtroom was small. Franz and Pearl were seated at a long table, and the plaintiff was nestled behind a duplicate version in front of them. There was a witness stand facing them, a judge who was sitting on an extremely tall chair, and a clerk of the court. There were empty chairs on the far side of the room for jurors, and benches in the back for the spectators, although there were few in number. There were no attorneys; both the plaintiff and the defendant were representing themselves. The proceeding was really more like a hearing than a trial. After all, there was no money involved. The plaintiff was given his opportunity to speak first.

"I am a major in the United States Army Officers' Reserve Corps, and I am studying for an exam which could make me a colonel," the plaintiff said proudly. "But this gentleman makes so much noise when he sings that I just might fail the test. I filed a complaint with the Police Department because I simply couldn't bear the noise anymore."

"I can see from this summons that you don't even live in the same apartment building as the gentleman you are accusing," the judge said.

"That's correct, but his voice carries."

"Does he sing at odd hours of the night?"

"No. He sings mostly in the afternoons and evenings. But he disturbs me, and he is a nuisance."

It was Franz's turn to speak next. Pearl had told him to address the judge as "*Your Honor*," to show respect, she'd said. Franz was still having trouble articulating his thoughts in English, but he was getting better at it.

"Your Honor, I am an opera singer. Here is a document that proves that I am," Franz said, showing the judge the paper that certified him as an official opera singer in Austria. "Of course, with the war . . . and Hitler . . . I suppose that the document is no longer good. . . . Anyhow . . . in the great opera houses of Vienna and Prague, I have sung; and I have just immigrated here to New York City. I earn my living with my voice: It is my instrument, and I must practice using it. I should be able to do whatever I like in the privacy of my home."

"Not if it disturbs the peace and tranquility of the people around you," the major said, standing up.

"Please sit down, sir," the court clerk advised.

"He bothers other people in my building too."

"But does he have a very *BIG* voice?" the judge asked inquisitively.

"*V-E-R-Y* big," the major answered, as if having a big voice was detrimental.

"*Thank you!*" Franz responded, accepting the remark as a compliment. So the judge smiled and the spectators laughed.

"I've made a decision," the judge then announced. "You can sing, Mr. Jung, but you must not do it after ten o'clock in the evening. Your neighbors have the right to sleep."

"That won't do any good," the major shouted. "He rarely sings past ten anyhow."

"If you want to dispute my ruling any further, I suggest that you find witnesses who are also troubled by Mr. Jung's singing," the judge proclaimed. "As for now, my decision stands."

At about the time of the hearing, my parents decided that they wanted to be completely American. They wanted American names. It would have been

*natural for them to change "Jung" to "Young," but they didn't. My father
still hoped that his voice would return, and he wanted a name that would
be easy to pronounce. He was afraid that people would pronounce "Jung" as
"Junk." So I presume that he had heard the name "Delmar" in Cuba. It was
a Latin name that would be easy to pronounce in any language, he told me.
So although my parents apparently did not legalize the change until later, on
all of the paperwork I have found, and on all of the letters from people who
wrote them at that time, my father became "Frank Delmar" and my mother
became "Frances Delmar."*

*I rarely heard my father call my mother "Frances" when he talked to her.
He always called her either "Franziska" or "Franzi" (pronounced "Frahnzi").
Once in a great while, he would call her "Frances" or "Franci" (with an "a"
sound as in "Frances" and the letter "c" to match the "c" in "Frances) when
around Americans.*

*My mother called my father "Franz," "Franzl," or "Frank." She seemed
to like his American name.*

*All of their European friends called my mother "Franzi" and my father
"Franzl," "Franz," or "Frank." And all of their new American friends called
them "Frank" and "Frances."*

*Their American names were legalized when they became United States
citizens. So I still do not understand it, but their papers started saying "Frank
Delmar" and "Frances Delmar" beginning in New York.*

*For this memoir, it is not difficult for me to change my father's name to
"Frank" because he worked and everyone called him "Frank." But for some
reason, it is very difficult for me to refer to my mother as "Frances" since
my father didn't call her by that name, and I called her "Mother." She just
didn't seem like a "Frances" to me. So I am using the name interchangeably
with "Franziska," "Franzi," and sometimes, though rarely, "Franci." I guess
anything goes.*

Frank continued singing at public schools and going to Dr. Mayer-
Hermann for injections, but his voice was steadily deteriorating. He'd
had a bad spring: his postnasal drip was worse, not to mention his hay
fever. He'd decided to teach voice. He'd placed an advertisement in *The*

New York Times, stating that he was auditioning potential students. A lot of young people answered the ad because there was no charge for the audition. But in most instances, the audition was the last time that Frank saw any of them, even if they had been accepted. Frank did have one student though: Thomas P. Martin. Thomas was Arthur Fleischer's son. He had studied conducting at the Konservatorium and had accompanied Frank, then Franz, when Franz took lessons from his father. Arthur Fleischer had immigrated to San Francisco, but Thomas had settled in New York with his American wife, Ruth. He was setting up various conducting engagements in Chicago, St. Louis and Cincinnati, and was considering translating some operas into English. He wanted to know more about vocal technique so that he could translate and conduct from the vantage point of the singer. He was tall and slender with dark hair, and he was a baritone. On this particular afternoon, Frank appeared depressed.

"I think we should stop for the day," Thomas said, standing next to the piano. "I don't think your heart is into this. . . . But I know how to cheer you up. Come outside and I'll show you my new car. My father-in-law just gave it to me."

So Thomas and Frank went out onto Eighty-second Street. "Now look at that," Thomas said, pointing to the automobile that was parked in front of them. "Have you ever seen anything so beautiful?"

It was a 1940 pitch black shiny-painted Pontiac. "Come and look at the motor," Thomas said, lifting up the hood. "Have you ever seen anything so beautiful?"

Frank attempted to smile in order to be polite. "Yes, it's beautiful," he said. But of course, he knew absolutely nothing about automobile engines.

When they went back inside, Frank became more serious again. "I'm so frantic," he said. "I try to hide my emotions from Franzi. But I never wanted to get married until I could support her. I spent so many years working toward that aim, and we were married when I finally thought that I would be able to take care of her – that was if we could get out of Europe, which we did. Under normal circumstances, André Mertens would have kept me busy with engagements here in the United States;

and one day, I probably would have been able to sing Beckmesser and Alberich at the Met. But now, look at me: I'll never be able to sing on a stage again, and I can't even attract students. . . . . Franzi wanted to be a designer, and now she has to work long hours doing alterations in the tailor shop down the street. She's working below the minimum wage, and the tailor – who could be her father – is making passes at her. How could I have known that I would lose my voice? How could I have known?"

"The problem is that you're not a well-known opera singer here," Thomas Martin said. "If you were, you would be able to reap in the students with your name alone. Maybe you need to go somewhere that doesn't have a *Broadway* and a great opera company like the Met. Maybe you ought to go to a place like Knoxville, Tennessee."

"Knoxville, Tennessee?" Frank said. "What on earth am I going to find in Knoxville, Tennessee?"

"Students," Thomas said.

"Students? How do you know that anyone in Knoxville, Tennessee wants to learn how to sing?"

"Because I have a cousin who lives there. She's a second cousin. She was born in America, but she spent some time in Vienna studying voice with my father."

"I seem to remember meeting her there," Frank said pensively.

"Then she married someone who lives in Knoxville," Thomas continued. "I'll write her. She's the socialite-type; maybe she'll be able to help you find some students. In fact, maybe she'll want to be your first."

That was in August. Frank really didn't give the suggestion much thought. The war was escalating. Holland and Belgium had surrendered to the Germans, the Allied troops retreating to Dunkirk on the northern coast of France. Next, the British and French rescued the Allied troops, evacuating them to England. And then Norway surrendered, France signed an armistice, and the Germans attacked Great Britain. As a result, the United States government sold the British a large supply of weapons and ammunition.

"Hitler is everywhere," Franziska said when she arrived home that night. "It seems that the concentration camps are really becoming death camps. It was bad enough when the Jews were dying from starvation, disease, and mistreatment; but now the Nazi brutality is intensifying. There are so many shootings, and . . . I simply shudder when I think about it. I'm so glad that we're in New York."

"Sometimes I wonder if I am," Frank responded.

"I don't even mind working for Sebastian anymore," Franziska said, not having listened to Frank's remark. "Sure, he's a little bit flirtatious, but he's harmless. I enjoy being able to walk to the shop every morning, and I like stopping for groceries at the stores along Columbus Avenue on the way home. This is really a quaint neighborhood. The little markets are sort of like those in Prague."

"How can you be so optimistic?" Frank blurted out. "You could be a seamstress for the rest of your life."

"No, I don't think so," Franziska responded. "Something wonderful is going to happen. You'll see."

CHAPTER THIRTY-THREE
HIAS to the Rescue – Again

New York City
August to September 20, 1940

"$\mathcal{J}$t's all right. I understand," Franziska said. "Let's go to sleep."

"I can't sleep," Frank uttered. "I've turned out to be some great husband. First, I can't support you, and now I can't make love to you."

Frank was the one who had wanted to be intimate. He'd been tired of thinking about his problems; and there she was, as beautiful as ever, in a long, flowing powder blue crepe nightgown.

She'd lit some candles, and he'd put on a phonograph record. Then they'd gazed into each other's eyes for what seemed to be eternity.

"You're more beautiful to me every day," Frank had whispered to her while brushing her cheeks with the tip of his finger, then stroking the small crevice below her chin. "The more we go through life together, the closer I feel toward you. . . . I'm sorry."

That's when she'd told him that it was all right and that they should go to sleep.

"As soon as you either get your voice back or find some new direction, everything will be fine," she said.

"But I want to take care of you."

"You are and you will. . . . Don't be so hard on yourself."

375

She nestled her head against Frank's chest and closed her eyes. He kissed the top of her head and fell asleep.

Frank hadn't talked to Thomas P. Martin in days. Then Thomas telephoned one evening. "Pack your bags," he said.

Thomas explained that he had written his cousin, Senta, and that she had called to tell him that she would be delighted if Frank and Frances moved to Knoxville, that she would help them get settled and would introduce Frank to some potential students.

"It's a grand opportunity for you," Thomas said. "You'll be able to have some immediate success, and the experience will be good for you whether your voice comes back or not."

Frank thanked his friend, but said that he'd have to discuss the matter with Franziska, and that they'd make a final decision in a few days. Frank had never mentioned Thomas's suggestion to Franziska before. The idea had seemed so implausible to him at the time, and he'd doubted that Thomas would actually pursue it.

"Franziska . . . there is something that we have to discuss," Frank said.

"All right. What is it?" she asked.

They were sitting at their small dining room table, eating a piece of *Apfelstrudel*.

"Thomas P. Martin has a distant cousin who lives in Knoxville, Tennessee. She has offered to help me find some students there."

"Are you trying to tell me that you want to move to Knoxville, Tennessee?" Franziska asked.

"I don't know," Frank responded. "I'm trying to find out exactly what you think about the proposition."

"You've kind of caught me off guard. I thought that we were going to stay in New York. I thought that we were through with traveling."

"So did I. But I can't earn a living here unless my voice comes back. The vocal students here want to study with someone who has a name and a reputation."

"That's true."

"And I've had a very bad spring here. My hay fever couldn't have been worse. Maybe the climate will be better for me in Tennessee. Maybe my voice will improve."

"I want you to have hope, but I don't know if moving from place to place is the answer."

They couldn't make up their minds. They were beginning to feel comfortable in New York City, but their bank account was dwindling. They sat at their dining room table talking into the wee hours of the morning and drinking one cup of coffee after another.

"All right," Franziska said. "If we decide to move to Tennessee, where are we going to get the money to relocate?"

"We could ask Ilona and Hans."

"No, I don't think that we should do that."

"Maybe you're right. I don't want to feel indebted to them for the rest of our lives."

"How about the Hebrew Immigrant Aid Society?"

"HIAS?"

"Didn't Egon Eisenstadt say that HIAS was helping him?"

"I think so. Why don't we go there tomorrow before we make up our minds?" Frank suggested.

"You mean today," Franziska answered. "It's already morning. And since today is Saturday, I don't think that we'll be in luck."

"We can go there Monday, then."

"You mean *you* can go there on Monday. As long as we're in New York, I don't want to lose my job."

So on Monday, Frank went to the HIAS office, and then he rushed to the tailor shop where Franziska was working. The shop was located at the bottom of an apartment building that was on the same side of Eighty-second Street as their apartment, just a couple of doors from Columbus Avenue. A purple canvas awning extended over the width of the store, identifying it with a telephone number and the words: *"Tailoring & Alterations."*

Franziska was sitting in the front of the shop by one of the windows.

She was stitching on a sewing machine and smoking, her back resting on a pillow that she had brought from home.

"What are you doing here?" she asked when Frank pranced through the door. They always spoke to each other in German.

"I've come to take you somewhere for *Mittagessen*."

"I can't leave for another half hour," Franziska said, crushing her cigarette in the ashtray beside her. "Where did you have in mind?"

"Fifteen West Eighty-second Street," Frank said. "We need to talk."

"All right. I'll meet you there as soon as I can."

Just then, Sebastian came out from the back of the shop. "This is my husband," Franziska said, introducing Frank to her boss, suddenly switching to English.

"I'm Sebastian," the tailor said. "Frances is always so charming to be around, and she is a diligent worker. Whatever I want from her, she does."

Frank felt his face getting flushed. He was recalling every time Franziska had told him that Sebastian had tried to get fresh with her. He was angry. How dare this little old man make passes at his wife! Frank wanted to punch the tailor. But instead:

"It's interesting that someone else appreciates my wife as much as I do," he said.

At first, Franziska simply looked at Frank a bit perplexed. Then she uttered a short laugh without even opening her mouth. In actuality, the noise sounded more like a grunt or a snort.

"Oh, I *d-o-o-o* appreciate her," Sebastian said, making matters worse.

Frank actually raised his arm to take a swing, but Franziska quickly grabbed it. Smiling, she said: "Why don't you go home and put that left-over goulash in the oven? I'll see you there in twenty minutes."

So Frank responded: "Frances may have a surprise for you when she returns, Sebastian."

However, that comment did not meet with Franziska's approval. Frank was jumping the gun. "Good-bye, Franzl," she said. "Remember the goulash . . . the goulash." So Frank walked out of the tailor shop.

Fifteen minutes later, Franziska marched into the apartment. "I have forty minutes," she said. "I have to be back at the tailor shop in forty-five. So what are you making such a fuss over? Are you trying to make me lose my job?"

"One thing has nothing to do with the other," Frank responded. "I have some news to tell you, and then . . . maybe you'll want to give Mister Sebastian notice. Maybe it doesn't matter if you lose your job. I just didn't want him to get away with his behavior."

"Go on. . . ."

" I went to the HIAS office today, and the woman I spoke to said that the organization would pay for our moving expenses and then some."

"Do we have to pay the money back?"

"I don't know. But I'm sure that we don't have to pay it back until we're able. So why worry about it? HIAS is going to give us the money, and Thomas's cousin is going to find me some students. What do we have to lose?"

"But I thought that you wanted to be with your family."

"We can visit them."

"So you really want to do this?"

"Yes! I do."

Franziska had her doubts. She wondered what Knoxville, Tennessee was like. Would they be able to make friends there? Would Frank really be able to attract students? Would she be able to find a job?

Yet Frank was definitely less depressed. For the first time in a very long time, he was looking toward the future with hope.

"Okay," Franziska said. "We'll go. I think that it's important for us to go."

They made all of their preparations. They told everybody that they were leaving, and they began to pack. Frank even wrote a letter to André Mertens, who had also immigrated to New York, where he was now a full-time artists' representative at the Columbia Concerts Corporation. Mertens couldn't quite get used to Franz's name change, but he tried and responded with:

COLUMBIA CONCERTS CORPORATION
OF COLUMBIA BROADCASTING SYSTEM
113 West Fifty-seventh Street, New York, N.Y. – Circle 7-6900

August 22, 1940

Mr. Francis Delmar,
15 West 82nd Street,
New York, N. Y.

Dear Mr. Delmar:

This is to thank you for your kind wishes.

I am so sorry to hear that you were ill all the time. However, I hope that the climate in Tennessee will help you. Give me a ring as soon as you are back.

With best wishes and kindest personal regards,

Very sincerely yours,

André Mertens

"You see . . . it's all over," Frank said after having read the letter to Franziska aloud. "It's as if I've died, and now I have to mourn over my own demise."

"Yes, but you're going to be reborn again . . . in a new city with a new career."

"So you *are* telling me to give up."

"No, I'm not. I just want you to focus in a new direction, and I don't want you to make any false presumptions. If you move forward enthusiastically without expecting your voice to return, then you will be able to live from day to day with some tranquility, and you will be able to become successful at something new. Then if you are able to rediscover your voice, you will be overjoyed. However, if you expect that your voice will return and it doesn't, you will not be successful in Tennessee as a teacher, and you will always be unhappy. I am optimistic, but I don't know what the future will bring."

"You're so wonderful," Frank said. "You always know what to say."

"That's because I've known you since I was fifteen years old," Franziska said.

At that moment, Frank went over to her and gave her a big hug. "Now let's get back to work," she said. "We have a brand new trunk to fill."

Then the telephone rang. It was Thomas P. Martin.

"She what?" Frank said a few minutes into the conversation. "She doesn't want us to come to Knoxville? But why? *She's* the reason that we decided to go there. We've made all of our plans. We're supposed to leave in less that two weeks."

But Thomas Martin couldn't give Frank a tangible reason for his cousin's change of heart. Maybe Senta discovered that she couldn't find any students – maybe it was hard to find students for a teacher without a name who was a refugee. Perhaps her husband wanted her to put her time to better use. Frank was convinced that he would probably never know the real reason. Yet he wasn't about to blame his friend, Thomas. Thomas was only trying to help and meant the very best for him.

"What do you *mean* she doesn't want us to come to Knoxville? What's her reason?" Franziska asked upon hearing the news. "We're packing. We've told everyone that we're leaving. We've given up our jobs . . . this apartment. HIAS has given us money. What are we supposed to do now?"

"I don't know," Frank said. "How am I going to find the students on my own?"

They didn't know what to do. They didn't sleep that night. They both felt desperate.

Franziska took a bath at five o'clock the following morning. She was dressed and ready to go at six – only she didn't know where to. Frank, on the other hand, decided not to get dressed at all. He wanted to stay in his pajamas all day. In fact, he lay on the bed until afternoon with the curtains closed and the lights dimmed. And Franziska didn't even attempt to dissuade him; she was too busy cleaning.

But the next day, they were determined to pull themselves together and make a decision: Were they going to leave, or were they going to stay?

They went to the HIAS office. Maybe somebody else could make the decision for them. Maybe HIAS would want the money back.

The people there were wonderful. They told Frank and Frances to keep the money and go. They would contact some members of the Knoxville Jewish community and arrange everything. "When you arrive at the station, someone will be there to pick you up," one of them said. "Don't worry, we'll find you some students."

Could what they were saying really be true?

Frank and Franziska didn't believe in fairy tales. But they had to take a chance. With such evil going on in the world, could there really be such charity? They had to take a chance.

CHAPTER THIRTY-FOUR

"The Star-Spangled Banner"

Knoxville, Tennessee
Chattanooga, Tennessee
February 1941 to December 7, 1941

"*O*h how funny – ah, ha, ha! Is this matter – ah, ha, ha! So excuse me – ah, ha, ha! If I laugh, sir – ah, ha, ha, ha, ha, ha . . ."

Frank was teaching voice to a talented soprano in a room at the Church Street Methodist Church in Knoxville. The soprano was singing Adele's laughing song, "Mein Herr Marquis," from Johann Strauss's comic operetta, *Die Fledermaus*.

"Lighter . . . more lyrical," Frank interrupted the soprano and the accompanist. "Let's try it again."

Since arriving in Knoxville, life had been passable for Frank and Frances. Just as the people from HIAS had projected, a Jewish couple was indeed at the railway station to welcome them. But the couple did much more for them than that. Sam and Ada Averbuch befriended them, helped them find an apartment on Magnolia Avenue, and even provided them with some of the furnishings. The Averbuches were well-heeled. They owned a clothing store on Knoxville's main thoroughfare, Gay Street; a house on Cherokee Boulevard which backed onto the Tennessee River; and a boat that was docked there. On many weekends, Frank and Franzi were invited to the couple's posh home in the affluent

Sequoyah Hills neighborhood. And on many of these occasions, they were invited to take short excursions on the family's impressive yacht.

But it was Joyce and Roy "Britt" Brittain who helped Frank the most with his new career. Frank had advertised in the local newspaper, and Joyce and Britt had become his first students. When they'd answered Frank's ad, he still hadn't found a studio. They introduced him to the Reverend James A. Bay at the Church Street Methodist Church, and Frank instantly had a place to teach.

The church stood regally on the corner of Henley Street and Main Avenue atop a mound of downy-green grass. Designed in the neo-Gothic tradition, the pinnacled tower, rising high above the quartz stone and limestone-trimmed structure, rendered a vision not unlike the statuesque churches of Europe. The sanctuary emitted an image of the classic Middle Ages as well: simple and dignified with pews of oak and aisles of sandstone. But it was in a room on the same floor as the sanctuary – just outside its doors – where Frank made his new professional home. It was in this simple room with walnut cabinetry, a few chairs, and a piano, that Frank embraced his first students.

"Oh how funny – ah, ha, ha! Is this matter – ah, ha, ha! So excuse me – ah, ha, ha! If I laugh, sir – ah, ha, ha, ha, ha, ha!"

"Much better, Joyce," Frank said when the soprano came to the end of the bar. "Keep on singing."

But while Frank was teaching voice, Franziska was selling cosmetics. "May I assist you with something?" she asked a woman standing in front of the perfume counter.

She had taken a job as a salesgirl in the cosmetic department of Miller's Department Store. As there were no openings in women's dresses, she'd accepted the position that was available.

"Why that's downright kind of you, ma'am," the customer answered. "What fragrance would you recommend?"

Miller's Department Store was a brick and stone landmark in downtown Knoxville. The Edwardian-style building on Gay Street was ornamented with sculptured rosettes and ancient Greek maidens

– *canephoroe* – that seemed to support the structure's roof. The window displays were inviting, and people from all over the Tennessee traveled to shop at Miller's.

But Frank hadn't wanted Franziska to take such a menial job. If she couldn't work toward becoming a designer, he didn't want her to work at all. Maybe he'd make enough money as a voice teacher so that she wouldn't need to. But Franzi had insisted. She'd eventually be able to work in the dress department, she hoped. Then she'd be closer to reaching her goal.

"Smell this," Franziska said to her customer, placing a dab of perfume on the inside of her wrist and then holding her arm over the counter.

"*How divahne!*" the woman said in a Southern drawl.

"It's French perfume of the highest quality."

"Ah'll take it," the woman decided. "Mah husband will love it."

"But Dr. Acuff, do you think that ever will return my voice?" Frank asked his new physician after the doctor had examined his vocal cords by holding a mirror inside his mouth.

"I don't know," the doctor replied. "If we could only discover the cause . . ."

"Yes, that's the dilemma," Frank responded.

"I don't detect any polyps, nodules, ulcers, or paralysis. That only leaves your postnasal drip and allergies," Dr. Acuff said. "Maybe you should consider going to Mayo Clinic at some time in the future. The clinic is at the forefront in medical research and diagnosis."

"I've heard so," Frank answered. "But the distance – all the way to Minnesota."

"From your history, I'd say you've traveled a lot farther than that."

"Yes, but the costs . . ."

"I'm sure something could be arranged. Just keep the suggestion in the back of your mind," Dr. Acuff said.

He was an elegant man, Frank thought, always well-dressed. But his style and status never restricted him from revealing his empathetic side.

Dr. Acuff saw Frank often and never charged him. He was the type of man who was simply interested in the well-being of his patients. And his office was conveniently located in a Renaissance-style building, in walking distance from the Church Street Methodist Church. Frank liked Dr. Herbert Acuff, and Dr. Acuff seemed to like Frank as well.

"I spent six months at Mayo Clinic doing research and postgraduate work," he told Frank. "It just might be worth a try."

L A W R E N C E T I B B E T T

February 6, 1941

Mr. Frank Delmar
2930 E. Magnolia Avenue
Knoxville, Tenn.

Dear Mr. Delmar:

Thank you for your letter.

I'm sorry to hear about the trouble you are having with your throat. I believe the only solution is a series of careful exercises under an expert. It is too intricate to describe in a letter or I would be glad to do so.

I hope with rest and careful exercises your difficulty will clear up. You may be sure that you have my very best wishes.

Sincerely,

Lawrence Tibbett

"You see, Franzi: Lawrence Tibbett thinks that I'm losing my voice because I don't know how to sing. He thinks that I have poor vocal technique," Frank told Franziska after he read the letter to her in the living room of their small apartment.

They still always spoke German to each other when they weren't in the company of those who spoke English.

"I told you not to write him," Franzi said. "You don't know him well enough. He doesn't have the whole picture."

"I only wrote him because I'm so desperate. He was a colleague of mine. Even though I never performed with him, he sang in Prague and we said hello to each other a few times. I thought he could give me a clue that might solve my problem. But now I'm even more exasperated. Everyone that I've ever known in the operatic world probably believes that I'm losing my voice because I'm a bad singer. That simply is not true. But I can't face any of them nevertheless, because the doctors can't give me a medical reason to disprove their theories."

"First of all, with the war going on in Europe, most of the people you know in the operatic world have far more important things to do than wonder what has happened to your voice, or to you, for that matter. So don't flatter yourself so much. We have to start a new life here, and you have a new career."

"Yes, but it's related to what I've already accomplished as a singer. I can't run away from my past. You read what that reporter wrote about me in the local newspaper when we first arrived: '*A Viennese bass-baritone who has sung operatic roles in the capitals of Europe and South America has come to Knoxville, hoping the climate will heal his throat and restore his voice. He is Frank Delmar, 31, who was in Prague in 1938 when Czechoslovakia mobilized for war, only to be disarmed and dismembered by the treaty of Munich.*' "

"You've memorized it?" Franziska said in amazement.

" '*He suffered from bronchitis, lost his opportunity to sing, and was advised to leave New York for the South. . . . He plans to teach singing until his voice is restored, and will open a studio in the educational section of the Church Street Methodist Church.*' "

"Well, aside from the comment about your bronchitis, the story seems pretty accurate."

"I had to say something to save face."

"You worry too much about what people think," Franziska said. "However the article has been good publicity for you. I'm sure that it's helped you to recruit some students."

"But back to the main issue at hand: There is definitely something medically wrong with me. I am not and never have been a bad singer. My technique is not causing me to lose my voice. I wouldn't be able to teach singing in Tennessee if I thought that it was."

"Swing low, sweet chariot – coming for to carry me home. Swing low, sweet chariot – coming for to carry me home. . . ."

Frank was teaching singing to a bass with a somewhat average voice, but with good intentions. On this particular day, Frank was not teaching in Knoxville though. He was in a room in the educational building at the First Methodist Church in Chattanooga.

Joyce and Britt had moved there. And hoping to continue their singing lessons, they'd arranged for Frank to teach on Mondays and Tuesdays at the stately neo-Gothic-style church on the corner of McCallie and Georgia avenues. So every Monday, Frank took the train to Chattanooga, taught, spent that night with Joyce and Britt, and then returned home the following day. Britt was a salesman – he sold Scott tissues – and Joyce was a stenographer for the Tennessee Valley Authority (TVA), a government corporation created by Congress to develop the resources of the Tennessee Valley. Ray Jones was also an employee of the TVA – he worked in the mailroom – and he liked to sing. He liked to sing Negro spirituals.

Frank was really unfamiliar with that genre. So sometimes it almost seemed as if Ray Jones was teaching him.

"You have to count," Frank interrupted Ray Jones. "Look at the time signature: four beats to the measure, and every quarter note has a beat. Make sure that you pay attention to the dotted notes. Here . . . I'll mark your music."

"Ah understand what you're doin'," Ray Jones said, "but everyone just sings these songs the way they feel 'em."

"But you have to be accurate for the accompanist," Frank said.

"From my understandin', it's the singer who leads the accompanist," Ray Jones said, causing a smile to cross Frank's face. "After all, an accompanist isn't exactly an orchestra with a conductor."

Ray Jones was right, of course. Frank often led his accompanists when he wanted to go faster or slower, and they followed him, yet the relationship between pianist and singer was a collaborative one. But Frank still wanted his student to show some respect for what was written on the sheet music.

"When I think you've learned this song more precisely, I'll bring in the accompanist," Frank said. "Then you'll be able to be a little more flexible. But you must learn the music the way it's written first."

As time passed, Ray Jones and Frank became good friends. Since Ray was often Frank's last student of the day, the two often talked for a while afterwards. Ray wanted to eventually move to California, where he said it would be easier for him to excel in the workplace. "There's less discrimination against Negroes there," he'd said.

On one occasion, Frank invited Ray to have dinner with him at Joyce and Britt's apartment. "Whah, sir, I couldn't," he'd answered. "A Negro *never* socializes at the home of a white man."

Frank was astonished.

"How can such discrimination exist in a free country?" Frank asked Britt that evening at the dinner table.

"It stems back to all of those years of slavery in the South," Britt answered. "Some people still haven't gotten over the Civil War."

Britt coincidentally reminded Frank of Clark Gable in the Civil War epic, *Gone With the Wind*. Britt was an attractive man, and Joyce was a fetching-looking woman. They had a modest apartment on Cameron Hill which, also coincidentally, was the site utilized by the signal corps of both armies during the Civil War. There was no better view of the city than from the park at the top of the hill.

"But this is America," Frank said, "where everybody is supposed to be equal."

"That may be true," Britt commiserated, "but in the South, people still live and socialize in segregated groups."

"I shudder to think what would happen if they didn't," Joyce agreed.

"Look, I'm very liberal-minded," Britt continued. "Our maid, Bessie, uses the telephone all the time, and I never even wipe it."

Frank instantly felt the anger rising within him. These people had been so good to him. How could they be so closed-minded?

The next day, Frank's last student of the day canceled. Frank usually took the train back home to Knoxville; but on this day, he could leave earlier by bus. As he was paying the fare to the driver, he could hear his name echoing from the back: "Franzl . . . Franzl," someone was shouting. It was Doktor Peter Gottesmann. He was standing and waving his hand.

"Doktor Gottesmann!" Frank said walking toward him. The two embraced and then sat down together.

"What are you doing here?" Frank asked. "Did you ever find any of those golden treasures you were looking for in the jungles of Panama?"

"I had to cut my expedition short," Doktor Gottesmann said. "I was bitten by a poisonous snake and almost died. I was sick for a very long time, but I finally pulled through."

"Oh, I'm so sorry to hear of your misfortune," Frank said. "But I'm glad that you're all right."

"Yes . . . well, that mishap put an end to my treasure-hunting days, but I'm happy to be in America now."

"But why Tennessee?" Frank asked.

"I wanted to see the country before deciding where to settle down," Doktor Gottesmann said. "I've worked as a busboy wherever I've stopped."

"So what's next on your agenda?"

"I've just about finished traveling now. I started out in New York City, and I'm going to go back there before I make my final decision."

"I started out in New York City too, but life is full of surprises," Frank said, then explained his situation.

"And how is Franzi?" Doktor Gottesmann asked. "I remember how lovely she was."

The two continued talking as the bus passed Cleveland, Athens, Sweetwater, and Lenoir City before arriving at the Union Bus Terminal on Gay Street in Knoxville. They talked about Hitler, and they talked about the war in Europe. The Germans had invaded Yugoslavia, Greece, and the Soviet Union, thus ignoring the Nazi-Soviet Nonaggression Pact; and mass shootings of the Jews were being carried out by the SS mobile units of the Reich police force. Passage of the Lend-Lease Act had enabled the U.S. government to sell, lend, or lease weapons, aircraft, or ships to any government fighting to maintain freedom. And the signing of the Atlantic Charter went one step further in establishing a commitment between Great Britain and the United States toward the destruction of Nazi tyranny and the establishment of peace.

Frank never even had a moment to look out of the window and glance at the scenery because his conversation with Peter Gottesmann was so intense. Could the United States stay out of the war? The Japanese and Chinese had been fighting for years, and the U.S. government had maintained its neutrality until concluding that Japan's conquests had become too widespread. Then President Franklin Delano Roosevelt stopped the sale of oil to Japan and froze all Japanese assets in the United States.

"America will go to war," Doktor Gottesmann maintained. "I don't see a way out."

But Frank declined to take a position.

Doktor Gottesmann definitely had an astute mind, but he was nothing like any other lawyer Frank had ever known. He was a colorful person: an adventurer and a wonderful storyteller.

"The best of luck to you," Frank said as they were getting off the bus at the terminal in Knoxville. "There's my streetcar. I'd better rush or I'll miss it."

"Yes, run and catch it," Doktor Gottesmann said. "I'm sure that we'll bump into each other again."

Frank and Frances were sitting in the Bijou Theatre at the Knoxville Symphony Orchestra's first concert of the season. It was three o'clock in the afternoon on Sunday, the seventh of December in 1941. It seemed like an ordinary day to them: Neither had read the newspaper that morning or turned on the radio. Frank didn't normally like to go to theaters anymore, especially when music was part of the program, but at least this performance didn't include opera. Frank's accompanist, Elsa Stong, was one of the soloists; and her mother, Bertha Walburn Clark, was the conductor.

The Baroque music was carrying Franziska into another world. Her fantasy: early eighteenth century court music being played at a formal gathering held in the palace of a sovereign. She could envision the members of nobility dancing gracefully as they listened to the music in their elaborate costumes. Yet in actuality, she was hearing Arcangelo Corelli's Concerto Grosso in G minor, which was really composed to be performed in a church on Christmas night.

Next, Eugenia Buxton played Sergei Rachmaninov's Second Piano Concerto, which seemed to swell and swell to an impassioned climax that was so real and beautiful that the emotions Franziska felt were hard to define.

Then after intermission, the orchestra culminated the performance with Ludwig van Beethoven's Fifth Symphony. It was as if fate was knocking at the door, Franziska thought, while listening to the symphony's four-note motif. As the movements progressed, the music seemed to imply a struggle, heroic energy, and then a triumphant victory. Everyone applauded enthusiastically, almost begging for an encore.

Then Bertha Walburn Clark spoke into a microphone: "As I am sure most of you are aware, the Japanese attacked Pearl Harbor this morning and declared war on the United States and Great Britain. We must brace ourselves for the months ahead. Please join me with the orchestra in paying tribute to our great country."

Bertha Walburn Clark returned to the podium. And as soon as the people in the audience heard the introduction to "The Star-Spangled Banner," they stood and then sang:

Oh say, can you see, by the dawn's early light,
What so proudly we hailed at the twilight's last gleaming?
Whose broad stripes and bright stars, thro' the perilous fight,
O'er the ramparts we watched were so gallantly streaming?
And the rockets' red glare, the bombs bursting in air,
Gave proof thro' the night that our flag was still there.
Oh say, does that star-spangled banner yet wave,
O'er the land of the free and the home of the brave?

The Southern Railway Station/Terminal.
(*Courtesy of Thompson Photo Products, Knoxville.*)

Turning Point

Knoxville, Tennessee; Rochester, Minnesota
Fort Oglethorpe, Georgia
February 3, 1942 to Fall 1943

$\mathscr{T}$he day after the Japanese attacked Pearl Harbor, the United States declared war on Japan. And a few days after that, Germany and Italy declared war on the United States. No one knew what to expect. Wives and mothers feared that they would lose their loved ones on the battlefield. Frank had registered with the Selective Service Board and was willing to fight for the Allies, but he hoped that he wouldn't be obliged to. He'd had enough excitement in his life and didn't want to leave Franziska alone. He was reluctant to admit his true feelings to anyone though. But he was actually glad that America was in the war, because now, for the very first time, he believed that Adolf Hitler could be defeated.

It was a snowy Tuesday evening the beginning of February. As she did every Tuesday evening, Franzi finished her day at Miller's Department Store, walked up Gay Street to the Southern Railway Station, and waited in the terminal building for Frank to arrive from Chattanooga. When he didn't disembark from his usual train, she wasn't worried. She assumed that he'd be on the next one, so she just sat patiently smoking a cigarette. And she was right.

"Psst . . . Psst," she uttered as Frank walked into the terminal building, brushing the snow from the shoulders of his overcoat.

He smiled, walked over to her, and gave her a kiss.

"What happened?" she asked. "Did you miss your train?"

"As a matter-of-fact, I did," he answered. "Joyce was my last student, and I gave her some extra time."

"It's probably too late to catch a streetcar," Franzi said, smashing her cigarette into an ashtray. "But I'm dressed warmly, so even if it isn't, why don't we walk instead? It's such a lovely evening, and I feel like breathing in the crisp air."

So they left the Dutch Colonial-style terminal building with its chiseled stepped gables. They walked up Gay Street and then along Magnolia Avenue. The snowflakes were falling so delicately that they seemed to float like feathers in the wind. Frank was holding a small suitcase in one hand; his other arm was around Franziska's waist. They talked about all they'd been through and reminisced about the time they'd chased each other and thrown snowballs in a very vacant Charles Square in Prague. That seemed so long ago. As they were walking, they somehow felt as if they were in another world. They felt peaceful as if they had no worries or cares. And they felt close.

Then the snowflakes began to fall much more abundantly. They stopped for a few minutes to take refuge under the overhang of a storefront. Suddenly a glaring light was shining in their eyes. It was the headlights of a police car. An officer was walking toward them.

"Good evenin'," the officer said. "Where are you-all goin' so late at naht?"

"Home," Frank said. "I just returned from Chattanooga; and by the train station, my wife picked me up." Frank's English was getting so much better. But when he saw the police officer, he became nervous.

"Where are you-all from?"

"Originally from Austria," Franziska answered.

The police officer had a blank look on his face.

"Germany," Frank added.

"But aliens aren't allowed to travel," the police officer stated.

"I have a letter here," Frank responded, taking an envelope out and handing it to the officer.

"Yes . . . this is very official. It says that you can travel, and it's from the U.S. attorney's office."

"It was such a lovely night that we decided to walk home," Franziska said.

"Do you-all live far?" the officer asked, handing the letter back to Frank.

"We live on this street," Franzi said, "but we still have quite a walk ahead of us."

"Look, it's too late for you to catch a streetcar, so I'll drive you home," the officer declared.

So Frank and Franziska climbed into the police car, and the officer drove them to their apartment. Then he escorted them up a walkway and directly to their door.

They lived in a small two-story brick building with wooden accents. The entrance to their apartment – Number Two – was on the far right side.

"Thank you so much for driving us home," Franziska said. But the police officer didn't make any effort to leave.

Franzi took the key out of her purse, slid it into the keyhole and turned. Then she pushed the door open and walked inside.

"Thanks so much for driving us home," Frank repeated.

The police officer nodded.

"I'm going to Chattanooga again next Monday. Maybe you'd like to drive us home once more on Tuesday when I return," Frank suggested laughingly.

The police officer apparently didn't appreciate Frank's humor. He didn't utter a word. He simply nodded his head again and walked back toward his car.

"That police officer certainly didn't trust us," Frank said once inside the apartment. "He wanted to make sure that we really live here . . . that our key would actually open the door."

"This is wartime," Franziska answered. "We could be dangerous enemy aliens or spies. The government has established certain rules and regulations regarding foreigners, and the police have to administer them. He was just doing his job. He was just being careful."

"I guess you're right," Frank said. "I guess I'm just tired of all of the rules and regulations."

Frank received a typed letter from Thomas P. Martin.

325 West 45th Street
The Whitby
New York City

Febr. 12, 1942

Dear Delmar,

 I must apologize for not having answered your letter before, but, as you can imagine, there is so much work during the season at the Metropolitan [since I have been named assistant conductor] that it is hard to keep up with correspondence.

 I am very glad that you like our translation of The Magic Flute; we tried to be as close to the original as possible and at the same time do justice to the music in every respect. In a short time the vocal score will be on the market, edited by Schirmer. . . .

 If you come to New York, get in touch with me. I will be very glad to see you and hear you, too. You will always be able to find me at my former address . . . in case we should have moved from this apartment.

 I am, of course, very happy to be at the Met; the engagement came as a great surprise to me, shortly before the first performance of the "Flute," just after I had come back from Chicago.

 Please give my regards to your wife! I am really glad that you apparently are successful as teacher. I am sure that you developed your method to a high degree.

Best regards to both of you from both of us!

Yours

Thomas M .

Every hour for three days, Frank could hear a twenty-three-bell carillon chiming from the tower that topped the building he was in. He had refused to give up trying to determine what had caused the loss of his voice, so in February of 1943, he took Dr. Acuff's advice and went to the Mayo Clinic for an evaluation.

The multistoried brick and limestone building was a little intimidating to him at first. But the soft-colored lobby was calming, and the nurses and receptionists were cheerful. It was Frank's final day under observation at the clinic. He was sitting in the office of his primary doctor.

"Well, we've examined you thoroughly these last few days," Dr. Williams said, sitting behind his desk. "We do detect some infection and postnasal drip, and you appear to have numerous allergies, but that is really all that we can find."

"Could these problems cause me to lose my voice?" Frank asked.

"I don't know," Dr. Williams said. "But I'd like you to try some treatments."

"What type of treatments?" Frank asked.

"Injections every couple of days. Would you be willing to learn how to give yourself shots?"

"Yes, absolutely. I'll try anything to help restore my voice."

"Good!"

"But my doctor in New York gave me injections at least twice a week."

"These will be different. I'll speak to your physician in Knoxville, and he'll show you what you have to do."

"Thank you so much," Frank said. "Now I have some hope again."

"And during the hay fever season, I want you to take some ephedrine; stay indoors as much as possible; and maybe try using an air filter. But as I said before, I'll explain everything to your doctor in Knoxville."

Franz left Rochester, Minnesota feeling uplifted. People from all over the world had been helped at the Mayo Clinic. Maybe he would be a success story as well.

"Frank, I'm home," Franziska called as she entered through the front door.

"I'm in the kitchen," Frank answered.

She walked through the living room, the dinette, and into the kitchen. There was a pot of boiling water on the stove where Frank had sterilized a hypodermic needle. He was standing in his undershorts, meticulously injecting some medication into his upper thigh. Franziska didn't say anything because she didn't want him to make a false move and hurt himself. She went directly to the stove, turned it off, and then she continued walking into the bedroom.

MAYO CLINIC
ROCHESTER, MINNESOTA

June 15, 1943

Mr. Frank Delmar
2930 East Magnolia Avenue
Knoxville, Tennessee

Dear Mr. Delmar:

The flushing of the face after the injection of nicotinic acid is to be expected and is a normal reaction. I am sorry to hear [from Dr. Acuff], however, that you have not gotten any improvement in the drainage from your nose. Since you have had no beneficial effects from our treatments, I think you might as well discontinue them. I am sorry to say that I have nothing further to suggest from the standpoint of treatment and I do not believe that a return here would be of any value. . . .

I regret that I have to write this letter to you as I know how important your voice is to you.

Yours very truly,

Henry L. Williams, M.D.

Many young men were being called in for active duty. There were always lists of draftees in *The Knoxville News-Sentinel*.

At the beginning, the Japanese were victorious – in Hong Kong, Manila, Guam, and Singapore – but in the spring of 1942, they started to lose their momentum. And less than a year later, the Germans lost ground as well when the Soviets drove them from Stalingrad. And soon after that, the Axis forces in Africa surrendered to the Allies.

But Hitler's relentless resolve to exterminate all of the Jews in Europe did not subside. More concentration camps were emerging – most were really annihilation camps – and the Jews deported to them were gassed en masse.

Frank's classification had changed. Franziska feared that he would be called to serve at any moment. And in August of 1943, he was.

"Oh, please, sir, don't let my husband fight in the war," she said to the man sitting behind the desk in the Selective Service office in Knoxville. "We've emigrated from Vienna, Austria. It has taken us years to attain the proper visas to enter the United States. We lived in Cuba for almost a year waiting. My husband has been through so much. He was an opera singer, and then he lost his voice. We've had to start all over again here in Knoxville. He's a voice teacher now, just down the street at the Church Street Methodist Church. Please don't take him away from his students."

Franzi had talked Frank into going with her to the Selective Service office, to try to have his classification changed back to what it was. But Frank didn't realize that she was going to make such a scene. He was actually a little embarrassed.

"Please, sir," she pleaded. "He's been under a doctor's care."

But the man in the office explained that he didn't have the authority to change anyone's classification. "Your husband will have to report to the place designated," the man said. "The officers at the induction center will determine his status."

"Oh, please, sir!" Franziska cried. "I'll be all alone here. Don't take my husband away from me."

"Now ma'am, you're getting hysterical. Please try to calm down."

Frank didn't know how to respond to Franzi's outburst. He placed his arm around her and tried to comfort her, but she broke away from him, sobbing.

"If my husband is hurt, I won't know what to do," she cried. "I won't know what to do."

"I've been rejected! I've been rejected!" Frank shouted, pushing the door open to the apartment.

Franziska came running into the living room, practically jumping into Frank's arms, he in turn lifting her and swinging her around. The two laughed and kissed and hugged for a few minutes and then almost fell onto the sofa.

"I'm so happy," Franziska said. "How did you do it?"

"It was the letter. . . . I think that it was Dr. Acuff's letter. I have to thank him again."

"He didn't write anything that was libelous though."

"No, he didn't. But the way he phrased the details about my physical condition and allergies must have made the medical officer at the base wonder if I would be able to withstand the rigors of military life."

Then Frank began singing the aria Figaro sings to Cherubino in the *The Marriage of Figaro*, the aria that takes place after Cherubino has been ordered to join the Count's regiment.

Franzi laughed when she heard it, and then they hugged some more. "But seriously," she said, "describe for me what actually happened."

"Well, about forty of us took the train from Knoxville to Chattanooga," Frank explained, "and then a truck drove us to the induction center at Fort Oglethorpe. There were men there from all over Tennessee. Then after completing some paperwork, we went to some temporary wooden barracks nearby, to the mess hall for something to eat, and then back to the barracks. You know me – the bunks were so uncomfortable that I didn't sleep the whole night. Then in the morning, we were led back to the induction center - more paperwork - and then some non-commissioned officers marched us to the hospital."

"Sounds pretty boring so far," Franziska said.

"It wasn't boring for me. I was so worried and excited that I thought my heart was going to pop out of my chest."

"Go on. . . ."

"Well, the hospital was very nice, sort of American Colonial-looking. But the process of taking the physical was really quite demeaning. We had to strip. There we all were in a line, completely naked except for our shoes."

Envisioning the picture, Franziska couldn't help but smile.

"How can you make fun of me in that situation?" Frank asked. "I was so excited that I thought I was going to faint."

Franzi nodded her head, trying not to laugh. After all, Frank always felt faint in moments of crisis.

"Now stop that," Frank said.

"I can't help myself," Franziska uttered. "I was just remembering the time you almost fainted in Colón, when you thought that we weren't going to get tickets to sail on the *Chiriquí*."

"Well, this incident is a little bit different. . . . Anyhow, since I couldn't lie down, I kept on bending over instead, pretending to tie my shoelaces in order to get the blood to rush up to my head."

"And . . ."

"When it was my turn, I handed Dr. Acuff's letter to the medical officer. He read it and then barely examined me. He took my blood pressure, listened to my heart, and hurriedly looked into my ears, nose, and throat. He asked me if I had any allergies, infections, or inflammations of the throat and vocal cords. And when I said, 'Yes, all of them,' he rejected me on the spot. He said that he was sorry, but he didn't think I would have the stamina that would be required of me to effectively serve in the Army."

The corners of Franziska's mouth were curving upward ever so slightly.

"My feelings of dizziness immediately subsided, and I no longer felt faint. I told the medical officer that I was sorry too – that I had felt obligated to serve the country which had become my refuge and home, the country that had saved me from a foreseeable doom. Then I thanked him for his candor. I went back to the barracks to retrieve the few items that I had brought with me. I took a bus to Chattanooga, and I boarded the first train that I could find which would rush me home to be with you."

Franziska's onyx-colored eyes were serious now. The tears were rolling down her cheeks. "Oh, Frank," she said, wrapping her arms around her husband. "I am so lucky to be here in America with you. I want us always to be together."

There was a rental sign thrust into the grass in front of Frank and Franziska's apartment building. Their apartment was for rent.

Although they had enjoyed living in Knoxville, they still preferred larger cities. Frank's career wasn't progressing very well because some of his students had been drafted. And he was finally facing the reality that his voice might never return. It was time to break away and try to start all over again somewhere else.

San Francisco sounded good. Arthur Fleischer lived there. But when Frank had written him, Arthur Fleischer had answered with a letter suggesting Los Angeles instead. He'd written that although San Francisco was a lovely, cosmopolitan city, the climate was far better in Los Angeles – more sun and less rain. The climate would be better for Frank's throat. And since Hollywood was the home of the movie industry, Arthur Fleischer thought that Frank would be able to find more opportunities there.

It was settled: Frank and Franziska were moving to Los Angeles in November. To their astonishment, the Averbuches wanted their furniture back. Thus they would be leaving Knoxville exactly as they had come – with little else except their clothing – and they would say their good-byes to the Averbuches at the railway station.

Hollywood Hope

Los Angeles, California
February 1944 to September 1945

$\mathcal{F}$rank was propelling a pick toward the ground. Upon impact, he drove the sharp instrument deep into the soil, thus breaking up the dirt and rock around his target. He repeated the maneuver over and over again, his arm duplicating its circular locomotion almost by rote. He was a laborer – a laborer in one of his made-to-order European suits – a laborer who was digging a ditch on the backlot of Twentieth Century-Fox, one of the most prestigious studios in Hollywood. The foreman was egging him on. "Keep on working," the foreman said. No time to even wipe the perspiration from his brow. Oh why hadn't he accepted Otto Preminger's offer a few weeks before? He might have become an actor. Otto Preminger's office was so close to where he was toiling so laboriously now, on the very same lot. If he could only relive his meeting with the famous director, he'd respond quite differently now.

Otto Preminger had been so cordial to Frank, probably because they were both from Vienna, and neither wanted to return. There were other similarities as well. Otto Preminger had performed as an actor at the German Theater in Prague, and also at the Stadttheater in Aussig. What a coincidence!

Preminger had wanted his secretary to escort Frank to the casting department. "No! No!" Frank had said. "I don't want to be an actor."

"You don't?" Otto Preminger had responded, somewhat astonished. "Then what do you want to be?"

"Since I've lost my voice, I don't want to do anything in front of an audience, even if the audience is a camera," Frank had explained.

He presumed that Otto Preminger wanted to cast him in the role of a German or Nazi. After all, he had a thick accent. But the thought of portraying a Nazi repulsed him. "I'd like to work behind the camera," he'd said.

"Then I cannot help you. All of those jobs are unionized, and I have no influence with those unions," Otto Preminger had responded with a hint of disgust in his voice. After all, he was offering Frank the opportunity of a lifetime. Frank was well-suited for the job: As an opera singer, he'd been trained to act as well as sing. The transition would have been simple. But what did Frank know about the other crafts? Nothing! Yet he left Otto Preminger's office unaware of what he'd forgone, and completely unappreciative of how generous the charismatic, temperamental director had been.

"Keep on working," the foreman shouted, thus returning Frank into reality. A number of men were standing on either side of him doing exactly what he was doing. Frank thought that they were probably preparing the soil for a pipeline. But he was not in a position to ask questions, so he continued to exhaustedly propel his pick into the ground, repeating his motions over and over again until well after dark.

"I will not allow you to go back there," Franziska told Frank that evening in their apartment.

They had rented a furnished studio apartment in West Hollywood, near Melrose and Fairfax avenues. It wasn't a bad-looking building. And during the war years, apartments were hard to find. They were paying thirty dollars a month, and they had to give the landlord an extra thirty to secure the lease. The main room was furnished with a sofa and coffee table, and the bed sprang out of the wall. Frank was lying on it faced down. He was naked from the waist up, and Franziska was crouched over him, massaging his back with mineral oil.

"Oh, that feels so good," Frank said. "Now I know that I'll be able to stand up straight and walk again. I wasn't so sure a few hours ago."

"You have to go back to the union and ask for another job," Franziska told him in German. They still always spoke to each other in German. "That friend of Evelyn's doesn't have to work nearly as hard as you did today. Evelyn told me that he just sweeps a little."

Evelyn was Freddie Lowe's wife, and Freddie was Frank's second cousin. Although Frank had never met his distant relative while in Europe, Olga Jung had written him that Freddie had settled in Los Angeles. So as soon as Frank and Franziska arrived, they contacted him. It was Evelyn who had recommended that Frank register with Local 727. But she didn't know that the job would be so physically demanding. The other motion picture unions were far more difficult to penetrate. But because so many young men were being called off to war, a laborer was a desirable commodity.

"All right, I'll go to the union tomorrow," Frank said while Franziska continued to knead his back as if it were a mass of dough. "Maybe I can do something else that's less strenuous."

This time, Frank was on the backlot of MGM. He'd been working there for three days, pulling nails out of old pieces of wood from demolished sets. He'd traveled through some of MGM's oldest streets, where the buildings looked like they'd been bombed. Most of the sets only revealed partial façades and framework. Frank wondered if the movie moguls planned to finish constructing the buildings or to simply tear them down. He was doing such a diligent job that they promoted him.

On this, his fourth day at MGM, he was in the paint shop. It was really more like the interior of a partially dismantled set. He was wearing work pants, an old shirt with rolled-up sleeves, a rubber apron, and a cap. And there was more paint on him than there was in the buckets. He spent most of his day washing brushes and paint containers with lacquer thinner. After using the strong solvent to clean the brushes, he gave them a final cleansing with soap and water, patted them, and then laid them down to dry. He scoured the old paint containers with a scraper, and then washed them twice with the very same pungent solution. His nose was running, and his eyes were burning and tearing. Even his skin burned. But he worked until the end of the day.

"*I c-a-n't! I c-a-n't!*" Frank shouted as he opened the door to his apartment and collapsed on the couch.

"What happened? Why are you so excited?" Franziska questioned, leaving the kitchen to join him.

"When I was working at Fox, you told me not to go back there even though I thought that I should. So I didn't. But now, no matter what you say, I'm not going back to MGM. I'm not going back there."

"What happened?"

"I can't tolerate the chemicals. My eyes are watery and I can't stop sniffling. I came to Los Angeles because of the climate. If there is any chance to heal my throat, I thought that it would be in Los Angeles. I am not going to voluntarily work at a job that exacerbates my problems."

"Calm down, Franzl. Calm down. No one is forcing you to go back into a situation like that."

"But how are we going to survive? I have to work! And I have to work right now."

"I'm looking for a job. Everything will be all right."

"How are we going to pay the rent?"

"Try not to worry so much. Take off those dirty clothes and take a nice shower."

"I can't get the smell of all that paint thinner out of my nose."

"Just take a shower, Franz."

There had finally been an Allied breakthrough in the war: "D-Day," it was called. The Allies had invaded Normandy, captured St. Lô, and soon later liberated Paris. Everyone in the United States was extremely optimistic.

Frank finally had a steady job at the largest costume house in Hollywood. Western Costume Company provided all of the top actors and actresses with clothes for their latest films. Evelyn Lowe worked in the office there and suggested that Frank apply for a job. But when he was only offered seventy-five cents an hour, he telephoned Franziska for advice. She told him to take the job – after all, he could always quit – and so he began as a stockman the following week.

The old six-story Western Costume Company building was near the corner of Melrose and Bronson avenues, just a few steps away from Paramount Pictures. Every day as Frank ate the lunch that Franziska had packed for him, he walked into the little U-shaped secluded area in front of Paramount and wondered what it would be like to work on one of the stages beyond the studio's grand archway and wrought-iron gate. Once in a while, he joined the Paramount community by eating a sandwich at Oblath's Café, or by purchasing a shirt or tie at Geller's.

He spent the first few months learning where all of the costumes belonged, as there was a designated place for every garment. When a suit had to be placed back in stock, Frank had to know in what period it was worn – the 1860s or the 1920s, for example – and then he had to know in which aisle to hang it. He soon became so knowledgeable that studio costumers began to ask for his assistance at fittings. He was meeting numerous movie stars now, and they all seemed to like him. He knew what he was doing, yet he was never too aggressive.

On this particular day, Frank was fitting fifteen extras with a costumer who was preparing a World War II film for Twentieth Century-Fox. Frank had pulled twenty infantry uniforms off the racks. And as each extra entered the dressing room and tried on a uniform, the tailor marked and pinned what needed to be altered while Frank jotted down the changes on a tag.

"Okay," the tailor said. "That should do it. Let's go on to the next one."

"I think the shoulders need to be taken in," Frank said.

"We can probably get away with leaving them the way they are," the costumer responded. "Extras' clothes don't have to fit as well as if they were made for actors. Whether the tailor alters the jacket or not, the camera will never pick up the difference."

But when the last extra walked in, Frank didn't have a costume to accommodate him. Frank needed a size fifty-two field jacket and size forty-two combat trousers.

"Well, I guess you won't be able to work on this picture," the costumer said to the extra with a deadpan expression on his face.

"Central Casting sent me. I have to work on this picture," the extra blurted out excitedly. "I need the money."

The costumer was joking, of course. Nevertheless, Frank was obliged to do some quick thinking. "I'll be right back," he said.

A few minutes later, he returned with a uniform in the correct size. The fabric looked the same as all of the others, but the uniform was cut differently and exhibited different insignias. "Try this one on for size," Frank said, cutting off the insignias. "The tailor will be able to make it look just like all the others. And I know that we can fit you with combat boots, a helmet, and a haversack."

The costumer was impressed. Frank had saved the day. He was a hard worker, and he was determined to succeed in America. "You can take your clothes off now," Frank told the extra as he was leaving the dressing room with the costumer and tailor.

"Sure. . . . Thank you," the extra said.

Frank was proud of himself. For the very first time on a job, he had forgotten that he was a singer who had lost his livelihood. He'd actually enjoyed himself this afternoon. He felt vital and needed. He was alone now, placing the tags with their alteration directives on the costumes and hanging them on a rack. One more, and he could roll all of the uniforms into the tailor shop.

He walked into the last extra's dressing room to retrieve his final costume. The extra was standing there stark-naked. "Oh, pardon me," Frank said, turning around, planning to walk out. But instead of leaving, he stood there for a minute, thinking. He'd given the extra plenty of time to get dressed, yet the extra was standing there as if he were posing for a nude portrait.

"Excuse me," Frank said, turning back around. "I'm curious. . . .

Could you please tell me why you haven't gotten dressed yet? I just came to take your costume out."

"Well, you told me that I should take my clothes off, so that's what I did," the extra said. "I try to follow directions."

"I meant that you should take the uniform off and then get dressed in your own clothes," Frank explained, smiling. "Maybe my English isn't so clear."

"Oh, it's clear," the extra said.

"Well, maybe it's too clear then," Frank answered, trying not to laugh."

And he never uttered those very same words to another actor or extra again.

There was a rumor that Germany would be defeated before the end of the year. Hitler's attempt to impede the Allies in Belgium had failed, and the Allies had moved into the Rhineland. In addition, they had liberated the victims of Buchenwald.

United States troops had wiped out Japanese resistance on the island of Iwo Jima and had landed on Okinawa soon later.

And Soviet troops had captured Vienna, freed the victims of Auschwitz, and entered Berlin.

The month was April; the year was 1945. President Franklin Delano Roosevelt had just died of a cerebral hemorrhage, and Harry S. Truman became the thirty-third president of the United States.

Frank and Franziska were standing in the chambers of U.S. District Judge Howard S. Blair. They were in the neoclassic-style United States Courthouse on Spring Street in downtown Los Angeles. The eighteen-story white stone building housed the main post office, numerous governmental departments, and federal courts. The building's central section – accented with numerous dark-shaded windows – was stacked high above a much wider foundation. Doric columns and eagle carvings added decoration. And on either side of the entrance doors, the United States flag hung gracefully atop a flagpole with a base of bronze. The massive structure evoked a patriotic feeling from all of those who entered its marble and travertine-embellished lobby, and Frank and Franziska were no exception. Today was a very special day for them, and they were dressed accordingly: Frank, in a nice new suit; and Franziska, in a more feminine version. They were extremely nervous as they stood in the judge's chambers, surrounded by shelves and shelves of volumes which spelled out the laws of the land. They'd studied hard, and they'd fulfilled all of the requirements.

"Please raise your right hand," the judge said, holding his hand up, waiting for Frank and Franziska to imitate him. And then he recited:

"I hereby declare under oath that I renounce all allegiance and fidelity to any foreign monarch, potentate, state, or sovereignty of whom or which I have heretofore been a subject or citizen;

"That I will faithfully support and defend the constitution and laws of the United States of America in the presence of and against all foreign and domestic enemies;

"And that if required by law, I will bear arms on behalf of the United States, perform noncombatant service in the armed forces of the United States, and will execute work under civilian direction when the work is of national significance."

The judge paused for a few seconds and then asked: "Do each of you take this obligation freely, without mental reservation or intent of evasion, so help you God?"

Neither Frank nor Franziska uttered a word. There was silence. Frank didn't know if he should speak; Franziska didn't know if she should speak. Then, suddenly: "We do!" Frank said in a booming voice.

"Please let your wife speak for herself," the judge responded.

"Oh! I do!" Franziska exclaimed. "I do!"

"Well, in that case, congratulations to you both," the judge declared. "You've just become citizens of the United States of America."

Frank and Franziska were delighted. They smiled and laughed and shook the judge's hand. And on the way out of the courthouse, they smiled and laughed some more.

⌒≈⌒

The United States of America was the country of freedom and hope and power. The Axis forces had heretofore discovered America's strength. Benito Mussolini had been killed. The German forces in Italy had surrendered. And Adolf Hitler had reportedly committed suicide. Frank and Frances were elated. There would never be any more clouds in the sky for them. Within days, Germany had surrendered unconditionally, and the concentration camp victims had been liberated. But nothing could atone for the millions who were lost. Frank and Franziska wondered what had happened to their aunts and uncles and cousins. Many of their relatives had disappeared.

Frank was working at Western Costume Company, and Franziska had taken a job as a salesgirl in the cosmetic department of Saks Fifth Avenue in Beverly Hills. She still hoped to one day continue pursuing her career as a designer. But for the time being, she and Frank needed to earn and save some money. She received a salary and commission, and on some weeks, earned more than Frank. Movie stars galore frequented her department. And although expensive perfumes were a rare commodity during the war years, a few bottles were always hidden under the counter for the wealthy, glitzy Hollywood clientele. Every evening, Franziska would tell Frank about the famous male film stars who had been shopping for their wives or girlfriends. But Frank was never impressed, because after all, he might have fitted that very same movie star the day before.

They also started talking about having children. Franzi wanted to keep on working. She wasn't ready, she always told Frank. She knew that having a child would be a financial burden, and she wanted to wait until they were more secure. But Frank continually attempted to talk her into trying to get pregnant.

"If something happens to me, I don't want you to be alone," he always said, remembering the fuss she'd made at the Selective Service office in Knoxville.

"Nothing's going to happen to you," she always responded. "We have plenty of time."

It was a warm summer and they spent many weekend afternoons lying around the pool at the Ambassador Hotel. The massive

European-looking castle-like structure was located on Wilshire Boulevard, midway between Beverly Hills and downtown Los Angeles. It was the place to see and be seen: where *Gone With the Wind* had won eight Academy Awards, and where Buster Crabbe had supposedly trained for the Olympics, and Bing Crosby and Jack Benny supposedly had proposed to their significant others. In addition, actress Marion Davies is said to have ridden a horse through the Ambassador's elegant lobby to impress William Randolph Hearst – the very same lobby that Frank and Franziska crossed almost every weekend on their way to the Olympic-sized swimming pool.

The war would be over soon – that's what the news commentators on the radio were predicting. The United States and British governments had called upon Japan to surrender unconditionally, but the Japanese had wanted a negotiated peace. The U.S. government responded by dropping the first atomic bomb on Hiroshima. With the Japanese still refusing to surrender as specified in the Potsdam Declaration, the Soviets invaded Manchuria, and the United States dropped another atomic bomb on Nagasaki. The Japanese then surrendered unconditionally.

Frank and Franziska were lying around the pool at the Ambassador Hotel the day that the war officially ended. The Japanese had signed the surrender agreement. Everyone was talking about it. Some of the women were throwing their swimming caps into the air. One man screamed at the top of his lungs and jumped into the pool. Franzi was wearing a halter-neck swimsuit of knitted black wool. She slipped a sporty coat dress over it, and Frank threw a shirt and pants over his swim trunks. They walked through the lobby and down the long pathway which led them to Wilshire Boulevard, where they planned to catch a bus. The people were ecstatic. They were dancing on the sidewalks and in the streets. Frank even started fox-trotting with Franziska. It was like New Year's Eve and Mardi Gras, all rolled into one.

"I love you so much," Frank sang as he pranced around playfully with Franziska.

"We've come a long way," she answered. "I'm glad that we've made it this far."

CHAPTER THIRTY-SEVEN

Eliot Ness, DeMille, and Me

Los Angeles, California
Near Cairo, Egypt
March 1946 to August 1963

*T*hey were asleep. At least, Frank was. Frances was thinking about having a baby. Maybe Frank was right. Maybe it was time. And for some unknown reason, she intuitively believed that this was the night that she could become pregnant. So she began by giving Frank a few soft, affectionate kisses on his face – his forehead, his cheeks, his nose, and then his lips.

"Mmmm," he murmured, still appearing to be very much asleep.

She continued by kissing his eyes delicately, and then once again, his lips. But this time Frank caught her by surprise. She had edged her body so that it was angled ever so partially on top of him, so that he could feel her breasts resting daintily on the side of his bare chest as she kissed his lips sweetly. He then murmured "Mmmm" again, wrapped his arms around her, pulled her atop him, and kissed her passionately. She loved him when he was strong like this.

He had stripped off his sleepwear now, and she was straddled so that he could feel the cool softness of her silk nightgown draped over him and the warm sexual intimacy of her body underneath. There was no need for foreplay. He could feel her honey waiting for him. They both knew that they were ready, so the two began their passionate journey toward ecstasy, with him taking the reins from her and becoming the aggressor, then positioning her so that there could be no mistake.

"I want to get pregnant. Right here and now!" Franziska uttered longingly. "Let me carry a part of you inside of me."

"Really? Oh, how wonderful!" Frank said in the midst of his ardor. "I'll grant you your wish. I promise I will!"

And so they added a new dimension to their lovemaking that night. And a few weeks later, when Franziska announced to Frank that she was indeed pregnant, they were overjoyed. They would raise this little girl or boy to be kind, giving, and honest, and to follow his or her dreams with strength and conviction.

"Oh, I wish that I could hold my baby," Frances said, lying on the bed in one of the patient rooms at St. Vincent's Hospital in downtown Los Angeles.

"You will . . . soon," Frank answered, bending over his wife and kissing her lovingly on the forehead.

"I just couldn't keep her inside of me any longer. She was so anxious to come out and see the world. How could I keep it from her?"

Franzi felt comfortable at St. Vincent's. The Italian Renaissance-style building almost seemed European-looking to her. And although the building was only twenty years old, its arched windows and doorways lent age and character to its façade. The hospital staff was friendly and warm, and the nurses – many of them Sisters of Charity – made the atmosphere one of peace and good will.

"When our neighbor answered the telephone yesterday instead of you, I was shocked," Frank said. "And when she told me that your water bag had broken and that her husband had taken you to the hospital, I was stunned. I ran into the tailor shop and shouted, 'We're in labor. We're going to have a baby!' Everyone there laughed, and my boss called out: 'So what are you waiting for? Go!' I'm sure glad that we bought that new Dodge this year, because I wanted to get to the hospital fast."

"Well, you made it. That's all that counts," Franziska said. "I'm glad that I didn't have a hard time. I just hope that little Carol Jeanie is healthy. The first thing that I asked Dr. Henley was, 'Does she have all of her fingers and toes?' And when he said 'Yes,' I was relieved. Oh, Frank . . . she's so little. Two months early and only four pounds fifteen ounces – I know that Dr. Henley said she'll live, but I'm worried."

"She'll be just fine."

"I hate having to leave without her."

"I'm sure that you'll be able to visit her, and before long, we'll be able to take her home."

"I can't stand it, Frank. I feel like I'm a prisoner in my own house. The nurse won't let me near my own baby."

The scene was not one of tranquility. Franzi and Frank were sleeping on their bed in the main room, and the nurse and the baby were in the kitchen: the nurse, on a cot; and the baby, in her crib.

"The nurse won't let me touch Carol Jeanie either," Frank said. "We have to understand that because she was premature, she's very susceptible to disease. The nurse will only be here a few more days, and then we'll have our little bundle all to ourselves; and pretty soon, I'll bet that you'll be screaming to have the nurse back."

"No! Never!" Franzi answered. "We've decided that I'm not going to work anymore, that I'm going to always be here for Carol Jeanie. Being a mother is going to become my vocation. I'm going to be the best mother you've ever seen."

"Daddy! Daddy! Don't go and leave me, Daddy! Don't go and leave me!"

Carol Jeanie was crying and making quite a scene at Los Angeles International Airport. I was already seven years old.

My father was the head costumer on the biblical epic, *The Ten Commandments*, and he was on his way to Egypt. Soon after I was born, he'd quit his job at Western Costume Company because the department head of wardrobe at Universal had wanted him to work as the set man on the film, *Pirates of Monterey*. He knew that if he worked on films, he wouldn't have steady employment; however he wanted to progress in the industry, so he took a chance. And he was lucky. By the time he began to prepare the costumes for Paramount's *The Ten Commandments*, he'd dressed Ronald Colman, William Holden, Charles Laughton, Rod Cameron, Robert Taylor, and Stewart Granger. And he'd worked at Universal, MGM, and Paramount.

In *All the Brothers Were Valiant*, Robert Taylor and Stewart Granger played brothers, and there really was sibling rivalry on that set. Neither of them wanted to be shorter than the other. So when Robert Taylor noticed that Stewart Granger was the taller one in a shot, he asked my father to have the heels on his boots made higher; and likewise, when Stewart Granger discovered that Robert Taylor was taller, he asked for lifts. If my father would have honored the wishes of both movie stars, they would have each been eight feet tall by the end of shooting. Oh, well, my father did his best to please both of them.

"Daddy! Daddy! Don't go and leave me, Daddy!"

I spoke accent-free English because my parents rarely spoke German at home. They only spoke the language when they were arguing or when they didn't want me to understand. They didn't want me to develop an accent. To this day, I regret their decision.

"Daddy! Daddy! Don't go and leave me, Daddy!"

My parents and I were standing behind a chain-linked fence, looking at the airplane behind it.

"Time to board," we heard someone say.

The gate was opened, and people started walking toward the aircraft. "Well, I guess this is good-bye," my father said, drawing my mother toward him and kissing her. "And as for you, my little Cutie, how about giving your daddy a big hug?"

I looked up at my father with tears filling my eyes. And when he lifted me up and hugged me, he could see that the tears were trickling down my cheeks.

"Now you have to be a big girl and take care of Mommy," he said to me. "And I'll be home before you have a chance to miss me."

He set me back down on the ground and gave Franzi one more short kiss on the cheek. He showed the passenger agent his boarding pass and started to walk through the gate.

My mother was standing there with her arms around my shoulders. I broke away from her, ran after my father, and grabbed on to the legs of his pants. "You can't go, Daddy!" I cried.

My father picked me up and carried me back to my mother, who was standing just outside the open gate.

"Mommy needs you to be with her now," he said to me. "And when I come home, I'll bring you a big surprise."

He kissed me on the forehead and set me down. He gave my mother a loving glance and then walked back toward the stairway that would lead him into the airplane.

Again I started to run through the gate. But this time I was intercepted almost immediately by a passenger agent. "You can't come in here," the agent said. "It's not safe."

I quickly turned around and ran back to my mother, throwing my arms around her skirt and crying.

"If you don't calm down, you won't be able to see Daddy take off," she said. So I almost instantaneously ended my tantrum. I watched my father as he walked up the stairway and entered the aircraft. And then when the plane taxied to the runway, I remained standing by the gate with my mother, waving until the airplane took off, and continuing to wave until it was out of sight.

Producer-Director Cecil B. DeMille was in the midst of shooting the "Exodus" scene from *The Ten Commandments*, when Moses led the Hebrew slaves from Egyptian bondage to freedom. Giant megaphones were being used to broadcast Cecil B. DeMille's every command to the extras. Each word was translated to them in Egyptian Arabic. There were six cameras strategically placed to capture the visual image of the grand migration. The cameras were shooting the scene from different heights, distances, and angles. Later, with the imposition of close-ups, dialogue and music, the editors would mold the image into the story.

Thousands of extras – as Israelites – were following their deliverer,

Moses, moving away from the city gateway, which was guarded by massive dark-colored stone sphinxes and flanked with huge reliefs of Egyptian leaders riding their chariots to victory. The Israelites were following a processional route lined with sphinxes. And a long shot was capturing the entire vision: men, women and children of all ages and sizes – some strong, others weary from years of hard labor; flocks of geese and herds of oxen; donkeys hauling carts and wagons; old people hobbling on crutches; young people with heavy loads on their shoulders; barking dogs, bleating sheep, and camels; herdsmen and shepherds; and Moses.

The locally recruited assistant directors were mingling among the extras, costumed to blend in while giving the extras directions. These were not ordinary extras: For most, this was their very first film. They were local inhabitants who had been drawn in by the glamour of being among Hollywood filmmakers and by the stipends that were offered to them. The property men had provided them with all of the necessary props: carts and wagons laden with everything from hay to golden calves; plants and planters; animal cages; yokes to carry pails of water; baskets filled with food, clothes, and household goods; staffs to support their bodies; and the list of items went on like an unending dictionary.

The costumers were playing an integral part on this location as well. Their work had begun in the wee hours of the morning. Collapsible dressing rooms had been set up for the men and the women extras, and the costumers had given each of them something appropriate to wear. Frank was supervising approximately fifty wardrobe men – most of them, Egyptian residents – and designer Dorothy Jeakins was overseeing the wardrobe ladies, much fewer in number. That morning, they had dressed the extras in loincloths, short and long tunics, and caftans; cloak-like wraps and blankets; belts and waist-sashes; and finally, sandals and simple head coverings made out of cloth. It had been an exhausting morning.

But now that shooting was under way, Frank was able to relax. He and many other members of the crew could now simply become spectators. He'd positioned himself behind a camera and was watching the action. He could see the magnificence of the vision enfolding: the Hebrews departing from Egypt with the city gateway and sphinxes in the background, and Charlton Heston, as Moses, in front. And later, as the Israelites moved away from the land of the Pharaohs toward the desert, a reverse shot captured them from behind. The Pharaoh's walls were no longer within the camera's view, only the thousands of Israelites walking between the sphinxes with merely the desert and hills in front of them.

"Okay . . . cut!" Cecil B. DeMille told his camera crew, his declaration instantly relayed through a megaphone.

There was a rumor that Mr. DeMille wasn't feeling well. Makeup artist Frank Westmore was guiding him down from the camera platform positioned on top of the city gate.

"That's a wrap," the first assistant director shouted, his words immediately translated into Arabic.

The crew and extras dispersed; and a few hours later, no one would have ever guessed that thousands of people had spent the day making a movie on that spot near Cairo. Only the grandiose set remained as a testament.

"This is my daughter," Frank said, introducing me to actor Robert Stack. "She's visiting the set today."

I looked up into Robert Stack's eyes and smiled. He seemed so tall to me in his *Eliot Ness* suit, vest, and fedora.

"It's a pleasure to meet you," he said. "I think that Leonard Kantor has written an excellent script, so I'm sure that you'll enjoy the shooting. Now you make sure that your dad lets you stand where you can see everything. If he doesn't, just come to me and I'll find you a place with a clear view."

"Thank you," I said. I was a shy thirteen.

My father was the costume supervisor on *The Untouchables*, and we were on a sound stage at Desilu-Culver. My father had made a conscious decision to work on television shows instead of movies because he didn't want to go on so many long locations: He wanted to be with his family more. Before *The Untouchables*, he'd been the key costumer on *The Adventures of Jim Bowie* and *Yancy Derringer*, both series taking place in the 1800s in Louisiana. He enjoyed working on shows that required historical costumes. His job entailed breaking down each script by writing down the types of costumes needed for every character in every scene; preparing a budget; directing fittings; purchasing or renting most clothes at costume houses, while designing other clothes and having them made; and finally, supervising his set people so that the actors and their costumes were matched accordingly.

My father had positioned me next to one of the cameras, just far enough behind it to be out of the view of its lens. He was standing next to me.

The gaffer was setting up the lights.

Then: "Quiet on the set," the first assistant director said. "Roll sound. . . . Roll camera."

It was the clapper's turn next: "Scene Five, Take One," he said, clapping the slate.

Then the director said, "Action."

It was a party scene at Madam Flora's establishment in a suburb of Chicago during the Prohibition era. Al Capone's empire was crumbling, and the new man in town, Charles "Pops" Felcher, was hoping to become his successor. Pops was sitting at a small round table with his lawyer, Archie Grayson. It was like New Year's Eve. The band was playing. Everyone was all dressed up. The room was decorated with tinsel. And the waiters were buzzing around, uncorking bottles of champagne. Madam Flora shouted for everyone to shut up, including the band. She had a brassy personality and voice. She was wearing a long black evening dress with a low neckline that was trimmed with appliqué lace and embroidery. It looked kind of like a nightgown.

"Cut!" the director said. "There's something missing on that dress."

My father perked up. "Sabine . . . Sabine." He called for the set lady.

"Yes, Frank. Here I am," she said.

"Isn't there a boa that's supposed to go with that dress?"

"Why, yes."

"Will you please go and find it?"

A few minutes later, a peach-colored feathery boa was draped around Madam Flora's neck, with the floating ends hanging almost to the floor.

"Okay, let's do it again," the director said.

"Places everybody," the assistant director called out. "Roll sound. . . . Camera."

"Scene Five, Take Two." Clap!

"Action."

The party scene proceeded again, and Madam Flora once again enunciated her "Shut up" line. Then she drew open what looked like a stage curtain. The words *"Pops We Love You"* were displayed behind it on a drop that appeared to be covered with gift-wrapping paper.

The gift was from Madam Flora and her girls to Pops Felcher. Handing Felcher the end of a long strip of ribbon that extended all the way to his gift, Madam Flora told him to give it a good pull.

And as Pops Felcher yanked the ribbon, a striking cat-like woman came jumping through the paper, the other end of the ribbon wrapped around her waist. She was Rusty Heller (actress Elizabeth Montgomery), and she wanted to be Pops Felcher's girl. She was dressed in a leotard of black sequins, black mesh stockings, a rhinestone collar, and a sequined cap with cat ears. She sat flirtatiously on Pops' lap, kissing him until he moved her over to Archie Grayson.

One of the mobsters shouted to Archie to throw her to him.

And then WHAMMO! The mobster hid under a table as federal agent Eliot Ness and his team of investigators pushed open the door and raided the place. Ness handed Madam Flora a search warrant and said he was looking for Augie Kleiner. A shady but respectable-looking man in a pin-striped suit said that Kleiner wasn't there, then told Ness that he was getting paid to spill beer, not interrupt private parties.

BAM!

Eliot Ness slapped the man across the face, clutched him by the collar, called him a "punk," and commanded him to answer the question.

Then Ness overturned a table and exposed Augie Kleiner underneath it.

"Take 'em all in," he directed his agents.

"Cut!" the director said. "Print it!"

⁓

Frank was standing on the stage of the International Ballroom in the Beverly Hilton Hotel. Actress Susan Kohner was handing him the Motion Picture Costumers' Award for Creative Artistry in Television Costuming for *The Untouchables*. He was receiving his union's statuette for the best men's costuming on a filmed television series for 1960. Since television costumers were unable to compete for Emmys, this was the most prestigious award that he could receive.

"Thank you so very much," he said. "I deserve it."

Everybody laughed.

"The people in this industry have shown me that in America, any man can succeed if he is conscientious and determined. My wife and daughter thank you, and so do I."

Everyone applauded. The orchestra played as Frank walked down the stairs at the side of the stage and returned to his table, then kissed Franziska on the lips as he sat down.

"Congratulations!" she said to him. "I'm proud of you."

"Me too!" Frank gleamed.

This was a big night for him. In fact, this was his very first black-tie affair in America. It was the Adam 'N Eve Awards Ball. All of the women were either wearing glamorous long evening gowns or stylish cocktail dresses, and almost all of the men were attired in tuxedos. My mother was wearing a sleeveless tight blue satin cocktail dress with a scooped neckline, and my father was wearing a black suit. He didn't own a tuxedo and hadn't wanted to rent one, so he was the nonconformist of the evening, although no one seemed to mind.

Having won his award at the beginning of the evening, he was able to relax as actors Barry Sullivan, George Murphy, and Gerald Mohr presented awards to costumers in other categories, and to actors and actresses whom the costumers' union had wanted to acknowledge, among them: Doris Day, Joan Crawford, and Dick Powell, who asked his wife, June Allyson, to come up onstage to join him. June Allyson almost had to decline her husband's request, though. She couldn't seem to locate her shoes, which were not on her feet, but were indeed under the table beside them.

Yes, it was a star-studded evening. And after the master of ceremonies concluded the event, Frank posed for pictures with some of the other award recipients.

However he felt the most gratified a few days later when he opened *The Hollywood Reporter.*

Congratulations . . . . .

FRANK DELMAR

On winning the Costumer's
Award "for creative artistry
in television costuming" for
Desilu's THE UNTOUCHABLES.

Bob Stack

and the gang

Not only was my father good at what he did, but he was liked and appreciated by the people in his profession. Maybe his life was turning out all right after all.

Freddie and Evelyn Lowe had moved to the San Fernando Valley. They'd opened a gift store in Reseda and had bought a house in Northridge. The city of Los Angeles was unlike most. It had some tall buildings, but it seemed to be growing outward instead of up. And as it continued to expand, more and more communities and suburbs were being created, each becoming a subdivision of the sprawling city. The San Fernando Valley – north of downtown Los Angeles, Hollywood, and Beverly Hills – was divided into many such communities, each blending into the other so that it was almost impossible to decipher where one ended and the other began. The land and vegetation were plentiful, and the summers were hot.

Evelyn liked to entertain on the weekends. She had a large backyard with a swimming pool, and a patio adjoined her kitchen and living room. It was a warm Sunday, and she was having a little party. Well, it wasn't really a party; it was more like a friendly gathering. The guests included Evelyn's distant relatives, Jean and Kurt Ralston; her friends, Dr. Leon and Ruth Gruneberg; and my parents and me. I was already 16, and I wasn't the only young adult at the party. Evelyn's son, Johnny, was there to keep me company, although he spent most of his time in his bedroom watching television.

Evelyn had set up a buffet of cold cuts on the patio. Her guests were sitting around some large round garden tables finishing the main part of their meal.

"Save some room for fruit and dessert," Evelyn advised cheerfully. Her lively mannerisms, quick wit and speech were so endearing that she was nothing short of adorable, and Freddie was obviously devoted to her. "I've made a *Sachertorte,* and Franzi has brought some open-faced fruit tortes from *Benesch*," she continued.

Soon later, my father started to talk about the new television series that he was working on. "I've been given the opportunity to design more," he said. "A lot of the costumes have to be made, and they are all historical. Each episode dramatizes an event in American history."

"What's the name of the show?" Freddie asked.

"*The Great Adventure.* The first episode will be telecast next month."

"The series sounds interesting," Kurt Ralston said. He was a hairdresser. "I've always been interested in period costumes and hairstyles."

Evelyn was starting to clear one of the tables. "Let me help you," my mother offered, entreating me to bring some of the plates into the kitchen as well.

Quite a bit later, the sun started to set, and we were all eating dessert. The women had put lightweight wraps over their swimsuits, and the men were now wearing sporty shirts and trousers. My mother had a cigarette in her mouth. She was lighting it.

"Cigarettes are so bad for you," Dr. Gruneberg said.

"Are they really?" she asked. "I've been smoking for years. A good cigarette somehow finishes off a meal."

"Yes, but you don't just smoke them after meals," Frank said. "You smoke them all day long. You somehow restrained yourself when I was singing because you knew that the smoke was bad for my voice. But lately . . ."

"Now Franzl, I don't smoke *that* much."

"Yes, you do."

"And I could stop in a minute if I wanted to. I just don't want to."

"There are studies which indicate that cigarettes are extremely hazardous to your health," Dr. Gruneberg said.

"In what way?"

"Smoking is now being linked to cancer, cardiovascular diseases, chronic bronchitis, and emphysema."

"Oh . . ."

"And people are becoming dependent on the nicotine."

"I have to admit that my smoking has become a habit, but it's not an addiction. Like I said before, I could give it up at any given moment."

"Then why don't you give it up right now?" Frank asked.

"Like I said before," Franzi repeated, "because I don't want to."

"You mean you'd rather risk getting lung cancer or having respiratory problems?" Dr. Gruneberg questioned.

"Well, I have to make my own decision, and I can't do that right here on the spot."

"Do you know what your lungs look like? They could already be black from all of the tar and nicotine," Dr. Gruneberg said. "If I could cut you open right here and now, I'll bet that I could confirm that."

"Don't give me the shivers," Franzi said. "I'm glad that you can't."

"But a simple X-ray would prove my point just as well," Dr. Gruneberg asserted.

"I've heard enough," Franzi declared. "I'll think about what you've said, but why don't we change the subject, please?"

My mother continued to smoke the cigarette that she'd lit because she had a point to make. She wasn't going to allow anyone to bully her.

"I hope that Dr. Gruneberg can scare some sense into you," my father remarked.

"Oh, stop it, Franzl. Maybe he already has."

Then Evelyn cut in, attempting to alter the topic of conversation. "Carol Jeanie, dear, why don't you go into the house and ask Johnny if he wants a piece of the open-faced blueberry torte that your mother has brought. Tell him that she really only brought it just for him."

"Okay," I said, opening the sliding glass door and disappearing into the living room.

My mother had set her cigarette in the ashtray. She brought it to her lips every once in a while; however for the most part, she let it burn out. She'd been intimidated, so she didn't smoke another cigarette for the entire evening.

"We really have to be going," she told Evelyn at about half past eight. "We have a long ride ahead of us, and Franzl has to be at work early to-morrow morning. . . . Good-bye, everyone," she said standing, my father and I then following her lead.

"It's been nice seeing you again," Jean Ralston said to me. "You've grown up to be a lovely young lady. You look just like your father."

"Thank you," I replied, not knowing if I'd been given a compliment or not. I had my father's brown hair and hazel eyes. And although my father was nice-looking, my mother was quite beautiful.

"Don't forget our little conversation about the color of your lungs." Dr. Gruneberg reminded my mother again.

"I promise to remember," she answered as she opened the sliding glass door. "We'll see you all soon again!"

My father, mother, and I walked through the living room to the front door, and Freddie stayed with us until we reached our car.

"Drive safely," he said. "And please think about what Leon said to you, Franzi. Having cancer is no fun."

My mother did think about what Dr. Gruneberg had told her. After that afternoon and evening, she never lit another cigarette again.

Dr. Wilhelm Mayer-Hermann, my father's doctor, in a painting by Otto Dix at the Museum of Modern Art in New York. Mayer-Hermann was the laryngologist of many famous Broadway stars and opera singers who performed at the Met. (*Digital Image © The Museum of Modern Art/ Licensed by SCALA / Art Resource, NY; and Otto Dix © 2012 Artists Rights Society, ARS, New York / VG Bild-Kunst, Bonn.*)

A photo of the automobile Thomas P. Martin showed my father as described in Chapter Thirty-Two. I couldn't believe there was actually a photo of it. (*Courtesy of Mary-Anne Martin.*)

COLUMBIA CONCERTS CORPORATION
OF COLUMBIA BROADCASTING SYSTEM

Metropolitan Musical Bureau, Inc. • Haensel & Jones
Evans & Salter, Incorporated • Concert Management
Arthur Judson, Inc. • Community Concert Service
Wolfsohn Musical Bureau of New York, Incorporated

113 WEST FIFTY-SEVENTH STREET, NEW YORK, N.Y. • CIRCLE 7-6900 • CABLE: COLCONCERT

August 22, 1940

Mr. Francis Delmar,
15 West 82nd Street,
New York, N.Y.

Dear Mr. Delmar:

    This is to thank you for your kind wishes.

    I am so sorry to hear that you were ill all the time. However, I hope that the climate in Tennessee will help you. Give me a ring as soon as you are back.

    With best wishes and kindest personal regards,

Very sincerely yours,

Andre Mertens

AM:mw

The real letter from André Mertens to my father dated August 22, 1940.

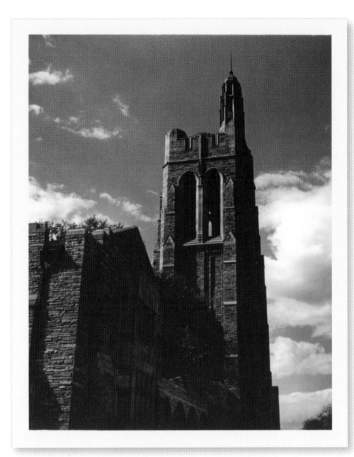

A 1941 photo of the Church Street Methodist Church where my father taught voice in Knoxville, Tennessee.

Miller's Department Store in the '30s in Knoxville, Tennessee on Gay Street. (*Courtesy of Thompson Photo Products, Knoxville.*)

LAWRENCE TIBBETT

February 6, 1941

Mr. Frank Delmar
2930 E. Magnolia Avenue
Knoxville, Tenn.

Dear Mr. Delmar:

Thank you for your letter.

I'm sorry to hear about the trouble you are having
with your throat. I believe the only solution is a
series of careful exercises under an expert. It is
too intricate to describe in a letter or I would be
glad to do so.

I hope with rest and careful exercises your difficulty
with clear up. You may be sure that you have my very
best wishes.

Sincerely,

Lawrence Tibbett

The real letter from baritone Lawrence Tibbett to my father.

The program cover of the concert my parents attended at the Bijou Theatre on December 7, 1941, the day the Japanese attacked Pearl Harbor. Note the photo of the pianist Eugenia Buxton, and the credit for the conductor of the Knoxville Symphony, Bertha Walbern Clark, who was the mother of my father's accompanist, Elsa Stong. (*Courtesy of the KSO.*)

325 West 45th
The Whitby
New York City

Febr. 12, 1942.

Dear Delmar,

   I must apologize for not having answered your letter before, but, as you can imagine, there is so much work during the season at the Metropolitan that it is hard to keep up with correspondence.

   I am very glad that you like our translation of the Magic Flute, we tried to be as close to the original as possible and at the same time do justice to the music in everyvrespect. Ina short time the vocal score will be on the market, edited by Schirmer, and you as well as anybody else will be able to make use of it.

   I share your opinion in respect to translations, but it will take a long while until everybody will be convinced. We are working on other ones, but I cannot tell you now on which one. We finished the " Entfuehrung" which will be performed for the first time on a smaller stage in New Jersey, with Lorenzo Alvary as Osmin and Hans Busch as stage director.

   If you come to New York, get in touch with me, I will be very glad to see you and hear you, too. You will always be able to find me at my former address (14 Reservoir Ave, Jersey City, Tel:Journal Square 4 -5800) in case we should have moved from this apartment.

   I am, of course very happy to be at the Met, the engagement came as a great surprise to me, shortly before the first performance of the "Flute", just after I had come back from Chicago.

   Please give my regards to your wife! I am really glad that you apparently are successful as teacher, I am sure that you developed your method to a high degree. I heard from Bing, too, he seems to be very successful, too.

     Best regards to both of you from both of us!

       Yours

      Thomas M.

Thomas P. Martin's actual letter to my father dated February 12, 1942.

EAR, NOSE AND THROAT SECTION

DR. H. I. LILLIE
DR. B. E. HEMPSTEAD
DR. H. L. WILLIAMS
DR. K. M. SIMONTON
DR. H. A. BROWN
DR. O. E. HALLBERG

MAYO CLINIC
ROCHESTER, MINNESOTA

A-1-256-056   June 15, 1943

Mr. Frank Delmar
2930 East Magnolia Avenue
Knoxville, Tennessee

Dear Mr. Delmar:

The flushing of the face after the injection of nicotinic
acid is to be expected and is a normal reaction. I am
sorry to hear, however, that you have not gotten any
improvement in the drainage from your nose. Since you
have had no beneficial effects from our treatments I
think you might as well discontinue them. I am sorry to
say that I have nothing further to suggest from the standpoint of treatment and I do not believe that a return here
would be of any value to you.

I doubt very much that any other climate than the one you
are in would be more beneficial to you. I regret that I
have to write this letter to you as I know how important
your voice is to you.

Yours very truly,

Henry L. Williams, M. D.

HLW:ZG

The actual letter from Dr. Henry Williams to my father from Mayo Clinic,
dated June 15, 1943.

Western Costume Company's historic old building on Melrose Avenue in Los Angeles next to Paramount. (*Courtesy of Western Costume Company.*)

My mother's certificate of United States citizenship. Her change of name by "Order of Court" can be found on the back.

My father's certificate of United States citizenship -- one of the most eventful days of my parents' lives. His change of name can be found on the back.

My parents in 1945, either in a suburb of Los Angeles, or in Santa Barbara, California for a weekend outing.

Toddler Carol Jeanie with her mother.

Baby Carol Jeanie with her mother.

Cecil B. DeMille filming *The Ten Commandments* in Egypt from a camera perch, 1954. (*Photographed by Ralph Crane / Time & Life Pictures / Getty Images*)

Makeup artist Frank Westmore helps Cecil B. DeMille walk across a plank to a camera stand while shooting the Exodus scene from *The Ten Commandments*. (*Photo by Ralph Crane / Time & Life Pictures / Getty Images*)

My father with the famous costume designer Dorothy Jeakins on location in Egypt while filming *The Ten Commandments*. (*Photo from my father's collection.*)

A photo of my father receiving the Motion Picture Costumers' Award for Creative Artistry in Television Costuming for *The Untouchables* from actress Susan Kohner at the Beverly Hilton Hotel, 1960. Emmy Awards were not yet presented to costumers. This award was the highest award my father could receive. (*Photo by John J. De Ninno.*)

My father holding the award with actor Robert Stack.

Bob Hope Rates High For Season

Claiming the highest rating on any network this season, Bob Hope returned for his first special of the season Monday night to leave his opposition in the Arbitron race practically standing still as he racked 33.7 and 31.9 for his two half-hours. Audience share on the first turn was a whopping 51.2 despite a loss of sound on the first portion of the show.

In direct opposition, premiere of hourlong "Surfside 6" drew second place with 15.9 and 19.1. CBS took the cellar with 12.3 for a Senator Lodge special and 14.2 for return debut of the Danny Thomas Show.

Other top raters of the evening were which clobbered ——— Griffith Show (26.6) new series, "Dante" (13.5), second half of "Adventures in Paradise," and "Cheyenne" (22.0 and 27.9), and "Pete and Gladys," with 17.4.

Pasadena Workshops

Applications are being accepted for the Pasadena Playhouse Acting Workshops under the direction of Gail Shoup, senior director and instructor in history of theatre and play direction. Workshop 1 is scheduled to begin Oct. 10, with 15 sessions, 7:30 - 10:30 p.m., designed to help the beginner in determining his qualifications for a professional career. Workshop 2, to develop the actor with some training, opens or Oct. 11.

Pageant *Spotlights* Huston

Director John Huston and United Artists' "The Misfits" are spotlighted in a nine-page layout in October issue of Pageant Magazine. The article by Peter Meyerson is titled "The Incredible John Huston."

TV WRITING DEALS

Sam Marx and Lewis Meltzer have sold original teleplay, "A Cool Line to Catiman," for MGM's "The Islanders," and "Bullets Cost Too Much" to Screen Gems for "Naked City."

Producer Peter Kortner has bought two teleplays for "Domestic Relations," by Richard DeRoy, and "End of a Mission," by Richard Fielder, for Four Star's June Allyson Show.

William Fay signed to write "Double Checkmate" for Revue's "Checkmate" series, through H. N. Swanson Agency.

Producer Vincent M. Fennelly has purchased original teleplay, "Songs My Mother Taught Me," by Kay Lenard and Jess Varneol, for "Stagecoach West."

TV DIRECTING DEALS

Frank McDonald, "Escort to Santa Fe" segment of "Wells Fargo."

Donald Gold, "Trail to Indian Wells" episode of "Two Faces West."

Joe Jackman, "The Firebug" stanza of "Manhunt."

Charles Haas, "Strange Disappearance of Judge Seward," segment of "Roaring 20's."

Virgil Vogel, "The Money Driver," G.E. Theatre episode.

Robert Sinclair, "Kakua Woman" segment of "Hawaiian Eye," scripted by Robert J. Shaw.

the NOTE BOOK

With his newest Atco release, "Bobby Darin, For Teenagers Only," just out, Darin takes special pains to dispel the impression that he has turned his back on the teenagers. The new album is a tribute to the younger element who first discovered and rooted for him. In addition to Darin's picture in color on the covers, there are several fan photos of him inside—and a large, folded full-length color picture of him that can be framed. Two numbers in the album, "You Know How" and "Somebody to Love," were written by Darin himself.

Oliver Berliner, president of Tropicana Records, leaves today for Chicago SF, NY and Mexico to promote Ray ——— album. In NY he will present the annual Emile Berliner Award for sound engineering achievement at the Audio Engineering Society convention.

Vanguard has released an album titled "Chocolate Covered Matzohs," an Evening With Herschel Bernardi, who plays Police Lieut. Jacoby in the "Peter Gunn" TV series. It's a choice collection of song, humor and story-telling by a gifted and versatile artist.

Colpix has released Jimmy Darren's single of "Come On My Lover" b/w "Man About Town."

Jimmy Shigeta's "I've Got Somebody To Love" being released this week on the Silver Slipper label.

World Pacific Records has released an LP by The Don Randi Trio titled "Feelin' Like Blues." This will mark the first album for the group currently appearing at The Losers on the Strip.

Jerry Rosen and his Orchestra will play for the annual Latin American Consular Assn. Ball at the Beverly Hilton on Friday.

Decca will release composer Alex North's "Love Theme" for "Spartacus" as single Nov. 3.

Jane Morgan will record an LP album for Kapp Records from the stage of the Cocoanut Grove during her engagement there starting Nov. 9. Dave Kapp flies in from NY to supervise the session.

The Roger Wagner Chorale Group has been signed by MGM to sing the main title song for "Cimarron." Song was written by Franz Waxman and Paul Francis Webster.

Fourteen new albums are being released by Capitol this week: Dean Martin, Stan Kenton, Fred Waring, Nancy Wilson, Cathie Taylor, Ron Goodwin, Don Baker, Tommy Collins, Louvin Bros., Mickey Katz, Rene Bloch, Van Alexander and Michael Paige.

Sam Honigberg Moves

The public relations firm of Sam Honigberg & Associates has moved to new headquarters at 468 No. Bedford Drive, Beverly Hills.

'Peter Gunn' Takes Lead In Arbitron

"Peter Gunn," returning Monday night, was a decisive leader in the Arbitron ratings, for its period, with a 19.2 average and 35% of audience, against 11.8 average and 20.7% of audience for Milton Berle's bowling show, and 11.7 average with 21.3% of audience for "Presidential Countdown."

Disney Signs 3 Corcorans

Kevin, Brian and Kerry Corcoran have been signed by Walt Disney to portray the three Boone children in his new TV series, "Daniel Boone," starring Dewey Martin and debuting this fall on "Walt Disney Presents."

NITERY NOTES

The Pat Brady Trio (Pat, Hal Keller, Ed Mihelich), which has appeared on TV and in niteries here, will appear Fridays, Saturdays and Sundays at the Malibu Sports Club, at Malibu Pier.

Phil Phillips is at the piano nightly, 5-11, at the Diablo Room, 1125 So. Beverly Drive, recently taken over by Bill Miller.

A bust of Tony Martin, by sculptress Lia Di Leo, will be placed on display in the lobby of the Desert Inn, Las Vegas.

Pianist Dave Kenner has returned to entertain nightly in the Corker Room at Stanley Burke's restaurant in Sherman Oaks.

Roberta Day and Chuck Sedacca, just closed at the Dunes in Las Vegas, opened engagement last night at the moore.

Night Club Review

CIRO'S

Current layout shapes as a moderate draw for the Frank Sennes showplace. While faring quite adequately, both acts (Pattie Moore & Ben Lessy, with Ruth Olay an added attraction have been seen to better advantage elsewhere.

Coming off on top are Miss Moore and Lessy, a couple of pro's in anybody's theatrical book. She's the delightful foil to his rubber-leg cavorting about stage. Seen heretofore at Billy Gray's Band Box, the pair are serving up primarily the same material, although here the room seems to lessen its effectiveness to a degree. Yet the ——— retain their basic humor, and the vocal blending harks to vaudeville of high order.

Miss Olay was not working to an overly receptive audience at the opener, and it should in her performance. A talented singer, she'd be wise to liven up her act here with more of the jazzy, upbeat tunes that she does so well. Predominance of the soft-sell, at least for her, is for the smaller room. Winner with the spenders was her rousing attack on "Wish I Could Shimmy Like My Sister Kate."

Brian Farnon's orchestra (9) provides the excellent backstopping throughout. Liberace 88's his way in on Monday.　—Neal Graham.

Swanson Reps Boyington

Gregory "Pappy" Boyington has signed for representation with H. N. Swanson Inc.

A congratulations memo in *The Hollywood Reporter* from Bob Stack and the gang. (© *The Hollywood Reporter. 97685*)

(Photo by C. Swatosch.)

My great-aunt Clementine Freund with her husband, Moritz, before being taken to Theresienstadt.

CHAPTER THIRTY-EIGHT

A Sad Farewell
from Theresienstadt

Read in Los Angeles, California
December 1963

I wrote briefly in the second chapter that my grandmother, Olga, had six sisters and a brother. My father was very close with his cousin Robert Freund, who was the son of his Aunt Clementine, or Tina Werner Freund. I do not know under what circumstances Robert entered the United States, but he and his wife, Toni, lived in New York. He imported fine fabrics from Europe, traveling there a few times a year. But during every Christmas season, he visited Los Angeles with Toni, and they always stayed at the Ambassador Hotel. After dinner when my mother and father dropped them off at the hotel, we would sit in the car for what seemed to be hours. They would talk and talk, and I would always fall asleep.

On one of these trips, Robert shared this letter with my parents. It was not dated. It was the last letter Robert received from his mother, my great-aunt, before she perished in the Theresienstadt ghetto and concentration camp with Robert's father, Moritz. The letter was also addressed to her other son, Otto Freund, who had been arrested in Vienna by the Nazis, was sent to Dachau in June 1938, was transferred to Buchenwald in September 1938, and was fortunate to have been released in February 1939 when he returned briefly to Vienna, went to London, and ultimately immigrated to Australia.

431

Between November 1941 and April 1945, approximately one hundred forty thousand Jews were deported to Theresienstadt. Thirty-three thousand Jews died there. Eighty-eight thousand were sent to other camps to be exterminated, including Auschwitz.

The letter here has been translated from the original in German to English. I am not familiar with some of the names. Most were related to Robert on his father's side. I do know that Antschi was another one of my great aunts who was deported to Theresienstadt and perished. My father, aunt, and grandmother are mentioned at the end. My father read the letter with great sadness.

My beloved Children,

Oh, how long I have wanted to write to you, to speak directly to you once, in case we did not have the great good fortune to see you again, my most precious ones. I have no idea whether you received any news about us. We received no answer from either Lucas or Dr. Friedjung.

Since July 23, we are living here in . . . a very sad life and we suffer terribly because of our separation from you, since seeing you again is so remote, and yet the thought of it is the only thing that sustains us. In the midst of this hard time of our life, we are very fortunate that our good relatives are in the truest sense of the word our saviours. Foremost is dear good Antschi, who succeeds in doing incredible things for us that are quite beyond description. Papa's nieces visit him daily and are exceptionally nice; they do a lot for us, and we are thankful to them for many things. Berta W. (Weinberger), Frau Dr. F. (Fertigova), is an angel – she takes care of us like a daughter, and I will never forget that. The Brands are also very nice and help us with food as much as they can. I used to be able to say that thank God we are in good health. But unfortunately, I can no longer say that about Papa. He has had several bouts of the bad diarrhea prevalent here, and these have weakened his heart very much, and now he is lying down with swollen feet, which worries me terribly.

Oh, children, I have such a heavy heart -- if only I could speak to you. We both want to, but will we ever come to you? I am often gripped by fear. If God so wills that we never see you again, my beloved ones, then I painfully bid you farewell and bless all three of you. God grant you health and shield you from cares. I particularly ask dear Toni to always be a good wife to you and also to stand in for me as a mother. And stay close with Otto -- this thought comforts me in my misery.

I must also tell you how much, dearest children, I thank you for your love. Not all children are like you, and I am very proud of you. All that you, my dear good Robert, have done for us is exceptional and we will never forget it, and the great happiness you gave your parents should be a source of comfort in your life. God grant it to you, my dear good child. Similarly we know the kind of child Otto is, and may life bring him many good things.

Dear Papa is somewhat better today, but I am very worried. Life here is destructive to one's health and you would also not recognize me. God help us at long last – we are so terribly unhappy. God knows whether my poor sisters are still alive. Aunt Karo was hardly well and would not have survived the hardships. Uncle Berthold (Robert's father's brother) died on 15 September simply from weakness. The Weinb. (Weinbergers) and Brands are doing relatively well. The son of Ella W. (Weinberger), Dr. Robert W. (Weinberger), has a top position and Liesl Brand is well employed -- the young help the old. Oh, how wonderful it would be if we were to live to experience coming to you. I want only to see my children one more time and then would gladly die.

This letter is in case we do not live to see you again, my beloved ones. You must correspond with Vinzi. She can always be reached through Wrabetz. We were very moved by her kindness to us, as were Ruda and Bettina. The Ecksteins are with the aunt. God knows how they are. Oh children, what we have been through. How can one endure this. It is only a question of time.

May my motherly blessing be with you all your lives. I kiss you a thousand times and very sadly bid you farewell.

With everlasting love,

Your parents

I wish all the best to Aunt Olga, also to Uncle Walter, Else, Ilona, Franz, Grete and Sonia.

My grandmother Olga Werner Jung (fifth from left) with her six sisters. My great-aunt Clementine "Tina" Werner Freund (far right) wrote the letter. Antschi Werner Fischer (far left) also perished.

Original Letter in German

Meine geliebten Kinder,
Ach wie lange will ich Euch schon schreiben,einmal mit Euch
direkt sprechen,für den Fall,dass wir nicht mehr das grosse
Glück hätten,Euch,meine Teuersten,wiederzusehen.Ich weiss
ja nicht,ob Ihr von uns Nachricht hattet,wir bekamen weder
von Lucas noch von Dr.Friedjung Antwort.
Wir leben seit 23.Juli hier in ....ein.recht trauriges
Leben und leiden furchtbar unter der Trennung von Euch,denn
ein Wiedersehen mit Euch ist so entfernt und dieser Gedanke
ist doch unser einziger Halt.Bei allen Härten dieses Lebens
haben wir ein grosses Glück,denn unsere guten Verwandten
sind im wahrsten Sinne des Wortes unsere Rettung.An der
Spitze die liebe gute Antschi,welche Unerhörtes für uns
leistet,es ist ganz unbeschreiblich.Papas Nichten sind
täglich bei Papa und sind ungewöhnlich brav,sie tun sehr
viel für uns und haben wir ihnen sehr viel zu verdanken.
Berterl W.,Fr.Dr.F.ist ein Engel,sie kümmert sich wie eine
Tochter um uns,ich werde ihr das nie vergessen.Auch Brands
sind sehr brav und helfen uns bei der Ernährung wie sie
können.Ichkonnte auch immer G.s.D.sagen,dass wir gesund
sind.Aber leider kann ich das von Papa jetzt nicht sagen.
Er hatte einigemale die hier üblichen so bösen Durchfälle,
die sein Herz sehr geschwächt haben,und jetzt liegt Papa
mit geschwollenen Füssen,was mir furchtbaren Kummer macht.
Ach Kinderlen,ich habe so ein schweres Herz,wenn ich mit
Euch reden könnte? Wir wollen es beide,werden wir es erleben
zu Euch zu kommen?Oft packt mich die Angst.Wenn es Gott so
fügt,dass wir Euch,meine Geliebten,nicht mehr sehen sollten,
dann nehme ich einen schmerzvollen Abschied von Euch,und
segne Euch alle drei.Gott soll Euch gesund lassen und Euch
vor Sorgen bewahren.Die 1.Toni bitte ich sehr,Dir immer
eine gute Frau zu sein und mich auch als Mutter zu vertreten.
Und haltet mit Otterl zusammen,dieser Gedanke ist mir in
meinem Jammer eine Beruhigung.

Auch muss ich Euch noch sagen,wie sehr ich Euch,teuerste
Kinder,für Eure Liebe danke,es gibt nicht immer solche Kinder,und ich kann auf Euch sehr stolz sein,was Du,mein lieber
guter Robert,für uns getan hast,ist wohl einmalig,wir werden
es Dir niemals vergessen,und es soll Dir im Leben ein Trost
sein,dass Du die Eltern sehr beglückt hast.Gott soll es Dir
lohnen,mein liebes gutes Kind.Ebenso wissen wir,was Otterl f
für ein Kind ist,das Leben soll ihm noch viel Gutes bringen.

Dem 1.Papa geht es heute etwas besser,aber ich mache mir
sehr viel Kummer,die Gesundheit ist hier bei diesem Leben
zerrüttet,auch mich würdet Ihr nicht erkennen.Gott soll uns

doch endlich helfen,wir sind ja so unglücklich.weiss Gott,
Ob meine armen Schwestern noch leben,Tante Karo wohl auch
kaum,sie wird die Strapazen nicht ausgehalten haben.Onkel
Berthold ist am 15.September nur an Schwäche gestorben.Weinb.
und Brands geht es relativ gut,der Sohn von der Ella W, Dr.
Robert W.ist hier an erster Stelle,ebenso ist Liesl Brand
günstig beschäftigt-die Jugend hilft den Alten.Ach wie
herrlich stelle ich es mir vor,wenn wir es erleben könnten
zu Euch zu kommen,nur einmal noch meine Kinder sehen,dann
gerne sterben.
Dieser Brief ist für den Fall gedacht,dass wir es nicht
erleben,Euch meine Geliebten,wiederzusehen.Mit Vinzi
müsset Ihr korrespondieren,sie ist durch Wrabetz immer zu
erreichen.Sie war rührend brav zu uns,Ruda und Bettina
ebenso.Ecksteins sind bei der Tante,weiss Gott,wie es ihnen
geht.Ach Kinder,was haben wir erlebt.Wie soll man das ertra-
gen? Es ist nur eine Frage der Zeit.Mein mütterlicher Segen
soll Euch durchs ganze Leben begleiten---
ich küsse Euch tausendmal und nehme sehr traurigen Abschied
von Euch.
           In unendlicher Liebe
                           Eure Eltern.
Tante Olga wünsche ich alles Gute,
ebenso Onkel Walter,Elserl,Ilonka,Franzerl,
Greterl und Sonia.

෨

As a postscript, according to a website of records and digitized documents sponsored by the Terezín Initiative Institute, National Archives, Prague, and confirmed to me by a letter from the National Archives – Moritz and Clementine Freund were deported from Vienna to Theresienstadt (or "Terezín" in Czech) on the twenty-second of July in 1942.

Moritz Freund died on the twenty-second of March, 1943. Clementine Freund died two days later.

CHAPTER THIRTY-NINE
Snapdragon

Los Angeles, California
July 1975 to March 1996

*M*y father was recuperating from a heart attack in a room at UCLA Hospital. He was hooked up to a cardiac monitor and had an IV in his arm.

"I wonder if people have sent me all of these flowers because they care, or because they're simply being politically correct," he said.

The years had brought Frank success in his profession. He was highly regarded for his historical costuming on *The Great Adventure* television series and then for *Profiles in Courage*. He had been department head of costumes at CBS Studio Center for a decade now. At the beginning, the job was overwhelming to him. He was preparing wardrobe plots and budgets for most of the movies and television shows that were filmed on the lot. He supervised all of the costumers, tailors, seamstresses, and stock people; and for the most part, was the one who hired and fired them. He was responsible for their mistakes, and at times, the burden was an ominous one. Yet in spite of the responsibilities inherent in the job, his secretary and employees loved him, probably because he never abused his power. He was a compassionate human being all the way through, right down to the core.

"They're sending you the flowers because they appreciate you," my mother said. "They want you to get well and come back to work because they know how good they have it. If you had to be replaced, your department would never be the same."

"Oh, how you flatter me, Franzi. You make me feel like I'm indispensable. But I don't know if I really believe that."

"That isn't what I meant to do. I simply wanted you to be aware that the people who work in your department appreciate you. The only one you're really indispensable to is me."

My mother rose from her chair and stood at the side of my father's bed. Then she reached over and placed her hand affectionately on his cheek. He kissed her palm.

"Hi, everybody!" I said as I entered the room after a bit of eavesdropping.

I was all grown up now and no longer living with my parents in their home near Beverly Hills. I had graduated from UCLA with a degree in theater arts, acted a little in local theater and film, but was a teacher, working on a master's degree in psychology. All of my friends, including my parents, were calling me "Carie" now.

"How are you feeling, Dad?" I asked.

"Much better," my father answered. "The doctor thinks that I'll be able to go home in a few days."

"Oh, that's wonderful," I said.

"How was your class, honey?" my mother asked.

"Interesting. I'm glad that it's summer so that I don't have to teach tomorrow. I'm going to study in the Biomed Library and then come up here to visit you."

"When your dad comes home, I'm going to start him on a whole new regimen. No more butter, eggs, and rich desserts; no more pork, lamb, and fatty red meat; but lots of fruits and vegetables and exercise."

"Sounds like a plan," my father said.

"You're going to be back at work before you know it," Franzi said.

About half an hour later, my father wanted to sleep. My mother would have ordinarily remained sitting on the chair beside him, reading or doing needlework, but she wanted to talk to me. So the two of us left my father alone to rest while we walked down the hall and talked.

"You haven't been sleeping enough," I told my mother. "At the beginning, you stayed here all night, and now you're here from eight in the morning until after eleven. You're going to get sick, and then you won't be able to help Dad."

"I know what you're saying is true. But your father means everything to me. He's all that I have."

My mother looked so tired and lost and sad. She was already sixty-four years old. Her graying hair was now tinted somewhere between blond and brown, and she was dressed in a very worn and wrinkled pants suit. But she still had those expressive almond-shaped onyx-colored eyes, and she was still beautiful.

"I'm going to keep your father alive," she uttered. "The doctor said that the heart attack caused extensive damage to his heart, and you know that he's had fibrillations for years. . . ."

Her voice trailed off, and she had to brace herself by holding on to the railing on the wall.

"Mother, are you all right?" I questioned, frantically placing my hands on my mother's shoulders to support her.

"Yes, just tired," she said, beginning to cry.

"The worst is over, Mother. You said that Dad might be able to go home in a few days. He's going to be okay."

"I know he is; I know he is," she said. "I was trying to be so strong before. Maybe I was just holding all of this inside of me. Maybe it needs to come out."

For the first time in my mother's life, she was looking into my eyes with need. She had never allowed me to see her vulnerable side before. But this evening, she couldn't help herself. I held her for a few minutes and then helped her to a chair. Then I sat down beside her.

"I hope that one day you will love someone as much as I love your father," she said.

I couldn't do anything but look into her eyes. I had never seen her in this light before. I was unable to talk or move. My parents had always been so prim and proper. They had rarely kissed or even held hands in my presence. I had always known that they loved each other, but I had rarely seen them display any kind of physical affection. I loved them both, but until my father's heart attack, I had never thought about what life would be like without them. They had given me so much. They'd spoiled me with clothes and given me ballet, acting, and piano lessons. They'd given me everything I'd ever wanted, and they'd showered me with their love. Maybe I'd always taken these things for granted. The memories suddenly seemed to shoot explosively through my mind so that as I stared into my mother's eyes, my own began to fill with tears. Then the two of us embraced as if for the very first time, with a clearer avenue of communication, and with a more mature love for each other than ever before.

"You are so fortunate to have found Dad," I said. "Nothing is going to happen to him. But just remember that I'm here, too; and just as you've protected me my whole life, I'm old enough and strong enough now to take care of you."

The two of us were sitting face to face now. My mother's composure had returned.

"You *are* all grown up, aren't you?" she said to me with a sudden maternal gleam of pride in her eyes. Then with a surge of strength: "Your dad is going to be all right; I'm going to be all right; and we're both going to protect each other and you for a long time to come. It was lovely to hear what you just told me; however it made me feel much too elderly. I'm not that old yet, and neither is your father, so why don't you tell us both the same thing in about fifteen years? Until then, let us just be your mother and dad."

The two of us walked back into my father's room arm in arm. I kissed them good night and left.

"You know, we've raised quite a daughter," Franzi said. "We can really depend on her."

"You're the one that deserves all the credit," Frank answered. "You were always there for her when she came home. You sacrificed having a career for her. I was always working long hours. . . . Yes, you deserve all of the credit."

Then the nurse came in, checked the electrodes on Frank's arms, legs, and chest, and gave him an EKG. Soon after she'd gone, a nurse's aide brought in a dinner tray, set it down on my father's bedside table, and left. My mother opened all of the little containers for him and watched him eat, sneaking in a few bites here and there for herself. When finished, he was exhausted, probably because he was still so weak. Another health-care worker removed his tray.

"Do you remember when we met at that five o'clock tea in Vienna almost fifty years ago? We were so young."

"Of course, I remember," Franzi answered.

"I knew right away that I wanted to spend the rest of my life with you."

"You know – I think that maybe I did, too."

"And now I might be coming to the end of my life. I can't imagine not waking up, not seeing your beautiful face anymore. I can't imagine . . ."

"Then don't."

"I'm so tired again. I think that I'll take another little nap."

A few minutes later, Frank had dozed off, and Franzi was sitting on the chair beside him doing needlework. She just kept doing it and doing it and doing it as if she were in a trance. Her eyes were glassy and she was having trouble focusing. She placed her needlework back inside her bag, and then just sat in her chair staring blankly into space. She sat that way for a long time, not doing anything, not appearing to be thinking. Then she closed her eyes, her head tilting to the side, and she fell into a restful sleep.

My father did go back to work. My mother had kept her promise: She'd nursed him back to health and then kept him on a strict diet. I had married and divorced, causing my parents much worry and anxiety. They'd wanted me to be happy, but my ex-husband and I had come from different worlds. The marriage was not meant to be.

"A toast – let's toast to Frank's future."

It was Frank's retirement party – it had been ten years since his heart attack. CBS Studio Center had become CBS/Fox and then CBS/MTM. When Frank decided to retire, he was told that there would be no replacement. The person in charge of the property department would now oversee costumes and art. It was time for him to retire. His heart was weak and he was already seventy-five.

The toast was being made by Bernie Pollack. Frank had nurtured Bernie when he first became a costumer, and now he was a motion picture designer. When Frank's secretary had called Bernie to tell him about the party, he had said that he wouldn't think of missing it.

The party was being held in Frank's department at the studio, in what appeared to be a one-story ranch-style house fronted with grass and trees. The only thing lacking was a picket fence. The house contained Frank's office; a much larger area with desks for his secretary and the costumers on the lot; one tailor shop for men and one for women; a costume storage area; and dressing rooms. The desks had been covered with decorated paper tablecloths and had become the receptacles of cold cuts, salads, potato chips, and spiked fruit punch; and there were balloons hanging all over the room.

"Yes, a toast to Frank's future," Bernie said, holding up a plastic glass of punch. "To the man who has taught me almost everything I know."

At the beginning, it was difficult for my father. He was used to getting up in the morning and going to work, and my mother was accustomed to having the freedom to come and go whenever she had a sudden fancy or whim. But they adapted quickly because they were aware of their priorities. They had spent their entire lives loving and protecting each other. He was the most important being in her life, and she was the most precious entity in his. And because they could never forget that they were now facing the twilight of their lives, they were resigned to holding on to every moment that they shared together. Each tried not to think about what life would be like without the other because that somehow seemed intolerable. Instead, they lived for each other and enjoyed the sunshine of every day.

He developed a passion for living that he had never before experienced. He had an insatiable desire to know everything that was happening in the world, from the facts about a presidential election to the details of the Olympic Games. *Newsweek*, *Time*, and the television became his resources of knowledge. And his newfound interests served to give Franziska the free moments that she so yearned for herself: to putter in the garden, to work on petit point, or to do something as simple as marketing. They didn't have a lot of friends – they only needed each other. He for her and she for him – that's all there was; that's all they ever wanted.

Frank's heart became weaker though; he had a leaking heart valve, and his heartbeat was more irregular. He was taking all kinds of medications. And Franzi had developed some sort of respiratory ailment. X-rays revealed that her lungs were scarred and that her airways were obstructed, yet the doctors could never seem to determine the causes. So they just kept living from day to day – she, always wondering how she would survive without him, always trying to prepare herself for the inevitable outcome; and he, simply trying to protect her, never admitting to himself that she would ever leave him.

The years continued passing – his hair was a little grayer; his hairline, somewhat receding – and the doctors couldn't understand how he was surviving. His heart was working so arduously, unable to pump enough blood to meet his body's needs. Yet he was enduring like an Olympic swimmer on his last lap before the finish. And it was all because of her. They were a team, and she simply wouldn't let him go. But then she broke her hip, and next she contracted pneumonia.

"I will not be staying in this hospital for more than a day," she told the nurse as she was lying down on the bed in her room at Cedars-Sinai Medical Center. "I'm not that sick. I don't know why the doctor insisted that I come here."

She was a tyrant to the nurses taking care of her: "I need a bath every day, and I need plenty of hot water for tea. . . ."

But they put up with her; and by the end of her stay a week later, she'd mellowed. Since she'd been unable to control what was happening to her, she'd succumbed.

That's when Frank had discovered how seriously ill she really was. She'd been going to their regular family physician, and she was seeing a pulmonary specialist as well, but she'd never told Frank how sick she truly was. She'd refused to accept the severity of her condition; and even if she had, she would have never burdened Frank with the doctors' prognoses. Until her bout with pneumonia, she'd still always looked wonderful – her hair had been tinted red – and she'd been driving almost every day into Beverly Hills.

"Her lungs are so badly scarred that I don't know how she is living such a normal life without oxygen," her doctor told Frank in the hospital.

"But what does she have? And what is it from?" he asked the doctor.

"It's hard to put a label on it: something like emphysema."

Whether or not her smoking had caused her lung disease was uncertain because she'd stopped the habit so many years before, but the smoking might have indeed been a contributing factor, the doctor concluded.

After she came home, she was never the same. Even though she was free of the pneumonia, she always felt weak and out of breath. She spent more and more of her time sitting on top of her bed doing needlework and watching television, and less and less of her time going out. Pretty soon she stopped leaving the house altogether, except to go to her doctors.

And Frank took care of her. At the beginning, he only left her to go to the market. But later, when she was afraid to be alone, I did the shopping instead. I was already forty-eight years old, and my mother was eighty-three.

Soon my mother's domain became even smaller. She would no longer even leave the bedroom for her meals. She'd always loved the house. She'd decorated it herself and spent years furnishing it. Every inch reflected her taste. It was a small ranch-style frame and stucco house, but the furniture, drapes, and wallpaper were elegant and royal, with touches of gold-colored imperial Vienna throughout. It had a U-shaped floor plan: the curved or horizontal portion in the middle was a combined living and dining room which faced a lovely Oriental-type garden and backed the den; one vertical side enclosed the kitchen, while the other incorporated the two bedrooms and master bathroom. A journey into the kitchen was simply too far an excursion for Franziska to attempt. And even a walk into the living room – its walls bedecked with her elaborately framed needlework – was too exhaustive for her to undertake.

She just remained partially lying, partially sitting on her bed, her back propped up by a pillow against the headboard, hour after hour barely moving, sometimes turning her head ever so slightly to look out at her garden.

"Come outside with me," Frank said one afternoon, trying to cheer her up. "Come and look at the snapdragons that the gardener has just planted."

She looked up at him with a half-smile. "I don't know if I have the strength," she said.

"Seeing the lovely flowers will make you feel stronger. Come," he said. "Put your feet over the side of the bed and I'll help you on with your slippers and robe."

She was so thin now – she was barely eating. Frank cloaked her with her robe, placed her pink satin slippers on her feet and almost lifted her into a standing position. Then he placed his arm around her and guided her to the sliding glass door. He opened it and led her onto the patio, down two short steps, and into the garden. Oh, how she loved her garden!

"Here we are," he said. "Look! Aren't they beautiful?"

He bent down and pulled one small section off a snapdragon. He squeezed on either side of the two little blossoms, and the flower opened its mouth as if to speak. "I will you to smile," he said, as if he were a ventriloquist and the snapdragon had been the mouth of a puppet. "And you *will* get better."

Franziska did smile. In fact, she somehow found the strength to laugh. But then her face grew serious again. "You really think that I'm going to get better, Franzl? "Is that what you think?"

My father didn't know what to tell her. The doctor hadn't given him much hope. His goal was simply to keep Franzi with him as long as she did not suffer. He believed that telling her the truth would be detrimental to her morale. "Yes, I really think that you will feel better," he lied. "I really do."

But it was impossible to determine if Franziska believed him. She gave him a half-smile, but there was still an expression of doubt on her face. He helped her back into the bedroom and into her bed, and she rested with much more serenity for the rest of the day.

However, a couple of weeks later, when Frank tried the same strategy again, Franziska refused to leave her bed. That's when he knew that her condition was progressing more rapidly. And soon after that, after her eighty-fourth birthday, she was no longer able to visit either of her physicians. Her breathing was much more labored, and it was impossible for her to live without the oxygen machine that was hooked up in the other bedroom – its constant droning sound echoing throughout the house; its tubing extending through the hallway into her bedroom, culminating with a plastic cannula which pushed oxygen through her nose into her lungs.

"Am I going to *die* this way?" she always asked Frank. "Am I going to *die* this way?"

And he always responded, "No, of course not. You will get better. You will get better."

But she didn't. Her expressive onyx-colored almond-shaped eyes now communicated something different than ever before. They said, "I'm like a little, lost deer in the forest. Please come and rescue me – I'm scared."

And Frank did try to rescue her. Oh, how he tried. But she just continued to get worse. Whenever Frank heard her desperately calling for help, he immediately rushed to her bedside. He took care of her: He cooked for her. He washed her nightgowns and changed her bed linens. He fed her, lovingly trying to force some nourishment into her, and he tenderly bathed her. There were no doctors anymore, not even a compassionate telephone call: just the two of them together; and on some evenings, a visit from me.

"I've brought you a delicious treat," I would say, going into my mother's bedroom with a piece of hazelnut torte on a plate."

"Oh, I couldn't," my mother would answer, as if she'd just eaten a sumptuous meal and simply had no more room for dessert.

"But I went especially to *Viktor Beneš* to get this for you," I would say. "Won't you please at least taste it?"

So my mother would then take a few bites, say how delicious the pastry tasted, and then set it aside for later.

My father didn't understand all of the things that were happening to my mother. He was reluctant to call her doctors, because since she couldn't go to them, they had lost interest in her condition. It was not only her inhaling that was so noticeable to Frank, but her exhaling as well. She would push the air out against her partially pursed lips as if she were blowing out the candles on a birthday cake. It was as if she was trying to expel all the air that was inside her so that she could inhale deeply and fill her wanting lungs with oxygen. My father also noticed a strange repetitive sound that she uttered both when she was speaking and when she was supposedly silent. The sound was similar to the one made by a child holding an imaginary gun and imitating the gunshot noise reverberating from it; only my mother's vibration was much more breathy. Was that what they called the death rattle? My father didn't know, and he had no one to ask. His responsibilities were becoming overwhelming. Even though he was practically carrying my mother to the bathroom, by the time she returned to her bed, she was always gasping and could barely catch her breath.

Frank finally called the family physician, and his secretary offered to speak to the doctor about securing some sort of help for my mother. At last! A health aide from the home-care agency at the hospital began coming to the house a few hours every week to ease my father's burden. But my father was sick himself and could have used more medical assistance, more direction from a doctor. My mother was dying. What could he do to stop the process? She was his air, his oxygen. Sometimes he just went into the second bedroom and cried.

Then he walked back down the narrow hallway to my mother, and they spent hours holding hands and remembering. How would he be able to sleep in their bedroom without her? The beautiful gold velvet bedspread was so permanently folded inside out on the bench at the end of their adjoining beds. But the green-and-gold-striped velvet chairs, Italianate furniture, plush gold silk drapes, and damask wallpaper would never allow him to forget the way it had been: the way she'd looked and smelled when she was getting ready to go out with him for a special evening, dabbing the scent of perfume discreetly on her body, and slipping into her evening wear. How could he ever forget? He never wanted to. He just didn't want to face having to remember what it was like to touch her. But he could still hold her now. They could still talk about the past.

Yet she knew that she was about to leave him. Nobody had to tell her – she just knew. She was so frightened that she often held on to his wrist with all of her strength. Maybe if she held on tightly enough, she wouldn't be torn away. They reminisced about the first time they'd met and the first time they'd made love; about Franz's performance as Figaro in the Musikverein; about the *Opernball*, their wedding, Cuba, and me – the memories of a lifetime.

"Hello, Doctor: I'm calling because Frances is so very sick. I don't know what to do anymore."

"I'll talk to the pulmonologist, and I'll call you back."

It was Christmastime. I had brought my mother some poinsettias which were sitting on the bureau across from her bed. She loved the rich red color of their leaves.

She was still alert. She still wanted to see a sample of the wallpaper that I had picked out for my condominium and a piece of the fabric that I was using to upholster my sofa. She still wanted to live to see me married and happy. She still wanted to be alive.

"I have talked to the pulmonologist," the doctor told my father by telephone. "We think that you should put Frances in a private hospital. Then we would be able to watch over her and give her morphine to ease her breathing, and she could remain there until she slips away peacefully without any pain."

Frank suddenly had a choking feeling in his throat. He could feel the tears welling up in his eyes. "NO!" he was screaming inside. "SHE *CAN'T* GO YET! *I'M* NOT READY! *SHE'S* NOT READY!"

"I . . . I don't know what to say to you, " Frank said softly into the telephone. "How long would she . . . how long does she . . ."

"That's hard to say – maybe a few weeks."

A few weeks, my father thought to himself in disbelief. *That's impossible.*

"NO!" he said to the doctor. "She has always told me that she wants to die at home in her own bed. I want to honor her wishes. I'll let nature take its course."

"Maybe you need time to digest what I've said. Maybe you should think about it."

"NO!" Frank responded. "I've made up my mind."

As the weeks passed, my father surmised that the doctor's prediction had been wrong. My mother was still alive. My father wondered if putting her in the hospital on morphine would have hastened her death. He wasn't a doctor, so how could he know. He didn't want Franziska to suffer. But she was still so alert and cognizant of everything that was going on around her. She was still watching television. In fact, when he was asleep at night, she watched the TV without the sound – that's what she told him. Yes, she was where she belonged – she was in the house she loved with the man who adored her.

But in March, my father tried to accept the inevitability of the situation. My mother's body was shutting down. Even the commode by her bed now seemed too exhausting for her to utilize. Her hair was long, gray, and unstyled, but it was not unkempt. Every day, my father sat on the bed next to her, combing and stroking her hair, and then looking into her now somewhat vacant eyes and telling her how much he loved her. And even though she looked back at him as a child looks to her father, she was warmed by his gentleness, and she understood his pain.

"Always get along well with Carie," she said. "Don't ever fight with her. The two of you only have each other, so I hope that you will be good to one another."

My father didn't say anything. He simply placed his palm on my mother's cheek.

"And please don't forget me. Come and visit me often."

"You're going to get better," my father said, choking back the tears. "This spring . . . you're going to get better this spring."

CHAPTER FORTY

Home

Los Angeles, California
April 10, 1996 to April 14, 1996

$\mathcal{I}$ was feeding my mother creamed spinach. I cooked it for her after my father told me she was no longer eating. My mother was trying so hard to force every spoonful down. She wanted to live, and she wanted to feel the benefits of the nourishment.

She was so frail, propped up by a pillow against her headboard. As I brought each spoonful of spinach to her mouth, I could see her quivering, and could hear the jerky, breathy gunshot-like utterances emanating from her lips. Her gray hair, although somewhat brittle, rested gracefully atop the shoulders of her flannel-lined pink satin nightgown. Her face was gaunt; her onyx-colored eyes, wide but vacant; and she was pale.

"Thank you," she uttered very slowly and softly, just above a whisper. "Your father doesn't know how to feed me. He puts too much on the spoon and then thrusts it into my mouth."

"I see," I answered with a momentary half-smile.

"But don't tell him that I told you. He's so loving. He just doesn't have any maternal instincts."

My father was in the kitchen. I had brought him something to eat, too.

451

"I don't want any more," Franziska said somewhat breathlessly.

"Are you sure?" I asked, setting the half-full dish of spinach on the nightstand.

Franzi nodded her head. Then she patted the empty part of the bed next to her. I looked at her a little perplexed at first, but then understood and sat down.

"I realize how sick I am," she said, grasping my hand. "I want you to know that I love you, and wherever I go, I will always watch over you."

At that moment, my eyes began to fill with tears. I knew that my father didn't want to acknowledge to my mother that she was dying. He didn't want her to be more unhappy than she already was, and he wanted her to have some hope. "There's always a slight chance for a miracle," he'd said to me. And although I didn't know if my father's decision was the right one, I honored it.

"I love you too," I said, hugging my mother. "You're going to stay right here and get better, because I need you."

"I'll always be your mother, and I'll always be with you, " she said, her dark eyes misty with tears.

"Please, Mother . . ."

"You know this isn't at all what I thought was going to happen. I was always so sure that your father would be the one to go first, and I worried that I wouldn't be able to survive without him. And now I'm the one who's leaving instead."

"Please don't talk like that, Mother."

"You're going to need each other, so please be good to him, honey, and I know he'll come through for you."

"You're going to get better. I know you are."

"Promise me that you'll take good care of him. That was my job for more than sixty years. He's going to need you. He's going to need you so very much."

"Please, Mother . . ."

"Promise me!"

"All right, I promise," I said, almost breaking down. "I promise. But I know that you're going to get better!"

"And now, will you open the drawer of my nightstand, please?"

"I don't understand."

"Just open it."

So I obeyed.

"Do you see the letter there on top?"

"Yes."

"I wrote it awhile back when I realized that I could be dying. Would you please give it to your father at the appropriate time? I've saved all of his letters, but I doubt that he still has any of mine. Let this be my last gift to him."

I took the letter out of the drawer slowly. "*To My Dear Husband*," the writing on the envelope said.

I no longer tried to refute my mother's contention that she was dying. I simply held on to the letter as if it were a treasure. Then I kissed my mother on the forehead.

"Your wish is my command," I said, hugging her. "I love you."

A few days later, a hospice nurse from Cedars-Sinai Medical Center came to the house to evaluate Franziska's condition. My father and the nurse and I were sitting around the dinette table in the kitchen.

"I'm glad that your home-health aide finally got the ball rolling," the hospice nurse said. "I'm surprised that your doctor didn't mention anything to you about our services. We could have been helping Frances for months already."

My father glanced at me with a displeased look on his face.

"Another nurse will be here tomorrow, and a hospice doctor will visit her on Monday."

"That's wonderful," my father said, a little more encouraged. "Frances hasn't been seen by a doctor since before Thanksgiving, when she became too ill to leave the house."

"I see," the hospice nurse said. "Mr. Delmar, you need to know that Frances is terminally ill."

"I know," Frank said.

"And she has very little time left."

"I know that too," he said with a solemn expression on his face. "I've just been trying to avoid facing the truth."

"The morphine I've given your wife will help ease her breathing, and she may sleep. Our goal is to keep her comfortable and free of pain."

"I understand," Frank said. "Please don't let her suffer."

"We won't, Mr. Delmar."

⌒⋙⌒

That evening, after everyone had left and Frank was alone with Franziska, he serenaded her in German with "An die Musik."

> *Oh dearest art, how often in dark hours of sadness,*
> *When life's cruelties have encircled me,*
> *Have you inspired a warm new love in my heart,*
> *And brought me into a far better world!*

He hadn't sung the *Lied* in years – he hadn't sung anything in years – and of course, he no longer had much of a voice. But as he sat next to Franziska in the stillness of their bedroom, holding her hand and singing pianissimo, they were able to travel back in time, and his voice sounded to her just exactly as it had always been.

> *Often a soft sigh rising from your harp,*
> *A sweet and blessed chord sent from you*
> *Has disclosed heavenly visions of better times for me.*
> *O dearest art, for that I thank you now.*

As they were looking into each other's eyes, they had visions of themselves dancing at the Kursalon in Vienna, riding on the *Riesenrad* at the Prater, making love in the foliage of the Lobau, saying their wedding vows at the magistrate's office in Prague, and traveling into train stations and out of ports: Yes, Frank's "An die Musik" serenade was enabling them to remember their lives when they were young.

"I'm going back," Franziska said when he had finished singing. Her voice was trembling and breathy, yet euphoric. "I'm going home."

"No," Frank said. "You can't leave me, and I'm staying here."

"You'll come back home one day too," Franziska said, beginning to doze off. "Then we'll be together again, my dear Franzl. We are destined to always be together."

Frank kissed Franziska's hand and laid it gently next to her body. Then he kissed her forehead. Even now, she looked beautiful to him. He fell asleep sitting at her bedside.

It was Sunday afternoon. When I saw my mother, I knew that the end was near. The covers were pulled back, and she was lying on an absorbent cloth which had been placed over her sheet. I had always seen my mother in a nightgown. Today, the nurse was helping her into a clean one, and I could see how thin and emaciated her body truly was. She looked up at me but didn't say anything. Her large almond-shaped eyes told the whole story: She was as helpless and defenseless as a diapered baby.

It broke my heart to see her like this. She had always taken care of me and been there for me when I sought the answers to so many much-contemplated questions. Who would I turn to now? I pushed the thought out of my mind. I was being selfish. I wasn't the important one now. Yet I felt so all alone. Never mind! What could I do to help her?

I sat quietly on one of the gold-and-green velvet chairs, watching. My father was standing next to my mother. Then he suddenly sat down on the second velvet chair and began taking his pulse. Seeing Franzi like this was affecting him deeply.

"Are you all right?" I asked.

"I think so," he responded. "My heartbeat was just feeling irregular. I'm okay now."

The nurse was repositioning Franzi on the bed and covering her from the waist down. Then she gave my mother some drops of morphine.

"Frances should rest peacefully now," the nurse said. "The hospice doctor will be here tomorrow morning. You can use the morphine as needed."

The nurse packed up her supplies and left. It was evening by then, and my mother had fallen asleep. I decided to spend the night there.

But the droning noise from the oxygen machine would make it impossible for me to sleep in my old bedroom. I'd sleep on the couch in the den, I decided. I just couldn't go home and leave my parents alone.

I went back into the kitchen with my father to get something to eat. He really didn't want much, so I just opened a can of sardines and served them on toast. Even the kitchen had been my mother's creation: the stained wooden cabinets, the goldish-colored cobblestone-patterned linoleum, and the cheery yellow-and-white wallpaper behind the oval dinette table.

"Oh, I'm going to miss her," my father said, suddenly putting his head in his hands and crying.

I had been clearing the dishes off the table. I couldn't really remember ever having seen my father cry before. "It's all right, Dad. I'm going to miss her too," I said, placing my arm around my father's shoulders to comfort him.

"We've spent our whole lives together. I met Franzi when I was seventeen . . . in another world. We've gone through so much together. . . . You know my past, but she was there. She was there to hear me sing. She risked her life to marry me. And if it wouldn't have been for her strength and fortitude, I doubt that I would be here today."

"I understand, Dad. I'm going to miss her too."

"I don't think I really want to live without her. What am I going to do?"

"You have to be strong, Dad. That's what you're going to do. Mother would want you to be strong."

"I don't know if I can," he said. "I don't know if I can."

At that moment I remembered the letter that my mother had given me. Maybe this was the appropriate time. "Dad," I said. "I have a letter for you from Mother. I originally thought that I would give it to you whenever she died, but I think that this might be the right moment."

I took the letter out of my purse and gave it to my father. Then I sat down at the dinette table next to him and watched him read it silently.

My dear Franz,

I always thought that I was put here on this earth to take care of you. And when you became ill, I decided that I alone had the power to keep you alive. But I always wondered how I would survive if anything ever happened to you. I must confess that this doubt may have motivated me to work even harder these last few years to keep you healthy. So please, Franzl, forgive me for my selfishness.

Now that I have come to the realization that I will probably predecease you, I have worried greatly about your physical and emotional stability. But you have Carie, and she has you, so you must take care of each other, and I will watch over the both of you.

Your job on this earth is not yet finished. Years ago when you were losing your voice but still tried to sing a few phrases of the "Four Serious Songs" to your mother in New York, you refrained from finishing the first Lied because you didn't want to sing of rejoicing about your own works. You felt that your life was over without your voice, and that you would never have any more accomplishments. Oh, Franzl, look at all that you have achieved! You worked your way up to the top of your profession. You made a new life for us in America, and you gave us a beautiful daughter. If you would only sing "Vier ernste Gesänge" now, I know that you would finish singing the whole cycle.

This is the last thing that I ask of you: After I die, please sing "Vier ernste Gesänge" whenever you are grief-stricken and sad that I have left you. The words in the third Lied – taken directly from the Old Testament (Ecclesiasticus 41, 1-2) – will tell you that death is a welcome sentence to an old man (or woman) with failing strength who can hope for nothing better. Therefore please accept my death, not with anguish, but with the understanding that death was better for me than a life of suffering. If you come to that realization, you will find peace within yourself, and you will be happy that God has taken away my pain.

And when you sing the last Lied, the words – taken from the New Testament (1 Corinthians 13, 1-3, 12-13) – will remind you to be thankful that we met, oh, so many years ago, and that from that moment on, we were blessed to love each other our whole lives through.

Again, take care of Carie – that is your job now – and she will take care of you. And one day, when it is the right time for you to come to me, when Carie has found your equal, I will be waiting for you with outstretched arms. We will both be strong again. And we will sleep together always, under a canopy that will forever shield us from harm.

This is my last gift to you, my dear husband. Keep it and treasure it, for it comes from deep within my heart and soul.

Thank you for all that you have given me! My love is eternal, and I am with you always.

Franziska

Tears were welling up in my father's eyes. When he was finished reading, he sat for a few moments without moving. He folded the letter, placed it back in the envelope and into his pocket. "I want to go back to your mother now," he said, standing, sighing, and looking quite spent.

I was curious about the contents of the letter, but I respected my father's privacy too much to ask. I stood up, readying myself to finish clearing the table. My father hugged me and held me for a very long time. No words were spoken, but I instinctively knew that he was going to be all right now. Whatever my mother had written to him, it must have been personal, moving, and uplifting. Maybe one day he would share the letter with me. But for now, I was relieved to see the change in his behavior.

My father finally released me. "I'm going back to your mother now," he said.

And I was soon washing the dishes.

"Carie . . . Carie!"

It couldn't have been more than five minutes later. My father was calling me from the living room.

I stopped what I was doing, dried my hands on a dishtowel, and ran to meet him.

"There's something different about your mother. Come! Come!"

We hastened through the living room, down the hallway, and into the bedroom.

Yes, there definitely had been a change. My mother was lying on her back taking deep, loud breaths, and her chest was heaving.

We just stood there at first, not knowing what to do.

"Franziska, are you in any pain?" my father shouted.

My mother's eyes were closed and she wasn't responding to him. The tubing from the oxygen machine was at her side. The machine hadn't seemed to do much good lately. My father placed the cannula into her nose anyway.

"Franzi, can you hear me? Are you asleep?"

No response. Was she in a coma? We felt helpless.

My father tried elevating her head on the pillow. Then he attempted to shoot a drop of morphine under her tongue with an eyedropper, but he was unsuccessful and the morphine rested on the top of her tongue instead.

My mother's mouth remained open. She wasn't swallowing. She seemed to be gasping. The morphine remained a pool atop the crevice of her tongue.

I was sitting on the chair next to her, spellbound. I stood up and touched her forehead soothingly, but her heaving movements frightened me so that I sat down again.

The breathing was so deep and loud, and she was making some sort of repetitive clicking noises as well. Was she making these crackling sounds with her tongue? Or were they emanating from her lungs or chest?

My father held my mother's hand and took her pulse. Her heartbeat was weak, and her hand felt quite cool. He pulled the covers over her.

"I didn't want Franzi to suffer," my father cried out to me. "But I can't figure out if she is or if she isn't. She seems to be in a coma. I don't know – can she hear me?"

"I think she's unconscious, Dad. I don't think that she's in any pain."

But there was no one there to answer my father's questions, no one there to assure him that Franziska was indeed not suffering. The hospice doctor wasn't due until the next day.

We were both sitting and waiting now. We'd lost track of the time. Franziska was working so hard to stay alive. She didn't want to leave us.

"It's all right, Mother," I finally uttered. "Dad and I will take care of each other. You can let go now. Let yourself rest."

I didn't know if my mother could hear me or not, but I wanted to comfort and relieve her from care. Then a few moments later, her breathing abruptly changed. After she had taken one of her regular deep breaths, she closed her mouth, swallowed, and stopped breathing. It was as if all of the air was being sucked out of her. She was so pale and sallow. And during those never-ending seconds, my father and I were holding our breath as well, worrying that this could possibly be the dreaded moment that we'd feared, the moment that we'd been preparing ourselves for, but didn't want to face. The silence was excruciating for us. But then Franziska opened her mouth and inhaled. She began to breathe loudly and deeply again. We were extremely relieved.

The pattern reoccurred a few minutes later though. Yet this time, the room remained silent; only the slight humming sound of the oxygen machine was still audible.

For one minute, for two, for three – Franziska was not breathing. My father grasped her wrist, desperately trying to find her pulse.

"I don't feel anything!" he said to me. "I don't feel anything!"

Then he tried to locate the pulse on her neck.

"Nothing," he uttered. "Nothing."

Franziska lay there motionless as my father removed the cannula from her nose. Her life had slipped away.

"Franzi! Franzi!" my father cried, draping his arms around her.

The tears were running down my cheeks as well.

"We've taken every journey in our lives together. But this last journey,

I cannot take with you. I am so sorry, my dear sweet Franziska. I am so sorry that I can no longer protect you."

My father was crying uncontrollably now.

"Good-bye, my beloved," he said, kissing my mother on the forehead. "Good-bye."

Epilogue

The Memorial Park
Los Angeles, California
October 14, 2012

$\mathcal{M}$y dear parents, once upon a time, there was a little girl who was blessed to have the best mother and dad that anyone in the world could ever have. They showered her with love, dressed her in beautiful clothes, and taught her all of the social graces. They taught her to be kind and respectful of all others, to be a moral person, and to be giving. But most important, they made her feel special. And even though this little girl had no siblings and few relatives, she never felt wanting. She loved her parents just as much as they loved her, and she was sure that they would never leave her.

But then one day, they did – first one, then the other. Although the little girl had grown up to become a fine woman, she still had no siblings and few relatives, and had never found true love. She was so lonely. She visited her deceased parents often, attaching vases of flowers to the knobs under their plaque, and sitting for hours on a stool beside their resting place. She read them poetry and the words to German *Lieder*. She told them about her dreams and aspirations, and then she cried:

"You left me, Dad, before you were supposed to. Why did you do that? Mother wanted you to stay with me until I found a man to share my dreams with, a man who could be your equal. That's what she wrote in her final letter to you."

And then the little girl, now a woman, apologized to her father for having read the letter which she'd found in the drawer of his nightstand. But, you see, when the woman had said her final good-byes to her father, she'd laid the letter beside him so that he could keep it for all times.

And then the little girl, now a woman, cried out once again:

"I am so lonely, Mother. Sometimes when I lie in bed at night unable to sleep, I close my eyes, hold on to my pillow, and cry. Then I imagine that you are bending over me, stroking my hair as if I were a child. I call out in the darkness of my bedroom. But when I open my eyes, you are never there. Never there to soothe me, to calm me, to protect me."

And then the little girl, now a woman, apologized to her mother for being so childish:

"I'm supposed to be a grown up, and I suppose that to the world at large, I am. But there's a child inside of me that wants to be nurtured. Sometimes I just don't want to be strong."

While the woman's father was still alive, she began to travel. She went to Vienna: to Pötzleinsdorfer Strasse and to Blütengasse Neun. She went to the Kursalon, the Musikverein and the Staatsoper, and she walked along the Kärntner Strasse, always imagining that both of her parents were promenading beside her. And then she went to the Czech Republic: to the theaters where her father had sung, and to the place where her parents were married.

And when she came home, she was a much richer person. Then she went to Zürich, Milano and Genova, and later to Venezuela, Panama, and Cuba. She was never lonely because she always pictured that her parents were nearby. And again, she came home much richer because of the experiences.

Day after day for more than three years, she typed her parents' passionate story on her computer, reading chapter after chapter to her dear old father, often interrupting to care for him after a stay at the hospital, grateful that he was able to still reminisce with her. And when she read the final pages to him, he was moved to tears.

The book remained unpublished while he was dying, but he kept it close to him and read parts of it over and over again, sometimes holding it very close to his eyes, peering at the pages with a magnifying glass. And when he did die, the little girl, the woman, buried the manuscript with him because it was his story.

So of course, my dear parents, by now you know that the little girl, the woman, is me. Whether I find true love or not, at least I know that Dad has enabled me to discover who I am and where I've come from. And can you imagine? People will soon be reading your story and seeing pictures of you, your passports with the big red "J" on them, and many other items that document historically that you were indeed Holocaust survivors; were locked up in Triscornia; and that you, Dad, lost your operatic voice and career, but it was your voice that saved your life so that you could begin anew with Mother in America.

And so for the first time in my life – as the U.S. war continues to escalate against terrorism – I understand the insecurities that you both felt when you became innocent victims fleeing from evil. The actions of the extremist Adolf Hitler were allowed to flourish then, thus causing a terrorism the likes of which the world had never known before. And even though other radical personalities have since threatened our very endurance, we have learned that history must not repeat itself. The importance of lasting relationships and the value of love have been re-awakened inside of us, as well as a sense of patriotism in pursuit of the American dream. So much like you, the challenges I face are making me stronger and more compassionate.

After you died, Dad, I discovered in the local Jewish newspaper that payment of restitution money would be given to the former Austrian Holocaust survivors and their heirs. I filled out numerous forms documenting your losses, crying in the process, and I received historical papers from the Austrian archives that gave me proof of our family's existence. Later I received monetary compensation from the General Settlement Fund for Victims of National Socialism. Never before have I felt more close to you. You are with me every minute of every day. And I am so very proud of my heritage. Although I remain alone, thoughts of you keep me moving forward as I pursue new endeavors.

No, Dad: You weren't supposed to leave me, not until I met your equal, not until you could share my joy with Mother. Yet I understand how you longed for your Franziska and were compelled to hasten to her. And although she could not take her final journey with you, at least you were able to take yours to her. I find solace in knowing that you have been reunited, and that you will rest in peace with each other for eternity. And if I do find the right person for me one day, I know there will be a way for me to share my happiness with you. Until then, I remain peaceful and content – because you have given me my foundation and remain the source of my strength.

I will love you both my whole life long and beyond. I thank you for all that you have given and taught me. You have made me who I am today.

Please forgive me if I choose to believe that you are watching over me like the stars to a planet, for I feel the warmth and luminescence of your light, and in my heart, your glow will never fade away.

APPENDIX
CHAPTER NOTES

Author's Afterthoughts, Observations, and Clarifications

RE: Introductory Note and Epilogue:

—I began writing *Serenade* in 1998 as a novel based on my parents' lives since they were not famous. My mother had passed away, but my father was alive. After my father died, I decided that I wanted to include photographs and copies of documents, passports, and actual letters. Most of the novel had been truthful. So I changed the fictional names of the main characters to those of my parents. I contacted archivists and did more fact-finding. I then reworked various events and moved them around, thus forming new chapters, to be accurate. I added my voice and narrative in the first person.

The book still reads like a novel with creative nonfiction narrative and dialogue, which help tell the story. But even down to the dates that various operas were performed, it is accurate. As a memoir, or nonfiction memory, I believe the book has more historical validity now and tells the true story of my parents who lived a very real but atypical Holocaust love story. Their story is unique because they were never in a concentration camp. My father's voice saved his and my mother's lives. And I, as the daughter of Holocaust survivors, carry their story with me every day and every hour of my life.

RE: Throughout the Book:

—Most of the letters printed or referred to throughout the book in the text are actual letters my father received. Some are included in the illustrations. Those include letters written by opera director Walter Eberhard; my grandmother, Olga Jung; conductor-libretto translator Thomas P. Martin; opera agent-managers André Mertens and Nelly Walter (Columbia Concerts Corporation of Columbia Broadcasting, CAMI); opera agent-manager Wilhelm Stein (Dr. Artur Hohenberg); baritone Lawrence Tibbett; Dr. Henry L. Williams, Mayo Clinic; and others.

—All of the quotes from operas, *Lieder*, and poetry were translated into English by my German-speaking father and I. I read various librettos and scores for each selection; and with the aid of my father and the common dictionary, I created the language of *Lieder* and opera that is written in this memoir.

—Some of the German-language street names could either be written as two words, two words with a hyphen, or as one word. I attempted to use the most common spellings.

Prologue:
—First quoted selection: Franz Schubert's "An die Musik," D. 547, with words by Franz von Schober.

—Second quoted selection: Schubert's "Der Wanderer" with words by Schmidt von Lübeck.

Chapter One - A Café and More:
—Sometimes the "u" in "Jung" was written with a "v-like" hook over it. Suetterlin writing was a type of script that was taught in German and Austrian schools from 1915 to about 1941. It was called "German handwriting." After the middle of the century, it was considered antiquated. The typed "u" did not have the hook.

—"An der schönen blauen Donau" ("On the Beautiful Blue Danube"): Composed by Johann Strauss II.

—"Geschichten aus dem Wienerwald" ("Tales from the Vienna Woods"): Composed by Johann Strauss II.

Chapter Two - Pötzleinsdorfer Strasse 130:
—Pötzleinsdorf is in the eighteenth district.

—Franz Jung address at birth was Ferdinandstrasse 29 in the second district.

—Siebenbürgen: German name for Transylvania.

Chapter Three – Blütengasse 9:

—Blütengasse Neun is in the third district.

—In Austria, "Perger" is pronounced "Pairger" or like the fruit: "Pear-ger." In the United States, the name is pronounced "Purr-ger," like the sound a cat makes.

—Heinrich Perger's original family name in Czechoslovakia was "Pereles." He must have changed it when he moved to Vienna.

—Franziska Perger's address at birth was Rembrandtstrasse 27 in the second district.

—Franziska had both Austrian and Czech birth certificates and documents. On all of her Czech documents, her name was "Františka Pergerová."

—Stefanie Perger was also known as Steffi Perger. Fritz Perger was also known as Fred.

Chapter Five – Bits and Pieces:

—The idea for the first lines of Franz's letter came from the Hugo Wolf *Lied*, "Heut Nacht erhob ich mich um Mitternacht," German translation by Paul Heyse. The concept is similar to "Last night I rose at midnight," but the words in the letter are different.

Chapter Six – Discovery:

—Regarding the long quote on opera technique: *Kammersänger* Arthur Fleischer, my father's voice teacher, was born in 1881 and died in San Francisco, California in 1948, where he was a successful voice teacher after a long renowned operatic career in opera houses including the Wiener Staatsoper, Volksoper, and the Berlin Kroll-Oper. In reality, the words on technique could have been quotes from my father, because he learned his technique from Fleischer. Yet through the years, my father perfected the technique, and he left me an audiotape and essay that described it. So since my father was a student in this chapter, I let his teacher tell him how to sing, and I hope that his teacher would agree if he were alive to read it. If not, then I hope he would accept my apology. The description is my father's interpretation of how he was taught.

—Naturally, I was not at the rally depicted at the end of the chapter and could not hear what was said. I devised the quotes based on my research from the books in the bibliography and from Adolf Hitler's own words in *Mein Kampf*.

Chapter Seven - The Lobau:

—The verse is from William Shakespeare's Sonnet 75.

Chapter Eight - Wiener Staatsoper; Burgtheater:

—My father saw Giuseppe Verdi's *Don Carlos* (*Don Carlo* in Italian) at the Wiener Staatsoper on the sixth of April, 1934, with a libretto by François Joseph Méry and Camille du Locle. My mother saw Schiller's *Don Carlos* at the Burgtheater in June 1932. My father told me that the subject really concerned them. They were together the night that Chancellor Dollfuss was killed.

—In the depiction of *Don Carlos* in this chapter, Elisabeth and Carlos do not begin the opera in the forest of Fontainebleau. The act is often eliminated.

Chapter Nine - Musikvereinsgebäude:

—Schubert's "Die Forelle," D. 550 ("The Trout"): Text by Christian Friedrich Daniel Schubart.

—My father told me about the Marian Anderson recital. He said that the hall was not crowded, but that after the critics heard Anderson's voice and spread the news, the theater was filled for the subsequent concert a few days later.

I have tried to determine when this concert occurred. I finally gave up and simply placed it in 1935. According to the archival records in the Musikverein, Marian Anderson had three recitals in 1935. The first was on the twenty-second of March. The second and third were spaced close together on the twenty-first and twenty-eighth of November. But that would not make sense since my father said he saw Ms. Anderson's début performance in Vienna, and few people knew anything about her until after the first performance. Plus, I found an article in *The New York Times* by Herbert F. Peyser that said: "But a sensation of the Vienna music season, and to date perhaps its most dramatic event, has been the début here of the colored contralto from Philadelphia, Marian Anderson. In less than two weeks she has given two recitals. The first was attended by a handful. The second was mobbed." And to confuse the issue even more, that article in *The New York Times* was dated the tenth of March in 1935, which was before any of the dates from the records in the Musikverein. In fact, at the top of the article, which seems to be a group of reviews from Vienna, there is the date of 17 February 1935. So then I checked with the Konzerthaus, although my father heard Anderson in the Musikverein, and she sang there on the sixth of December in 1936 and on the twenty-sixth of November in 1937, which were still later dates. So I just placed the recital in 1935.

Also, my father said that Marian Anderson's recital was in the Brahms-Saal, but the archival records indicate that it was in the Grossen Saal.

—"Der Tod und das Mädchen": Text by Matthias Claudius.

—There were no records of performances given by students in the Neues Wiener Konservatorium, so 1935 is as accurate as I could be.

—Wolfgang Amadeus Mozart's *The Marriage of Figaro*: Libretto by Lorenzo da Ponte after the Beaumarchais comedy.

Chapter Ten - Beginnings:

—I did not know Appenzeller's first name, so I made it "Gustav."

—"Der Doppelgänger" is part of Franz Schubert's *Schwanengesang* cycle (D. 957).

—"Erlkönig" may mean "Erl King," "Alder King," or "Elf King" when translated into English. It is often written in two words, in two words with a hyphen between them, or sometimes as in German, in one word.

Chapter Eleven - The *Opernball*:

—According to my father, the Appenzellers owned the dress shop. He often went there to pick my mother up after work, and he confirmed the story written in this chapter. However, I could only find Berta Appenzeller's name, which is on a website that lists victims of the "Theresienstadt" (or "Terezín") concentration camp, devised by the Terezín Initiative Institute, National Archives, Prague. Before deportation on the fourteenth of August in 1942, Berta's listed address was Neubaugasse 46, so I connected her name to the store, since my father could not remember it. Her death certificate, also on the website, indicates that her name was "Bertha," so that is the name I have given her in the book. She died ten days after deportation. This information was confirmed by a letter to me from the National Archives. I have attempted to be accurate regarding the owners of the Appenzeller dress shop.

Chapter Twelve - Björling:

—Mozart's *Don Giovanni*: Libretto by Lorenzo da Ponte.

—The "Catalogue Song" is also known as the "Catalogue Aria," the "Catalog" aria, the catalog aria, and various other versions of the same thing. My father called it the "Register" aria.

Chapter Thirteen - Paul Eger:

—Paul Eger (1881-1947) was the general director of the New German Theater (Neues Deutsches Theater) from 1932 to 1938. He left Prague in fall 1938 for Switzerland where he died with failing health in 1947.

Chapter Fourteen - Beckmesser:

—In the first letter dated 5 September 1937, Schubert's "Ständchen" is in the *Schwanengesang* cycle. Words are by Ludwig Rellstab.

—In the second letter dated 15 September 1937, the verse is from William Shakespeare's Sonnet 47.

—Regarding the third letter dated 15 October 1937, I possess portions of music reviews without the dates or names of the newspapers. The *Aussiger Tagblatt* was a local newspaper in Aussig.

—In the third letter dated 15 October 1937, with reference to Franz Allers: Allers (1905-1995) left Czechoslavakia in 1938 for New York where he became the conductor and music director of many hit

Broadway musicals by Alan Jay Lerner and Frederick Loewe, including *My Fair Lady* and *Camelot*. After 1962, he returned to conducting opera in the United States and Europe. He resided in Munich at the time of his death.

—Much of the performance information on the New German Theater has been lost, although a history book of the theater with some dates has been published. *Die Meistersinger* was performed on 5 January 1938. There could have been more than one dress rehearsal. I did not know the date or time, so I approximated based on the norm. My father simply told me that he had covered for a dress rehearsal of *Meistersinger*.

Chapter Fifteen – Henlein and the King:
—Verdi's *Aïda*: Libretto by Antonio Ghislanzoni.

Chapter Sixteen -- Annexation:
—"We are yielding to force. . . ." From Paul Hofmann, *The Viennese* (New York: Anchor Press, Doubleday, 1988), p. 231.

—"As Führer and Chancellor of the German nation . . ." From Paul Hofmann, *The Viennese* (New York: Anchor Press, Doubleday, 1988), p. 236.

Chapter Seventeen – Dr. Bartolo:
—*Anschluss* means the joining, connecting, and in this case, the union of Austria with the German Reich. The word "annexation" means adding to something: the incorporation of one country into the territory of another. Austria became a province of Germany: the province of Ostmark (Eastern March), gaining independence after World War II.

—I do not know exactly when Olga Jung moved to Sieveringerstrasse 12. I tried to find the address and think that I did, although the building was somehow camouflaged by the building on the corner with the address of Weinzingergasse 1.

—My parents were living in Smíchov. When I went to Prague, no taxi driver could find their address, which was Nábřeží Legií 22, XVI. Years later I figured out the problem. The district numbers in Prague change and the boundaries change within them. Smíchov is now District V. My Czech girlfriend also told me that the streets change as well. "*Nábřeží*" means "embankment." "*Legií*" means "Legions." There is a Bridge of Legions, for example. So the district number and street seemed nonexistent, but the district is there; only it is District V. I found the district, just not the address in it.

Mail and telegrams were addressed to Franz Jung, but "c/o Fried." He must have either been the owner or manager.

—Gioacchino Rossini's *The Barber of Seville* (*Il Barbiere di Siviglia*) is based on the play by Beaumarchais. Libretto by Cesare Sterbini.

—My father performed Dr. Bartolo in *Barber* the end if April, on 27 April 1938, according to the archived records from the theater in Aussig, which is now Ústí nad Labem. According to the archivist, this was the last performance of *Barber* before the season ended. It was performed on a Wednesday. The season calender concluded on 30 April 1938.

My father told me that the incident happened during a matinée performance, which led me to believe that it was on a Sunday. He told me that he thought it occurred in about mid-May or after, when there was evidence of troop movement on the northern border of Czechoslovakia. Henlein broke off negotiations with the Czech government on the ninth of May, and on his return from London on the fourteenth, he met with Hitler at Berchtesgaden. Tensions between Czechs and Germans escalated during May due to Joseph Goebbels' propaganda efforts. I also had the feeling that my father performed Dr. Bartolo more than one time as he did other scheduled operas, but according to the chronology that I received from the archivist, there was only one performance of *Barber*.

I have placed the performance as indicated by the theater, and as a matinée. It is possible that my 93-year-old father did not remember the date. His photographs as Dr. Bartolo are dated April 1938. But he remembered the incident vividly. He told me that he had been very excited by the situation, and there was definitely tension and crisis in the Sudetenland in April already.

—André Mertens headed the agency, André Mertens & Company,

and he was the general European representative of the Columbia Concerts Corporation of Columbia Broadcasting System. By 1940, he had immigrated to New York, where he became an artists' manager at Columbia Concerts Corporation, and later, a vice president. Columbia Concerts became known as Columbia Artists Management Incorporated, or CAMI, which is one of the largest and most prestigious agencies for performing artists and opera singers in the world. Mertens represented great artists including Leontyne Price. He died in 1963 at the age of 59.

Chapter Eighteen – Mobilization Day:

—My father told me that the Palestine Opera was being formed and organized at the time of this chapter. According to some sources, it was already in existence although it was Walter Eberhard's first attempt at becoming its director. Mordechai Golinkin was the first visionary to bring opera to Palestine and was one of the directors of the Palestine Opera, which was also called the National Opera of Palestine.

—I am not sure of the consul general's name.

Chapter Nineteen – Broken Glass and a Café:

—I do not know the date of the incident when my father was practicing the role of Alberich. The New German Theater produced the *Ring* in January 1938. My father could have been a cover for those performances, but he didn't indicate that he was. January seemed too early for the incident to have occurred. So I approximated.

—Hermann Göring: "A petty segment of Europe is harassing the human race. . . ." From William L. Shirer, *The Rise and Fall of the Third Reich* (New York: Simon & Schuster Inc., 1988), p. 383.

—Adolf Hitler: "The Germans in Czechoslovakia are neither defenseless nor abandoned. . . ." From Gordon A. Craig, *Germany* (New York: Oxford University Press, 1978), p. 705.

—I described the Pergers' immigration to Australia as told to me by my father. As a side note, my father told me that Paul and Fritz Perger had married. However Fritz's wife went to Czechoslovakia and stayed with her uncle before immigrating to Australia.

—Regarding the letter/agreement from Nelly Walter (1901-2001) on behalf of André Mertens, dated 22 November 1938: the letter appears to have been written from Paris. When the Germans marched into Paris, Walter went into hiding with her mother in Marseille. She was sent to a concentration camp, escaped, and immigrated to New York City in 1946 when André Mertens gave her a management position at Columbia Artists Management Incorporated (CAMI). Later, as a vice president of CAMI, she represented many great artists, including Renata Tebaldi, Cesare Siepi, José Carreras, Ferruccio Furlanetto, Giuseppe Di Stefano and Ettore Bastianini. She was instrumental in shaping the careers of Plácido Domingo, Leonard Bernstein, and many other great singers.

—Mail to Franz at Petrská 24, including the Nelly Walter letter, was sometimes addressed to him "c/o Koopmann," who must have been the owner or manager.

Chapter Twenty-One – The Hideaway:

—My father did not remember the name of the bank he went to in Zürich. I visited a number of them in 1999. I chose Bank Leu to describe because of its architecture, but I have no evidence to believe that Bank Leu was the correct location. In 1990, the bank became a subsidiary of Credit Suisse. In 2007, Credit Suisse merged its four independent private banks – Clariden, Bank Leu, Bank Hofmann, and Banca di Gestione Patrimoniale – with Credit Suisse Fides, to form a single unit known as Clariden Leu.

Chapter Twenty-Two – Good-Bye . . . :

—The libretto of Giacomo Puccini's *La Bohème*: By Giuseppe Giacosa and Luigi Illica, based on Henri Murger's *Scènes de la vie de bohème* and his play with Théodore Barrière, *La vie de bohème*.

—I do not know where the *Rialto* docked. It is unclear whether or not my parents boarded the *Rialto* on the Ponte Andrea Doria embarkation pier at the Stazione Marittima. After extensive research, I attained a document describing the ship's general journey. It appears that it did depart from Genova. However, my father believed that he and my mother left from Nervi, formerly a small fishing town adjacent to Genova.

It is more likely that they embarked from the Stazione Marittima in Genova, however.

Chapter Twenty-Three – On the *Rialto*:

— "Der Wegweiser" is part of Schubert's *Winterreise* cycle (D. 911).

—Georges Bizet's *Carmen*: Libretto by Henri Meilhac and Ludovic Halévy after the novella by Prosper Mérimée.

Chapter Twenty-Four – Cine General Salom:

—The Cine General Salom was named after General Bartolomé Salom who was the general in chief of the army of Venezuela in the War of Independence.

—I wrote at the end of the chapter that Boleslav Manowski was not the name of the man who was so gracious to my father, although the signature on the postcard could have been a similar name. I chose to use a name to enhance the realism of the story. I did find an article that said that the owner of the theater was General Briceno, but my father said that the owner was Polish and was a businessman; however it is possible that he was the gentleman my father spoke of. He naturally spoke fluent Spanish. Also, there was an excerpt which was a chapter in Adolfo Aristegueta Gramcko's book, *Elves, Fairies, Witches and Puerto Cabello*. It stated that Charles Martell attended the box office. The illegible signature on the postcard could possibly be his, judging from the letters that are perceivable.

—"Because": Composed by Guy D'Hardelot (Helen Rhodes).

—"I'll Be Seeing You": Music by Sammy Fain. Lyrics by Irving Kahal.

Chapter Twenty-Six – Triscornia:

—Various names describe the synagogue and Jewish community center in Havana that I visited. The Gran Sinagoga de la Comunidad Hebrea de Cuba is also known as Sinagoga Beth Shalom. The community center is called El Casa de la Comunidad Hebrea de Cuba, and the whole complex is known as "El Patronato."

—Dr. Federico Larado Brú was president of Cuba from 1936 to 1940. Fulgencio Batista y Zaldívar was president of Cuba from 1940 to 1944.

He rose to power in 1933 during the "Revolt of the Sergeants" and became chief of the armed forces. Thus he controlled the presidency and had the power, making Brú a puppet president. But Brú made the decisions regarding the *St. Louis* (Chapter Twenty-Seven) since Batista did not interfere.

Although the passengers were taken in by various countries, many of them perished in death camps when Hitler's armies invaded Western Europe.

—To describe Triscornia, I used a document given to me by Maritza Corrales, a Cuban writer I met at the Jewish synagogue in Havana. She told me she secured it from the American Jewish Joint Distribution Committee of New York. The organization was working with the Joint Relief Committee in Havana to provide assistance to the refugees in Triscornia. The document shows a more pessimistic description of the camp than I portrayed. Many people had amoebic dysentery and what was described as "seasonal grippe." There were cases of whooping cough, jaundice, and incidences of heart problems. There were bedbugs and lice. The Joint Relief Committee was sending one thousand oranges and one thousand bananas or pineapples to Triscornia each day, and eggs, sardines, milk, and butter. The organization was also providing valuable medication to the sick. Some people perished from weakness.

I focused on the wonderful relief efforts made by the Hebrew Immigrant Aid Society (HIAS) because that is the organization that was so invaluable to my parents. It is the organization they always felt indebted to. However, I have read articles and documents that show the incredible efforts made by the American Jewish Joint Distribution Committee and the Jewish Relief Committee. So I must mention them all here with my gratitude.

Chapter Twenty-Seven – Good And Bad:

—Max Schenirer was known as Mack Shearer once in the United States. He married Dora Kohn, and she became Dora Shearer. Dora remarried after Mack Shearer's death and became Dora Kohn Shearer Warren.

—Again *The Marriage of Figaro* (*Le nozze di Figaro*): Libretto by Lorenzo da Ponte.

—"Rauschender Strom . . ." From Schubert's "Aufenthalt" or "The Resting Place," which is part of the *Schwanengesang* cycle. Words by Ludwig Rellstab.

—I do not know the name of the lawyer my father wrote to in Prague to secure his and my mother's quota numbers.

—Paul Csonka (1905-1995): After years of hearing my father mention the name of "Csonka," I suddenly found him on the Internet. He was the son of the largest oil importer in Austria and Hungary, but there was a rumor that he might have been the illegitimate son of Kaiser Franz Joseph. I knew that he and his father had been business partners with one of my father's uncles. I even have a letter written from agent André Mertens to my father in Cuba in which Mertens sends his regards through my father to Csonka (in illustrations). But Csonka was not destined to remain in the family business. He had a love for music – composed and conducted. He formed the Salzburg Opera Guild which performed all over Europe. Although raised Catholic, he had one Jewish ancestor and settled in Havana, Cuba, where he is found in this chapter.

I do not have a time table, but Csonka built up the Opera Nacional de Havana and directed Havana orchestras. According to various sources, he brought Plácido Domingo, Jussi Björling, Elisabeth Schwarzkopf, Clemens Krauss, and other great opera singers and conductors to Havana.

Fidel Castro approached him to become the national director of music in Cuba when he was in his 50s, but he fled to the United States instead. He formed the Civic Opera of the Palm Beaches (Palm Beach Opera) and developed a roster of singers, which included Beverly Sills, Domingo, Luciano Pavarotti, Robert Merrill, Anna Moffo, Licia Albanese, and others. There is an annual scholarship given by the Palm Beach Opera in his name.

I heard Csonka's name mentioned many times. My father had no idea what had become of him because after my father lost his voice, he was psychologically disengaged from the opera world.

Chapter Twenty-Eight – Saving Face:

—Verdi's *Rigoletto* is based on *Le roi s'amuse* by Victor Hugo. Libretto by Francesco Maria Piave.

—Walter Herbert: Baritone Walter Herbert was one of my father's best friends while a student at the Neues Wiener Konservatorium and thereafter. My father always referred to him as "Herbert." I called him "Walter" in the book because I have a letter from my father's agent, Wilhelm Stein, dated 4 May 1938 (in illustrations), and he refers to Herbert as "Walter" in the letter. In most later sources Herbert is named "Ralph" Herbert and listed as a bass-baritone. He sang at the Volksoper in Vienna and then in Cuba. Naturally the incident in this chapter is true, and based on how my father remembered it.

Ralph Herbert (1909-1995) made an illustrious career for himself in most of the companies in the United States, including the Met. He became proficient in many of the roles my father sang (ie. Alberich and Klingsor). He taught at Mannes College of Music, the Manhattan School of Music, and was on the faculty of the University of Michigan School of Music.

Chapter Twenty-Nine – The Park:

—"Bei mir bist du schön": Composed by Sholom Secunda with lyrics by Jacob Jacobs. Later, new lyrics by Sammy Cahn and Saul Chaplin.

—"Fascinating Rhythm": From *Rhapsody In Blue* by George and Ira Gershwin.

—"Lullaby of Broadway": Music by Harry Warren. Words by Al Dubin.

—"The Continental": Music by Con Conrad. Words by Herb Magidson.

Chapter Thirty – The Voice of Freedom:

—"Vier ernste Gesänge": Composed by Johannes Brahms.

Chapter Thirty-One – Encounters:

—Hatschek: I was unable to find Hatschek's first name.

Chapter Thirty-Two – Trials and Tribulations:

—I do not know at which high school my father sang. The John Jay High School was a possibility.

—Thomas Philipp Martin (1909-1984) was Arthur Fleischer's son. He was a staff conductor with both the Metropolitan Opera and the New York City Opera. He was associate chorus master at the Met and director of musical studies at the City Opera.

After graduating from the Neues Wiener Konservatorium, he conducted at the Volksoper and then toured the United States with the Salzburg Opera Guild, mentioned previously as the company formed by Paul Csonka.

Martin is also known for his numerous libretto translations from German and Italian into English with his gifted journalist wife, Ruth Kelley Martin.

Thomas attempted to help my father by giving him a new direction. My father was always grateful.

Chapter Thirty-Three – HIAS to the Rescue – Again:

—Senta's full name was Senta Greene.

Chapter Thirty-Four – "The Star-Spangled Banner":

—*Die Fledermaus*: Music by Johann Strauss, Jr. Libretto in German by Carl Haffner and Richard Genée based on the French farce *Le Reveillon* of Henri Meilhac and Ludovic Halévy, which stemmed from the German comedy by Roderich Benedix: *The Prison*.

—"Swing Low, Sweet Chariot": Negro Spiritual: Wallis Willis. Harry T. Burleigh did an arrangement.

—"The Star-Spangled Banner": Words by Francis Scott Key. Music by John Stafford Smith.

Chapter Thirty-Five – Turning Point:

—Although the doctors could never truly determine the cause for my father's loss of voice, he did tell me that somewhere along the way (which could have even meant after he moved to Los Angeles), a doctor had told him that his vocal cords looked like the vocal cords of an old man.

Chapter Thirty-Six - Hollywood Hope:

—I do not know the exact wording of the oath used when my parents became United States citizens. This section of Chapter Thirty-Six was paraphrased from a document sent to me by the U.S. District Court on Spring Street in Los Angeles – the Central District (formerly the Southern District in 1945), also known as the U.S. Courthouse. The clerk's office sent the oath of citizenship to me.

Chapter Thirty-Seven - Eliot Ness, DeMille, and Me:

—"The Rusty Heller Story" was the first episode of the second season of *The Untouchables* in 1960. In addition to Robert Stack and Elizabeth Montgomery, who was nominated for an Emmy, Charles "Pops" Felcher was played by Harold Stone; Archie Grayson was played by David White; Walter Winchell narrated. Ness's agents were Paul Picerni, Nicholas Georgiade, Abel Fernandez, and Steve London. Walter Grauman directed. The producers were Jerry Thorpe, Lloyd Richards, and Josef Shaftel. Production managers were Argyle Nelson and Marvin Stuart. The assistant director was Vincent McEveety.

—I am not sure of Dr. Leon Gruneberg's first name. It may not have been "Leon."

Chapter Thirty-Eight - A Sad Farewell From Theresienstsadt:

—In reference to the letter: my great-aunt Antschi's full name was Antschi Werner Fischer. It is unclear if she died in Theresienstadt or Treblinka (a Nazi extermination camp in Poland). According to the website of records and digitized documents sponsored by the Terezín Initiative Institute, National Archives, Prague, and to a letter to me from the National Archives — someone named Anna Fischer (who may have been Antschi Fischer) was transported from Vienna to Theresienstadt on the tenth of July in 1942. She was moved to Treblinka a few months later, where she was murdered. So Antschi died either in Theresienstadt or Treblinka.

—The digitized copies of records posted on the website sponsored by the Terezín Initiative Institute in Prague indicate the word "murder" as the cause of death of those who perished in Terezín.

Chapter Thirty-Nine – Snapdragon:

—My father has sometimes been credited as "costume designer." He was a member of the Academy of Motion Picture Arts and Sciences.

—I believe that today, the doctors would label my mother's ailment as having been a form of COPD (chronic obstructive pulmonary disease). The term became more prevalent after the 1990s.

In Conclusion:

—Some critics may categorize this memoir as a novel. The events and people are real, even if my father could not remember all of the names. The dialogue and embellished scenes give life to truth. I do not mind if a reader "*feels*" like he or she is reading a novel. My goal is to allow the reader to enjoy the *Serenade* experience. My narration and the actual illustrations substantiate my claim that this is indeed a truthful nonfiction memoir.

ACKNOWLEDGMENTS

The process of writing *Serenade* has been the most singularly significant happening and journey in my life. It has changed and enriched me forever. From a novel to truthful memoir, I needed to nail down exact dates and events, which I did with the help of some knowledgeable archivists. Some of those mentioned may have retired or changed positions, since this book has taken years to create, but their names are worthy of acknowledgment.

I must begin with my father, Frank Delmar. Naturally, I thank my mother as well; however, my father was there for me every step of the way until his death. He provided me with photographs, documents, and letters. But mostly, he provided me with his love and endless devotion to this project.

Next I must praise my graphic designer, Jamie Saloff, who worked tirelessly with me to create the *Serenade* look. She answered my numerous questions about the publishing process with patience, and I am very fortunate to have found her.

Much thanks also to Mary Fisher who created the cover my mind was envisioning, and to my wonderful team of professionals, including Carolyn Anderson, Chris Raines, Mirko Bonet, Kathleen Brown, Rachel Palmer, and Diane Musto.

Marvin Chau at Henry Printing & Graphic made my illustrations fly across the miles and into the pages of this book. Thank you for adding and sending and adding and sending so that the illustrations almost tell the whole story.

Since I traveled to each locale described in this memoir, I must thank the late Dr. Paul Claussen who directed policy studies in the Office of the Historian at the United States Department of State. I telephoned his office with a question one day, which led to his long-lasting friendship and support during my journey from airport to airport and port to port.

That said, I will begin at the beginning with Vienna, Austria. Thank you to Elizabeth Krotouski and Jakub Opalski for enabling me to see everything on my extensive list. Thank you to Michael Schwab and to Robert and Judith Zafir for welcoming me into their homes, which were once the homes of my parents. Thank you to Franklin Fanning and Vivien Cooksley for informing me about what it might have been like to be a student at the prestigious Neues Wiener Konservatorium, and to Daniela Franke at the Österreichisches Theatermuseum, Ilse Kosz at the Gesellschaft der Musikfreunde, Marie-Louise Löffelhardt at the Staatsopermuseum, and Felix Brachetka at the Volksoper.

In Prague, I am indebted to the staff of the Hotel Palace Praha. They went far beyond my hotel needs. Even years later, when I telephone the hotel with a question, there is always someone there to oblige me. Thank you Nina Schlossarová for that.

When I go to Prague the next time, I will visit Sasha Stogevska. When I was unable to find information, she located the appropriate sources for me. One such person was Tomáš Vrbka at the Documentation Centre of the Státní Opera Praha.

While in Ústí nad Labem – Aussig at the time of my story – Blanka Housová and Vlasta Kralová made me feel welcome. I would also like to acknowledge Vladimir Kaiser, who provided me with additional information.

Dr. Jan Binar, of the Rotary Club Mánes, brought my parents' wedding reception to life. And Ivana Hlausova and Martin Klucar answered my endless questions at the Czech Consulate in Los Angeles.

Thank you to Mariel Baumann at the Opernhaus Zürich, to Matteo

Sartorio at the Teatro alla Scala, and to Lorenzo Buccellati, the Consul General of Panama in Milan.

I could have never toured Puerto Cabello the way I did without the preparatory organization accomplished by Jadwiga Romanowska in Caracas, which led me to my guide, Nerio Plazola, and to Giovanni Godobo and Mirtha Onez.

As for Panama, Wayne Baxter drove me around the port of Cristóbal, Colón, the Panama Canal area, and Panama City, which was when I met Ricardo Dupuy, who was an official at the port of Cristóbal. What a fascinating day I had! In addition, I talked to Raphael Guardia at the Associated Steamship Agents, and to Carolina Mouritzen at the Panamanian Consulate in San Diego.

I feel extremely privileged to have been able to visit Havana, Cuba legally from Miami. I am indebted to Jeffrey DeLaurentis, who was the First Secretary of Politics & Economics in the U.S. Interests Section when I was there in 1999. He has held various Foreign Service posts, has been the Deputy Assistant Secretary of State for the Bureau of Western Hemisphere Affairs, and was sworn in as the Alternate Representative of the United States for Special Political Affairs in the United Nations in 2011. I was in good hands. He introduced me to my guide Nilda Carreras from the Cultural Affairs Department, who graciously accompanied me around Havana, which included to the apartment where my parents had lived and to what was once the spot of the immigration camp, Triscornia. Under the direction of Carlos Díaz La Rosa, the vice director of SUMARPO at the time (Maritime Port Supplies), I was able to wander around the area to create a vision for myself for the Triscornia chapter. But I could not have derived that vision without the help of Adela Dworin at the Gran Sinagoga de la Comunidad Hebrea de Cuba (Sinagoga Beth Shalom), who introduced me to Cuba's Jewish past, or without the invaluable information imparted to me by Maritza Corrales, a Cuban historian and writer.

I also want to thank the Friedländers - Michal, Albert and Dorrit - for information on the Pension Friedländer, and to Robert Witajewski, the former Deputy Director of the Office of Cuban Affairs for the Cuban Interests Office in Washington, D.C. My trip to Cuba was a fruitful one.

It seems apt for me to mention the help I received while writing the travel chapters in memory of the *S.S. Rialto* and the *Chiriquí*. I want to thank the maritime historian and author, Mark Goldberg, who wrote *Going Bananas: 100 Years of American Fruit Ships in the Caribbean*, and maritime experts Bill Kooiman (San Francisco), and Michael Cropper and Ping Bodine in Los Angeles. I received significant information about the *Chiriquí* from Magnes Welsh at Chiquita Brands International and from Nancy Van Orman, the daughter of one of the ship's captains.

Back on solid ground, thank you to John Pennino at the Metropolitan Opera, for providing me with archived information and press releases. And a thank you to Dr. Else Goldstein for taking me back to the days of her colorful father, Dr. Wilhelm (William) Mayer-Hermann.

I especially enjoyed the very history-conscious residents of Knoxville, Tennessee, who displayed great pride in their city. Thank you Candra Phillips, who at the time of my visit was a research librarian for the Knox County Public Library System; Sally Polhemus at the McClung Historical Collection; and David Douglas of the East Tennessee Historical Society. Thank you Loretta Best and Kelly Woods for some church information, and to Mark Tucker, Jennifer Barnett and Carol Taylor of the Knoxville Symphony Society, for enabling me to capture a moment in history.

In Chattanooga, archivists John and Mary Lee Germann clued me in on the First Methodist Church. And the research librarians at the Chattanooga-Hamilton County Bicentennial Library were also helpful.

Thank you to Bill Taylor of the Sixth U.S. Cavalry Museum for a history of Fort Oglethorpe, and to Sue Bales and Peggy Stanfield for their hospitality.

Back at home in Los Angeles, I am grateful for the direction I received from the research librarians at UCLA and at the Central Library of the Los Angeles Public Library. Thank you to Ethel Pattison, Los Angeles International Airport's airport historian, and to the staff of the Museum of Television and Radio. I appreciated talking to respiratory therapist George Raber, and to the very empathetic, warm and nurturing Paula Hinz, a licensed clinical social worker who specializes in Hospice issues.

I am indebted to my cousin John Friend from Down Under for family details, and to Marion Marchal, my cousin through marriage who is my real cousin at heart.

I never expected the wonderful written compliments I received from the people I hold in such high esteem. Thank you Frederica von Stade, E. Randol Schoenberg, Yitzchok Adlerstein, Vladimir Chernov, Rabbi Jerry Cutler, Peter Kazaras, and Paul Lawrence Rose. Your graciousness overwhelms me.

I am so very grateful to my friends for their support and encouragement during the process toward publication. Many read my manuscript before publication. They were forever patient, and always attempted to answer my questions with objectivity. Their insightful comments were invaluable to me. Much appreciation goes to William and Ligia Toutant, Patsy McNally, Dana Dvorak, Rebecca Bowne, Howard Richman, Barbara Friend, Joan Schiff, Art Kress, Diane Gerry, Stuart Tower, and others. If I was negligent in mentioning the name of someone who helped me, the negligence was unintentional, so please forgive me. I am very grateful and appreciative of every single person who has helped me create a step on my *Serenade* staircase.

SELECTED BIBLIOGRAPHY

Books, Plays, Poetry, Screenplays, Articles:

Björling, Anna-Lisa, and Andrew Farkas. *Jussi*. Portland: Amadeus Press, 1996.

Blum, Daniel. *A New Pictorial History of the Talkies*. New York: G.P. Putnam's Sons, 1968.

Brooks, Tim, and Earle Marsh. *The Complete Directory to Prime Time Network TV Shows, Fourth Edition: 1946-Present*. New York: Ballantine Books, 1988.

Byock, Ira. *Dying Well: Peace and Possibilities at the End of Life*. New York: Riverhead Books, The Berkley Publishing Group, a division of Penguin Putnam, 1997.

Caruso, Enrico, and Luisa Tetrazzini. *Caruso and Tetrazzini on the Art of Singing*. 1909. Reprint, New York: Dover Publications, 1975.

Connors, Martin, ed., and Jim Craddock, ed. *VideoHound's Golden Movie Retriever*. Detroit: Visible Ink Press, 1998.

Craig, Gordon A. *Germany: 1866-1945*. New York and Oxford: Oxford University Press, 1978.

Fischer, Klaus P. *Nazi Germany: A New History*. New York: Continuum, 1996.

Fletcher, Andrew J., Robert Berkow, ed., Mark H. Beers, ed. *The Merck Manual of Medical Information: Home Edition*. New Jersey: Merck Research Laboratories, a division of Merck & Co., 1997.

Friedländer, Saul. *Nazi Germany and the Jews, Vol 1: The Years of Persecution, 1933-1939*. New York: HarperCollins, 1997.

Frischauer, Willi. *Behind the Scenes of Otto Preminger*. New York: William Morrow & Company, 1974.

Gold, Annalee. *75 Years of Fashion*. New York: Fairchild Publications, 1975.

Goldberg, Mark H. *Going Bananas: 100 Years of American Fruit Ships in the Caribbean.* New York: The American Merchant Marine Museum Foundation – North American Maritime Books, 1993.

Gorsline, Douglas. *What People Wore: A Visual History of Dress from Ancient Times to Twentieth-Century America.* New York: The Viking Press, 1952.

Hartman, Rev. Louis F., ed., and Rev. Francis T. Gignac, ed. *The New American Bible With Revised Book of Psalms and Revised New Testament.* Iowa Falls, Iowa: Catholic World Press, World Publishing, 1997.

Herman, Lewis, and Marguerite Shalett Herman. *American Dialects: A Manual for Actors, Directors, and Writers.* New York: A Theatre Arts Book, Routledge, 1997.

———. *Foreign Dialects: A Manual for Actors, Directors, and Writers.* New York: A Theatre Arts Book, Routledge, 1997.

Hines, Jerome. *Great Singers on Great Singing.* 1982. Reprint, New York: Limelight Editions, Proscenium Publishers, 1995.

———. *The Four Voices of Man.* New York: Limelight Editions, Proscenium Publishers, 1997.

Hines, William E. *Job Descriptions for Film, Video & CGI, 5th Edition.* Los Angeles: Ed-Venture Films/Books, 1999.

Hitler, Adolf. *Mein Kampf.* 1925. Reprint, Boston: Houghton Mifflin Company, 1971.

Hofmann, Paul. *The Viennese: Splendor, Twilight, and Exile.* New York: Anchor Press, Doubleday, 1988.

Holden, Amanda, ed., Nicholas Kenyon, ed., and Stephen Walsh, ed. *The Penguin Opera Guide.* New York: Penguin Books USA, 1996.

Holy Bible, The: King James Version. New York: Ivy Books, Ballantine Books, a division of Random House, 1991.

Ionazzi, Daniel A. *The Stagecraft Handbook.* Cincinnati: Betterway Books, 1996.

Jones, J. Morris, ed., and David C. Whitney, ed. *The World Book Encyclopedia.* 1917. Reprint, Chicago: Field Enterprises, 1955.

Keller, Ulrich. *The Building of the Panama Canal in Historic Photographs.* New York: Dover Publications, 1983.

Kennedy, Michael. *The Concise Oxford Dictionary of Music, Fourth Edition.* Oxford and New York: Oxford University Press, 1996.

Klemperer, Victor. *I Will Bear Witness: A Diary of the Nazi Years, 1933-1941.* Translated by Martin Chalmers. New York: Random House, 1998.

Langellier, John P. *The War In Europe: From the Kasserine Pass to Berlin, 1942-1945: The Illustrated History of the American Soldier, His Uniform and His Equipment.* London: Greenhill Books, Lionel Leventhal Limited, 1995, and Mechanicsburg, Pennsylvania: Stackpole Books, 1995.

Lehmann, Lilli. *How to Sing.* Translated by Richard Aldrich. 1902. Reprint, New York: Dover Publications, 1993.

Mackenzie, Aeneas, Jesse L. Lasky, Jr., Jack Gariss, and Fredric M. Frank. Cecil B. DeMille, producer-director. *The Ten Commandments.* Final shooting script. Los Angeles: Paramount Pictures, Dec. 21, 1954.

McConathy, Dale, with Diana Vreeland. *Hollywood Costume: Glamour! Glitter! Romance!* New York: Harry N. Abrams, 1976.

Michaelis, Ruth. *The German Lied.* Würzburg, Germany: Stürtz Verlag AG, 1977.

Morton, Frederic. *A Nervous Splendor: Vienna.* 1979. Reprint, New York: Penguin Books USA, 1980.

Osborne, Robert. *50 Golden Years of Oscar: The Official History of the Academy of Motion Picture Arts and Sciences.* La Habra, California: ESE California, 1979.

Peacock, John. *The Chronicle of Western Fashion: From Ancient Times to the Present Day.* New York: Harry N. Abrams, 1991.

———. *20th Century Fashion.* New York: Thames & Hudson, 1993.

Peyser, Herbert F. "Double Bill in Vienna." Review of recital by Marian Anderson. *New York Times,* 10 March 1935 (Vienna, 17 February 1935). Music Section, X6.

Sanborn, Pitts. *The Metropolitan Book of the Opera.* New York: Simon and Schuster, 1937.

Schiller, Friedrich. *Don Carlos and Mary Stuart.* Plays translated by Hilary Collier Sy-Quia and Peter Oswald. Oxford and New York: Oxford University Press, 1996.

Shakespeare, William. *The Complete Works of William Shakespeare*. New York: Chatham River Press, 1975.

——. *Shakespeare's Sonnets*. New York: Washington Square Press, Pocket Books, a division of Simon and Schuster, 1967.

Shirer, William L. *The Rise and Fall of the Third Reich: A History of Nazi Germany*. 1959. Reprint, New York: Simon & Schuster, 1988, 1990.

Simon, Henry W. *The Victor Book of the Opera, Thirteenth Edition*. 1929. Reprint, New York: Simon and Schuster, 1968.

Slide, Anthony. *The New Historical Dictionary of the American Film Industry*. Lanham, Maryland: Scarecrow Press, 1998.

Smyth, W.H. *Sailor's Word-Book: An Alphabetical Digest of Nautical Terms*. London: Conway Maritime Press, 1996.

Snyder, Louis L. *Encyclopedia of the Third Reich*. 1976. Reprint, New York: Marlowe & Company, n.d.

Wilcox, R. Turner. *The Dictionary of Costume*. New York: Charles Scribner's Sons, 1969.

Wilson, John Morgan. *Inside Hollywood: Behind the Scenes*. Cincinnati: Writer's Digest Books, 1998.

Woodford, Peggy. *Schubert: The Illustrated Lives of the Great Composers*. New York: Omnibus Press, 1984.

Zweig, Stefan. *The World of Yesterday*. 1943. Reprint, Lincoln, Nebraska: University of Nebraska Press, 1964.

Guidebooks:

Brook, Stephen. *Eyewitness Travel Guides: Vienna*. New York: Dorling Kindersley Publishing, 1994.

Doggett, Scott. *Lonely Planet: Panama*. Oakland: Lonely Planet Publications, 1999.

Dorais, Leon, State Director for Southern California, James Hopper, State Director for Northern California, and Employees of the Federal Writers' Project of the Works Progress Administration for the State of California. *California: A Guide to the Golden State*. 1939. Reprint, New York: Hastings House, 1942.

Dydyński, Krzysztof. *Lonely Planet: Venezuela.* 1994. Reprint, Oakland: Lonely Planet Publications, 1998.

Dykeman, Wilma, Jerrold Hirsch, and Employees of the Federal Writers' Project of the Work Projects Administration for the State of Tennessee. *The WPA Guide to Tennessee.* 1939. Reprint, Knoxville: The University of Tennessee Press, 1986.

Fiennes, Peter. *TimeOut Guide: Prague.* New York: Penguin Books USA, 1997.

Gody, Lou, ed., Chester D. Harvey, ed., James Reed, ed., and Employees of the Federal Writers' Project of the Works Progress Administration in New York City. *The WPA Guide to New York City: The Federal Writers' Project Guide to 1930s New York.* 1939. Reprint, New York: The New Press, 1992.

Labrut, Michèle. *Getting to Know Panama.* El Dorado, Panama, Republic of Panama: Focus Publications, 1997.

Schacherl, Lillian. *Prestel Guide: Vienna.* 1991. Reprint, Munich: Prestel, 1993.

Scores, Librettos, Music Collections, Sheet Music:

Bizet, Georges. *Carmen: Opera in Four Acts* with words by Henri Meilhac and Ludovic Halévy. Ruth and Thomas Martin, English trans. Libretto, New York: G. Schirmer, 1959.

Burleigh, Harry Thacker, arranger. *The Spirituals of Harry T. Burleigh.* Miami: Warner Bros. Publications, n.d.

De Curtis, Ernesto, music and Giambattista (G.B.) de Curtis, lyrics. "Torna a Surriento" or "Come Back to Sorrento." Claire Stafford, trans. Sheet Music: Miami: Warner Bros., 1947.

Leoncavallo, Ruggiero. *Pagliacci.* Opera score in two acts. Joseph Machlis, trans. New York: G. Schirmer, 1963.

MacMurray, Jessica M., ed. *The Book of 101 Opera Librettos.* New York: Black Dog & Leventhal Publishers, 1996.

Mozart, Wolfgang Amadeus. *Don Giovanni.* Opera score in two acts with words by Lorenzo da Ponte. Ernest Roth, ed., Edward J. Dent, trans. New York: Boosey & Hawkes, n.d.

———. *The Marriage of Figaro.* Opera score in four acts with words by Lorenzo da Ponte. New York: Dover Publications, 1979.

——. *Three Mozart Libretti: The Marriage of Figaro, Don Giovanni and Così Fan Tutte.* Robert Pack, trans., Marjorie Lelash, trans. Libretto, New York: Dover Publications, 1993.

Neapolitan Songs. New York: Amsco Publications, 1938.

Rossini, Gioacchino. *The Barber of Seville: A Comic Opera in Three Acts.* Libretto by Cesare Sterbini. Ruth and Thomas Martin, English trans. Libretto, New York: G. Schirmer, 1962.

Strauss, Johann. "Mein Herr Marquis: Adele's Laughing Song." From the operetta, *Die Fledermaus* with words by Carl Haffner and Richard Genée. Estelle Liebling, ed., Lorraine Noel Finley, trans. Sheet music, New York: G. Schirmer, 1939.

Verdi, Giuseppe. *Aïda: Opera in Four Acts.* Score with words by Antonio Ghislanzoni. Walter Ducloux, trans. New York: G. Schirmer, 1963.

——. *Don Carlo: Opera in Four Acts* (sometimes five acts). Score with words by François Joseph Mery and Camille du Locle. Walter Ducloux, trans. New York: G. Schirmer, 1958, 1963.

——. *Rigoletto: Opera in Four Acts.* Score with Libretto by Francesco Maria Piave after Victor Hugo's play *Le Roi s'amuse.* Ruth and Thomas Martin, English trans. New York: G. Schirmer, 1957.

Wagner, Richard. *Die Meistersinger von Nürnberg (The Mastersingers of Nuremberg): An Opera in Three Acts.* Score arrangement by Karl Klindworth. Frederick Jameson, trans. New York: G. Schirmer, 1932.

——. *Die Meistersinger von Nürnberg.* John Gutman, Libretto trans. New York: G. Schirmer, 1963.

——. "O du mein holder Abendstern" ("To the Evening Star") from the opera, *Tannhauser.* Dr. Th. Baker, trans. Sheet music, New York: G. Schirmer, n.d.

Discography (Compact Discs):

Beethoven, Ludwig van. *Beethoven: Symphonien Nr. 5 & 6 "Pastorale."* Berliner Philharmoniker conducted by Herbert von Karajan. Hamburg: Polydor International, 1984. Deutsche Grammophon Compact Disc 439 004-2.

Björling, Jussi. *The Ultimate Collection.* RCA, 1999. Compact Disc 74321 63468 2.

Brahms, Johannes, and Hugo Wolf. *Alexander Kipnis Sings Brahms & Wolf.* Compact Disc MONO 89204 (2CD).

Corelli, Arcangelo. "Concerto grosso fatto per la notte di Natale, Op. 6 No. 8." Berliner Philharmoniker conducted by Herbert von Karajan. Hamburg: Polydor International, 1972. Deutsche Grammophon Compact Disc 419 046-2.

Kipnis, Alexander. *Alexander Kipnis: Opera, Lieder.* Nimbus Records, 1997. Compact Disc NI 7885-6.

———. *The Art of Alexander Kipnis*: An insert of a long lost record album by Seraphim. Words to Franz Schubert's "Der Erlkönig" in English and German from a poem by Johann Wolfgang von Goethe, David Money, trans., 1961. Words to Johannes Brahms' "Vier ernste Gesange" ("Four Serious Songs").

Rachmaninov, Sergei. Rachmaninov: *Piano Concertos 2 & 3.* Played by Vladimir Ashkenazy. Legends 1963. London: Decca, 1999. Compact Disc 289 466 375-2.

———. *Piano Concertos 1-4.* Played by Vladimir Ashkenazy with the London Symphony Orchestra, conducted by André Previn. London: Decca, 1972. Compact Disc 444 839-2.

Schubert, Franz. *Schubert: Die schöne Müllerin, Winterreise, Schwanengesang, Lieder.* Sung by Olaf Bär with Geoffrey Parsons, piano. With accompanying booklet with printed words trans. by William Mann and Richard Wigmore. EMI Classics, 1997. Compact Disc 4 CD set. 7243-5-66145-2-9.

———. *Schubert: Dietrich Fischer-Dieskau, Lieder.* Germany: EMI Records, 1990. Compact Disc CDMB 63566.

Wagner, Richard. *Das Rheingold: Bayreuther Festspiele.* Orchester der Bayreuther Festspiele conducted by Daniel Barenboim. Germany: Unitel, 1992, Teledec Classics International, 1993. Compact Disc 4509-91185-2.

Videography (Videocassettes):

DeMille, Cecil B., producer and director. *The Ten Commandments.* Los Angeles: Paramount Pictures, 1956. Videocassette of film produced by Motion Picture Associates. ISBN 0-7921-0124-1. Also, 9736-06524-3.

Kantor, Leonard, writer, Jerry Thorpe, executive producer. "The Rusty Heller Story," Episode of ABC TV series *The Untouchables*. Los Angeles: Desilu. Aired October, 1960. Video viewed at The Museum of Television & Radio, Beverly Hills, California.

Mozart, Wolfgang Amadeus. *Don Giovanni*. Wiener Philharmoniker conducted by Herbert von Karajan. Directed by Michael Hampe; Claus Viller, video director. Recorded at the Salzburger Festspiele, 1987. SONY Classical, 1991. Videocassette S2HV 46383. Also, 41-048356-82.

———. *Le Nozze di Figaro*. Orchester der Wiener Staatsoper conducted by Claudio Abbado. Stage prod., Jonathan Miller. Production director, Attila Lang. Brian Large, video director. Recorded at Theater an der Wien. Prod. by ORF, BR and NHK with Wiener Staatsoper, Wiener Festwochen and Sony Classical, 1992. SONY Classical Videocassette 41-046406-82. Also S3HV 46406.

Puccini, Giacomo. *La Bohème*: Opera in Four Acts. Libretto by Giuseppe Giacosa and Luigi Illica. San Francisco Opera prod. Orchestra of San Francisco Opera conducted by Tiziano Severini. Francesca Zambello, director. Brian Large, video dir. R.M. Arts. A KULTUR Videocassette film ISBN 1-56127-002-4.

Rossini, Gioacchino. *Il Barbiere di Siviglia*. Metropolitan Opera and Orchestra from the Met, conducted by Ralf Weikert. John Cox, stage prod., Brian Large, video dir., Peter Gelb, exec. producer, 1989. Deutsche Grammophon, 1990. Videocassette 072 514-3.

SuperCities Prague: Magnificent, Exceptional, A Hidden Treasure. London: International Video Network. Videocassette ISBN 1-56345-221-9.

SuperCities Vienna: An Empire Set to Music, The Legacy of the Hapsburgs. London: International Video Network. Videocassette ISBN 1-56345-212-X.

Verdi, Giuseppe. *Aïda*. Metropolitan Opera and Orchestra conducted by James Levine. Stage prod. by Sonja Frisell. Brian Large, video dir., Peter Gelb, exec. producer, 1989. Deutsche Grammophon, 1991. Videocassette 072 516-3.

———. *Don Carlo*. Orchestra e coro del Teatro alla Scala conducted by Riccardo Muti. Stage production and video director, Franco Zeffirelli. Video recorded live at La Scala, 1992. EMI Classics, 1994. Videocassette 7243 4 77779-3 6.

———. *Rigoletto*. Wiener Philharmoniker conducted by Riccardo Chailly. Film-video directed by Jean-Pierre Ponnelle on location in Mantua. Unitel, 1983. London, Decca, 1990. Videocassette 071 501-3 LH.

Vienna. New York: World Video Travel Guide, 1986. Videocassette WVTG 005.

Wagner, Richard. *Die Meistersinger von Nürnberg.* The Australian Opera with the Elizabethan Philharmonic Orchestra conducted by Charles Mackerras. Michael Hampe, stage dir., Peter Butler and Virginia Lumsden, producer-directors. Public Media: Home Vision, 1990. Videocassette ISBN 0-7800-0621-6. Also, 37429-0507-3.

SELECTED INDEX

*"Illus." means the entry has illustrations on inserted color pages.
Page numbers in italics refer to other illustrations.*

ABOUT THE AUTHOR

Carol Jean Delmar is an opera and theater critic, author, and actress. She has contributed cover stories on opera singers Susan Graham, Vladimir Chernov, and Ferruccio Furlanetto to *Classical Singer* magazine, and feature stories on entertainment and education to the *Los Angeles Times*. She is a former staff writer for the *Los Angeles Daily News* and has blogged on the *Huffington Post*. Carol Jean holds a bachelor's degree in theater arts from UCLA and a master's degree in psychology, which she utilized while being a teacher and counselor in the 1970s. Her reviews can be read on OperaTheaterInk.com and OperaOnline.us.

Carol Jean is interviewing world-renowned opera singers for a nonfiction book she is writing on vocal technique. She resides in West Los Angeles in the home where she was raised.

www.SerenadetheMemoir.com